Marxist Intellectuals and the Working-Class Mentality in Germany, 1887–1912

Marxist Intellectuals and the Working-Class Mentality in Germany, 1887–1912

Stanley Pierson

Harvard University Press
Cambridge, Massachusetts
London, England
1993

Printed in the United States of America
10 9 8 7 6 5 4 3 2 1

This book is printed on acid-free paper, and its binding
materials have been chosen for strength and durability.

Library of Congress Cataloging-in-Publication Data
Pierson, Stanley, 1925–
Marxist intellectuals and the working-class mentality in
Germany, 1887–1912 / Stanley Pierson.
p. cm.
Includes bibliographical references and index.
ISBN 0-674-55123-0
1. Socialism—Germany—History. 2. Communism and intel-
lectuals—Germany—History. 3. Kautsky, Karl, 1854–1938.
I. Title.
HX273.P44 1993
335′.00943—dc20 92-41089
CIP

To Gordon and Louise Wright

Contents

Preface

Studies of European socialism before World War I have largely ignored a fundamental problem—the paradoxical place of middle-class intellectuals in movements which were predominantly working class. The problem was central to the Marxism from which these movements drew much of their inspiration. For the intellectuals assumed, in the Marxist vision of radical social transformation, a special responsibility. Having grasped Marxist theory, they were assigned the role of equipping the workers with the understanding necessary for them to fulfill their historical mission. The intellectuals were charged, in short, with the task of remaking the working-class mentality.

In this book I explore the attempt of the intellectuals within the German Social Democratic Party to realize that goal. Fully committed to the task, the intellectuals soon discovered, however, that their presence within the party generated ongoing controversy. By examining their struggles to raise the workers to a new socialist consciousness, I seek to provide a new interpretation of German Social Democratic development during the critical years before World War I.

My interest in the problem of the intellectuals arose out of two earlier studies of the British socialists. I turned to the German movement, the largest of the European socialist movements, because it offered materials for a study of the problem in depth. Not only were the socialist intellectuals in Germany keenly aware of their function within Marxist theory, but they recognized more clearly than elsewhere the dilemmas resulting from their presence within the party. Their hopes, their setbacks, and the ways in which they dealt with them provide the focus for this book.

At the outset of the inquiry I was encouraged by Carl Schorske, whose treatment of the German Social Democrats remains indispensable for understanding the party's development. Along the way I received considerable help from Vernon Lidtke, whose books and articles on the German movement have left all who study the Social Democrats in his debt. Numerous conversations with other scholars in Europe and the United States have also aided the project. I mention in particular discussions with Akito Yamanouchi, during a summer in Amsterdam, and with Martin Jay, during a year in Berkeley.

I owe much to the staffs of the International Institute of Social History in Amsterdam, the Archive of the Social Democratic Party in Bad Godesberg, the Bundesarchiv in Coblenz, the Hoover Institution, the Stanford University library, the libraries of the University of California, Berkeley, the Library of Congress, Widener Library of Harvard University, and the University of Oregon library. For permission to quote from unpublished materials I thank the administrators of the Institute in Amsterdam, the Bundesarchiv in Coblenz, and the Leo Baeck Institute in New York City.

My research has been supported by grants from the Fulbright Commission, the National Endowment for the Humanities, the American Council of Learned Societies, the American Philosophical Society, and the University of Oregon. For help in the preparation of the manuscript I thank Carol Pritchett, LaVerne Norman, and Marlene Koines. I am greatly indebted to Catherine Heising for her skill in word processing. Alexander Mathaes corrected many errors in my use of the German language. I am especially grateful to my colleague Roger Chickering for a close and critical reading of an earlier version of the manuscript. The manuscript has also profited from the careful editing of Elizabeth Gretz at Harvard University Press.

Finally, it is a pleasure to acknowledge Gordon Wright, who started me on the road to historical study many years ago and who exemplifies the best qualities in humanistic scholarship. Those who know Louise Wright's gifts for hospitality will understand why she is included in the dedication. My wife, Joan, has, as ever, been unfailing in her support even as she followed her new vocation.

Marxist Intellectuals and the
Working-Class Mentality in Germany, 1887–1912

Introduction

"FEW among the active Social Democratic intellectuals," wrote Henri De Man, "ever lose the depressing feeling that one is suffered as a guest in a foreign house, whose inhabitants have other habits."[1] De Man thus identified a fundamental problem in the Marxism from which the European working-class parties in the late nineteenth century drew much of their inspiration. The problem was both theoretical and practical. How did Marxist theory explain the position of intellectuals, drawn mainly out of the middle classes, in predominantly working-class movements? And what was the role of the intellectuals in the struggle to realize socialism?

Marx and Engels had provided a general answer to the theoretical question in the *Communist Manifesto*. Intellectuals within bourgeois society, having grasped the laws of historical development, would break away from their class and join the workers. These deserters from the bourgeoisie would, by virtue of their education, their skills in analysis and exposition, help the proletariat become aware of its social condition and its historical task.

In view of Marx's insistence on the decisive influence of material or economic factors in shaping human thought this explanation has seemed to some of his critics logically inconsistent and, indeed, a reversion to idealism. Hence, for the sociologist Alvin Gouldner, the "paradoxical authority of intellectuals" in the proletarian movement became a "repressed problematic in Marxist theory."[2] The "Marxist scenario of class struggle could never account for those who produced the scenario." Later Marxists were, therefore, "constrained to avoid" the issue; the result was "embarrassment covered by silence." But long before Gouldner made the problem central to his critique of Marxism others had questioned the adequacy of Marx's view of the intellectuals. Even before the turn of the century Werner Sombart rejected the claim that the educated recruits to the movement were drawn mainly by rational considerations.[3]

The practical question—the role of intellectuals in the working-class struggle—also presented difficulties. They arose early, during the eighteen forties, when Marx confronted working-class leaders who dismissed the intellectuals as outsiders, ignorant of the real interests of the workers.[4] When Marx identified the proletariat, arising inexorably out of the inner dynamics of capitalism, as the primary agent in modern history, the question of the intellectuals lost much of its significance. Abstract, theoretical considerations were superseded by the self-understanding acquired by the workers in the practical struggle. "The proletariat," as Walter Adamson has observed, "schooled by . . . praxis . . . educates the theorist—indeed, quite possibly is the theorist."[5] In Marx's emerging conception of historical materialism and the dialectical relationship between consciousness and practice, the socialist intellectual could, at most, help the workers to grasp the meaning of their own activity.

Following the failure of the revolutions of 1848 Marx reaffirmed the relative independence of theory and the intellectual.[6] His confidence in an "anti-philosophical common sense" had proved mistaken.[7] The proletariat had been deceived by "mere appearances"; to gain access to those aspects of social reality which remained "hidden to ordinary consciousness," outside educators were necessary. But Marx's renewed stress on the importance of the intellectual helped to break up the most important of the early organizations through which he attempted to mobilize the workers—the Communist League. At the critical meeting in London in 1850 Marx and his supporters were attacked by working-class leaders who charged that those who "fight with the pen" inhibited men of action.[8]

After withdrawing from the practical struggle in order to pursue his studies of capitalism, Marx restated his belief in the indispensable role of the intellectuals in the mid-sixties when he participated in the International Working Men's Association.[9] Convinced, as he told Engels, that it represented the real forces in modern history, he became the chief theorist of the new organization. Although he worked mainly in the background, Marx soon confronted attempts to exclude nonproletarians from influential positions in the association. At its first international conference, in Geneva in 1866, the delegates narrowly defeated a motion, aimed at Marx, to prevent anyone but workers from holding elective office or even serving as delegates.

Marx and Engels continued to face distrust and suspicion from working-class leaders who complained that interlopers from the middle classes were confusing the minds of the workers or seeking to exploit them for their own political goals. Only men with "calloused hands," so the argument went, could understand and represent the interests of the workers. Distrust of middle-class intellectuals was expressed in a series of attempts to establish exclusively proletarian parties—in Germany at the end of the sixties, in Italy a few years later, and subsequently in France, Russia, and Belgium.[10] In France, which provided the name for this outlook—"ouvrierism"—hostility toward middle-class intellectuals persisted as a characteristic of the labor movement into the twentieth century.

Participation in the working-class movements had convinced Marx and Engels that the proletariat, lacking the guidance of theory, would go astray. Conditions under capitalism prevented the workers from acquiring the intellectual skills necessary to understand their social situation. The correspondence between Marx and Engels abounds, as Schlomo Avineri has observed, with "allusions to the workers' intellectual limitations, stupidity, and narrow mindedness."[11] By the early seventies Engels, in particular, was concerned about the scarcity of the educated recruits needed to help the workers become aware of their historical role.[12]

Marx and Engels also worried, however, about the reliability of the intellectuals who were joining the movement. The educated recruits did not always adopt the ideas which the two thinkers believed expressed the socialist and proletarian outlook. Hence the warning which the German Social Democratic leaders received from Marx and Engels in a "circular letter" in 1879.[13] Scrutinize the middle-class recruits, the party leaders were told. They should demand that these individuals discard all the "remnants of bourgeois . . . prejudices" and "make the proletarian way of seeing their own." What was meant by a "proletarian way of seeing," however, was a working class informed by Marxist theory.

The "proletarian way of seeing" did not come easily to the intellectuals who entered the socialist movement in these years, for they often brought to the working-class struggle distinctive values and aspirations. To understand those values and aspirations it is necessary to consider the new place of intellectuals in Europe during the nineteenth century.

The emergence of intellectuals as a distinct group with distinct functions has been a special feature of modern history. As such they have been subject to ongoing sociological study and reflection. This work offers insights into the relationship of Marx and Engels and their followers to working-class movements. This perspective also illuminates the dilemmas arising from the efforts of intellectuals to carry out the Marxist project.

The sociology of intellectuals has focused mainly on what Karl Mannheim, its most influential figure, described as the "relatively free-floating intellectuals."[14] Here was a type of individual who lacked any clear or fixed position in the social structure. Having been "set adrift," either through the workings of economic and social forces or out of personal inclinations, these intellectuals existed "between the classes."[15] By virtue of their ambiguous social status and their special abilities, however, the "free intellectuals" were uniquely equipped to deal with the needs of groups undergoing radical social change. Lacking direct access to any vital and functioning section of society, these intellectuals often sought new social ties.[16] And through their capacity for "vicarious participation in a great variety of social movements," they could serve classes or groups which were attempting to understand or assert their place in a society where many of the old guidelines had disappeared. As "apologists" for new social groups, the free intellectuals were largely responsible for formulating the new ideologies of the nineteenth century.[17]

For Theodor Geiger, a contemporary of Mannheim's, the free intellectuals functioned primarily as critics of modern society.[18] The distinguishing feature of this "new cultural type" was a capacity to judge social practices in terms of fundamental values and meanings. "Like no other group," these intellectuals felt the "antimony between thought and reality," between "spirit and power."[19] Even when, as the "creators of all the ideologies," intellectuals entered the service of a particular class, their critical function remained central. As a result they were often viewed with suspicion by those whose cause they served.

For a third sociologist, Edward Shils, the distinctive mark of the intellectual has been a "fascination with the sacred or ultimate ground of thought and experience" together with an "aspiration to enter into contact with it."[20] Indeed, the "need to penetrate beyond the screen of immediate concrete experience" and connect with a general symbolic order has been, according to Shils, characteristic of intellectuals in all societies.[21] The modern intellectual might pursue his truth as philosopher or as scientist or through some other basic inquiry, but he was, like his predecessors, engaged in a religious quest. In a world where traditional religious meanings had lost much of their influence, a striving for the sacred or the ultimate grounding of life has continued, Shils argued, to inform the work of modern intellectuals.

Viewed from this sociological perspective, the free intellectuals have exercised three more or less distinct functions—as apologists, articulating and justifying the interests of social groups, as critics, both of existing social practices and their own philosophical assumptions, and as a new clerisy, engaged in the definition or redefinition of fundamental truths.[22] Each of the three functions has presupposed a relative detachment from practical concerns in order to reflect on the general state of human affairs. Even the apologists, occupied with the interests of a section of society, have usually claimed universal validity for their belief systems. In each of the three functions, however, the intellectuals have become vulnerable to special hazards—to the extremisms encouraged by an abstract or logical view of human experience and what Robert Michels described as the tendency for "mental work" to become "dissociated from hard reality."[23]

Each of the three drives which sociologists have identified with the modern intellectual can be found in the early development of Marx. Indeed, the extraordinary power of Marxism as an ideology can be traced to its capacity to synthesize the three functions. By combining claims about the ultimate grounding of life with both an apology for working-class interests and responsibility for carrying forward the critical enterprise, however, Marx introduced basic conflicts into his socialist theory. It was left to his intellectual disciples to struggle with the resulting dilemmas.

Initially Marx had taken a path which would establish him in the characteristic German form of the new intellectual stratum in Europe—the Bildungsbürgertum.[24] Marked off from other sections of the middle classes by its academic education and by an intense pride in its cultural leadership, the Bildungsbürgertum included the upper levels of state employees—civil servants, university professors, and the clergy—as well as those in the legal and medical professions and, less clearly, artists, creative writers, and journalists. It was largely Protestant in background. But the concept of "Bildung," the forming, deepening, and perfecting of one's own personality, was drawn mainly from the neoclassical humanism associated with the Weimar of Goethe and Schiller.[25] As a partly secularized version of the old religious attitudes and feelings, German humanism invested culture with many of the qualities formerly identified with Christianity. The emphasis on inward cultivation was reinforced during the first half of the nineteenth century by the persistence of absolutist forms of government in the German states and by the comparative absence of the opportunities for political participation enjoyed by the middle classes in France and Britain. Indeed, a disdain for what seemed the vulgar and materialistic realm of politics, accentuated by the failure of liberal initiatives at mid-century and after, increasingly characterized the Bildungsbürgertum even as it claimed the cultural and spiritual leadership of the German people.[26]

During the second half of the century that leadership was threatened by the economic and political developments that were transforming Germany. The Bildungsbürgertum was more and more on the defensive as its humanistic values collided with the scientific and technological orientation associated with rapid industrialization. As the economic basis and the social prestige of this older cultural elite weakened, its "relatively coherent mentality" disintegrated.[27]

Marx, like a number of young intellectuals, had anticipated the crisis of the Bildungsbürgertum. Following a period of romantic rebellion at the universities of Bonn and Berlin, he had discovered in Hegelian philosophy a system of thought which pointed the way toward personal and social reintegration.[28] But during the early eighteen forties, having been denied the academic career he sought, Marx moved to the margins of middle-class society, joining other free intellectuals in the attempt to translate Hegelianism into a program for radical political change. In his early journalistic work Marx renewed the critical drive in Hegelianism, directing it not only against the political and religious institutions which Hegel had reaffirmed but against his philosophical premises as well. Like other left-wing Hegelians, Marx also renewed the quest for fundamental truths.

The process through which Marx developed his analysis of the emerging capitalistic world and provided a powerful new rationale for workers who were struggling to assert their interests in the new industrial system need not be recapitulated here. But the critical and the apologetic drives in Marx's system of thought depended on his claim that he had discovered, in historical materialism, an ultimate grounding for human development. Having disposed of traditional religious, ethical, and philosophical views, Marx presented a new vision of human possibilities.

Two problems in Marx's synthesis presented special difficulties for the socialist intellectuals examined in this book. One was philosophical. Did the historical development described by Marx mean, as he indicated in his writings during the mid-forties, the end of philosophy?[29] Were the traditional philosophical issues—epistemological, ethical, metaphysical—superseded by the growing capacity of the proletariat to grasp reality directly by means of practical activity? Or was this, as later critics argued, a case of arrested philosophical development—a failure on the part of Marx to think through the implications of his own premises?[30] Toward the end of the century a number of the socialist intellectuals reopened the philosophical question.

The second problem concerned the preparation of the proletariat for its historic task. Just how did the workers gain the knowledge needed for a successful revolution? What amount of theoretical understanding was required for the proletariat to act effectively? Or, in view of the increasingly deterministic bent of Marxist theory, could the problem of education be ignored, reduced, as Adamson has put it, to "a kind of sidelines cheerleading for the larger historical forces in the field"?[31] These questions too occupied socialist intellectuals, all the more so because their own place in the movement was at stake.

The two problems—philosophical and educational—did not become urgent until Marxism gained a significant following among the German Social Democrats and became the official ideology of the party. That process was under way during the seventies and eighties. Although Marx had based his analysis of capitalism on the British experience, his findings were being confirmed by the rapid industrialization of Germany. The disruption of old ways of life was accompanied by new forms of economic exploitation and social insecurity. The economic crisis of the early seventies and the severe unemployment over the next two decades seemed to confirm the correctness of Marx's analysis. When the two pioneering socialist organizations in Germany came together at Gotha in 1875 to form a united party they drew heavily on Marx's ideas in defining its program. Bismarck's attempt, three years later, to stifle the new party by means of repressive legislation gave additional force to Marx's prediction that a brutal class struggle would dominate modern history.

Engels gave a new clarity to the Marxist ideology in the late seventies when he adapted it to the positivistic assumptions of contemporary science.[32] Seeking to counter the strong appeal of a Berlin philosopher, Eugen Dühring, to Social Democratic leaders, Engels expanded Marxist theory into a comprehensive interpretation of reality.[33] In his *Anti-Dühring* he extended the dialectical process which, according to Marx, characterized social development to the realm of nature. Both the social and the physical realms were, in Engels' restatement of Marxism, governed by objective, rigorously causal laws. In an effort to strengthen the political and psychological appeal of Marxism, Engels had transformed it into a world view. Thus Marx lived to see, in George Lichtheim's words, "a form of the theological world view, against which he had rebelled earlier, reinstated by Engels with his silent acquiescence."[34] But Engels had simply made explicit Marx's claims to have discovered the ultimate grounding of human development.

By means of the *Anti-Dühring* Marxism "first began to be adopted by the European socialist movement."[35] In placing economic determinism at the center of Marxism, however, Engels had greatly weakened the critical impulse in the theory and made the position of the intellectual more problematic. The significance of human consciousness and the will had been radically devalued. If historical forces were unfolding with the certainty of natural laws, what was the role of the intellectual?

In the form presented by Engels—positivistic and deterministic—the Marxist ideology made steady headway during the eighties.[36] It owed much of its appeal to the claim that socialism constituted a new world view. Particularly in August Bebel's simplified version of the ideas of Marx and Engels in his *Women under Socialism,* the new ideas began to reach the working classes.[37] Popular treatments of Darwinian biology, with which the Marxist ideas were frequently blended, enhanced the appeal of socialism. Indeed, the battle against traditional religious views on behalf of the socialist and scientific world view threatened at times to preempt the political struggle of the Social Democrats.[38]

Despite the severe restrictions placed on the Social Democrats and the persecution and exile of many of their leaders, the party maintained its presence in the German parliament and increased its electoral support. In 1890, when Bismarck left office and the antisocialist legislation was not renewed, the German Marxists were confident that their ideas, empowered by irresistible economic forces, would steadily win over the workers and transform society. A year later, at the Erfurt conference, the Social Democrats adopted a new party program based firmly on Marxist principles. Its chief authors, Karl Kautsky and Eduard Bernstein, had learned their Marxism directly from Engels.

The late eighties and the early nineties were crucial years in shaping the relationship of the intellectuals to the party. The party's changing political position brought to the surface the latent tensions—philosophical and practical—within its ideology. The resulting dilemmas were addressed most directly not by the party's chief theorists, Kautsky and Bernstein, but by young, academically educated recruits. They not only had attempted to master the intricacies of Marxist theory but were determined to communicate the new ideas to the workers.

These young intellectuals were, in most cases, born in the sixties. They came mainly out of the provincial lower middle classes and had entered universities during the eighties. The section of German society from which they came was particularly vulnerable to the social and economic changes under way as new capitalistic modes of production displaced many of the old forms of economic activity.[39] With the narrowing of customary economic and social prospects, a growing number of young men in the lower middle class entered the universities in search of careers. They helped to swell enrollments which were already expanding to meet the educational needs of a changing society.[40] One consequence, however, was a surplus of candidates for the professions of law, teaching, medicine, the clergy, and the civil service. In the closing decades of the century there were frequent complaints that educated young men were unable to follow the careers for which they had been trained.[41]

In some cases the young socialist intellectuals experienced this frustration. The charge that capitalism was creating an "intellectual proletariat," comparable to the "reserve army" of the working class, was common in the socialist literature of the nineties and beyond. Resentment arising from blocked careers was, no doubt, a significant factor pushing educated individuals toward the movement. The strength of this factor was suggested too by the disproportionate number of young men of Jewish background among the socialist intellectuals.[42] They often experienced, in addition to the other obstacles to entering the professions, the widespread discrimination against Jews in Wilhelmine society.

Yet vocational setbacks do not go very far in explaining the decisions of the educated recruits.[43] Thousands among the academically educated were unable to enter the professions in these years. Only a few joined the socialist movement. A number of these turned to the Social Democrats as students. Others had started promising careers within their chosen professions only to break away to work for the party. In some cases the rational considerations stressed by Marx and Engels may have been decisive; often, however, ethical or idealistic impulses seem to have been crucial. But the motives of many of the educated recruits remain obscure. The idiosyncratic nature of their conversions to socialism was suggested by a Social Democrat who was especially active in recruiting the academically educated. Looking back over two decades of work for the party, Adolf Braun observed: "Among the academics who have come to us it was . . . often only a chance or accident, often only a 'being caught up' by the movement, to which one then dedicates heart and head for life."[44]

For these young intellectuals the Social Democratic party offered many opportunities. Most often they worked as journalists and editors, finding positions in the socialist press which, during the nineties, came to include a wide range of publications. There were periodicals devoted to contemporary economic, social, and political affairs as well as periodicals devoted to problems of theory. A central party newspaper was supplemented by scores of provincial dailies and weeklies. Pamphlets and books were one of the means by which socialist intellectuals undertook the task of interpreting and applying the teachings of Marx and Engels. Through their growing influence in the local branches the young intellectuals also assumed important roles as speakers and organizers. During the mid-nineties they became prominent in the debates and discussions at the party's annual conferences. By the turn of the century they were an important part of the Social Democratic Fraktion (the party's representatives) in the German parliament.[45] Several of the young intellectuals carried out research for the trade unions or served as "labor secretaries," a position which developed after 1900 to advise workers about their legal rights and social benefits.

The number of the academically educated in the German party was small in comparison with those in the French and Italian socialist parties. The most important attempt to analyze the social composition of the Social Democrats—that by Robert Michels in 1906—concluded that the German party was, to a higher degree than other parties, proletarian.[46] Even in the local parties in which Michels identified a significant number of academics, the educated recruits constituted no more than 1 percent of the membership. And this was true only in the larger cities such as Berlin, Leipzig, Munich, Nuremberg, and Frankfurt, where an intellectual could join the party "without immediately going hungry." When intellectuals did participate in the movement, however, they often rose rapidly to influential positions as editors of party newspapers or as representatives to elected bodies. Among the eighty-one Social Democrats elected to the Reichstag in 1903, thirteen had an academic education.[47]

During the eighteen nineties the young intellectuals began to see themselves as a distinct element within the party. Their growing self-awareness was reinforced by the perceptions of other Social Democrats. The terms used to describe the intellectuals were various—academics, brain workers, literary types, or simply intellectuals. But such terms, employed in the party press, at the annual party conferences, and in the correspondence and memoirs of leading Social Democrats, set them apart. The terms were frequently pejorative; the educated recruits were viewed by many as a "foreign body" within the movement.[48] What was referred to as the "Akademikerproblem," the question of the proper role of the academically educated, had become by the end of the century a subject of controversy.

The young intellectuals who entered the party during the late eighties and early nineties possessed a strong sense of mission. They saw themselves as crucial mediators in the transformation of working-class consciousness forecast by Marx. Indeed, they were engaged, to use the terminology of Geiger, in an effort to displace an older "mentality" by "ideology."[49] The former represented the "direct, unreflective . . . stamp of knowledge and value" which the individual received from his "social environment"; the latter referred to an "expressly formulated belief system." One task of the intellectual, therefore, was to erase pre-ideological habits of thought and feeling and create within the working class a new Marxist understanding of society, the self, and reality—in short, a new mentality.

In their pursuit of this goal the younger intellectuals soon clashed with the older party leaders. And that clash brought to the surface the latent tension within the Marxist ideology—between its promise of a radically new way of life and its function as an apology for working-class interests. The conflict also reactivated the critical spirit intrinsic to Marxism.

The Protest of the Young Intellectuals

IN HIS essay "The Stranger," Georg Simmel described the situation which often faces a newcomer to an established movement.[1] His position "is determined basically by the fact that he has not belonged to it from the beginning, that he imports qualities into it which do not and cannot stem from the group itself." He remains, therefore, something of an outsider. Yet his lack of rootedness in the "peculiar tendencies of the group" enables him to confront it with a "special quality of objectivity." Less restrained "in his actions by habit, piety, and precedent," the stranger is "freer, practically and theoretically." He can judge the practices of the movement more clearly in terms of its principles and its goals.

Simmel's description of the stranger fits the experiences of a number of young intellectuals who joined the Social Democratic party in the eighteen eighties and after. The practices of the party, shaped by nearly two decades of struggle, were now fairly well defined. Governmental repression, the restraints placed on the Social Democratic organization and its propaganda work, had confined the activity of the party to parliamentary politics. And it was this activity which the young intellectuals judged in the light of their understanding of the writings of Marx and Engels. Not surprisingly, the newcomers, little touched by habit, piety, and precedent within the party, were soon at odds with its leaders.

The *Berliner Volks-Tribüne,* the Übergangsmensch, and the Inner Movement

The results of the legal disabilities which Bismarck had imposed on the Social Democrats were paradoxical.[2] By demonstrating that the German state was hostile to the aspirations of the workers, the repressive legislation confirmed the Marxist analysis and heightened the appeal of

Marxist ideas. And yet by limiting the work of the party to electoral campaigns, the laws had meant a growing emphasis on the party's parliamentary activity. Marxists might reconcile their revolutionary aims with the party's political role by claiming that the Reichstag provided a "window" through which to address the workers. But the Social Democratic leaders increasingly viewed parliament as a means of advancing the immediate interests of their working-class followers. During the mid-eighties the intransigent and heroic stance of the earlier years gave way to a more positive view of the legislative process, both within the Reichstag and in those state assemblies where the party was represented. The Social Democrats were developing a policy which was, in the words of Vernon Lidtke, an "ambivalent parliamentarianism."[3]

The ambivalence became more pronounced during the late eighties as the German government renewed the antisocialist laws and stepped up its repression. Even after the party's Reichstag Fraktion, numbering twenty-four after the election of 1884, was cut in half three years later, August Bebel and the other Social Democratic leaders continued to follow a course of political accommodation. For some of the Marxists within the party such a course seemed to contradict their revolutionary principles.

The contradiction was felt most keenly by the young educated recruits. They found a vehicle for their concerns in a new socialist weekly, the *Berliner Volks-Tribüne,* which began publication in July 1887. Over the next several years its editor, Max Schippel, provided guidance and a forum for a group of young Marxist intellectuals and other radical elements among the local Social Democrats. In the columns of the paper they discussed aspects of Marxist theory and attempted to apply it to German history and to contemporary economic and social issues. They also questioned the policies of the Social Democratic leaders.

Schippel had studied political economy at the universities of Leipzig, Basel, and Berlin.[4] Initially attracted to the state-centered socialist views of Johann Karl Rodbertus and Albert Schäffle, he had been converted to Marxism in 1886 and joined the Social Democratic party. Impressed by his zeal for the cause and by his abilities, the Berlin Social Democrats soon pushed him onto the staff of the local party paper, the *Volksblatt.* For some months Schippel served as its political editor. But he grew impatient with the caution of the paper's chief editors and their preoccupation with the practical aspects of the party's work. In starting the new paper Schippel denied that he wished to "battle the *Volksblatt*" but promised that the new *Volks-Tribüne* would avoid the tendency to get lost in details and would provide "a whole and deep outlook on public life."[5] The *Volks-Tribüne* soon gained a readership and an influence which extended beyond Berlin.

The *Volks-Tribüne* dealt with the immediate concerns of the workers—the struggles of the trade unions and the activities of the Social Democratic representatives in the Reichstag and other elected bodies. But the special appeal of the paper derived from its broad and deep conception of the socialist movement. Convinced that the present society was destroying itself, writers in the *Volks-Tribüne* declared that socialism was "much more than a stomach question"; it entailed a complete transformation of "cultural, social, and intellectual life."[6] They compared the new spirit arising within the proletariat to the "new life" which had emerged during the "decline of the heathen world."[7] Signs of a cultural and spiritual renewal could be seen in the work of contemporary writers—Zola, Maupassant, Dostoevsky, Tolstoy, Ibsen, and Björnson—as well as in the new Naturalist literature in Germany.

Schippel was eager to strengthen the alliance, described by Marx and Engels in the *Communist Manifesto,* between the proletariat and the middle-class intellectuals who had broken away from their class. And he aligned the *Volks-Tribüne* with those elements in the party which were most committed to the Marxist doctrines. When an October 1887 meeting in St. Gallen, Switzerland, of the Social Democratic leaders ended with a strong revolutionary statement, the *Volks-Tribüne* celebrated the demise of the party's "right wing."[8]

Convinced that the "party of the future" required the "enlightenment of the masses," Schippel set out to instruct his readers in Marxist ideas.[9] The able group of young intellectuals who shared his goal included Paul Kampffmeyer, Conrad Schmidt, Paul Ernst, Hans Müller, and Bruno Wille. Three of these figures—Kampffmeyer, Schmidt, and Ernst—along with Schippel himself had undertaken serious study of Marx's economic theory. Their efforts to transmit and apply the ideas of Marx were expanded in 1889 when Schippel created the Arbeiter Bibliothek, a series of pamphlets designed for working class readers.

Marxists who contributed to the *Volks-Tribüne* accepted the economic determinism expressed in the writings of Engels and Kautsky. The working-class movement, as one writer declared, had "nothing to do with . . . logic or morality"; it was "as much a product of capitalism as the steamship."[10] To gain knowledge of socialism the workers needed only to observe economic realities. Indeed, the proletariat alone was fully capable of judging social developments critically and grasping the facts that ensured the victory of its class. The "most difficult and abstract theory" was becoming the "flesh and blood" of the German workers.[11]

Economic determinism did not rule out a vital role for the movement's educated recruits, however. Contributors to the *Volks-Tribüne* were much occupied with the plight of young men with academic backgrounds. They had often been educated, one writer observed, at great cost to their lower middle-class families who, aware of the declining prospects in their own economic world, hoped to prepare their sons for positions in one of the professions.[12] But the young men coming out of the universities frequently found themselves victims of the laws of supply and demand; their attempts to enter such fields as law, medicine, teaching, the clergy, or the civil service failed because of a surplus of candidates. Those who discussed this dilemma in the *Volks-Tribüne* conceded that the academically educated were still inclined to "look down on their comrades with calloused hands." But they also contended that "the brain workers . . . will enter our ranks" when "their condition reaches the level of the manual worker."[13]

Schippel and his colleagues held that the intellectual proletariat and the industrial proletariat were complementary revolutionary forces. They warned against the tendency to view the working-class movement in a "one-sided way."[14] "Both sides" were necessary for the transformation of society. "Armed with knowledge," the intellectual proletariat would help to clarify the struggle of the workers.[15] The modern revolution was an "intellectual revolution" in which "words are soldiers, speeches are battalions." In a talk delivered in Berlin in 1889, Schippel envisioned the two proletariats "striding forward together as pillars of fire" toward the "world historical goal."[16]

The young intellectuals gathered around the *Volks-Tribüne* expressed with a special intensity the deepening political and cultural uncertainties of some sections of the German middle classes. Earlier hopes for a genuine parliamentary system had been frustrated as the industrial and financial leaders accepted the dominant role of the traditional ruling groups. And the old meanings and values, embodied in the Bildungsbürgertum, were losing their force in a world where many were looking to science for new authority.[17] For young men who had left provincial middle-class homes to attend universities and then found their way to Berlin in search of further education or careers the sense of social alienation and personal crisis was particularly acute. Their condition was a central theme in many of the Naturalist novels of the period.[18] One can turn to that fiction to gain insight into their existential anxieties, their social estrangements, and, in some cases, their discovery of socialism. This "pre-ideological" state can be explored by means of a novel which "circulated like a gospel" among the intellectual proletariat during the early nineties, Hermann Conradi's *Adam Mensch*.[19]

The character Adam Mensch saw himself as a typical "modern man," a "proletarian of the spirit."[20] After he had earned his doctorate he had failed to find any clear vocation. He had left behind the narrowness and monotony of his petty-bourgeois upbringing without finding a new place in society. He kept himself afloat financially by tutoring, by contributing articles, reviews, and poems to newspapers and journals, and by lecturing on cultural and social topics. He toyed with various ideas and projects—the theory of Marx, the problems of the working classes, the writings of Nietzsche. Adam Mensch spoke of writing a "modern Bible," for the old scriptures were clearly obsolete. But the new world view toward which he aspired was still unclear; he could not find any firm principles. Indeed, he remained deeply divided. Strongly attracted to aesthetic experiences, to artistic creation, he was conscious too of the scientific claim that his personality was determined by biological or environmental forces.

Adam Mensch had lost his former simplicity, his sense of direction and practical purpose, but he still felt the pull of traditional morality. His life was one of constant self-laceration. Capable of acts of generosity, he inevitably succumbed to brutal egoistic drives. Hence his betrayal of the woman he seduced and his inability to establish relations of genuine mutuality with other human beings. At the end of the novel he remained in a state of suspense; the "old false catechisms were still too strong" while the "higher ethical point of view" to come was "still too obscure within him."[21]

The predicament described by Conradi appeared, with many variations, in the novels of the new generation of German writers. Their central figures often suffered, like Adam Mensch, from a lack of social ties or firm convictions. They moved erratically between extremes on the moral spectrum—from cynicism and nihilism at one end to altruism and idealism at the other. But such a young man could also be viewed, to use a term employed by Conradi and others, as an "Übergangsmensch," a man of transition.[22] He lived between two historical eras; the middle-class world out of which he had come was in irreversible decline, but a new way of life had not yet become clear.

The Übergangsmensch was, therefore, a "candidate for the future." And for a number of the heroes in the Naturalist novels the socialist movement was the future. In the working classes they saw new creative energies; socialism held the promise of social and cultural regeneration. Given the sympathy for socialism expressed in many of the novels, frequently autobiographical in nature, it was not surprising that a number of the Naturalist writers developed close ties with the young Marxist intellectuals. Leading figures of both groups settled in the Friedrichshagen suburb of Berlin, where they came together in discussion circles.[23] Many of the creative writers—Arno Holz, Johann Schlaf, Gerhard Hauptmann, John Henry Mackay, Wilhelm Bölsche, and the Hart brothers, Julius and Heinrich—formed friendships with Schippel and the contributors to the *Volks-Tribüne.* The paper celebrated the "literary revolution" under way; the work of the Naturalists confirmed the belief of

Schippel and his colleagues that profound cultural changes would accompany the economic and social transformation described by Marx. The *Volks-Tribüne* published pieces by several of the new German writers.

The fiction of the Naturalists also recorded the difficulties involved in the efforts of young intellectuals to develop close ties with the workers.[24] The barriers between the classes, together with the two groups' contrasting hopes and expectations, were often too great to be bridged. A revealing account of the difficulties was published later by one of the ablest of the young Marxists associated with the *Volks-Tribüne,* Paul Ernst.

Ernst had come to Berlin in the mid-eighties to continue his theological studies.[25] Later he recalled his shock and sense of moral indignation at the scenes of social misery and degradation he encountered on the streets of the city. Before long, tormented by religious doubt and stirred by literary ambition, he abandoned his plan to enter the ministry. He had discovered, moreover, other young men and women—students, would-be writers and artists, aspirants to the professions—who shared his moral indignation and his sense of social estrangement. They came together to discuss social and literary matters, the questions posed by modern science, and the changing relations between the sexes. Some, like Ernst, turned to the socialist movement.

In an autobiographical novel written at the turn of the century Ernst described the attempt of his hero, Hans, and a friend to gain "a closer acquaintance with the actual workers."[26] The two young men went to a meeting of shoemakers at which "a lecture on the materialistic conception of history" was being presented. At first they were viewed "with distrust by the workers" and stayed in the background. But when they explained why they had come, they were welcomed. The lecture was delivered by an older worker who spoke with "great intellectual effort." It had "little to do with the Marxist theory but it came from the heart"; he spoke of a future where the workers would have access to culture, where envy and oppression would disappear, and where all men would live as friends. After the meeting closed with the singing of the *Marseillaise* the two visitors left, having discovered a cause to which they could devote their lives.

Hans, however, did not find fulfillment in the movement. His experience there convinced him that the "deep gulf" between the classes was "unbridgeable": "There was actually little they could say to each other . . . they stood against each other almost as people of different tongues, who, by means of a few generally understood sounds and signs, assured each other of their friendship."[27] Hans discovered that the hopes of the workers rarely reached beyond the material comforts or the "modes of freedom and morality" characteristic of the class just above them, the petty bourgeoisie. The workers were deaf to the aspirations for a radically new way of living which energized the intellectuals.[28] Relatively free from the anomic state of the intellectuals, the workers retained, as one of the Naturalist writers observed, a "healthy one-sidedness."[29] "They were finished men" while "with me all was in flux."

The Naturalist writers, like many of their heroes, could not fully identify themselves with the material drives of the working-class movement. Seeking to portray their subjects with an exactitude inspired by science, the novelists showed little interest in the theoretical issues which occupied the Marxist intellectuals. And so the creative writers and the socialist intellectuals drifted apart—the authors to follow the demands of their artistic vocations, the Marxists to work for the proletarian cause.

The young intellectuals associated with the *Volks-Tribüne* did not dismiss aesthetic considerations. They viewed the coming socialist revolution as a total change—aesthetic and ethical as well as economic and political. At the same time the young Marxists were increasingly aware that the deeper socialist mission was being threatened by the party's involvement in conventional political activity. This fear found expression in the "inner movement," a growing spirit of opposition by the intellectuals in Berlin toward the "outer" political policies of the Social Democratic leaders.[30]

Shortly after starting the *Volks-Tribüne* Schippel warned that political activity might undermine the party's most important work. "Our future victory," he wrote, "lies entirely in this unshakeable conviction," that the "successful education of the masses, and that alone, has a real and fundamental meaning for us."[31] Parliamentary activity, he added, might lead socialist representatives astray, into a labyrinth of minor skirmishes at the cost of "their keen sense of the great ruling forces of public life." Schippel noted the seductive power of parliamentary manners; they tended to "deaden the feeling of class antagonism" and lead to a "loss of contact with the proletariat." Social Democratic participation in the Reichstag should be viewed chiefly as a means of propaganda and agitation; it served primarily to "awaken the sleeping self-consciousness" of the masses. If the workers were destined to "break up the old state, seize the reins, and create a new order of things," they must be prepared for that role through the "formation of understanding and will."

The education of the workers was, therefore, the central task. During 1888 and 1889 Schippel continued to warn against the illusion that parliament constituted anything more than a tool for the development of a "goal-conscious" working class, the "precondition of all cultural progress."[32] He even questioned the party's decision to take part in the Berlin municipal elections, on the ground that participation would contribute little to the all-important propaganda work. For his opposition he was summoned by local Social Democratic officials to a hearing in order to determine his reliability as a party member.

Schippel and the others who were active in the inner movement gave priority to "direct agitation among the masses." There were two ways to influence the working class—through the "spreading of ideas by word and writing, from laborer to laborer," and through the organization of trade unions. Schippel had come to view the unions as an alternative to political action. His pamphlet *The Use and Significance of the Trade Unions,* published during 1889, emphasized their function as schools for "character and spirit" as well as for the "economic and political education" of the workers.[33] Workers' very lack of the conventional understanding of political economy, he believed, was an advantage; they would learn more easily the lessons which experience within the trade unions taught about the nature of capitalism. The workers would gain as well the self-discipline and the solidarity needed for the struggle. Schippel welcomed the new tendency toward concerted action by the trade unionists. Responding to a resolution, passed at the first meeting of the Second International in Paris in 1889, trade union leaders in Germany made plans for a general work stoppage on May 1, 1890. During the early months of that year they found widespread support in the major industrial cities.

In the meantime, the political scene was changing dramatically. In January a majority in the Reichstag voted against a bill to extend the antisocialist legislation beyond September. This decision, together with a sharp rise in the Social Democratic vote in the general election in February and an increase of the party's representation in parliament from thirteen to thirty-five, helped to bring about the dismissal of Bismarck in March. The last major obstacle to the return of the Social Democrats to full legal status had been removed.

With the prospect of increased political opportunity for the party the question of tactics took on a new urgency. A serious conflict came in April when the party leaders torpedoed the "May 1 movement," the widespread preparations under way to celebrate the solidarity of the workers and symbolize their opposition to capitalism by means of a general work stoppage.[34] Social Democratic leaders, worried lest a strong display of working-class militance jeopardize the still uncertain prospects for a full restoration of their political rights, opposed such action. But members of the Fraktion, speaking for the party, waited until mid-April before urging the membership to limit itself to peaceful demonstrations on the evening of May 1. Many Social Democrats felt betrayed; the action of the parliamentary group gave new impetus to the "inner movement."

At first Schippel had identified the *Volks-Tribüne* with the May 1 movement. But having been elected in February by a constituency in his home city of Chemnitz, he was now a member of the Fraktion. After the statement by party leaders he softened his criticism of Social Democratic policy. By mid-May he was seeking to reconcile what he called the "two directions" in the party.[35] There was no necessary contradiction, he wrote, between immediate reforms and the revolutionary goals stressed in the inner movement. Neither side should identify its views with the whole struggle of the party.

Other young intellectuals associated with the inner movement were not so ready for a compromise. Moreover, the militant spirit, especially strong among the Berlin workers, was now spreading to other Social Democratic centers—to Magdeburg and Dresden—where the local party papers were being edited by young men who had been influenced by Schippel and the *Volks-Tribüne.* These intellectuals played prominent roles in the next stage of the protest against the policies of the Social Democratic leaders.

The Jungen Rebellion

In July 1890 members of the Fraktion, anticipating the full restoration of political rights in October, drafted a plan for the reorganization of the party. The plan, which established procedures for selecting delegates to the party's sovereign body, the annual conference, confirmed and strengthened the growing influence of its parliamentary representatives. One historian has even described the plan as an "inner party coup d'état."[36] The reorganization meant that Social Democratic policies would be shaped less and less by the party membership and more and more by political leaders, who were most attentive to the voters. The reorganization scheme was, in short, a system for the "increasing concentration of the Social Democrats on the parliamentary struggle."

To the socialist intellectuals associated with the *Volks-Tribüne* and the inner movement, the plan represented a further step in the process through which the party was surrendering to conventional forms of political behavior. In the prospect of a more centralized and disciplined party, they also saw a threat to their freedom as journalists. That freedom was crucial to what they viewed as their primary task—the education of the workers.

Bruno Wille voiced their concerns. In his article "October 1," published in the *Sächsischen Arbeiterzeitung* late in July, he charged that the party was undergoing a process of "corruption" that affected both leaders and the rank and file.[37] He warned that the new power sought by the Social Democratic leaders was likely to breed a band of "flattering careerists." It would discourage the "free, open, courageous men" needed to carry out the educational mission of the party. Wille's criticism initiated what the bourgeois press labeled the rebellion of the "Jungen," or young ones.

Wille was described by a contemporary as a "fierce apostle of the messianism of Marx and Lassalle," convinced that he had discovered a "third testament" for the liberation of mankind.[38] Born in Magdeburg in 1860, he had studied theology at the University of Bonn and then philosophy and natural science at the University of Berlin before completing his doctorate at the University of Kiel.[39] Moving back to Berlin in 1887, he assumed a leading role in a "Free Religious Congregation," took part in a recently founded "Ethical Club," and became a popular speaker before working-class groups. Drawn into the Friedrichshagen circle, he also began to contribute regularly to the *Volks-Tribüne.* In socialism he had found, a biographer observed, a "surrogate for the yearnings" which he shared with other "class-estranged intellectuals" at this time.[40] Convinced that the bourgeoisie was hopelessly decadent, he looked to the proletariat for social and cultural renewal. To raise the social and cultural awareness of the workers he organized, in the summer of 1890, the Freie Volksbühne, or Free People's Theater, designed to introduce them to socially relevant drama at prices they could afford.[41]

Wille was not a member of the Social Democratic party and his socialism, essentially ethical in nature, was idiosyncratic. But his very freedom from the Marxist emphasis on objective economic and social developments made it easier for him to fix on those aspects of socialism which were being endangered by the party's political practices. What mattered most to Wille and to the other young intellectuals who joined in his protest was the creation of a new understanding and a new will among the workers. Hans Müller, the co-editor of the socialist paper in Magdeburg, the *Volkstimme,* developed the point.

> We do not want the workers to be spineless admirers and trained to be steadfast applauders of our speakers, but men who are clear about each of their steps, who frankly criticize themselves and others. What makes our movement a powerful cultural movement are the self-thinking, self-acting, masses. The soldier knows discipline and he follows it because he must; the Social Democrat maintains discipline because he himself through his own reflection is convinced of the necessity of a definite tactic.[42]

For the Jungen intellectuals, political action was secondary to the task of preparing the workers for their historical role. "If," said one supporter of the protest, "the proletariat was the true grave digger of capitalism, the primary task was to bring the proletariat to consciousness and not to moderate capitalism."[43] Marxism demanded a fundamental break with the bourgeois world. To participate in legislative activity, Kampffmeyer recalled, was simply an "attempt to prolong the life of a moribund institution": "In the face of the bourgeois world the 'Jungen' saw only hypocritical features. And while the old bourgeois world was . . . already suffering from the convulsions of death, the new proletariat was aglow with the most ardent spirit of life and exuberant youthful energy."[44]

No aspect of the Jungen rebellion expressed so clearly the fear that the Marxist promise of a fundamental transformation of human existence was being lost than the charge that the Social Democrats were surrendering to a "petty-bourgeois" outlook.[45] This term had come to symbolize the way of life which the socialists believed they were leaving behind. Its function within the socialist vocabulary can be illustrated by means of two articles on "the psychology of the petty bourgeoisie" published by Bruno Schönlank in the spring of 1890.[46]

Schönlank was not one of the Jungen, but he was part of the influx of academically educated young men from the lower middle class who had entered the party during the eighties. Born in 1859 in a Jewish family in Thuringia, he had studied language and literature at the universities of Berlin, Kiel, and Leipzig and received highest honors for a dissertation dealing with the associationist psychology of Hartley and Priestley.[47] Seemingly headed for a brilliant academic career, Schönlank turned to the Social Democrats and became, during the nineties, the party's most imaginative and successful editor.

What distinguished the petty bourgeoisie, according to Schönlank, was its precarious social position; it was being ground down, as Marx had demonstrated, between the capitalists and the proletariat. A few, presumably intellectuals like Schönlank himself, might "slip out of their class" and discover the "intellectual revolution" expressed in the socialist movement.[48] But most members of this "doomed group," lacking insight into their condition, continued to cling desperately to the world of the possessors even as their own economic position became more and more wretched. As they "pined away in the stuffy air of the petty bourgeois world" their impotence was reflected in their unstable political behavior. While their anger and frustration might draw them momentarily toward the workers, more often they allowed themselves to be "used by the rulers against the masses."[49] They were particularly receptive to anti-Semitic and patriotic appeals.

Morally, too, the petty bourgeoisie were bankrupt. Their efforts to maintain forms of bourgeois respectability had led them into a "spiritual wasteland."[50] Hypocrisy provided only a thin covering for a way of life which had become inescapably individualistic and egoistic. Envy and fear toward the propertied were combined with hatred and scorn for the workers. They were, therefore, as incapable of effective moral action as they were of political action. Their "fists remained clenched in their pockets."

Schönlank conceded that the "backward conceptions" of the petty bourgeoisie had infected the working classes. But the approaching apocalypse, the inevitable "Götterdämmerung" of the bourgeoisie, would purge the workers of the "remnants of an alien idea world."[51] Schönlank's diagnosis thus displayed both the personal revulsion which he, like other young socialist intellectuals, felt toward the social world out of which they had come and their conviction that its death was clearing the ground for social and cultural rebirth.

Such a rebirth presupposed a radical disengagement from capitalistic institutions. Even the attempt to improve the living standards of the workers was suspect to the Jungen intellectuals. Not only did it raise false hopes that social conditions could be "significantly bettered on the soil of existing society," but it diverted workers "from the revolutionary path."[52] The workers, Wille warned, might be tempted "to deny their socialism for a mess of pottage."

Support for the Jungen rebellion came from working-class Social Democrats in Berlin, Magdeburg, and Dresden. In Berlin, which supplied the strongest backing for the protest, its leaders—artisans rather than factory workers—were carrying forward a local tradition of political radicalism. But even in the capital city the Jungen attracted only a minority of the Social Democratic rank and file. For party leaders, however, it was a challenge which could not be ignored, and it was quickly answered by August Bebel.

Bebel ignored the tactical and organizational issues raised by the Jungen and shifted the focus of the dispute to personalities.[53] The term "corruption," by means of which Wille described the transformation of the party, became for Bebel a charge of personal corruption leveled against the Social Democratic leaders. In this way he could respond by appealing to the feelings of loyalty toward leaders who had in many cases suffered persecution and imprisonment for the cause. His tactics seemed to confirm, in fact, one of the Jungen charges—that Bebel was assuming a dictatorial role in the life of the party.

Any serious discussion of the issues which divided the two sides was virtually impossible. The older Social Democratic leaders were convinced that their policies had been vindicated by the party's new political position. The rebels lacked, Bebel wrote, both "character and insight into the nature of the party."[54] Those figures who were most responsible for the development of the party's ideology—Kautsky and Bernstein—agreed. Without a "spark of experience and social-political knowledge,"

Kautsky observed, the young academically educated recruits brought little more than "good will."[55] Bernstein deplored their failure to "learn something about political propriety before they came to us." The Jungen protest indicated that the party was beginning "to attract careerists among the students."[56]

The Jungen intellectuals were confident that their understanding of Marxism was superior to that of the party leaders. And having measured their "practical behavior by the theoretical writings of the fathers," they saw that the "unity of theory and practice no longer existed."[57] The only hope of recovering that unity and the revolutionary promise was to alter the policies of the party, arrest the process of deproletarianization, and concentrate once more on the task of preparing the workers for the revolution.

In the ensuing contest with the party leadership the Jungen could not match the appeal of Bebel. His forceful speeches in the main centers of the opposition during August dispersed most of the support for the rebels. After losing the backing of local Social Democrats, the young Marxist editors—Ernst and Sommer in Dresden, Müller and Kampffmeyer in Magdeburg—resigned their posts. They had made little headway against habit, piety, and precedent within the party.

At a climactic meeting in Berlin late in August, attended by nearly ten thousand, Bebel and Wille confronted each other. The meeting completed the initial rout of the Jungen. It was difficult for Wille to get an impartial hearing in the face of an overwhelmingly hostile working-class audience as the two men debated the wisdom of the party's political practices.[58] Referring to Wille's claim that the party was keeping the worker in a "herdlike" condition, Bebel denounced it as an insult to the rank and file. His resolution reaffirming the policies of the Fraktion and rejecting the charges of corruption passed overwhelmingly. Wille admitted defeat. His only recourse, he declared, was to withdraw into his study and into the "inner core of his soul" and work there for "the goals of the party." But Wille also renewed his efforts to promote the "moral education" of the workers through his leadership of the Free People's Theater.

The Jungen protest continued. At the Social Democratic conference at Halle in October, spokesmen for the Jungen renewed the attack on the party's parliamentary activity.[59] But an attempt to persuade the delegates to elect a committee to deal with the differences within the party was unsuccessful. The Jungen found little support for their fears concerning the centralization of the party and the danger it presented to the independence of its press and journalists.

During the months which followed the Halle conference the Jungen opposition remained scattered and uncoordinated. In June of 1891, however, radical Social Democrats in Berlin and their intellectual allies renewed their effort to alter the course of the party. Both groups were angered by the timidity of the party's representatives in the Reichstag in promoting a bill to reduce working hours.[60] And they were outraged a short time later when the leading Social Democrat in Bavaria, Georg von Vollmar, called on the party to acknowledge frankly its reformist character and discard its revolutionary principles. Vollmar's "Eldorado speeches" confirmed the Jungen fears that the party was surrendering to a petty-bourgeois outlook.[61]

A series of protest meetings followed. During July an anonymous pamphlet elaborated the earlier Jungen charges that political activity was "systematically killing the revolutionary spirit" of the Social Democrats.[62] By suppressing "democratic thought and feeling" within the party the leaders were, moreover, preventing the growth of the proletarian consciousness without which socialism could not be realized. But the author of the pamphlet refused to accept the authority of majorities "at the cost of principle." The "present petty-bourgeois majority" within the party was "more or less accidental."[63] What was decisive, one of the Jungen said later, was the "goal-conscious minority," made up of those who were "true to the old principles."[64] The party was urged to recover its proletarian character before it was too late.

The party conference at Erfurt in October 1891 demonstrated that it was, at least for the Jungen, too late. In the course of adopting the new program, which combined the Marxist ideology with a series of proposals for piecemeal reforms, the Social Democratic leaders disposed of the Jungen.[65] Challenged to prove their charges of corruption against the party leaders—an impossible demand given the nature of their criticism—the Jungen spokesmen were put on the defensive. Nor could they respond effectively to the demand that they produce an alternative program. They were divided between those who wanted a purely agitational posture in the Reichstag and those who wished to renounce electoral politics altogether. But the Jungen saw themselves as guardians of the party's own revolutionary principles against its opportunistic political practices. They wished to serve simply as the party's "truest opposition." Finding little support from the delegates and faced with the threat of expulsion, the five Jungen representatives at Erfurt walked out of the conference.

There were no Jungen intellectuals present as delegates at Erfurt; the Jungen views were defended by working-class representatives from Berlin. But it was now clear to the rebels that the socialist cause and Marxist principles could only be saved by a new organization. Three of the intellectuals—Wille, Kampffmeyer, and Ernst—agreed to serve on a seven-man committee charged with the task of developing a constitution for a new "Independent" socialist party. The manifesto of the committee, published early in November, expressed once more the conviction that the socialist future presupposed a new working-class mentality: "We oppositional socialists place great value on the individuality of the workers. We want the horizons of the workers to be steadily widened through the discussion of all public questions. . . . We want him to form his own opinions . . . [for] the more the class distinction between the exploiters and exploited widens the more violent the class struggle becomes. The more the individuality of the worker develops . . . the more revolutionary he is."[66]

In their efforts to create a party made up of individuals "thoroughly conscious . . . of their own will and acts," the Independent socialists soon ran into difficulties.[67] Their attack on parliamentarianism had attracted anarchist elements on the fringe of the German movement. Soon the new party was the scene of a struggle between those who repudiated conventional political activity altogether and those who simply opposed the political practices of the Social Democrats. The victory of the anarchists in the spring of 1893 was followed by the dissolution of the Independent socialist party.[68]

But if the course of the Independents reflected the failure to find a viable alternative to the policies of the Social Democratic leaders, the rebellion had brought to the surface a basic tension within the Marxist ideology. Indeed, the ideology had come to function, as one historian of this development has recognized, in quite different ways. Marxist theory served the Jungen as a "scheme of explanation and a goad to action," features which reflected their belief that they had found an ultimate grounding for life.[69] But for the Social Democratic leaders, the ideology had begun to function as an apologetic for the party's organization and practices. The leaders were determined to hold on to their hard-won political gains; the young intellectuals fixed on the revolutionary vision.

To stress the deeper promise in socialism, the transformation of human existence, however, entailed a dilemma for the young intellectuals. What form of action, given the rejection of reformist politics, would bring the revolution? One answer was given by Wille. Unrestrained by the Marxist belief in the force of objective economic laws and the class struggle, Wille carried further the "moralistic and psychological" bent expressed in much of the Jungen critique.[70] What mattered most for Wille were the subjective qualities which went into the making of a new individuality. His idealism, his resistance to any outside claims on the individual, was reflected in his unwillingness to join the Independent socialist party.[71] Although he had helped to write its manifesto he refused to submit to the "procrustean bed" of a party.[72] Instead, he concentrated on the effort of the Free People's Theater to nurture new ethical and aesthetic qualities among the workers. His attempt to impose his "aesthetic pedagogy" on the members led, however, to a break with the Social Democrats associated with the theater.[73] Wille went on to develop the anarchist and elitist implications of his outlook by finding fresh inspiration in the writings of Max Stirner and Friedrich Nietzsche.

The young Marxist intellectuals who broke with the Social Democrats could not follow Wille's course. As Marxists they continued to acknowledge the force of objective economic developments and the central role of the proletariat.[74] Kampffmeyer, in fact, had attempted to formulate a new tactic for the Independent socialists. He saw in the economic associations of the workers the means of connecting economic determinism with the subjective qualities which the Jungen intellectuals viewed as indispensable. His analysis of the role of the trade unions, which led him to revise his Marxist beliefs, will be examined in the next chapter.

The intellectuals who participated in the Jungen rebellion were struggling to preserve those features of the Marxist ideology which had engaged them most deeply. They had been attracted particularly to the Marxist promise of a radically new way of life. In the light of that promise they protested against political practices that indicated a surrender to conventional attitudes and values. The Jungen intellectuals were reaffirming elements within the ideology which were being buried through participation in electoral politics. Thus Wienand has claimed that it was "the early Marx who lived again in the young opposition . . . the Marx for whom the essence of man lies in a 'free conscious activity' which enables him to produce his own world."[75] Although such a claim reads more into the Jungen protest than can be found there, it captures something of the significance of their challenge to the practices of the party.

Confident that they were faithful to the radical promise in the Marxist ideology, Ernst and Müller attempted to enlist Engels in their campaign against the "success-seeking parliamentarians."[76] But his indignant response to their appeal, together with his running commentary on the discords among the Social Democrats, indicated that Engels' Marxism left little room for the concerns of the educated newcomers. Engels evaded the emerging ideological dilemmas.

The Jungen Appeal to Engels

Following the death of Marx in 1883 his followers looked to Engels as the authority in matters of theory. He was in the years ahead occupied mainly with the task of completing the economic analysis presented in the first volume of *Capital* and preparing Marx's manuscripts for publication. Without this editorial work, he was convinced, the manuscripts would remain "a book of seven seals."[77] But Engels also attempted, by means of extensive correspondence, to guide socialist leaders across Europe and beyond. He was especially attentive to the progress of the German Social Democrats.

Engels also developed the ideas he had presented in the *Anti-Dühring.* His essay "Ludwig Feuerbach and the End of Classical German Philosophy," published in the *Neue Zeit* during 1886, offered a further clarification of his Marxist world view. Addressing the "paramount question" in the history of philosophy—the "relation of thinking to being"—Engels argued that the dialectical conception of materialism enabled mankind to grasp "the real world, to produce a correct reflection of reality."[78] Through "experiment and industry," he wrote, "we are able to prove the correctness of our conception of the natural process by making it ourselves." Although the history of society was different from nature, since the actors were "endowed with consciousness" and worked "towards distinct goals," here too there were "inner general laws . . . entirely analogous" to those "prevailing in the realm of unconscious nature."[79] "Accidents," individual passions and purposes, might "hold sway on the surface," but the inner hidden laws were always decisive. Engels held that the concept of the dialectic captured the essential character of social change and demonstrated that the "real, ultimate driving forces in history" could be traced to the modes of production.

Engels believed that dialectical materialism and the discovery of the "real interconnections in history" meant the end of the "demand for final solutions and eternal truths."[80] Religion, the old metaphysics, "idealistic crotchets" of all kinds, indeed, philosophy itself, had been "expelled from nature and history."[81] Engels had raised the dialectical conception of history to a new absolute; he had, Gareth Stedman Jones has observed, transformed Marxism "into the appearance of a finished system, a corpus of absolute knowledge which encompassed the whole of empirical reality."[82] The metaphysical claims and "idealistic crotchets which Engels believed he and Marx had thrown out the window, had returned by the back door."

Engels did not deny the influence of human consciousness and will in the historical process. But the nature of that influence remained unclear. In the Feuerbach essay he stated that ideas or concepts, the stuff of consciousness, were simply reflexes of the "dialectical motion of the real world."[83] What independent force then, if any, could human thinking exercise on a social process determined by the modes of production? Engels did not clarify the matter. The resulting ambiguity as well as his growing tendency to view the proletariat as the source of the new socialist consciousness was apparent in the conclusion to the Feuerbach essay: "Only among the working class does the German aptitude for theory remain unimpaired. Here it cannot be exterminated. Here there is no concern for careers, for profit-making, or for gracious patronage from above. On the contrary, the more ruthlessly and disinterestedly science proceeds, the more it finds itself in harmony with the interests and aspirations of the workers. . . . The German working-class movement is the inheritor of German classical philosophy."[84] In short, the laws of history, disclosed by Marx, were embodied in the German Social Democrats.

During the eighties Engels identified Bebel as the leader who united theory and practice most effectively. He was, Engels wrote in 1884, "the clearest head in the entire German party," capable of "using theory as a guide through the labyrinth of facts," not to be diverted from the true course indicated by Marx.[85] A decade later Engels still regarded Bebel as the "most clear-sighted, most sensible and most energetic man in the German party."[86] Bebel, in turn, looked to Engels for a fuller understanding of the meaning of his Marxist faith. But the extensive correspondence between the two men indicated that the ideology functioned in very different ways for Engels, who viewed the development of the Social Democrats from London, than for Bebel, the political leader, immersed in the practical problems of the party.

Although Engels had worried earlier about the lack of educated recruits, he was, by the early eighties, more concerned about the prominence of men from the middle classes in the party's leadership. The antisocialist legislation had forced the party to rely heavily on individuals with some measure of economic independence. Their presence threatened to dilute that strong class consciousness without which the proletarian party would not fulfill its historical role. Still, Engels was confident that the masses were sound.[87] The growing working-class consciousness would check any tendency for the Fraktion to lose sight of the true nature of the struggle. Until 1885 Engels believed that the Social Democrats would have to eliminate the "nonproletarian" element in their ranks in order to stay on course. He warned Bebel to prepare for a coming split in the party; to safeguard their revolutionary principles, Marxists should be willing to sacrifice numbers and short-term political advantages.[88]

In the late eighties, however, as Bebel and the other party leaders set aside their agitational tactic in favor of a more positive approach to legislation, Engels' outlook also changed. He accepted the "new tactic," the use of elections and parliament to promote the interests of the workers, convinced that it would not impede progress toward the revolution.[89] The steady increase of votes for the Social Democrats was evidence of an inexorable growth.

In matters of tactics Engels increasingly deferred to Bebel, confident that the party leader had "a wonderful nose" for political realities.[90] Both men began to view parliament as a crucial instrument in the process through which the proletariat would gain power. At times Engels outdid Bebel in the turn toward political pragmatism. His earlier insistence on proletarian purity gave way to the view that the Social Democrats needed a broader electoral base, one which included sections of the lower middle class and the peasantry. He even recommended electoral alliances with middle-class parties. By 1890 Engels had come to regard the Social Democratic vote in elections as a gauge to the development of a class-conscious proletariat; the elections registered the strength of revolutionary energies. Confident that the party would continue to claim an ever greater proportion of the electorate, Engels predicted that the Social Democrats would come to power by the end of the century.[91] Hence the eagerness with which he received the election results, telegraphed to him by Bebel.

The economic determinism central in Engels' formulation of Marxist theory made it possible for him to accept the "ambivalent parliamentarianism" of the Social Democrats. He granted a certain autonomy to the political process. Political developments were shaped mainly, however, by the growing antagonism between the forces and the relations of production. But here, as in his view of consciousness, the extent of that autonomy, or the ways in which the more fundamental economic forces might be influenced, remained unclear. Jones has argued that there was, in Engels' thinking about politics, as in his treatment of consciousness, a crucial gap. "The absence, on the theoretical plane, of any mechanism to connect the determination of the last instance by the economy and the relative autonomy of the superstructure, was reproduced on the political plane in an inability to produce a systematic theory of revolutionary politics."[92] This "political lacuna" and the reduction of politics to a secondary social phenomenon was reflected in Engels' comparative indifference to the complaints of the young intellectuals involved in the inner movement and the Jungen rebellion.

Engels showed no sympathy for those Social Democrats who, in the spring of 1890, were critical of the Fraktion's opposition to a work stoppage on May 1. It would be foolish, he assured Bebel, to engage in any provocative action at this crucial moment in the party's development.[93] When the Jungen protested against the reorganization scheme and the party's political policies, Engels was indignant, declaring that the rebels were showing a "reckless disregard for the actual conditions of the party struggle."[94]

Engels' scornful dismissal of the Jungen was ironic, for the rebels were protesting on behalf of the proletarian purity which, a few years earlier, had seemed to Engels to require a split within the party. The young intellectuals were especially worried about the contagion of bourgeois attitudes and values against which he and Marx had warned.

In view of the growing concerns of the young intellectuals, it was not surprising that Engels was urged to clarify the nature of economic determinism. Hence the inquiry in June from Conrad Schmidt, who had been greatly impressed by the critique of Marxism presented by Paul Barth in his doctoral dissertation at the University of Leipzig: "His criticism of the Marxist conception of history appears to me to be deeply penetrating. . . . Above all . . . it demonstrates that the economic does not determine the political in a one-sided way but that the political also determines the economic. . . . He cites very apt examples out of history."[95] Here and in subsequent letters Schmidt asked Engels to indicate the extent to which noneconomic factors could influence social development.

Doubts about economic determinism were soon expressed in another way by Ernst. Shortly after Wille had initiated the Jungen rebellion, Ernst published an article, "Dangers of Marxism," in the *Volks-Tribüne*.[96] A strict determinism, he wrote, might lead to "indifference and a weakening of revolutionary energies" within the working class. Ernst did little more than state the dilemma, but his article reflected the growth of a critical attitude among the younger Marxist intellectuals.

Later in the summer a mathematics student in Königsberg, Joseph Bloch, asked Engels to elaborate on the claim that the key to historical development was to be found in the mode of production: "I must ask you, therefore, if . . . the economic conditions overall, directly alone, and completely independent of persons, unalterably and irrevocably work as natural laws, or if other conditions can on their part determine or limit the course of historical development?"[97]

Engels' response to the inquiries of Schmidt and Bloch, in which he granted, as in the Feuerbach essay, some autonomy to consciousness, have usually been seen as evidence of his flexibility, his freedom from any dogmatic or extreme claims about the force of economic factors. A few years later, Bloch and others used Engels' letters to justify their efforts to soften the determinism in Marxist theory. But during the Jungen controversy Engels showed little sympathy for the concerns of the young intellectuals. When, at the end of August, Ernst and Müller claimed that he was on their side in the struggle against the "success-seeking parliamentarians," Engels was furious.[98] "If there were any doubts about the character of the newest literary and student revolt in our party," he wrote, "it must surely disappear in the face of the pyramidical insolence of this attempt to claim solidarity with me."[99]

Ernst then cited the preface to Engels' pamphlet on the housing question, published three years earlier, in which he had criticized the Social Democratic Fraktion for its petty-bourgeois character. How, Ernst asked

Engels, had the Jungen "represented other views than he and Marx himself" had held?[100] But Engels simply turned the charge of bourgeois contamination back on Ernst and Müller. Their "frantically distorted Marxism" could be traced to their social backgrounds; they were still burdened with ways of thinking which were alien to the working class: "Could they not see that their 'academic culture'—without a fundamental and necessary self criticism—entitled them to no official position . . . within the party . . . that positions of trust in the party are not to be conferred through mere literary talent and theoretical knowledge—in short, that they, the academically educated in general, have more to learn from the workers than these have from them?"[101] The "present rush of students and literary types into the party," he warned, threatened "all kinds of danger if they are not kept in appropriate limits."[102] For they were "using all the methods of publicity at the disposal of the movement in order to smuggle their members into the editorial chairs of the party newspapers and in that way dominate the party press": "Twelve years ago the socialist laws saved us from that developing danger. Now when those laws fall it is with us again. And this will explain why I defend myself with hands and feet against those who would identify me with such a clique."[103]

Engels' letters at this time were laced with invective directed against the Jungen; the rebels were cowards, upstarts, provocateurs, hidden anarchists, whose "incapacity was matched only by their arrogance."[104] And yet while this verbal abuse expressed Engels' impatience with the failure of the rebels to appreciate the practical aspects of the party's struggle, he too worried about the impact of a more centralized structure on the life of the party. "All shadings of opinion," he believed, should be allowed to express themselves, because this was the best way of ensuring that the new members, "green and raw," who had recently come into the party, could be educated.[105] Engels was committed, as he told a correspondent in 1889, to "free criticism"; it was the "living element within the party."[106] He cautioned Bebel against efforts to control the party press, because it might mean the kind of censorship among Social Democrats which they had fought in the form of Bismarck's legislation.[107]

Engels' lack of sympathy for the concerns of the Jungen intellectuals and his confidence in the free play of ideas within the movement can be attributed in large part to his economic determinism and to the belief that the possibilities for serious intellectual disagreement among Social Democrats were steadily diminishing. As the economic order advanced, human knowledge became more and more scientific. Basic philosophical questions had been settled. "Philosophy," he wrote in October 1890, "could only play first fiddle in undeveloped societies."[108]

It followed that the intellectuals, or theorists, so important in the earlier thought of Marx and Engels, were of declining significance. Engels still saw a role for the academically educated recruits. After all, the "whole of history must be studied anew" from a Marxist standpoint.[109] Engels encouraged the young intellectuals with whom he was in contact to apply the materialist conception of history to such areas as art, literature, politics, and past economic developments. He conceded, moreover, that there were problems in Marx's economic analysis which had not yet been resolved, and he lamented the fact that so few in the party were able or willing to undertake such study. But the future role of the intellectual in the development toward socialism would be limited to tasks which were technical or professional in nature. Social Democrats would require, as they began to gain power, chemists, architects, agronomists, engineers, and other specialists, including schoolteachers. As for the "rest of the educated," he observed in 1890, "we can do without them."[110] And with the collapse of the Jungen rebellion, the threat presented by the influx of bourgeois intellectuals into the party had disappeared. Hence Engels' optimism shortly after the party had, with his guidance, adopted Marxism as its official ideology at Erfurt.

> Until now we have been fairly happy to have been spared for the most part by the "educated people." Now that is different. Now we are strong enough to carry and digest any quantity of educated rubbish; and I predict that in the next eight to ten years we will have sufficient technicians, doctors, lawyers, and schoolteachers in order for party comrades to administer the factories and the great estates of the nation. Then our entrance into power will be relatively natural and smooth.[111]

Engels' reduction of the intellectuals to mere functionaries, executing the mandates of economic development, was the other side of his belief that the socialist consciousness was emerging among the workers. Events, after all, rather than "open propaganda" were decisive in their education.[112] Through direct experience with social and economic realities the workers gained a new understanding. The German workers were, according to Engels, at the forefront of this development. Rapid industrialization had made Germany the main battleground for the socialist future; in contrast to their counterparts in France and Britain, the German workers had not been demoralized by defeat.[113] "No European proletariat could have stood up so brilliantly" to the test of the socialist laws. Their confidence in ultimate victory made the German workers invincible.[114]

During the Jungen controversy Engels reaffirmed his "unconditional trust" in the workers. They would, by virtue of their practical experiences, always bring the movement "back on track."[115] The "process of clarification in the minds of the workers," he wrote early in 1891, was becoming "more rapid day by day."[116] A year later he observed that the workers were acquiring "instinctively and directly" a kind of understanding which the educated members in the party could only gain "laboriously and agonizingly."[117] Until he died Engels continued to see the proletariat as a purifying force, capable of correcting the mistakes of the leaders. The time was coming, he wrote in 1894, a year before his death, when the masses would gain a "degree of consciousness" sufficient to overcome the "sectarian squabbles and intrigues" to which the leaders were prone.[118]

Confident that the economic laws disclosed by Marx were unfolding with a "mathematical certainty," Engels dismissed the concerns of the Jungen intellectuals. Their fears that the party was, through its political policies, making its peace with conventional values and attitudes could be set aside in the belief that the socialist future was ensured by the deepening conflict between the forces and the relations of production. The class struggle was, therefore, becoming more intense; the gravitation of the workers to the Social Democrats was irreversible. The deepening economic crisis would leave most sections in the middle classes, including the intellectuals, no alternative but to turn to the socialists. Convinced that the collapse of capitalism was imminent, Engels and Bebel eagerly noted each sign that the economic system was in difficulty. At one point Engels assured the party leader that the capitalistic system was no longer capable of maintaining any level of prosperity for more than six months.[119]

But Marxism now served the two men in quite different ways. For Engels it still provided a reliable, scientifically sound, picture of present and future social developments. And while Bebel shared something of this faith, his uses of the ideology were increasingly determined by his role as a political leader. Later Bebel noted his unwillingness to follow the advice of Engels "on many important issues because I drew better insight out of the nature of things."[120] The "nature of things" referred to the immediate pressures—the needs, dilemmas, opportunities—encountered in the daily life of the party.

The divergent functions of the ideology can be illustrated by the different reactions of Engels and Bebel to the most important internal challenge faced by the Social Democrats during the early nineties—the call by the Bavarian party leader, Vollmar, in the summer of 1891, to the party to acknowledge its reformist character. Like the Jungen, but from the opposite side, Vollmar saw that the revolutionary goal within the Marxist ideology was losing any integral relationship to the party's practices; the commitment to revolution should, therefore, be discarded.

Engels regarded Vollmar's views as simply another expression of petty-bourgeois attitudes within the party. As such they represented a temporary aberration; they would soon "fall away."[121] What concerned Bebel, however, was Vollmar's threat to the spiritual cement of the party. He worried most about party unity, the danger to its political effectiveness. The same consideration demanded that Bebel avoid any clear confrontation with the Bavarian leader lest this alienate his large following in southern Germany. Hence Bebel's caution at Erfurt, where he reaffirmed the Marxist doctrines without, however, engaging the issue which Vollmar had raised—the gap between ideology and political practice. The party leader's conduct indicated, as his biographer has observed, that there were "more points of difference between Engels and Bebel than between the latter and Vollmar."[122]

Secure in his Marxist world view, Engels could ignore the problem which Vollmar and the Jungen had identified. He made little effort to gain the first-hand knowledge of party life that might have modified his beliefs. Bebel's wife, Julie, shrewdly noted the deficiency. Expressing her regret that Engels had decided not to visit them in Berlin and "follow the movement as an eye-witness," she remarked: "one must stand within it in order to gain a correct judgment."[123] Engels' Marxism had become increasingly doctrinaire and abstract. The result was, as the editor of his letters to Bebel observed, "the false prognoses and often grotesque distortions" of his last years.[124]

Shortly before the Jungen suffered their final defeat at the Erfurt conference, a writer in the *Volks-Tribüne,* identified only as "E.S.," declared that it was time to acknowledge the deep gulf between Marx's forecast and the development of the workers.[125] It had become clear that any hope for a "great mass . . . of conscious and economically schooled comrades . . . in the foreseeable future . . . would be a great self-deception." Despite twenty-five years of effort such knowledge was still "the possession of a comparatively small elite army." Those who believed that liberation would come "when the great mass of the proletariat" gained the "intellectual means to construct the socialist order" faced a dilemma. Even an "accelerating tempo" of education "under Social Democratic leadership" would take centuries and strain unbearably "the patience of the workers." The only solution, therefore, lay in a frank recognition of the decisive role played by recruits from the "intellectual proletariat."

Few among the young intellectuals were ready to accept this pessimistic assessment. But their clash with the party leaders had forced several of the educated recruits to reconsider their roles in the movement. At the same time they began to reexamine Marxist theory. In confronting the emerging dilemmas—practical and theoretical—the critics identified different issues and moved down different paths.

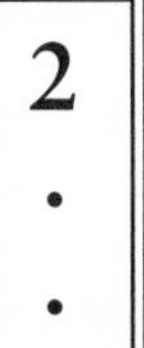

The Academics as Critics

FOUR young intellectuals were especially energetic and searching in their efforts to deal with the problems—practical and theoretical—which they saw emerging in Social Democratic development. Schippel, increasingly caught up in the political work of the party, attempted to adapt his Marxism to fit pressing practical problems. Kampffmeyer, having rejected parliamentary politics, turned to the trade unions as a more promising vehicle for advancing socialism. Schmidt focused on theoretical difficulties, seeking first to clarify an ambiguity in Marx's economic analysis and then taking up basic philosophical questions. Ernst, who ranged more widely than any of the young intellectuals, explored aesthetic, economic, and historical issues before setting out to test the Marxist ideology in the practical world.

Max Schippel: The Marxist Intellectual as Politician

Max Schippel's commitment to the socialist cause was suggested by a friend in describing their first meeting.[1] It was the winter of 1886–87. "I met him on a cold winter day in an unheated room . . . which surprised me because of its miserableness. . . . He kept his winter overcoat on and I followed his example." Schippel, the friend recalled, had recently given up a promising career as secretary of the Chemnitz chamber of commerce and was living on the "poor pay of a Social Democratic journalist." "We talked over the problems" of the movement "until late at night."

Born in 1859, Schippel, unlike most of the educated recruits, had grown up in comfortable middle-class circumstances in Chemnitz, where his father taught in a gymnasium. But by the early eighties, when he came to Berlin to study political economy with Adolph Wagner, he had already adopted the state-socialist views of Dühring and Schäffle. The latter, he recalled, "unclothed the prestige" of existing institutions and created the "exciting fantasy" of "taking over the economy in twenty-five years or so."[2] Even as he turned to Marxism and the Social Democrats, Schippel retained some of his earlier views, attempting in an article in the *Neue Zeit* to reconcile the ideas of Marx and Rodbertus. Engels scolded Kautsky for printing the piece without editorial comment and later included Schippel among those who threatened to infect the party with a sentimental and philanthropic outlook.[3] By 1887, however, Schippel had, as he told Bebel, abandoned all illusions about the possibility of "compromises between capital and labor."[4]

Schippel's relationship to the party was, as his editorship of the *Volks-Tribüne* demonstrated, marked by a strong spirit of independence. His determination to go his own way was evident in his correspondence with Kautsky during the eighties.[5] It was expressed too in his initial opposition to the party's political tactics. The primary task of the Social Democrats, he insisted, was propaganda: "Do we vote in order most of all to gain a joint influence upon bourgeois legislation and administration? Or do we vote especially for the purpose of educating the masses through the agitation before the election, to enlighten people as to their own interests and bring them into opposition to bourgeois tendencies?"[6]

Schippel's intellectual independence was evident as well in his attitude toward the trade unions. His economic studies had led him to doubt the Marxist belief that the end of capitalism was imminent and that the unions, therefore, would play a diminishing role in the working-class struggle. On the contrary, Schippel argued, the unions were indispensable for the economic and political education of the proletariat. Since "no class is born with the full knowledge of its historical role," the workers could only gain the knowledge they would need "through long experience."[7] The importance which Schippel attached to the unions was expressed in his initial support for the planned work stoppage on May 1, 1890, and in his criticism of the party leaders for their attempts to tone down the enthusiasm of the Social Democratic rank and file.[8] His role in the inner movement made Schippel a target for the anger of Bebel and others; the term "Schippelei" became a label for the dissenters in Berlin.[9]

During the late spring of 1890, however, Schippel softened his opposition to the party's policies. A year earlier he had been adopted, despite reservations about his "youthful impetuosity," as a Social Democratic candidate for the Reichstag in a working-class constituency in Chemnitz.[10] His brilliance as a speaker and his "great knowledge" had impressed local party leaders. And during the electoral campaign early in 1890 they proudly defended him against charges from his bourgeois opponent that he was a mere "hero of the pen" and a "world-estranged literary type." Schippel won the seat handily and joined the greatly increased Social Democratic Fraktion in parliament. His new political position probably accounted for his diminishing militance. Certainly by late May he was drawing away from the radical Social Democrats in Berlin and reassessing the party's parliamentary tactics. An article in the *Volks-Tribüne* defended the "double politics" of the party—its simultaneous pursuit of reforms such as the eight-hour day, as well as the goal of revolution.[11]

Schippel did not join the Jungen rebellion. He was sympathetic to their concerns—the authoritarian bent of the plan to reorganize the party, the "dictatorial tendencies of Bebel," and the threat to the independence of Social Democratic journalists. But when the Jungen leaders turned to him for advice and support, he backed off. Early in August he resigned as editor of the *Volks-Tribüne* after naming Conrad Schmidt, a moderate among the young intellectuals, as his successor. As the controversy developed it appeared to at least one of the Jungen leaders that Schippel "got cold feet."[12] His failure to show up at the meeting in Berlin at the end of August, where Bebel and Wille confronted each other, was seen by the Jungen as a betrayal.

After the Independents broke away from the party a year later, they directed much of their criticism of the Social Democrats against Schippel. In their paper, the *Socialist,* they reprinted substantial parts of the articles in which he had questioned the parliamentary tactics of the party.[13] His demand that Social Democrats concentrate on "mass agitation" was, according to the Independents, still valid. They were determined, therefore, to take up once more and develop the "fruitful ideas of Schippel" and devote themselves to the direct spread of socialist ideas.

Schippel's movement into the mainstream of party life was, at least in part, a result of decisions by the Social Democratic leaders. By providing him with a more secure position in the party press, they helped to separate him from the Jungen. In July, under pressure from Bebel and Johann Dietz, publisher of the *Neue Zeit,* Kautsky invited Schippel to become a regular paid contributor to the journal. Although Kautsky conceded that Schippel was the "best journalist we have in Germany," he was not enthusiastic about the move.[14] "I hold it to be an unfortunate idea," he wrote Engels, but he acknowledged that it was an attempt to "paralyze" Schippel and make him "undamaging for Berlin" by removing him from the *Volks-Tribüne.* Even Bebel, despite his support for the plan, still distrusted Schippel and continued to see his hand behind the Jungen protest.[15]

Schippel's contributions to the *Neue Zeit* as a Berlin correspondent dispelled Kautsky's doubts. "Schippel is better than I expected," he reported to Engels.[16] And Engels, whose suspicions of Schippel went back to the mid-eighties, observed in the spring of 1891 that the new contributor had "actually written a good article that one reads with pleasure."[17] Over the next few years Schippel wrote on a variety of issues—including the plight of various sections of the workers, German trade policy, the problems of the sugar industry. In the Reichstag, he became one of the party's chief spokesmen on economic issues. Schippel thus joined those who were shaping the party's political practices.

Schippel still believed, however, that the key to socialist advance lay in the "growing, always more brilliant unfolding of the world of the proletariat."[18] His conviction that the workers embodied radically new attitudes and values was expressed in his review of Paul Göhre's pioneering sociological study, *Three Months in a Workshop*. Göhre, a young clergyman who had worked incognito in a machine-tool factory in Chemnitz during the summer of 1890, presented an analysis of the lives of the industrial workers.

Schippel found much to praise in Göhre's study.[19] The author had portrayed with "surprising accuracy" the main features of modern factory life—the monotony of work, the absence of "creative satisfactions," the steady dissolution of "inherited moral, political, and social views" and "traditional family life."[20] But Göhre, according to Schippel, had "only half understood" the nature of the "forces which stir in the depths of economic life." He failed to see the "building up of quite different life habits" and human relationships.[21] Schippel scoffed at Göhre's suggestion that employers might play a "morally educational role." What was missing from the account was a Marxist understanding of the "revolutionary liberating process." The decline of specialization was making a new kind of education possible for the workers. "Daily experience and progressive reflection is tearing away the last veils" from the "devastating social forces" released by capitalism. The freedom of the workers from the "hunt for fortune" and the competitive struggle of the capitalists would enable them to develop a nobler ideal of character.

What Göhre lamented as the decline of traditional religious beliefs Schippel affirmed as a necessary step away from "an outmoded world view."[22] The "falling away from God," deplored by the clergyman, actually indicated the influence of natural laws, grasped by the workers as they built machines. The process through which scientific views were "sinking into the masses" was admittedly slow; their depressed social conditions prevented any "rapid theoretical deepening." But the future development was clear. The educational efforts of the Social Democrats, viewed by Göhre with a mixture of admiration and alarm, were, Schippel maintained, displacing the "old church ways."

To advance the education of the workers Schippel still assigned a special role to the trade unions. The republication of his pamphlet on the unions, in 1892, indicated once more his refusal to join other Marxists in discounting the significance of unions in the class struggle. With the revival of local party activity, however, their function in the movement had become uncertain. The issue was made more complicated by developments among the trade unionists.[23] Their efforts to achieve greater unity had led to the creation of a central body in 1890, the General Commission. To move toward a national organization, however, was also to depoliticize the unions. The German laws governing associations prevented political activity by unions which reached beyond local workers. In addition, the centralizing move met strong opposition from union "localists," many of whom had supported the radical opposition within the Social Democratic party during 1890. By 1892, however, the trend was clear. In March of that year the first national trade union congress, meeting in Halberstadt, adopted a plan which strengthened the authority of the General Commission. Its secretary, Karl Legien, became an increasingly effective spokesman for the independent role and the special claims of the trade unionists within the socialist movement.

Schippel welcomed this development. In a lengthy discussion of the Halberstadt congress he noted the crucial role which the unions had played while the antisocialist legislation was in force.[24] Not only had they taken over "a good part of the political agitation," but they had, owing to their relative toleration by the authorities, done much to "rebuild the institutions of the Social Democrats." They had been the "primary organization of the working classes." But Schippel noted that their role had necessarily been confined to the local level. And now, with the restoration of full legal rights to the party, the contribution of the unions to Social Democratic development was less clear. Schippel saw a danger of competition at the local level which would harm both the unions and the party. Unlike other Social Democratic leaders, however, he did not relegate the unions to a secondary role. They were "indispensable for winning . . . the backward" workers and of "decisive significance" for progress toward socialism.[25] Schippel still thought that progress would be much slower than most Marxists expected. The party would "experience many disappointments" if it did not maintain a close relationship with the unions. They were nurturing a socialist consciousness at a level where political activity touched, at best, only intermittently. There was no substitute for their educational role.

The trade union leaders were less and less willing to accept such a function. Not only were they increasingly inclined to concentrate on the immediate interests of their members—better working conditions, shorter hours, higher wages—but they had begun to distance themselves from the party in order to appeal to a broader section of the working class. In the face of demands by the Social Democratic leaders that the unions serve mainly as recruiting agencies for the party, the trade unions sought greater autonomy.

For Schippel the growing tension between the two branches of the movement presented a dilemma. At the Cologne party conference in 1893, where the question of the relationship between the unions and the party was discussed at length, he was caught in the middle.[26] He supported Legien's call for the party to take a more active part in promoting union membership. But he also criticized the unions for their tendency to dissociate their activity from that of the party. Indeed, much to the dismay of the Berlin trade unionists, who had looked to Schippel as their advocate in the debate, he refused to play that role. His position put him at odds with both groups.

Meanwhile Schippel was becoming ever more deeply involved in the party's political work, especially on economic issues. As he did so, however, ideological considerations tended to give way to purely pragmatic political concerns. No wonder that Bebel began to feel that Schippel dealt "too little with the principled side" of issues.[27] The party leader was especially upset in the spring of 1894 when Schippel responded in the Reichstag, on behalf of the Social Democrats, to a proposal to protect the wheat growers of eastern Germany from foreign competition. Schippel's brief criticism of the proposal was based on a problem—its lack of consistency with previous trade agreements—which seemed to Bebel completely irrelevant to socialist principles. Hence his complaint in a letter to Engels. Schippel, he wrote, had failed to seize the opportunity to attack the "parasitical nature of Junkerdom" and point out the "bankruptcy of private property."[28]

Schippel's abilities had, nonetheless, won him the grudging respect of the party leader. Bebel turned to Schippel when he became convinced that the Social Democrats needed a weekly paper which could address current political issues in depth. Neither the *Neue Zeit,* with its theoretical orientation, nor *Vorwärts,* occupied with the day-to-day activities of the party, served such a function. Although Bebel continued to distrust Schippel, he saw him as "the best editor we can get."[29] Kautsky agreed, noting that Schippel was the only one among the prospective candidates for the post "who has feeling with the masses."[30]

The new weekly, the *Sozialdemokrat,* began publication in February 1894. In an opening editorial Schippel defined its task.[31] The paper would be an "organ for practical agitation"; through comprehensive discussion of current issues it would contribute to the "growth of political responsibility" among the Social Democrats. The party needed to find new ways of applying its program and adjusting "its tactics to changing circumstances."

Within a few weeks Schippel initiated a discussion which shook the party to its foundations. By encouraging the Social Democrats to confront the "agrarian question," the editor demonstrated once more his intellectual independence. That independence was even more evident in the years just ahead, for his experiences as a politician were leading him to raise new questions about the party's practices and its Marxist ideology. His ventures in socialist self-criticism also earned him the bitter hostility of many Social Democrats.

Paul Kampffmeyer: A Marxist Alternative to Politics

Looking back forty years later, Kampffmeyer described the setting—Berlin during the mid-eighties—in which he and other young intellectuals entered the movement.[32] The initial socialist inspiration, ethical and religious in nature, had come from Ferdinand Lassalle. "Socialism," Kampffmeyer recalled, "was a holy land." But soon he discovered the Marxism of the *Neue Zeit,* recently founded by Kautsky. The new journal "took us beyond Lassalle" and "gave us what our hearts yearned for"—the "truths of scientific socialism." For Kampffmeyer, however, the full meaning of scientific socialism "had to be worked out"; the new truths only "opened to us little by little" through an intensive study of the writings of Marx and Engels.

Kampffmeyer was born in Berlin in 1864 and apparently came out of a secure middle-class background. An inheritance freed him from the need to earn a living and enabled him, following university study in Zurich, "to devote himself to scientific studies."[33] Genial and cultivated in manner, he immediately won, according to a younger contemporary, "the confidence of all whom he met."[34] Over a period of four decades, until the early 1930s, Kampffmeyer was one of the party's most prolific writers, serving as both a commentator and a historian of Social Democratic development.

Much of the attraction of the *Neue Zeit* for Kampffmeyer in the eighties lay in its conception of socialism as a broad cultural movement. The journal was "not only a fighting organ for a 'consequential Marxism'" but a means of acquainting the workers with modern literary and scientific ideas.[35] The prospect of sharing the literary and artistic heritage of Germany with the lower classes was, for Kampffmeyer, a crucial part of the socialist appeal. "What an enormous gulf," he wrote, "still separated the workers from the so-called educated in the eighties." The *Neue Zeit* offered a cultural bridge to the "stunted, intellectually undernourished soul of the proletariat" even as it clarified "the meaning of the daily economic and political struggle."

The *Neue Zeit* helped to break down the "walls separating the academics and the workers" and enabled the intellectuals "to get in step with the proletariat."[36] But Kampffmeyer also attempted, by means of close study of the early writings of Marx and Engels, to grasp the intellectual development culminating in *Capital.* The articles he wrote for the *Neue Zeit* during the late eighties were, in part, an outcome of his inquiry into the origins of Marxist theory. Drawing on the essays in the *Deutsche-Französiches Jahrbuch,* Engels' study *The Condition of the Working Class in England,* and other writings of the forties, *The Holy Family* by Marx and Engels and *The Poverty of Philosophy* by Marx, Kampffmeyer described the emergence of "scientific socialism" out of the "cradle of German philosophy" and the process through which Marx placed the Hegelian dialectic on the "ground of reality."[37] Marx, he concluded, had shown that the "historical tendency of capitalistic accumulation" prescribed "the route of march for the proletariat."

Kampffmeyer's letters to Kautsky during 1886 and 1887, written mostly from Zurich where he had gone to study, indicated his readiness to accept the guidance of the *Neue Zeit* editor in interpreting Marx.[38] He carried forward the strongly deterministic bent found in Engels and Kautsky. But in his reconstruction of Marxist thought, Kampffmeyer reinstated the ethical and humanistic elements which had largely disappeared by the time of the *Communist Manifesto.* In discussing the *Poverty of Philosophy,* for example, Kampffmeyer emphasized the way in which capitalism was, according to Marx, producing "a proletariat aware of its dehumanization" and thus opening the path for a "complete development of the human personality."[39] Through the work reductions made possible by modern technology, the workers would cease to be robots and leave "specialized idiocy behind."

Kampffmeyer also differed from Kautsky in his insistence that Marxists were committed to constant self-criticism. Marx, he observed, opposed "doctrinaire attitudes."[40] It was the nature of the dialectic to prevent any arrest of thought; it granted only "provisional reality" to the concepts through which theorists attempted to grasp "being." In Kampffmeyer's development as a socialist intellectual, the humanistic and critical impulses in the Marxist system of thought would become increasingly pronounced.

Kampffmeyer continued to write for the *Neue Zeit* during the late eighties, but he also joined the group of intellectuals around the *Volks-Tribüne.* There he applied Marxist theory to German economic development, contributing articles on the history of the housing industry and the impact of capitalism on traditional forms of agricultural life. Even among the peasantry Kampffmeyer saw the "flame of class-hatred arising."[41] Modern economic conditions were destroying the old "blind, slavish obedience" of the lower classes.

Although Kampffmeyer, like the other young Marxist intellectuals, concentrated on economic issues, he continued to identify socialism with a far-reaching cultural change. He was in close contact with the Friedrichshagen circle of writers and artists and was convinced that the Naturalists were creating a new socialist literature. When Wille founded the Free People's Theater, Kampffmeyer served on its executive. His concern with the inner qualities of socialism drew him into the Berlin opposition. Early in the summer of 1890 he joined Hans Müller in editing one of the main organs for the Jungen protest—the *Volkstimme* in Magdeburg.

Later Kampffmeyer recalled the main feature of the Jungen rebellion—the conviction that the party leaders were "turning away from the ultimate revolutionary goal" in favor of "an aimless drive for power."[42] Since parliament, like other bourgeois institutions, was in its death throes, its value lay simply in the opportunity it provided for propaganda which would energize the masses. Kampffmeyer also stressed the importance of Engels' pamphlet on the housing question as an inspiration for the Jungen. "It offered weapons for the battle . . . against the older" leaders. Indeed, Engels provided the catchword used most frequently by the rebels—"petty bourgeois Social Democracy."

The support which Kampffmeyer and Müller gave to Wille cost them their editorial positions.[43] Bebel's successful appeal to the local Social Democrats led to their resignations. But Kampffmeyer remained active in the movement, continuing to focus on the Marxist forecast of a radical change in the human condition. His pamphlet *Is Socialism Compatible with Human Nature?*, published in 1891, reaffirmed his belief that socialism would mean a "higher form of individualism."[44] Changes in technology were making it possible to throw off the "corrupting influence of a single occupation." It would no longer be necessary "to work at one job for a lifetime." Kampffmeyer paid special attention to the plight of contemporary intellectuals—victims of a "colossal emptiness" and a "one-sided development." Like the manual worker, the intellectual would "become a complete man" and find "a new harmony between spirit and body."[45] Kampffmeyer found additional support for his belief in a coming personal and social reintegration in the writings of Tolstoy.

Prior to the crucial Erfurt conference Kampffmeyer joined two other Social Democrats in Magdeburg in drafting a new party program.[46] Their proposals did not differ greatly from those in another draft, written by Kautsky and Bernstein, which was eventually adopted by the delegates. But the Magdeburg draft contained terminology and emphases which expressed the concerns of the Jungen. At several points it called attention to the cultural deficiencies of capitalism and to the need to nurture "socialist feelings and attitudes." In its provisions for more direct democracy in the party, the Magdeburg draft reflected the Jungen worries about oligarchical tendencies and the growing power of the Fraktion. Kampffmeyer and his colleagues also assigned considerable importance to the trade unions as instruments for the "socialization of the proletariat."

The expulsion of the Jungen spokesmen at Erfurt convinced Kampffmeyer and his closest associate, Müller, that the Social Democrats had surrendered their socialist principles. Müller summarized his and Kampffmeyer's views: "The battle that was fought out in Erfurt was a class struggle in which petty bourgeois socialism was finally victorious over the proletarian form. Since the Conference declared that nothing is to be altered in its tactics, it steers full speed ahead down the course of petty bourgeois opportunism."[47] Having concluded that the party had discarded its revolutionary aims, Kampffmeyer and Müller believed that a new party was needed. A few days after the conference they helped to write the manifesto for the Independent socialists. The "dictatorship of the Social Democratic executive," it declared, "stifled any independent thought" and thus prevented "the free movement of the proletariat."[48] For those who were organizing the new party the inner development of the workers remained uppermost. "The clarification of proletarian and socialist ideas," they wrote, "lies most on our hearts."

To carry out this task the Independents looked primarily to the trade unions. Kampffmeyer's pamphlet *The Significance of Trade Unions for the Tactics of the Proletariat* developed the new party's strategy.[49] He contended that the political activity of the workers had enabled them "to think as a class." But unlike the bourgeoisie, which had turned to politics only after gaining economic power, the workers were, as their more progressive sections had come to see, in danger of putting the cart before the horse. Kampffmeyer cited statements by Wilhelm Liebknecht to support his contention that the voting rights of the workers were illusory, granted by ruling classes who were confident that their economic position could not be threatened by political action. The state was, after all, as Marx taught, "simply an instrument of the dominant class."[50]

It followed that the real power of the workers lay "on quite another ground—the economic."[51] The "chief weight of the class struggle" should be borne, therefore, by the trade unions; these "threatened capitalism on its own ground." The strike, in particular, represented the "great economic means" possessed by the workers.[52] Together with other economic methods, including consumer boycotts, the workers would not only better their social and economic position but, more important, advance the cause of socialism. They would also carry out the task that mattered most to intellectuals like Kampffmeyer—the education of the workers. A trade union press could "unfold a strict socialist propaganda" unhampered by political expediency. The workers would become, through union activity, "self-acting, self-thinking" individuals and prepare themselves for the "great task of administering and managing" the means of production:[53]

> We must so train ourselves that all our future plans are built up on inner calculable factors and not on outer uncontrollable factors. The inner development of the worker, the strengthening of his consciousness of power, his goal-conscious activity, his capacity for the economic guidance of production, those are the really decisive, trustworthy elements, which one can use in social-political calculations.[54]

The "inner journey" of education was decisive. It would lead not only to a knowledge of specific branches of manufacturing but to insights into the workings of the whole economy. Such understanding would not "simply fall into the laps of the workers"; it "must be earned through their own activity."

The trade unions would also become "important economic components" in the future society.[55] Kampffmeyer did not attempt to describe that society lest he "fall into utopianism." Once the dominant economic apparatus "lay exclusively in the hands of the physical and intellectual workers," however, the need for a central political authority would disappear. The unions would not only supervise production but assume responsibility for the distribution of wealth.

Kampffmeyer believed that he was carrying out the logic of economic determinism. At the same time he was seeking to revitalize elements in the Marxist ideology which were tacitly being set aside by the Social Democratic politicians. He was, moreover, attempting to overcome a major difficulty in Marxist theory—the problem of explaining the way in which the working class gained the knowledge necessary to fulfill its historic mission.

As an Independent socialist, Kampffmeyer attempted to preserve Marxist doctrines. But when the new organization, under the influence of the anarchists, gave up on the proletariat, Kampffmeyer departed. He recognized, moreover, that the Social Democrats continued to hold the allegiance of most workers.[56] By the spring of 1893 he was turning back to the older party. In correspondence with Richard Fischer, who managed the party's publications, Kampffmeyer discussed ways in which the articles he had written for the *Volks-Tribüne* might be revised to serve as Social Democratic propaganda.[57]

Kampffmeyer still believed that the coming socialist society required a new mentality among the working classes. And he continued to see the trade unions as the main vehicle for that goal. But closer acquaintance with the economic associations of the workers—cooperatives as well as trade unions—led him to reconsider his view of Marxist theory and tactics. In the Marxist self-criticism which developed after 1895 he was a central figure.

Conrad Schmidt: Questions of Economic Theory and Philosophy

Writing to Kautsky in the spring of 1889, Engels described Conrad Schmidt as a very brave young man who "has come to us on his own . . . without encouragement, indeed, despite many indirect warnings on my part, simply because he cannot stand apart from the truth."[58] Two years earlier Schmidt had sent Engels a copy of his doctoral dissertation, which dealt with the wages of the workers. Later, during a three-month stay in London, he spent some evenings in the home of Engels. At that time Engels described Schmidt as "about the greenest youth I have ever seen."[59] But the relationship between the two men developed, by means of correspondence, into one of vigorous intellectual interchange and mutual trust. The older man became a confidant of Schmidt's as he struggled to find a vocation compatible with his socialist commitment and his interest in theory. When Schmidt published a study of the "average rate of profit" according to Marxist theory, Engels called it the "most significant economic achievement since the death of Marx."[60] He told Schmidt that he was one of the few among the younger generation who could "think theoretically."[61] Over the next several years, as Schmidt attempted to deepen his understanding of Marxist ideas, he relied on Engels for guidance. The correspondence between the two men indicated, however, Schmidt's growing doubts about Marx's economic analysis and the philosophical foundations of his theory.

Schmidt's idealism and his questioning spirit came out of his family background. His sister, Käthe Kollwitz, described their family life in Königsberg, where Conrad was born in 1863, as one in which strong religious beliefs did not hinder the discussion of new ideas and radical social views.[62] Their father, Karl Schmidt, had studied law and then had become a master mason when his liberal values proved incompatible with service in the authoritarian Prussian state.[63] After his father-in-law, Julius Rupp, founder of the first "free religious community" in Prussia, died, Karl assumed leadership of the congregation. Here the Lutheran faith had given way to an outlook, influenced by the city's most famous son, Immanuel Kant, which was strongly ethical in bent. The idealism of Conrad and his two sisters, Käthe and Lisa, found expression in their participation in the socialist movement.

During the mid-eighties Schmidt studied political economy and philosophy at the University of Berlin before completing his doctorate at the University of Leipzig. His dissertation, "The Natural Wages of the Workers," combined the interest in ethical and economic issues which characterized much of his writing for the movement.[64] After rejecting a purely mathematical attempt to calculate the economic value produced by the workers and the capitalists, respectively, Schmidt examined the wage theories and views of exploitation found in the two leading theoreticians of German socialism—Rodbertus and Marx. In making a case for socialism, Schmidt rejected the Marxist theory of value as an "undemonstrated hypothesis" in favor of the argument of Rodbertus, which was based on natural rights.[65]

After further study of Marxist thought, and through his exchanges with Engels, Schmidt concluded that he had misunderstood Marx. Close study of *Capital* also led him to reflect on an unresolved problem in Marx's economic analysis, acknowledged by Engels in his preface to the second volume of *Capital,* published in 1885.[66] There was, Engels conceded, an apparent contradiction between Marx's labor theory of value, according to which capitalists extracted surplus value from the workers, and the actual rate of profit. Surplus value and profit derived only from labor, or what Marx called "variable capital" in contrast to the "fixed capital" of raw materials and machines. But economists since the time of Adam Smith had shown that capital of equal amounts, whatever its "organic composition," or mixture of fixed and variable capital, yielded equal average rates of profit. How then to reconcile this characteristic of capitalist development with Marx's claim that profit rates would steadily decline? Although Engels challenged the Rodbertians, the chief rivals of the Marxists, to solve the problem, he assured his readers that the Marxist solution would appear in the third volume of *Capital.*

Schmidt took up the challenge. The effort, he wrote Engels, would help him grasp the Marxist way of thinking more fully.[67] It also led Schmidt to examine the mechanism through which capitalism was, according to Marx, destroying itself. Marx had seen in the tendency for fixed capital, chiefly in the form of machinery, to increase at the expense of "living labor," the source of surplus value, the inevitable decline in the average rate of profit.[68] Given that, as Marx put it, "the rate of profit is the motive power of capitalist production," the collapse of the system was ensured. In his efforts to overcome the contradiction between the law of value and the profit rate Schmidt was, therefore, struggling with questions which were of crucial importance in Marxist theory.

In 1889 Schmidt published *The Average Rate of Profit on the Basis of the Marxist Law of Value* and summarized his findings in the *Neue Zeit.*[69] The details of his analysis, which anticipated central features of the explanation presented in the third volume of *Capital,* are less important here than Schmidt's wholehearted endorsement of the Marxist claim that capitalism was doomed by its own internal workings. Schmidt concluded that the profit rate was "steadily sinking" and, since capitalism could not survive without the prospect of profit, the system was indeed disintegrating: "For the profit rate is the driving wheel of capitalist production. If it runs down the whole social machine must come to a stop . . . . Socialism is no utopia but, as any deep consideration of society always again shows, an unshakeable necessity anchored in circumstances."[70] For Schmidt, as for Engels, the Marxist law of value provided a "knowledge of our economic relations" comparable to the "law of the conservation of energy" for natural science.[71]

Engels' response to his study delighted Schmidt. Although "you have not solved the problem," Engels wrote, "we are close together."[72] And he assured Schmidt that his contribution would be acknowledged in his preface to the forthcoming third volume of *Capital*.[73] Schmidt was so pleased with Engels' letter that he sent it to his parents, hoping to overcome, in particular, his father's misgivings over his son's preoccupations.[74]

During the late eighties Schmidt still hoped to pursue an academic career. But his applications to study for an advanced degree at the universities of Halle and Leipzig were rejected, the former because Schmidt did not meet "confessional" requirements, the latter on ideological grounds. His Marxist study of profits had, so a former mentor informed him, banished him from "all university benches."[75] For a time Schmidt considered emigrating to America, but ultimately he decided against such a step and turned to journalism to make a living. Moving to Berlin, he began to write for both socialist and liberal newspapers. The move worried Engels. For one with a "scientific impulse like yourself," he wrote, journalistic work might make for superficiality.[76] He urged the younger man to find a way of continuing his studies in London. England remained, Engels observed, "the classical soil for the study of the laws of capitalistic production" and its decline. Schmidt himself was eager to return to London in order to deepen his economic understanding through close contact with Engels, and he was especially keen on helping Engels edit the unpublished writings of Marx.[77] He hoped to put together a package of journalistic assignments which would enable him to support himself.

Meanwhile Schmidt had entered the group around the *Volks-Tribüne*. Like Schippel and Kampffmeyer, he was also in close touch with the Naturalist writers and artists centered in the Friedrichshagen suburb. He shared with other young socialist intellectuals a strong belief in the cultural significance of their movement. A lecture on Spinoza, which Schmidt delivered before Wille's congregation during 1890, expressed his own philosophical quest.[78] He also served on the executive of the

Free People's Theater, convinced that it was encouraging "that form of literary creativity which correspond[s] to the essence of the working-class movement."[79] His belief that he lived in a time of profound spiritual transition was evident too in his response to one of the most notable novels of the period, *Tired Souls,* by the Norwegian author Arne Garborg. Here again the central figure was an Übergangsmensch, suffering from a complete loss of meaning in life. He was an intellectual for whom knowledge had led to an inability to act; the hero wavered between suicide and religious conversion.[80] To several socialist reviewers Garborg's novel seemed to capture the essence of bourgeois decadence.[81] It was, Schmidt wrote Engels, "a deep and exact analysis of the time."[82]

By the spring of 1890 Schmidt was working closely with Schippel as a paid editorial assistant for the *Volks-Tribüne.* He shared the concerns of the Berlin opposition and, to the regret of Engels and Kautsky, "allowed himself to be captured by the Jungen."[83] After he was chosen by Schippel as the next editor of the *Volks-Tribüne* early in August, however, Schmidt drew away from the rebels. Although he defended his paper against the attacks coming from the Social Democratic leaders, he followed a moderate course as the dispute heated up. By mid-September Engels could inform Kautsky that Schmidt had "kept his distance" from the "student squabble."[84] But Schmidt retained his ties with several of the Jungen intellectuals, particularly Müller and Ernst. He could not, as he told Engels, see "essential differences" between the rebels and the Fraktion.[85] He believed that the split had been "a great misfortune for the party."[86]

Schmidt was contemplative by nature and little drawn to political battles. He was concerned less with the tactical and organizational issues which divided the two sides than with ideas. He was eager, as he wrote Engels, to demonstrate the relevance of the materialistic conception of history to such matters as "religion, literature, historical writing, conceptions of sexual life, and philosophy."[87] But his confidence that all aspects of life could be traced to economic forces had been shaken, as mentioned earlier, by his reading of Paul Barth's Leipzig dissertation. Barth had attempted to show, by historical example, that political, legal, religious, and philosophical developments did not necessarily derive from "the economic base." To Schmidt it seemed a "penetrating critique" of Marxism.[88]

Schmidt continued to be torn between his need to make a living through journalism and his interest in theory. In November 1890, the offer of a position with a newspaper in Zurich promised to resolve the conflict. Engels approved of the move, noting that Zurich was an ideal place to gain insight into the workings of the international financial world.[89] Schmidt's position with the *Züricher Post* also enabled him to rekindle his hopes for an academic career, for it allowed time for formal study. In the spring of 1891 he enrolled in courses at the University of Zurich. When, in April, Kautsky attempted to bring him back to Berlin with the offer of an editorial post with the *Neue Zeit,* Schmidt decided to remain in Switzerland. "You have lost a valuable contributor," Engels wrote Kautsky; "he would have been completely your man."[90]

Engels was surely mistaken in his judgment. Over the next several years Schmidt's letters to Engels demonstrated his determination to establish for himself the soundness of Marxist theory. Through the formal study of classical political economy and German philosophy, he set out to understand the intellectual developments leading to Marx's mature formulations. He also began to work on a book in which the main features of Marxist thought—the method of economic analysis, the materialistic conception of history, and its philosophical foundations—would be presented in a systematic form.[91] These issues, he wrote Engels, were not simply "questions for scholars."[92] Like other young intellectuals, Schmidt was committed to the task of disseminating Marxist ideas in a form that made them accessible to the workers. He believed that the technical questions confronting the proletariat when they took over society would be much more difficult than those associated with achieving political power.[93] But as he attempted, during 1891 and 1892, to give systematic expression to Marxism, Schmidt experienced growing doubts about its adequacy. Both the economic analysis and its philosophical basis presented difficulties.

The "puzzle of the average profit rate," he wrote Engels, left him "with no peace."[94] He recognized too that the failure of Marx to explain the contradiction between his law of value and the actual profit rate had become the main target for his critics. Unless the problem was dealt with satisfactorily, he told Engels, the "enemy can dismiss the claim" that the Marxist analysis corresponded to reality.[95] Concern over the issue, he added, was "spreading among Marxist circles."

Schmidt continued, however, to defend the main lines of the Marxist analysis—answering a series of critics by means of articles in the *Neue Zeit* and other journals. Thus in the spring of 1892 he dealt with the new theory of marginal utility, which had emerged as the most serious challenge to Marxist economics.[96] Its psychological approach and consumer orientation ignored, according to Schmidt, the social and economic relationships which greatly limited the capacity of the workers to purchase "utilities." The article pleased Engels; he urged Bebel to send a copy to George Bernard Shaw who, along with other British Fabians, needed to be rescued from the new theory.[97] But Schmidt's continuing concern with the question of profit rates and his dissatisfaction with his earlier treatment of the problem were evident in a new attempt, published in the *Neue Zeit* late in 1892, to answer Marx's critics.[98] Again Engels found much to praise in the article while denying once more that Schmidt had solved the problem.[99] It is surprising that Engels did not acquaint Schmidt with Marx's solution, which was to be presented in the third volume of *Capital.* Schmidt could only remind his readers that his own efforts were provisional, and assure them that the forthcoming volume would end the debate.

Schmidt also began to question the philosophical basis of Marxism. At the University of Zurich he had undertaken the study of Kant and Hegel and, with guidance from Engels, explored the process through which Marx had "demystified" the dialectic.[100] But Schmidt could not accept Engels' form of materialism. Convinced that it simply introduced new metaphysical claims, he held, with Kant, that the "thing in itself" was "unknowable."[101] Marxist materialism, he told Engels, must "remain a theory of appearances." He had, in effect, rejected Engels' claim that traditional philosophical questions had been superseded by a direct, scientific knowledge of reality. Still, Schmidt saw no need for a "complete regrounding of Marxist theory."[102] And he did not give up his plan for a systematic treatment of Marx's ideas. What was needed was a book which would illuminate the scientific nature and the "spirit of Marxism" and show that it still bore "within itself a new world view."

Correspondence between Schmidt and Engels fell off during 1893. But the exchanges in 1894 indicated that Schmidt had abandoned the claim that Marx had discovered the "laws of economic development." He now granted to the theory of value simply a "fictional character," useful in pointing out tendencies in economic life but lacking the status of laws in any rigorous sense of the term.[103] Nor was Schmidt hesitant to draw the consequences from his altered perspective. In place of "necessity" or "blind working laws," one could speak only of hypotheses. Schmidt's skepticism about the claims made on behalf of Marx's economic analysis was not dispelled by the treatment of the profit rate presented in the third volume of *Capital,* published late in 1894. "Many points remain obscure," he wrote in a review.[104] Marx, he declared, "would have been the last to contest" the need for "continuing his researches."

In the face of Schmidt's criticism, Engels conceded that scientific conceptions, given the evolutionary nature of things, were only "approximations of reality."[105] To reduce the Marxist law of value to a fiction, however, was to "degrade" it and fail to see that it captured the real movement of economic life. In a letter to Schmidt a few months before he died, Engels was still trying to persuade his friend that the Marxist law of value was "something more than a necessary fiction."[106]

Schmidt's dissatisfaction with Marx's economic analysis did not "in any way cloud," he wrote Kautsky, his belief in the fundamental and "lasting significance of Marxian thinking."[107] Nor did it deter him from his plan to present the Marxist ideas systematically. But in denying that the Marxist doctrines mirrored real developments Schmidt had moved away from the economic determinism of Engels. Moreover, his turn to a Kantian epistemology had led him to pay more attention to those aspects of human consciousness which had been devalued and obscured in Engels positivistic formulation—the thinking process itself and the ethical qualities found in the working-class struggle.[108]

Schmidt's doubts about the adequacy of Marxist theory opened the way for a new view of socialist development. This was evident in an essay, "Socialistic Morality," published in the journal of the new Ethical Culture movement in Germany during 1894.[109] Here he focused on those qualities in the working-class struggle—"faithfulness to party," "willingness to sacrifice," "feelings of duty"—which could not be explained in terms of individual self-interest. There were, he argued, "super-egoistic" impulses, derived from the animal instincts which, in the process of biological evolution, worked for the "maintenance of the species." In human beings these impulses were becoming steadily more conscious and rational and, through their embodiment in the working classes, leading to "the freedom of the future race." Schmidt had not discarded the notion of the class struggle, but the Marxist emphasis on conflict and objective economic forces was giving way to a more optimistic and evolutionary view of social development.

In 1895 Schmidt returned to Berlin, having concluded that his prospects for an academic career in Switzerland were poor. Over the next few years he worked on the staff of *Vorwärts,* served as chairman of the Free People's Theater, and continued to reflect and write on the economic and philosophical issues which had emerged in his exchanges with Engels. Although he still saw himself as a disciple of Marx, he had adopted a much more critical stance toward the received version of Marxism. During the late nineties he would, like Schippel and Kampffmeyer, play a prominent role in the effort to revise the party's ideology.

Paul Ernst: Questions of Aesthetics and Practice

Writing about his early years in the movement, Paul Ernst emphasized the religious, indeed, millennial nature of his socialist faith. It was not the present that mattered "but a future, not the material but the spiritual."[110] Socialism offered "a community of the holy . . . much like that in which the old Christians believed." By identifying himself with the proletariat, Ernst recalled, he was participating in a "historical development, led by supra-personal forces," which would bring a new moral and social order. The time in which the socialist converts lived was comparable to that in which Christianity was growing out of the ruins of the Roman Empire. "I credited the working classes with qualities like those which emerged in the declining antiquity under the influence of the church."[111]

Born in 1866 in the Harz mining area, the son of a pit foreman, Ernst came to Berlin in 1886.[112] Having abandoned his plans to become a clergyman, he turned to the study of economics, history, and philosophy. He also joined the Durch circle, a group of young writers led by the Hart brothers and including several of the most talented figures among the Naturalist novelists, dramatists, and poets.[113] There Ernst became familiar with the work of Zola and Taine, Ibsen and Björnson, and Dostoevsky. Through the influence of Wille, also a member of the group, he was introduced to the work of the two thinkers who influenced him most—Tolstoy and Marx. The ideas of Tolstoy, particularly his faith in the common people and his gospel of physical labor, made a deep impression on Ernst.[114] For a time he thought seriously of becoming a factory worker in order to identify with the masses. But his reading of *Capital* opened an alternative path. Marxism provided a "firm conception" of life; it explained the "disintegrating world" around him and assured him that a new society was coming through the activity of the proletariat.[115]

By the winter of 1888 Ernst had given up his university studies. He decided to devote himself completely to the movement and to earn his living as a journalist. He had now joined the group around the *Volks-Tribüne,* contributing short stories and articles on both economic and literary subjects. His interpretation of Marxism was strongly deterministic. He was convinced that capitalism was destroying itself. In an extensive review of Schmidt's study of the average profit rate, Ernst complimented the author for demonstrating, even before the publication of the third volume of *Capital,* that Marx had identified a fundamental contradiction in the economic system.[116] Schmidt had shown how "one nail" was being driven into "the coffin of capitalism."

Persuaded that powerful objective forces were at work, Ernst left little room for the human will. He wrote in the spring of 1890, "We are nothing more than the instrument of history," charged with the task of "clearing away the stone which lies in the way of the rolling wagon."[117] Still, there was a need to promote "correct thinking" among the workers. Ernst attempted to further the educational work of the party. Along with his journalistic activity he lectured before working-class groups in Berlin and, having organized a class of forty or so, instructed his students in Marxist ideas. The effort, he later recalled, proved to be frustrating, for Marx "had said nothing about the way in which the proletariat ought to be prepared for its historical task."[118]

Ernst's application of the materialistic conception of history seemed to one of his young Marxist contemporaries in Berlin—the Austrian student Hermann Bahr—to be excessively rigid. When Ernst disparaged the plays of Ibsen and Björnson, greatly admired by most socialists because of their exposure of bourgeois hypocrisies, he was sharply criticized by Bahr. Ernst, he wrote, was one of the "Marxist epigoni," a mechanical follower of the great thinker.[119] Stung by Bahr's attack, Ernst wrote to Engels, seeking support for his claim that the Norwegian writers expressed a petty-bourgeois sensibility.[120] Engels gave him little comfort; he suggested that Ernst himself might be guilty of turning economic determinism into a "finished model," according to which historical facts could be "trimmed to size" rather than serve as a "guide to historical studies."[121]

Like the other young intellectuals who participated in the inner movement and the Jungen rebellion, Ernst was convinced that his grasp of Marxist theory was far superior to that of the Social Democratic leaders. The latter, lacking much understanding of the Marxist economic analysis and often still attached to the state-centered socialism of Lassalle, were becoming captive to "the needs of the hour," the immediate interests of the uninformed workers. Thus they neglected the crucial task—preparing the workers for the coming collapse of the state by helping them to form a "new understanding and will."[122] Having become co-editor of the socialist paper in Dresden, the *Sächsischen Arbeiter Zeitung,* Ernst joined the Jungen protest.

Although he took part in the struggle to preserve the Marxist promise of a radical transcendence of the existing way of life, Ernst had also begun to reflect on a dilemma within the ideology. His effort to teach the workers and his exchange with Engels had led him to question his own strictly rationalistic and deterministic form of Marxism. His article in the *Volks-Tribüne* early in August 1890 noted "a danger involved" in any "cold, logical" approach to socialism.[123] Marx had, to be sure, freed his followers from "all illusions and self-deception" and demonstrated that they were mere "waves on a flood." But if economic forces and, indeed, the activity of the enemy would bring the revolution, what was the use of the "enlightenment and organization of the masses"? A strictly deterministic outlook might in reality lead to "indifference and to a weakening of revolutionary energies." Ernst had concluded from his experiences in the movement that people became socialists not through "understanding" but through "feeling." "Illusions," he insisted, were necessary to energize the masses; unscientific as such factors were, they still had "a great role to play in Social Democracy."

Ernst's questioning of economic determinism drew a barrage of criticism, mainly from working-class readers of the *Volks-Tribüne,* who insisted that "strict knowledge" was the key to victory. Schmidt, now editor of the paper, soon ended the discussion. He criticized Ernst for his "one-sided" emphasis on "purely economic causes."[124] The actual impact of Marxist ideas on its adherents, he observed, was "just the reverse" of what Ernst feared. "The consciousness that the economic conditions work for us" did not lead to "inaction but to joyful activity for the great majority of the comrades." Schmidt thus passed over what for Ernst had become both a logical and a psychological dilemma.

Participation in the Jungen rebellion cost Ernst his editorial position in Dresden. And his new appeal to Engels late in August was met with anger and contempt. Engels publicly repudiated Ernst's rigid determinism; it was, he declared, based on a caricature of Marxist theory.[125] Privately Engels dismissed Ernst as a "schoolboy," captive to "such strong fallacies" that he could not write a column "without drawing the wrong conclusion."[126] Ernst's attempt to instruct the party derived, according to Engels, from "the self-conceit" common to "green youths." It would be much better for the party, he added, if Ernst confined himself to the writing of novels, dramas, and literary criticism; then he would "harm only the educated bourgeoisie."

Ernst, however, was already moving away from a rigidly deterministic viewpoint. His growing flexibility as a Marxist was most apparent in the essays on artistic and literary matters which he contributed to the Social Democratic press in the next few months. He continued to view socialism as a "whole world view," but he denied that artistic creativity could be explained in terms of changes in the modes of production. Hence his attempt to turn the tables on his earlier antagonist, Bahr, when the latter offered an economic interpretation of the rise of bourgeois forms of art.[127] What was lacking in Bahr's account, Ernst wrote, was a recognition that "inner psychological drives" were more important than "outer material circumstances" in shaping a work of art. Bahr, he declared, had turned the materialistic conception of history into a dogma.

In his essays on literary developments Ernst was increasingly occupied with aesthetic qualities, the form or style of a work of art, and the subjective element in the creative process.[128] He saw such features becoming more and more dominant in contemporary writers as Naturalism gave way to a quest that was private and personal. Ernst vigorously defended the special claims of art when Gustav Landauer, a leader of the Independent socialists, dismissed literary activity as irrelevant to the class struggle.[129] Not so, declared Ernst. The political and the literary realms were separate; a socialist agitator could enjoy good art even if it had no connection with the cause: "If one is a socialist should he enjoy only bread and water, and should one then all twenty-four hours a day be dissatisfied with the present and strive only for the future? Get out of my way, Herr Landauer, such fanaticism is simply intolerable. . . . Socialism should not lower the educational level of the cultivated, but raise the educational level of those who are excluded from cultural gifts."

Although Ernst, like other young socialist intellectuals, still saw socialism as a broad cultural movement, the relationship between economic and noneconomic factors was no longer clear to him. When Franz Mehring published his *Lessing Legend,* a pioneering application of Marxist theory to literary history, Ernst was critical. Mehring, he wrote, had "ignored the individual situation of the artist" and his mediating role, psychological and formal, which could not be traced to economic conditions.[130]

But if Marxist determinism was losing its hold on Ernst, he held fast to the class struggle. His Marxist confidence in the industrial proletariat left little room for the "intellectual proletariat" which, for Schippel and others, represented a necessary ally of the working classes.

He responded angrily when an anonymous pamphlet, published late in 1890, claimed that an "educated proletariat," made up of insecure individuals within the middle classes, was gravitating naturally to the Social Democrats.[131] It was a mistake, Ernst wrote, for the author to appeal to young doctors, lawyers, and journalists "to feel [themselves] as proletarian" and "join the battle of the workers." For there could be no genuine feeling of solidarity between the "reserve army" of refugees from the "declining petty bourgeoisie" and the workers. The educated recruits constituted a danger to the movement. They saw themselves as an "aristocracy of the spirit" and were only seeking secure places in the future socialist society. They were likely to be satisfied with reforms which stopped short of any "complete social transformation" and would "betray the workers." The "passionate distrust" which the proletariat felt toward these intellectuals was well grounded: "So the educated of our day will not be surprised if we reject its offered hand of brotherhood. In spite of many superficial similarities between its condition and that of the proletariat . . . it cannot be Social Democratic, as much as it might wish—and therefore belongs, despite all, for us, to 'one reactionary mass.'"[132]

Ernst was, of course, calling into question his own place in the movement. But he maintained that there were "rare recruits" among the educated who could serve the cause. He still saw his own role as one of bringing Marxist ideas to the workers. To that end he and Wilhelm Liebknecht planned to publish the short political writings of Marx. Ernst's view of the educational needs of the workers, however, soon clashed with that of Liebknecht. When Liebknecht had started a school for workers in Berlin that offered courses in stenography, accounting, and languages, Ernst was critical.[133] Such an enterprise, he declared, should concentrate on political education; its sole function was to "mobilize all forces for the battle we are engaged in."

Late in 1890 Ernst replaced Schmidt as editor of the *Volks-Tribüne.* It was a strategic post for advancing his view of the movement. But the Jungen rebels had dispersed, and the Social Democrats were in the process of redefining their program. During the first six months of 1891 Ernst refrained from criticism of the party leaders. In June, however, when Vollmar spoke out on behalf of a frankly reformist program, the Jungen forces were revitalized. Ernst quickly aligned the *Volks-Tribüne* with the renewed charges that the Social Democrats were losing their "proletarian character."[134] When, after the Erfurt conference, the Jungen leaders decided to form a new party, Ernst agreed to participate. But he soon had second thoughts and dissociated himself from the Independents. The venture seemed to him un-Marxist. He sympathized with the determination of Kampffmeyer and the others to nurture the "individuality" of the workers. To place primary emphasis on the subjective qualities of the workers, however, was a mistake. It was not the individual character of the worker that made him a revolutionary; material conditions were decisive. "Social Democracy," he wrote, "is the logical product of outer circumstances in the heads of the masses."[135] And so the *Volks-Tribüne* remained "on the side of the Fraktion and the party executive." Yet he deplored the action taken at Erfurt; it had cost the party several of its "most capable members" despite the lack of any "real difference of principles."[136]

In view of "the abuse we have taken from both sides," Ernst could claim that the *Volks-Tribüne* had exercised an impartial judgment in the dispute.[137] In actuality he had reached an impasse as a Marxist intellectual. Lacking any clear notion of the path ahead, he decided to resign the editorship. The decision was influenced by a personal tragedy—the death of his wife in childbirth. He was hurt too by a prosecution and fine for a story he had written. But Marxism no longer gave clear direction to his life. "I have not learned enough," he told Liebknecht.[138] He made plans to undertake further academic study before resuming his work for the movement. In the spring of 1892 he traveled to Switzerland, thus following the path of Kampffmeyer, Müller, and Schmidt, for whom Marxist convictions had similarly made formal academic work in Germany difficult.

Shortly after arriving in Zurich a chance conversation with a Polish student, Rosa Luxemburg, encouraged Ernst to study with August Oncken at the University of Bern.[139] Ernst's aim, much like that of Schmidt, was to gain a deeper understanding of the economic process through which capitalism was destroying itself. Oncken accepted Ernst's proposal to investigate the impact of technological advance on the condition of the workers. The resulting dissertation, Ernst recalled, examined the relationship between "rationalization" and "immiserization"—the way in which the position of the worker worsened despite the increase of efficiency through mechanization.[140] His study, he acknowledged, did not make any impression on the scholarly community. But it increased his grasp of economic issues. During the nineties he wrote on a variety of economic matters, ranging from the development of capitalism in Japan to the plight of German agriculture.

Ernst was still convinced that the socialist movement pointed toward a transformation of life as profound as that which occurred during the decline of the ancient world. Individuals at that time, he believed, were "just as spiritually lost" as those of the present.[141] In order to gain greater insight into the modern transition, Ernst gathered materials on the end of the Roman Empire. The results of his inquiry were presented in a series of articles published in the *Neue Zeit* during 1893.[142]

In the course of his study in Switzerland Ernst had concluded that much of what he needed to know "could not be learned out of books." His friendship with a maverick conservative social and economic thinker, Rudolf Meyer, led to an offer of work in agriculture management.[143] During 1892 and 1893 the two men worked together to improve the productivity of two large estates, one in lower Saxony, the other in Thuringia. The experience convinced Ernst that much of what the Marxists were writing about agrarian problems was nonsense.[144] When the Social Democrats began to discuss the agrarian question in 1894, Ernst took an active part.

In 1894 Ernst also tested his Marxism in another area—municipal administration. For a time he worked as a volunteer in the office of the mayor of Nordhausen. There he dealt mainly with problems associated with public relief for the poor. The experience was again, for Ernst the Marxist, disillusioning. "My veneration of the proletariat," he recalled, "suddenly appeared comical."[145] His Marxist faith was collapsing "piece by piece."

This period in Ernst's life ended with a nervous breakdown. He spent much of 1895 in a sanitarium. In 1896 he returned to Berlin, intent on resuming his career as a freelance journalist. He brought nothing back, he claimed later, "but lost illusions, doubts, and negations."[146] Ernst exaggerated. His articles for the Social Democratic press over the next several years still bore a strong Marxist stamp. His relationship to the Social Democrats, however, was now tenuous. He also decided that he had been mistaken in allowing Tolstoy and Marx to divert him from a literary career.[147] As a creative writer Ernst resumed the quest for a radically new way of living which had been for him, as for other young intellectuals, central to the Marxist appeal.

In their different ways Schippel, Kampffmeyer, Schmidt, and Ernst renewed the critical spirit within Marxism. At the same time they began to confront the difficulties involved in their attempts to transmit their Marxist faith to the working class and create a new mentality. But those difficulties can only be understood against the background of the Marxist orthodoxy developed by Engels and Kautsky and adopted by the party at Erfurt.

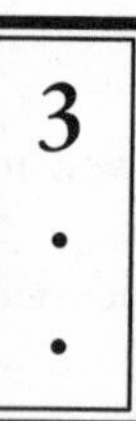

Two Paths for Marxist Intellectuals

AT THE Erfurt conference of 1891 Kautsky established himself as the party's leading theorist. But having formulated, with the aid of Engels, the Marxist principles embodied in the Social Democratic program, he faced his next task. Marxist theory, in any strict sense, was still the possession of a small group of Social Democrats. It was necessary to deepen the hold of Marxism on the life of the party.

Kautsky had been engaged in that work since the early eighties. In the years leading up to Erfurt he had developed an understanding of Marxism which would alter little. His interpretation of Marxist theory and his conception of the role of the intellectual did not, however, go unchallenged. It was called into question early by an Austrian compatriot and friend, Heinrich Braun. The debate between the two men during the eighties and early nineties helped to clarify "orthodox Marxism"; it also anticipated later disagreements among Marxist intellectuals.

Kautsky's Clarification and Dissemination of Orthodox Marxism

Kautsky adopted Marxism in 1879, after reading *Anti-Dühring.* "It enabled me to . . . understand *Capital* completely" and "gave my thought a basis of the greatest firmness and fruitfulness."[1] That basis had already been formed in large part, however, by the influence of Darwinian biology, the mechanistic materialism of Ernst Haeckel, and Thomas Buckle's positivistic philosophy of history.[2] Kautsky's encounter with Engels' treatment of Marxist ideas served, as he recalled, "only to deepen and modify" his pre-Marxist outlook.[3]

Educated at the University of Vienna, Kautsky had joined the young Austrian socialist party in 1875 at the age of twenty-one. His early writings for the movement were informed not only by current scientific views but by a romantic bent inspired by the fiction of George Sand. For a time his strong ethical orientation led toward anarchism. But his discovery of Marxism gave clear direction to his life. His decision to devote himself to the study of Marxist theory was aided by a wealthy German socialist, who provided support for Kautsky to move to Zurich in 1880. There he began to work with Eduard Bernstein who, in 1881, became editor of the *Sozialdemokrat,* the German party's monthly journal published, to avoid prosecution, in the Swiss city.

During the same year Kautsky made his first trip to London and entered the "intellectual workshop" of Engels,[4] who welcomed him as "one of the few in the younger generation" who actually wished to learn.[5] After closer acquaintance Engels expressed some doubts about Kautsky's abilities. He was, Engels wrote to Bebel, a "born pedant," a "hairsplitter," with a disposition to turn simple questions into excessively complicated ones.[6] "His scruples in matters of theory," Engels added, might impose severe limits on his ability to edit a party journal. In time, however, Engels concluded that Kautsky and Bernstein were the only Social Democrats who fully grasped Marxist theory. Bernstein seemed the better of the two; he lacked a university education and was not burdened, therefore, with the nonsense which Kautsky was struggling to unlearn.[7]

Kautsky soon discovered his life's work—"the propaganda, popularization and, insofar as my forces sufficed, the continuation of the scientific results of Marx's investigation and thought."[8] He was, at the same time, taking up the job which Marx had assigned to the intellectuals. No figure within the movement struggled so hard and so long with this task. "The problem of the intellectual in general and his special role in a working-class party," one observer has commented, "runs like a red thread through Kautsky's essays, books, and letters in all phases of his development."[9]

In 1883, as part of his efforts to fulfill this role, Kautsky founded the monthly *Neue Zeit.* He conceived its mission in broad terms; it would introduce its readers to contemporary scientific ideas, particularly those of Darwin, and to modern trends in cultural life. For several young intellectuals Kautsky served as a "schoolmaster," enabling them to fit their ethical and cultural aspirations into the "unified whole of Marxism."[10]

Still, the main purpose of the *Neue Zeit* was the enlightenment of the masses; it would show them "what Marxism is and is not." Although the workers "stood instinctively on the basis of the *Communist Manifesto,*" Kautsky wrote in 1885, reliance on "class instincts alone" would lead them astray.[11] It was the task of the intellectuals, those who could "use the pen," to bring "clarity and consciousness of goals" to the movement.

Kautsky's initial approach to the problem of educating the workers was highly rationalistic. There was "no real need to popularize Marxism"; Marx's writings were "clear and understandable enough."[12] What the workers needed was simply "an easily accessible summary," something they could read "without any great expenditure of money or time." Kautsky's book *The Economic Teachings of Karl Marx,* published in 1887, provided such a summary. The volume did much to spread Marxist ideas in Germany and elsewhere and established Kautsky as a leading authority of the theory. It was second only to Bebel's popular presentation, *Women under Socialism,* as a means of familiarizing the Social Democratic rank and file with the ideas of Marx.

Kautsky soon recognized that the task of educating the workers was more difficult than he had anticipated. Much of the difficulty lay in the Social Democratic party itself. Among the party's parliamentary representatives during the eighties, only Bebel and Liebknecht appeared to Kautsky to be genuine Marxists. The remainder were satisfied with an "uncritical, comfortable eclecticism."[13] Even the "educated comrades" were, with few exceptions, hostile toward the *Neue Zeit* and its efforts to propagate and clarify the Marxist doctrines. Many of the Social Democratic politicians clung to the state-socialist ideas of Lassalle and Rodbertus. Had it not been for Bebel's support, Kautsky believed, he would not have survived as the editor of the *Neue Zeit.* His relationship to Bebel was crucial to his attempt to carry out his educational mission.

It was a curious relationship. It entailed a deliberate separation of the two sides of the revolutionary struggle—practical activity and thinking—which Marx had attempted to integrate in his dialectic. Kautsky believed that he could best serve the cause by distancing himself from the immediate practical concerns which occupied Bebel. Responding to Liebknecht's fears that he would "lose his feeling for Germany" when, in 1885, he settled in London, Kautsky claimed that his "removal from the small battles" would enable him to see more clearly "the whole development of mankind" and view the German movement more accurately from the standpoint of the *Communist Manifesto.*[14] In a letter to Bebel he described their respective activities as a division of labor.

> You, in the midst of German development, in constant touch with the people, with exact knowledge of social conditions, carefully testing the material of the Reichstag and considering the material thus gained not from the standpoint of this or that electoral district but from that of the whole development of the proletariat—I, in constant association with Engels, using the treasures of the British Museum and thus in constant touch with the international course of development—I believe such a working together would make the *Neue Zeit* what it ought to be, the scientific representative of our party.[15]

The relationship between the two men has often been seen as complementary. Kautsky provided, one historian has observed, "a theoretical basis" for the "practical Bebel."[16] It was, however, a specious unity. At critical points in the years ahead the predominantly political concerns of Bebel would collide with Kautsky's determination to maintain the integrity of the Marxist ideology and, indeed, judge the development of the party in the light of its ideology.

Like Bebel and Engels, Kautsky had initially viewed participation in the Reichstag simply as a means of propaganda. But during the late eighties he also adopted a more positive conception of the political struggle, welcoming in particular the efforts of the Social Democratic representatives to strengthen the laws protecting freedom of speech and the right to assemble. Such freedoms were "the light and air of the labor movement," crucial to his own educational aims. Nor did Kautsky worry about the tendency for parliamentary activity to weaken the socialist convictions of the party's representatives. Like Engels, he was confident that the political process was governed ultimately by economic forces. What really mattered was the class struggle. From this standpoint parliamentary activity could only be viewed as a means through which the proletariat might achieve power.[17] Although Kautsky recognized that compromise was an essential part of legislation, he firmly opposed Social Democratic participation in coalitions. This would mean a loss of principle, a weakening of the discipline and solidarity necessary for victory. In a capitalistic state the party of the workers could only stand in opposition.

Kautsky showed no sympathy for the charge of the Jungen that the party's political policy was jeopardizing the Marxist goals. Wille, after all, displayed an "absolute ignorance of economics."[18] During 1890 and 1891 Kautsky was concerned mainly with the task of incorporating the Marxist doctrines into the new party program. His effort led, however, to a clash with Bebel.

Early in 1891 the *Neue Zeit* published, at the urging of Engels, and without consulting Bebel, Marx's criticism of the Gotha program of 1875. By publishing the critique, which contained a harsh denunciation of Lassalle, Engels and Kautsky hoped to set off the ideas of Marx more clearly in preparation for the party conference at Erfurt. Bebel was furious.[19] He feared the reaction of the Social Democratic rank and file, for whom Lassalle remained an inspiring figure. Kautsky, he declared, failed to appreciate the "influence which Lassalle exercised on the masses" and hence the danger of giving offense.[20] "You are theoretical and dogmatic," he told Kautsky, "and as much as you overvalue theory . . . you undervalue the practical."

At Erfurt, however, Bebel supported Kautsky's draft statement of Marxist principles which the delegates accepted, along with Bernstein's draft of the party's immediate goals. The two parts of the program were loosely joined.[21] Only the confidence that objective economic developments would transform the practical political struggle into a revolutionary force held the Erfurt program together.

In an extensive commentary on the theoretical section of the Erfurt program, published shortly after the conference, Kautsky presented the fullest statement of his Marxist convictions.[22] There he recapitulated the primary Marxist doctrines presented in the *Communist Manifesto* and *Capital*—the materialistic conception of history, the irreversible contradictions of capitalism leading to its collapse, the growing polarization of classes, and the emergence of the proletariat as the force which would bring a new socialist order. "Irresistable economic forces," he wrote, "lead with the certainty of doom to the shipwreck of capitalistic production."[23] In his restatement of Marxism, Kautsky emphasized the inward, psychological effects of modern economic change. What harrowed "men's souls most deeply" was the "insecurity of livelihood under capitalism." And he paid special attention to the plight of the "educated proletariat."[24] They suffered from disabilities much like those of the manual workers; their product—knowledge—had been reduced to a merchandise, and their access to professional careers was made ever more difficult by the growth of a "reserve army." For the "small property owner" who knew "no other way of keeping his sons from sinking into the proletariat than sending them to college," the prospects were rapidly diminishing. "The decline of the mass of educated people into . . . the proletariat can no longer be checked."

Kautsky's tendency to fuse the peculiar anxieties and aspirations of the intellectuals with the development of the proletariat was again evident in his discussion of the future socialist society. His portrayal of that future culminated in the claim that all members of society would be able to fulfil the traditional ideal of German intellectuals—"a harmonious, well-rounded development of physical and mental powers, a deep concern with the problems of nature and society, a philosophical bent of mind, that is, a searching for the highest truth for its own sake."[25] However, this was the future. In the present the laborer was robbed "of all intellectual activity" by the nature of mechanization.[26] But not, according to Kautsky, outside of his hours of work.

> One of the most remarkable phenomena of modern society is the thirst for knowledge displayed by the proletariat. . . . And this thirst for knowledge is entirely disinterested. . . . He seeks to understand the whole of society, the whole of the world. The most difficult problems attract him most; it is often hard to bring him down from the clouds to solid earth. . . . It is among the despised and ignorant proletariat that the philosophical spirit of the brilliant members of the Athenian aristocracy is revived.[27]

But if the proletariat was the modern bearer of Bildung, the ideal of self-cultivation, its capacity to grasp the full truth of Marxism was still limited. "At best a proletarian can do no more than appropriate for its own purposes a part of the learning of the bourgeois world."[28] He lacked the leisure necessary to carry independent scientific investigation beyond "the point reached by bourgeois thinkers." The workers needed, therefore, that "very small minority" of bourgeois idealists who "have not only the requisite theoretical insight but also the courage and strength to break with their class."[29]

Unlike Engels in these years, Kautsky reaffirmed the crucial role of intellectuals in the movement. They were charged with the task of providing the workers with a "clear conception of their historical function."[30] Without knowledge of the goal and insight into the laws of historical development, the proletariat would go astray. Kautsky thus rejected any fatalistic or purely mechanistic reading of the process leading toward the revolution.[31]

Kautsky's insistence on the independent role of the intellectuals and the need for a significant measure of theoretical understanding on the part of the workers did not fit easily into his economic determinism. His continuing demand for a new consciousness and will had no clear basis in the materialistic categories and the reflexive epistemology underlying his Marxism. One commentator has seen a "covert idealism" in Kautsky's thought.[32] "The revolutionary element," Walter Holzheuer has observed, "became an affair of correct consciousness," a "psychological revolutionism." Kautsky had fallen back on a commonsense assertion of human agency; he had tacitly drawn on the conventional mentality which his ideology was designed to replace.[33] Much of the grounding for his Marxist theory remained hidden.

In these terms, however, Kautsky could view the Social Democrats as a "church militant."[34] The party was a vehicle for a Marxist world view. It was made up of "bourgeois idealists" and that section of the working class which had become conscious of its exploited condition and developed a new will. Kautsky was convinced that the "socialist philosophy" was so suited to the "best minds in the working class" that they would, "as soon as they had the opportunity, willingly turn to it."[35]

If the Social Democratic party was a "church militant," socialists had "no reason to distrust parliamentary action."[36] Parliament was the "most powerful lever" that could be "utilized to raise the proletariat out of economic, social, and moral degradation." But the driving force of the movement lay outside of politics.

During the period following the Erfurt conference Kautsky resumed his effort, mainly through the *Neue Zeit,* to nurture a Marxist understanding in the party rank and file. The difficulties of that task, however, were becoming more and more apparent. Bebel was one problem. The party leader continued to complain that the *Neue Zeit* was "too doctrinaire and too little topical," by which he meant that it placed excessive demands on the minds of the masses and even on party members like himself, who had no time for its lengthy and highly specialized articles.[37] For Kautsky, in contrast, such articles gave the *Neue Zeit* its chief value. Current political questions, he argued, remained alive only for ten to fourteen days; an "academic, doctrinaire tone," Kautsky declared, was an inescapable feature of the *Neue Zeit*.[38] He continued to resist pressure to change the journal to a weekly and move it from Stuttgart to Berlin, where it would be closer to the immediate, practical struggles of the party.

The journal's remoteness from the everyday life of the party was corrected to some extent in the late summer of 1891, when Franz Mehring was hired to serve as its Berlin correspondent and write lead articles. In Mehring the Social Democrats had secured a talented and experienced journalist whose abilities complemented those of Kautsky. Not only could he provide incisive commentaries on public affairs, but his academic training in literature brought a new sophistication to the journal's treatment of cultural issues. Mehring's background and his temperament ensured, however, that his role in the party would be controversial.

In the eyes of Social Democrats Mehring's past was checkered.[39] As a progressive liberal journalist in the seventies he had expressed strong sympathies for the socialists. But in 1876 he had turned on the party, writing a pamphlet in which he denounced the Social Democrats as a threat to the nation. By the late eighties, however, Mehring was disillusioned with Bismarck's policies and, as an editor of a progressive Berlin newspaper, denounced the government's treatment of the party. In 1889 a dispute with a leading drama critic cost him his editorial post and led to his ostracism by the bourgeois press. Meanwhile, his study of Marxist writings had drawn him close to the Social Democrats. And after being courted by the party's leaders, he was offered a position with the *Neue Zeit* by its publisher, Dietz.

Kautsky accepted Mehring's appointment with some reluctance. But the newcomer more than fulfilled the hopes of those who had recruited him. His weekly lead articles, as Kautsky quickly recognized, gave the *Neue Zeit* a "freshness" and "topicality" which it had lacked.[40] Moreover, Mehring soon set out to apply Marxism to new areas. In January 1892 he began the series of articles later published as the *Lessing Legend,* in which he examined eighteenth-century Germany from the standpoint of the materialistic conception of history.[41] The essays were primarily an account of the rise of Prussia, but Mehring also attempted, through an analysis of economic and social life, to explain the cultural changes under way. Engels was delighted with the work. Mehring had shown how Marxist conceptions could guide the study of history. Mehring's "dissolution of the monarchic-patriotic legend," Engels wrote the author, was a contribution to overcoming class domination.[42] Soon Mehring began to contemplate a history of the force destined to replace the old authorities—the Social Democratic party itself.

For all his gifts and remarkable productivity, however, Mehring remained isolated among the Social Democrats. The distrust arising from his earlier betrayal of the party was not easily dispelled. Had it not been for "that cursed pamphlet," Kautsky observed, "he would be one of the first among us."[43] But Mehring's difficulties in the party stemmed even more from his own personality. He was, as Kautsky discovered, "pathologically sensitive," quick to take personal offense when disagreements arose and quick to turn "personal antagonisms" into "matters of principle."[44] His career as a Social Democrat was punctuated by quarrels with nearly all of those with whom he attempted to work closely. Even Bebel recognized the "danger of being intimate with him," for a time might come when confidences would be betrayed.[45] One of the closest outside observers of the German Social Democrats, the Austrian leader Victor Adler, continued throughout the decade to view him as a "dangerous intriguer" who had "no heart for the party."[46]

Kautsky, virtually alone among the Social Democratic leaders, was able to maintain a good working relationship with Mehring. The *Neue Zeit* editor thus gained not only a gifted collaborator but one who shared, for the most part, his conception of Marxism. Mehring joined Kautsky in the effort to make the journal both an authority in ideological matters and a means of educating the advanced sections of the German workers.

During the early nineties it was becoming clear, however, that the *Neue Zeit* was not reaching the party rank and file. Kautsky had conceded much earlier that the workers did not find theory interesting.[47] And in 1892 he acknowledged that its four or five thousand subscribers were mostly members of the bourgeoisie.[48] He now realized that his access to the majority of the Social Democrats lay mainly through the party cadre—journalists, speakers, and organizers. But here too Kautsky encountered difficulties in his efforts to transmit Marxist doctrines.

Liebknecht, whom Kautsky had replaced as the party's chief interpreter of Marx, was one of the obstacles. Although he had long lost, in the eyes of Engels, Bebel, and Kautsky, any credibility as a theorist, Liebknecht remained a force within the party. As editor of *Vorwärts* he now represented a barrier to the development of the common understanding of Marxism which seemed to Kautsky essential to the health of the party. Liebknecht regarded *Vorwärts* as a forum in which all sides of the questions dividing Social Democrats should be presented.[49] He did take a strong stand against the Jungen, but he refused to attack the "opportunists"—Vollmar and the trade unions leaders—whom Kautsky viewed as a greater threat to ideological integrity.

Nor could Kautsky count on the support of other Social Democratic journalists. A year after Erfurt he complained that the *Neue Zeit* was being boycotted by party editors because of its independent and critical spirit.[50] A quarrel with Schönlank, the most skilled and imaginative of the party's editors, suggested the difficulty of developing a common point of view. Relations with Schönlank also indicated the tendency for intellectual disagreements among leading Social Democrats to turn into deep personal antagonisms. Kautsky became convinced that his opponent had resorted to "lies and sneaky practices."[51] Charges of a personal nature also emerged during a vigorous polemic with another prominent Social Democratic journalist, Georg Ledebour, after the latter had accused Kautsky of seeking to be a "little pope within the party."[52] By 1893 Kautsky had come to see himself and the *Neue Zeit* as victims of a "literary clique" which was beginning to dominate the Social Democratic press.

Kautsky experienced periodic doubts about his mission. During 1893 and 1894 he thought seriously of returning to Austria. Such a move, he wrote Engels, would place him "in the middle of a great movement," enable him to receive fresh impetus from it, and check his tendency to become a "bookworm."[53] He felt, too, that his editorial responsibilities were keeping him from the theoretical and historical work for which he was best suited. Yet he could not identify any other Social Democrat to whom the *Neue Zeit* and its central task—the clarification and dissemination of Marxist theory—could safely be entrusted. As he considered possible replacements he concluded that they either lacked the editorial skills and personal qualities necessary, had shown tendencies to dilute Marxism, or both. Although Kautsky confessed, early in 1894, that he still "felt a stranger in the German movement," he decided that he could not desert his editorial post.[54]

That post had become, in his mind, even more important with the rapid growth of the party after 1890. The party was gaining a large number of workers who "know little more of our principles than our opponents."[55] It still suffered, moreover, from the neglect in the schooling of party members which had been unavoidable under the antisocialist laws. Recent recruits were especially susceptible to the tendency to "flatten out" the party's principles and fall prey to the "demagoguery of Vollmar." Without the kind of understanding provided by Marx, the German workers might "arrive at the condition of those in England," concerned "only with the immediate and the tangible and the practical."[56]

The obstacles Kautsky encountered in his efforts to clarify and transmit Marxist doctrines—the increasingly pragmatic course of Bebel, the indifference or ignorance of the workers themselves, and the hostility of other party journalists—did not diminish his sense of mission. He continued to believe that Marxism represented a new world view, a comprehensive set of truths for humanity. Not that his mind was closed to any alteration or correction of Marxist theory in the light of changing circumstances. He denied that Marxism was a finished system. The tolerance with which he had edited the *Neue Zeit* during the eighties, particularly his willingness to publish different viewpoints, continued in the nineties.

Having formulated the party's official ideology, however, Kautsky made it the test for correct thinking among Social Democrats. He showed little interest in the questions which Schmidt and other young intellectuals were raising. Admittedly uncertain in philosophical matters, Kautsky seemed to hold, like Engels, that the traditional questions had largely been eclipsed by modern science—by a direct grasp of the realities of the natural world and social development.

Kautsky's belief that Marxism expressed a comprehensive interpretation of life set narrow limits to his capacity for self-criticism. Moreover, his belief that the Social Democrats were the exclusive bearers of the new truths ruled out any meaningful dialogue with the bourgeois thinkers. This was a major point of disagreement with his friend Heinrich Braun, who shared Kautsky's commitment to the task of clarifying and spreading Marxist ideas. The growing disagreement between the two men sets off even more sharply the nature of Marxist orthodoxy. It also introduces, in Braun, a figure who would play an important role in the troubled relationship between the Social Democratic party and its intellectuals.

Heinrich Braun: Marxism as a Guide to Immediate Reforms

When Kautsky proposed, late in 1882, to start a new journal to "enlighten the masses," he received enthusiastic support from Heinrich Braun, an acquaintance from his school days in Vienna.[57] Braun contributed two thousand marks to help launch the *Neue Zeit* and accepted, alongside Kautsky and Liebknecht, editorial responsibilities. He also wrote the lead article for the first issue. He soon drew back from a leading role in the venture, although he and his wife Josefine continued to contribute articles and reviews. His ongoing interest in the *Neue Zeit* and its mission was apparent in his correspondence with Kautsky throughout the eighties. He also encouraged Kautsky's growth as a Marxist thinker. From a wealthy brother-in-law Braun secured the funds, a hundred marks a month, which enabled Kautsky to settle in London in 1885 and work closely with Engels.[58] The two men were, however, developing different conceptions of the way in which Marxist ideas could best be related to German life and different views of the function of the socialist intellectual.

Braun was born in a wealthy Jewish family in Vienna in 1854.[59] As a boy he displayed the rebellious spirit and the fierce sense of independence which characterized his later life as well. Sigmund Freud, an "inseparable friend" during his adolescent years, "compared him secretly to a young lion," a phrase which testified to Braun's personal force.[60] Freud recalled that Braun had "aroused revolutionary feelings within him." When, at the University of Vienna, Braun encountered socialist ideas in the lectures of Lorenz von Stein, he found a focus for his radical bent. At about the same time he entered a circle of young intellectuals who were caught up with the ideas of Schopenhauer, Wagner, and Nietzsche.[61] The circle included Victor Adler, the founder of the Austrian Social Democratic party at the end of the eighties, who married Braun's sister.

During the late seventies Braun studied law at the universities of Vienna and Göttingen and then completed a doctorate in political economy after further study in Strasbourg and Halle. For a time an academic career seemed to be opening up for him, but religious barriers and his socialist views blocked the way.[62] He continued his studies, however, freed by family wealth from the immediate need to make a living. In Marxism he had discovered a compelling interpretation of modern history. But unlike Kautsky he did not adopt Marx's theory as a total belief system. Braun had been influenced by the writings of the German mystics, particularly Meister Eckhart, as well as by the philosophical ideas of Spinoza, Kant, and Nietzsche. He rejected the economic determinism of Engels, insisting on the importance of ideas and, following Nietzsche, on the force of the individual personality. This outlook was reinforced by what his biographer described as the temperament of a "born autocrat."[63]

Yet Braun's commitment to Marxism was so strong that he made plans in 1882 to move to London in order to gain a deeper understanding of the theory through close contact with Marx and Engels. Kautsky encouraged him and attempted to smooth the way. He assured Engels that Braun was "completely reliable," that the distrust with which they customarily viewed "academically educated people" could be set aside.[64] When Engels expressed doubts about the proposal, Kautsky assured him that Braun stood "completely on the ground of Marx and the class struggle."[65] Family complications prevented Braun's move, but four years later he revived the plan to collaborate with Engels in developing Marx's ideas.

Braun's contribution to the first issue of the *Neue Zeit,* "The Problem of Worker's Insurance and the Conception of Lujo Brentano," suggested that his view of Marxism and its advance was quite different than that of Kautsky.[66] Kautsky saw the task mainly in terms of the inculcation of Marxist ideas; Braun wished to bring the Marxist analysis to bear on immediate social and political problems. To do so, he believed, required empirical investigation, the gathering of statistical data that would throw light on such problems as housing, unemployment, and poverty. The value of Marxist theory lay in its capacity to illuminate the relationship between economic developments and social conditions. Marxism also demonstrated the ways in which particular economic and social phenomena were integrally related to society as a whole. Both methods—empirical and wholistic—would guide legislators in improving the conditions of the working class.

To apply Marxist theory in this way entailed a view of the bourgeois opposition quite different from that of Kautsky. Kautsky considered Marxism to be a self-contained system of thought, tightly sealed off from bourgeois modes of thinking. Braun, however, saw possibilities for fruitful interchange. Not only did he believe that facts, statistical data, provided all reformers with a common ground, but he was convinced that the Social Democrats needed to refine their Marxist doctrines through ongoing debate with their critics. He was confident that such an interchange would demonstrate "the correctness of our views."[67]

Kautsky soon realized, as he informed Engels, that his relationship with Braun had not developed as he had hoped. Braun, he had concluded by the fall of 1883, was one of the "educated socialists" who had not "burned their bridges behind them."[68] Nevertheless, Braun's letters to Kautsky during the eighties indicated that they remained in close touch and shared a strong commitment to the advance of Marxism. Braun encouraged Kautsky in his studies, and Kautsky commiserated with Braun when, in 1885, a new plan to start an academic career failed. Later in the year Braun seriously considered joining Kautsky as co-editor of the *Neue Zeit.* Pressure for a change in editorial policy was coming from Liebknecht, who believed that Kautsky had lost touch with "those circles in Germany out of which the most fruitful contributors to the journal might come."[69] Liebknecht, in fact, wished to install Braun as sole editor. Informing Kautsky of the plan, Braun assured his friend that he would have no part of such a move. But he was critical of Kautsky's editorial policy: "You are an excellent writer and the best contributor to the *Neue Zeit,* but a very inadequate editor. . . . A journal ought not to have only a general program . . . it is even more important that it possess a special program which determines the attitude and content of the paper."[70] What was lacking in the *Neue Zeit,* according to Braun, was the discussion of concrete problems, such as protective legislation for the workers. An editor, he told Kautsky, should locate "suitable people," stimulate them to investigate particular social problems, and illuminate them both through statistical data and by means of theory. Without this, the *Neue Zeit* had become excessively general and abstract; hence its propensity for "unproductive polemics" and the absence of any "coherent direction." It had become a "mishmash."

Braun continued to stand, as he told his close friend, Paul Natorp, in the mid-eighties, "completely on the ground of Karl Marx."[71] But he was increasingly restive over the inability or unwillingness of Marxists to show that their theory could be applied to practical social and political issues. Social Democrats were vulnerable to the charge that their ideas were irrelevant to the problems of the day. "Passionately interested," as he wrote Kautsky in 1887, in overcoming this deficiency, he again proposed a move to London to collaborate with Kautsky and Engels.[72] To develop the "social and political side of Marx's theory" was even more important than the elaboration of his economic theory. If he could be assured that Kautsky and Engels were receptive, he wrote, he would be on his way. A short time later, apparently having heard that collaboration would be possible, he wrote that he would soon settle in London with his wife and two sons.[73]

Family problems again forced Braun to cancel the plan. But his determination, as he told Natorp, to "maintain full inner freedom and independence" in interpreting Marx and his commitment to practical applications of the theory made it unlikely that the three men could have worked together.[74] Before long Braun embarked on a course which demonstrated his sharp disagreement with Kautsky.

Braun had formed close ties with the German Social Democrats. Bebel was especially impressed with him and viewed Braun, so his biographer claimed, as a future leader of the party.[75] When representatives of the outlawed party held a secret conference in Switzerland in the fall of 1887, Braun served as secretary, evidence of the "unconditional trust" placed in him by Bebel and his colleagues. Writing to Kautsky shortly after the meeting, Braun expressed his satisfaction that the radical outlook of Bebel and Liebknecht had won a "complete victory" over the "weak, moderate element."[76] Bebel, in turn, expressed his confidence in Braun by asking him to take over the editorship of the party paper in Berlin, the *Volksblatt.*

Braun, however, had already decided to start a journal that would correct the deficiencies of the *Neue Zeit*. His proposed journal, he told Kautsky, would collect "facts relevant to the pressing problems of the day" and thus provide a firmer basis for the development of socialist theory.[77] He asked the editor of the *Neue Zeit* to help him with the project. When Kautsky refused, Braun was astonished and dismayed: "You are among the writers who count in our party. . . . A scientific undertaking of the kind we want to found will inevitably be influenced [through] your participation or through your keeping your distance."[78]

Only after Braun's assurance, supported by Bebel, that the new quarterly, the *Archiv für Soziale Gesetzgebung und Statistik,* would not compete with the *Neue Zeit* did Kautsky agree to help.[79] But the differences between the two men were again evident in Braun's description of his task as an editor: "I lay all weight on ability and leave behind the regard for party membership. I have from the beginning nothing against the representatives of *other* views than our own, if they can be validated scientifically. It would then be a matter of discussing the concerned questions so as to demonstrate the correctness of our views."[80] Such an enterprise was all the more necessary, Braun believed, because the Social Democrats were neglecting the hard intellectual work required to prepare for the socialist future. Only "independent investigation" could free the party from its tendency to fall back on a millenarian-like faith that economic forces were bringing a new social order.

By means of the *Archiv,* which began publication in 1888, Braun attempted, as the subtitle read, to provide a forum for the "investigation of social conditions in all lands." He was remarkably successful.[81] The *Archiv* was a pioneering venture in applied social science in Germany. Braun's Marxist approach to the undertaking was reflected in his emphasis on the condition of the workers under capitalism and in his effort to place that issue in the widest possible social and cultural context. But he demanded from his contributors an empirical basis for their inquiries as well as a commitment to scholarly objectivity.

Braun attracted a talented and diverse group of contributors. Articles by Social Democrats appeared alongside others by liberal social thinkers such as Lujo Brentano, and the most creative figures in the first generation of German sociologists—Ferdinand Tönnies, Max and Alfred Weber, Georg Simmel, and Werner Sombart. In Sombart, who became the most frequent contributor and a close friend, Braun had recruited a scholar particularly well equipped to undertake the project for which the *Archiv* was designed, connecting Marxist theory with the pressing social and economic questions of the day.[82]

The *Archiv* did not, however, advance that project significantly. Sombart's Marxism, like Braun's, remained open; Marxist claims that capitalism was being destroyed by its internal dynamics still needed to be examined and tested. Sombart, like Schmidt, was increasingly skeptical of the soundness of the Marxist economic analysis, even though he too attempted to salvage the notions of exploitation and the special mission of the proletariat.[83] Moreover, Braun's own attempts to bridge theory and practical life faltered, a result both of his absorption in his editorial duties and, according to his biographer, of his own limitations as a scholar. He was, she wrote, incapable of that "sense of proportion," the ability to stop at some point, give form to the material collected, and bring one's inquiries to fruition.[84] Braun proved, however, to be a skilled editor, combining a firm insistence on scholarly objectivity in dealing with the matter at hand with a respect for the independence and, indeed, the varied ideological perspectives of his contributors. Such an approach ensured that the pluralism which characterized the *Archiv* at the outset would not diminish significantly. Braun's confidence that the interaction of Marxists and non-Marxists would "demonstrate the correctness of our views," however, was not borne out.[85]

It was hardly surprising that Kautsky, who contributed an article to the first issue of the *Archiv,* was "not very edified by the society in which I find myself."[86] He was especially disturbed, he wrote Bebel, by Braun's willingness to give space to mere social reformers, to temperance advocates and the like: "That is not tolerance but weakness. We must use our slight means for the propaganda of our ideas, not for all possible ideas, even those of our enemies. The *Archiv* is on a very bad path. . . . Braun simply wants contributors who have a 'Name'; he had not found enough of them in our ranks, so now he must make his organ into an organ for academic careerists. I have no desire to contribute further to the *Archiv.* The devil take 'science' if it calls on us to propagate the opposite of that which we strive for." Convinced that Marxism required a radical break with bourgeois modes of social thought, Kautsky could only view Braun's editorial policy as a form of opportunism comparable to that which tempted the Social Democratic politicians.

As editor, Braun distanced himself from the Social Democrats, seeking to maintain at least the appearance of political neutrality. But he continued in the early nineties to follow the development of the party closely. He was not sympathetic to the Jungen, dismissing their protest as anarchistic. And despite his own concern with practical politics, he rejected Vollmar's call for an explicit reformist course. What concerned Braun most was the intellectual poverty of the Social Democrats. He attempted in various ways to correct the deficiency. Braun was instrumental in bringing Mehring into the party.[87] He provided help and encouragement to several of the young socialist intellectuals. When Schmidt, for example, attempted to put together a package of journalistic assignments that would support his study in London, Braun proposed that he become a regular contributor to the *Archiv,* reporting on trends in British social legislation.[88] In addition, Braun was responsible for the offer which Schmidt received from the *Züricher Post* as well as for the proposal to write a book on Marx.[89] Braun's younger brother, Adolf, who entered the German movement in these years, also sought to recruit intellectuals for the party.

Braun shared Kautsky's belief that the progress of socialism demanded that workers be raised to a higher level of understanding. For this purpose the *Archiv* had proved to be of limited use. It had drawn together a small circle of experts, but it had done little to enlighten the "crowd of unreflective citizens."[90] To reach a wider audience, Braun conceived the idea of a weekly paper which would, like the *Archiv,* promote understanding of social problems but do so in a more popular manner. He was motivated in part by the strike of the miners in the Rhineland in the spring of 1889 and by the "slight familiarity with the facts" displayed by all parties in the dispute.[91] Such failures to grasp the real nature of economic and social conditions, he felt, would have "fateful consequences for practical life and legislation." Hence the need for a paper that would help the general reader form "objective and penetrating judgments on actual questions." His proposed weekly, Braun told Sombart, would bring together in one place relevant information which at present was scattered—in specialized economic literature, in parliamentary reports, in trade statistics, both national and international. To present such material as fully and quickly as possible would also enable politicians to deal more effectively with such problems as child labor, care for the aged and the disabled, and the question of the proper length of the work week.

Braun was unable to start his weekly, the *Sozialpolitische Centralblatt,* until early in 1892. Before long, however, it was clear that he had exaggerated the power of disinterested social investigation to overcome ignorance, prejudice, and partisan loyalties. Social investigators who were willing to "go against their party" affiliations at an abstract, theoretical level shrank from direct applications of their findings to immediate political issues.[92] It proved much more difficult to maintain the disinterested posture of the *Archiv.* Nor was Braun's hope for a new kind of readership realized. The readers of scholarly periodicals, he wrote Sombart, were "weak-kneed and cowardly," able to tolerate "splendid temperaments like your own only with moans and groans." After three years Braun gave up the paper. His efforts to influence the treatment of immediate social questions by means of dispassionate inquiry had earned him only the hostility of all political groups.

Kautsky was especially angry. The doubts with which he had followed the development of the *Archiv* increased with the appearance of the

Centralblatt. Braun's appeal to socialist and nonsocialist readers alike clashed with Kautsky's conception of the movement. A note in the *Neue Zeit* welcomed Braun's weekly.[93] A few months later, however, it was criticized as opportunistic.[94] Kautsky's growing bitterness exploded in letters to Adler. The new paper came, he wrote, just as the fruit of his own ten years effort "to cram Marxism" into the party was beginning to succeed.[95] The *Centralblatt* threatened the new clarity which had been attained at Erfurt. What was especially galling to Kautsky was the respect which Braun was giving to academic social thinkers whom the *Neue Zeit* had been seeking to discredit. An article by Brentano on trade unionism in an early issue of the *Centralblatt* was a particularly flagrant example of the danger it presented to Social Democrats. Brentano held up the British workers as a model for their German counterparts because they had "not been enslaved by the Marxist orthodoxy."[96]

If Braun had pitched his paper simply to bourgeois readers, Kautsky observed, it might have been useful. Instead it had become an "organ for the systematic" and, indeed, "intentional corruption of the . . . movement."[97] It provided support for all that "is unclear and confusing in our party." The damage was most evident among the Social Democratic editors: "The fact is that among our editors it makes up the main scientific reading. . . . [It] is read more zealously than the *Neue Zeit.* And that is very natural. Our editors are overburdened with work. They have no time to read something which is not immediately useful; and therefore, they find more in the [*Centralblatt*] than in the *Neue Zeit,* for the reading of the first spares them work; the reading of the latter makes them work." The new weekly, according to Kautsky, was especially harmful to those Social Democratic journalists and agitators who were not "completely clear" about Marxist theory. Moreover, by printing articles from Braun's paper, the party press was "spreading the theoretical inadequacy." It provided "grist for the mill" for all party members who prided themselves on their ignorance in theoretical matters and "railed against the Erfurt program because of its philosophical character." Kautsky appealed to Adler to convince his brother-in-law that he was hurting the socialist cause.[98]

But Braun was seeking, as he told Adler, to place "bourgeois science in the service" of the working-class struggle in order to overcome the "shameful lack of intellectual capacities in our ranks."[99] During 1893 he offered a critique of the party in an article in the *Archiv.*[100] Noting the dissatisfaction with the Social Democratic press which had been expressed at a recent party congress, he charged that the press was not playing its proper role. Unlike the newspapers of the other political parties, the Social Democratic organs addressed readers with an "uncommon intellectual thirst and receptivity."[101] Party editors assumed, therefore, the chief responsibility for the education of the rank and file. Braun emphasized once more the party's intellectual stagnation. Social Democrats had become "locked up within the confines" of the ideas they had acquired earlier; they were not engaged in "ongoing scientific investigation."[102] To overcome the "ossification" which threatened, Braun called for greater internal discussion and constant interchange with their bourgeois opponents.

Braun was worried most, however, about the party's neglect of the "intellectual elevation of the masses."[103] Much like the Jungen intellectuals, he attributed this to the "one-sided, over-evaluation" of politics. The party was also suffering from its rapid growth. Enamored with "outer successes," Social Democratic leaders were ignoring the need for an "inner intellectual deepening."

Despite his conviction that the Social Democrats needed to connect their Marxist ideology with immediate political problems, Braun shared the belief, common to most socialist intellectuals, that the movement entailed a transformation of culture. Socialism, he wrote in 1892, was a "spiritual movement of elemental power," unmatched in Germany "since the Reformation."[104] The Social Democrats owed their growth to their capacity to express the "hidden yearnings of the masses." Despite his desire for dialogue with the bourgeoisie, Braun worried about the tendency for the masses to be seduced by conventional attitudes and values. He was convinced that socialists required a new conception of human needs and wants, what he called a new "theory of nourishment."[105] His own style of life was, in fact, strongly ascetic.

Yet in cultural matters as in practical affairs, the Social Democrats could not rely, according to Braun, "simply on the circle of their own followers."[106] Engels' assurance that the socialists were the "inheritors of German classical philosophy" applied to the entire German cultural tradition as well. Only by building on the "whole culture of the century" could the socialist movement bring "a new blossoming of intellectual life." Where Kautsky saw a radical break between socialism and traditional ways of thought, Braun insisted on continuity.

This difference was again the point of disagreement when Kautsky, angered by Braun's critique of the party, resumed his correspondence with Braun early in 1894. After scolding Braun for airing his view in a journal intended mainly for bourgeois readers, Kautsky dealt with the claim that the Social Democrats needed the help of bourgeois thinkers: "You have always endeavored to draw the "intellectuals" into our movement, and according to my view it has always been the most important task to view with mistrust the literary and student types, and to admit no one who is untested to a position of responsibility."[107]

It had become apparent to Kautsky, however, that intellectual capacity was not sufficient for the role to which Marx and Engels had assigned the educated recruits. "We are not only a party of scientific investigation," he told Braun, "but above all a party of struggle."[108] Knowledge was not enough. "We must also demand reliable" characters. The necessary qualities, he added, were "rarely combined with each other in the 'literary types' that seek places in the party."

The question of the reliability of the educated recruits had begun to trouble a number of Social Democrats. During 1894 and 1895 the "Akademikerproblem" arose in several ways. Kautsky decided it was time to look more closely at the relationship between the party and the new stratum of intellectuals developing in capitalistic society. Meanwhile the younger intellectuals, through their concern with the agrarian question, assumed a new significance in the life of the party.

Discovering the Akademikerproblem

FEARS that academically educated recruits presented a threat to the proletarian character of the movement surfaced first at the Cologne conference of 1893.[1] A warning came from Richard Fischer, a worker who had risen to an influential position in the party: "We need characters who have been tested, not people whose pasts we don't know; who were in the service of the enemy yesterday and may return to these tomorrow. These deserters [from their class] come to us because they have not found employment with the enemy and they will remain with us as long as they are paid. They will betray us in the first hour of danger."[2] The delegates' response, recorded in the conference proceedings, indicated that Fischer's feelings were shared by many.

The first serious discussion of the "Akademikerproblem" came, however, from one of the newcomers, Richard Calwer. In the fall of 1894 he published a pamphlet in which he examined the anomalous position of educated young men like himself in the movement. A short time later the question prompted a spirited debate at the party's Frankfurt conference. This episode in turn led Kautsky to reflect on the relationship between the Social Democrats and the "intellectual proletariat." But even as Kautsky addressed the issue, it was taking a practical form in the party's struggle with the agrarian question. Not only did the intellectuals play a central role in that discussion, but they presented the first serious challenge to the Marxist orthodoxy adopted at Erfurt.

Richard Calwer: Judging the Party in the Light of the *Communist Manifesto*

Richard Calwer grew up, like Ernst, in the fluid social sector where ambitious members of the working class might move into the lower middle class.[3] He was born in Esslingen in 1868, the son of a locomotive driver who had advanced to the position of foreman. The family was deeply religious, a fact that likely influenced Calwer's plans to become a clergyman. But after attending the universities of Tübingen and Berlin, he turned to the study of medicine at the University of Munich, and ultimately he left academic life without gaining a degree. There is no record of his conversion to socialism. By 1891 he was writing agitational materials for the party and had become co-editor of the paper in Braunschweig, the *Volksfreund.*

In these years Calwer was an orthodox Marxist, firmly committed to the views of Engels and Kautsky, and yet determined, much like the Jungen, to combat the influences which threatened the ideological purity of the party. His pamphlet *The Communist Manifesto and Modern Social Democracy,* published in September 1894, was designed for that purpose.[4] At the same time he was using the *Communist Manifesto* as a model with which to test the role of the intellectuals in the party.

Calwer's starting point was the claim by Marx and Engels that while the working class came to socialism "out of historical necessity," the "bourgeois ideologues" arrived "through study."[5] But did the converts from the middle class, Calwer asked, actually "come out of economic understanding"? "If this was not the case," as he believed, the proletarian movement was in danger. The intellectuals, who according to Marx and Engels were to enable the workers to become aware of their historical task, would not be able to fulfill their role.

Confident that the "basic ideas" of the *Communist Manifesto* were still valid, that it remained the "authority for the development of the proletariat," Calwer examined the Social Democratic press and its propaganda material.[6] He quickly concluded that the party's chief means for educating the proletariat was defective. "Our journalists," he wrote, still work mostly "out of the old standpoint," using the "same weapons" as their opponents.[7] Instead of recognizing, for example, that the capitalists were "not free," that they "must act according to immanent blind-working laws," Social Democratic writers often played the role of "moral preachers." Their inability to think and write in terms of the economic categories provided by Marx was reflected in their tendency to engage in personal invective. As a result the party press had become a "desert," "shallow," given to "twaddle," and "scarcely worth the paper it was written on."[8]

To explain the defects of the Social Democratic journalists, Calwer noted the ease with which young men like himself, though lacking much knowledge of Marxist ideas, could assume responsible positions in the party. "A good tongue" and a smattering of education were sufficient to gain a "firm place in our movement as an editor or writer."[9] So they came, Calwer observed, refugees from theological examinations as he was or, from the other professions, aspiring teachers and lawyers, who after hearing a few socialist lectures believed that they could serve the cause. Often, however, they simply brought petty-bourgeois attitudes into the party. For Calwer, as for the Jungen intellectuals a few years earlier, here was the chief menace to the integrity of the proletarian movement.

Signs of a petty-bourgeois sensibility were, according to Calwer, widespread among the Social Democrats. The sense of social impotence, characteristic of that sensibility, could be seen in the feelings of envy and resentment expressed in the party literature. The utopian bent, the propensity of Social Democrats to identify themselves with the fads of the day—vegetarianism, free thought, homeopathy, natural healing methods, and the like—were further evidence of ways of thinking alien to Marxism.[10] But petty-bourgeois attitudes were "constantly being formed within the proletariat itself" through the emphasis on practical reforms. Although Calwer did not question the party's political practices, he was critical of the short term, self-help methods of the trade unions and cooperatives.[11] Such methods favored the well-being of special groups at the expense of the class solidarity on which the triumph of the proletariat depended.

Although supposedly focusing on the petty-bourgeois sensibility as the main threat to the party, Calwer revealed his anti-Semitism when he took aim at the Jewish journalists in the party.[12] Who, he wrote, could "doubt the fact" that there was a "special Jewish character," a mixture of ambition and materialism? Calwer seemingly dissociated the party from anti-Semitism, but he suggested that the Social Democrats might be going to the opposite extreme—"philo-Semitism." The danger was twofold, in his view. The Jewish element was inclined toward sectarianism. It was "mainly Jews," Calwer noted, "who set the Independents in motion." But they were also given to opportunism. The party needed to be on guard against the "Jewish careerists in our ranks."

How then could the Social Democrats eliminate the influence of those who were "confusing the proletariat"?[13] The main remedy lay in the reform of the press. There were several obstacles. In too many cases the party paper was viewed as a financial operation rather than as a means of agitation; the position of the editors was subordinated to that of the business manager. Calwer also felt that free expression within the party was threatened by the move toward a more centralized organization. But if the Social Democrats were to follow the principles of the *Communist Manifesto*, the influence of petty-bourgeois elements within the party would have to be "broken." Only if they engaged in a more careful screening of their journalists could they address the critical problem—getting the "industrial proletariat to read."[14] It was the function of the party press to instruct the workers and enable them to "exist as a political class."

Calwer argued that the chief problem for Social Democratic journalists lay in "defective preparation." There was no substitute for "methodical, continuing schooling," indeed, for formal academic training.[15] University study was no guarantee that a socialist intellectual would gain the understanding needed. But without it a writer for the party was likely to degenerate into a mere literary trickster. Calwer called on the party Executive to take steps to strengthen the press along the lines he had suggested.

In the end Calwer reaffirmed the model presented in the *Communist Manifesto*. "Only if the pure proletariat and the Ideologues" worked "hand in hand" could the Social Democrats preserve their true character.[16] Individuals who had gained a "full understanding of the economic-historical movement" were needed to help the workers carry out their appointed task. But petty-bourgeois elements must be eliminated from the party.

Calwer sent a copy of his pamphlet to Engels, seeking, like the Jungen intellectuals, support for his assessment of the party. There is no record of Engels' reply. Probably he would have agreed with Mehring, who responded to Calwer's critique of the Social Democratic press in a lead article in the *Neue Zeit*.[17] Calwer, according to Mehring, had employed the *Communist Manifesto* in a stereotyped and mechanical manner. Had he followed the spirit of Marx and Engels he would have recognized that the Social Democratic party was the product of "definite historical circumstances," that any defect or "dark side" was inescapably bound up with its achievements. Although conceding the validity of much of what Calwer said, Mehring criticized him for his failure to explain the "rot" in social terms. Moreover, Calwer's unwillingness to name specific offenders in the party reduced his complaints to "mere lamentations." Calwer was guilty, Mehring concluded, of a moralistic and sentimental approach to the problem; his critique stood in sharp contrast to the outlook in the *Communist Manifesto*.

Calwer continued to insist that the proletariat required the aid of those trained in the methods of "bourgeois science." Two years later in his *Introduction to Socialism*, to support the demand for "strict scientific ideas" rather than mere enthusiasm, he cited Marx's quarrels with working-class leaders during the eighteen forties.[18] Before long, however, Calwer abandoned his doctrinaire view of the party's development. When he became, in 1898, a Social Democratic representative in the Reichstag, he began to move, much like Schippel, toward a much more pragmatic approach to working-class interests. But his pamphlet *The Communist Manifesto and Modern Social Democracy* had raised issues which were troubling a number of Social Democrats. At the Frankfurt conference in October 1894, the Akademikerproblem arose during a debate about the appropriate salaries for party officials.

The Frankfurt Conference: The Question of Salaries

Among the resolutions considered by the delegates at the Frankfurt conference were several calling for a salary limit of three thousand marks per year for party functionaries. It soon became clear that the proposals were aimed at the salaries being paid to educated recruits who were occupying the most important editorial posts in the party. A Berlin delegate explained: "The proposals . . . are simply an outcome of discontent in wide circles. . . . Always higher demands will be placed on the willingness of our comrades to sacrifice; no wonder that one also places demands for the same willingness of editors and officials—that one wants . . . to cut their salaries. We must indeed give expression to a general mood."[19]

The ensuing debate focused mainly on individuals with academic backgrounds who were, as one delegate observed, "crowding into the best positions in the party and crowding out the self-taught workers."[20] Salaries paid to the leading editors—seventy-two hundred marks to Liebknecht for editing *Vorwärts,* six thousand to Schönlank at the *Leipziger Volkszeitung,* and somewhat smaller figures to other Social Democratic journalists—seemed princely to workers, most of whom earned less than nine hundred marks per year. Hence the demands that the educated recruits be satisfied with lower pay.

Several delegates questioned the commitment of the intellectuals. They had, one speaker observed, "scattered like chaff in the winds" when the laws against the socialists were imposed.[21] Since the adoption of socialism required deep conviction, individuals who came out of the bourgeois class might be expected to work for the party without making special claims on behalf of their "intellectual gifts." Those who came "out of conviction" should, moreover, be willing to "begin as recruits rather than as officers."[22] If they turned "their backs on us" because they were not paid enough or lacked staying power, so much the better. The resulting "purification of the party . . . could only be welcomed."

One delegate, the trade union leader Legien, questioned the very distinction being made between "intellectual" and "physical" work. Such a separation, he declared, had not "been customary among us."[23] But another delegate contrasted the two types of work in a way that disparaged mental labor. The miner, after all, performed much more difficult tasks than "the man who sits in his office."[24] Still another speaker denied that the educated recruits should take credit for their achievements. They "forget that they owe their educations only to the money of their parents, that their education is a product of our society."

Against this wave of egalitarian sentiment, Bebel called on the delegates to be realistic. The party was still subject to the "laws of supply and demand" in seeking the skills it needed: "We live in a bourgeois society and will not come out of it in the immediate future. Our intellectual workers emerge from bourgeois society; if we want them to work for us the distinction between what they receive from bourgeois newspapers and what they receive from us cannot be too great. Otherwise they will remain where they are. One cannot reasonably demand that their idealism goes so far that they prefer a worse position to a better one."[25] Bebel noted the failure of the party leaders to find, after a search of some months, a suitable candidate for an important editorial post at *Vorwärts*. Another spokesman for the executive cautioned against exaggerating the problem. Only twelve of seventy-three major editorial positions in the party, he pointed out, were occupied by recruits from the middle class.[26]

The salary issue was not simply a matter of material reward. It was closely tied to the mode of existence to which the educated recruit was entitled. To what extent could he be expected to sacrifice his former way of life? This question was addressed by two of the young intellectuals in the party.

Wilhelm Peus had been a theological student in Berlin before joining the Social Democrats in 1890 and becoming a party journalist. In 1891 he had been arrested for statements deemed treasonable by the authorities and spent time in prison. So he spoke out of bitter personal experience when he responded to those who doubted the sincerity of the intellectuals. Individuals who came to the party with academic backgrounds, he maintained, had "more to lose than the workers."[27] They jeopardized "their whole existence when they joined the party." To ask them to get by on pay close to that of the workers was unreasonable; it would reduce them to the condition which made it so difficult for the worker to advance intellectually.

This point was developed by Eduard David, who had recently resigned a teaching position in a gymnasium in Hesse in order to work openly for the party. It was his first conference and he was encouraged to speak out, he told the delegates, because Marx, Engels, and Lassalle, after all, had been intellectuals. The party, he said, should recognize the distinctive needs of the intellectual—a library and a "special work place," for example—which required money.[28] He urged the delegates to compare the position of the intellectuals within the party with that of their counterparts in the bourgeois world. Such a comparison would demonstrate that service to the socialist cause demanded idealism, because intellectuals in the party accepted pay well below that which they could receive outside. So much for the charges, heard during the debate, that the educated recruits were living off "the pennies of the workers." For those of bourgeois background who considered joining the movement, David offered advice and a warning. "The academic must, indeed, if he comes to us, cast off his old skin and put on a new one" and, given the criticism he was likely to face, David added, "it had better be a thick one."

David also claimed that recruits like himself were entitled to "sufficient means to educate their children." It was not a claim that the party rank and file could easily accept: it suggested the persistence of bourgeois attitudes and ambitions among the intellectuals and, indeed, doubts about the imminence of socialism. Thus the disclosure that Liebknecht's son was studying to be a lawyer seemed to one working-class socialist in these years both astonishing and disillusioning.[29]

The delegates at Frankfurt rejected the proposal to limit salaries. But the problem of the intellectual had taken on a new importance as a result of the debate. A few weeks after the conference, Bebel, in commenting on the "distrust against the academics," urged the Social Democrats to welcome those "equipped for a scientific vocation," for their abilities, "indispensable for the class struggle," could be acquired "only with difficulty and often incompletely" by individuals who were self-taught.[30]

The dispute at Frankfurt also convinced Kautsky that the issue should be addressed. There were two major problems facing the party, he wrote early in 1895. Social Democrats needed to define their policy toward the landed population and toward the "different layers of the so-called intellectuals."[31] During the spring Kautsky examined the section of the bourgeois world where, according to Marx, the proletariat would find its intellectual allies.

Kautsky on the Relationship between the Party and Bourgeois Intellectuals

Prompted by the debate at Frankfurt, Kautsky first invited readers in the *Neue Zeit* to discuss the question of Social Democratic policy toward the "so-called intellectuals." The response, six articles in all, recapitulated the main points made earlier in the party's press. Capitalistic development, the contributors argued, had produced a surplus of the educated, a "reserve army" of candidates for the professions of law, teaching, the church, and civil service. Because of the intense competition for places, many individuals were being denied the way of life for which they had been educated and were being "pressed down to a proletarian existence."[32] Contributors disagreed, however, about the wisdom of the Social Democrats' seeking out these declassed intellectuals. The material interests which gave clarity and strength to the socialist convictions of the industrial workers, one writer declared, might be dangerous in the intellectual recruits; self-interest here might simply lead them to seek careers in the party.[33] But another writer argued that the Social Democrats, by virtue of their scientific approach to the problems of the day, could exercise a special appeal to the estranged bourgeois intellectuals. The party should make an effort to win them by developing pamphlets for the purpose.[34]

The discussion in the columns of the *Neue Zeit* during January and February 1895 lacked clear focus and conclusion. But it convinced Kautsky that the issue demanded systematic treatment. The three-part series of articles which he devoted to the question in the spring of 1895 represented the most important attempt of any Marxist thinker in the years before World War I to deal with the relationship of the socialist movement to the growing number of "free-floating intellectuals" within the bourgeois world.[35] This series also throws further light on his conception of the place of the intellectuals within the party.

Kautsky acknowledged at the outset that Marxist theory did not provide any clear "model of the proletarian movement of the present or near future."[36] The social scene was still fluid; between the proletariat and the bourgeoisie was "a series of population layers" which complicated the class struggle. It was the task of the theorist to study the social changes under way and draw practical conclusions for the party. Social Democrats needed to be clear "about what to expect" from other social groups, particularly the workers on the land and "the intellectuals." What were the prospects, Kautsky asked, for "winning the intellectuals"?

During the previous decade, Kautsky argued, the intellectuals had gained a new importance, not only in Germany, but elsewhere in Europe. And there could be no doubt about the desirability of drawing them into the ranks of the Social Democrats. Marx and Engels had answered that question decisively in the *Communist Manifesto*. They themselves had exemplified the process through which "a section of the bourgeoisie," having gained "a theoretical understanding of history," joined the proletariat.[37] Yet the relationship of the party to the intellectuals, as the recent conference had demonstrated, presented difficulties. Kautsky set aside the salary issue with the observation that a "modest bourgeois living standard" was necessary for the "brain workers . . . to realize their abilities."

From the standpoint of Marxist theory there were three questions to consider.[38] To what extent were the interests of the intellectuals the same as those of the proletariat? How far could the intellectuals "take part in the class struggle"? What "layers of the intellectuals" were "the easiest for us to reach"?

Kautsky first offered some general comments on the nature of the intellectual in modern society. The distinction between "intellectual and bodily work," he noted, was simply historical in origin. But it had led to a unique form of mental activity—"inherently enjoyable," "internally motivated," and requiring a "special kind of leisure."[39] In recent times, however, the character of intellectual work had changed in a fundamental way. While capitalistic development demanded a great increase in the number of intellectuals, it had also tended to separate them from any direct role in "economic exploitation." A "new class" of intellectuals had emerged, characterized by "special knowledge and abilities." But the supply of these "brain workers" had, through the pressures of capitalism on the middle classes, "grown even more rapidly" than the positions available. There was, Kautsky observed, an "over-production of intellectuals." Their growing dissatisfactions gave them a special importance for the Social Democrats.

"Mere dissatisfaction,"[40] however, was not sufficient to bind the intellectuals to the proletariat. Kautsky disagreed with those who claimed that the common interest between the two groups was leading to a "general solidarity." The "class-conscious revolutionary proletariat" was a "child of great capitalistic industry," while the intellectuals were much more diverse in their outlook; at the most they possessed only "vocational interests." There were many indications that they still considered themselves to be a "privileged class," separated sharply from the workers. Even among those "occupations and layers" of the intellectuals who were being proletarianized, the sense of belonging to a privileged class died hard; it might persist long after "its material conditions had disappeared." Social Democrats could not, therefore, expect to "win the intellectuals as a whole to socialism."

In considering the possibility of recruiting individuals, Kautsky was most interested in the "aristocracy of the intellectuals"[41]—the academically educated. And here he denied that the appeal to interests, central to his analysis thus far, would bring reliable recruits. Self-interest was likely to attract "unappreciated geniuses," "seedy literary types," "grumblers," and others who had failed to succeed in bourgeois society. How then to attract the right individuals? "Through no other method than that which had led many out of these circles to us . . . through insight into the historical justification of the goal of the struggling proletariat . . . through insight into the necessity of its victory. Only in this way can we draw useful members into the party . . . no matter how hungry and dissatisfied they are."

Thus Kautsky, like Marx and Engels in the *Communist Manifesto,* fixed on intellectual insight as the crucial factor bringing the intellectuals to socialism. Most of these intellectuals were, he conceded, still tied to capitalism and even hostile toward the proletariat. The intellectuals' "broader intellectual horizons," however, distinguished this group from other social groups:[42] "Through its greater capacity for abstract thought and through the lack of a unified class interest . . . it can more easily rise above class and class narrowness and be idealistic with respect to special interests . . . and grasp more readily the lasting interests of the whole society." Kautsky saw in the "socialists of the chair," German professors who favored some form of state socialism, and other bourgeois reformers evidence that the academically educated were beginning to rise above class interests. But at the same time he emphasized their limitations. Intellectual insight was not enough to bring a decisive break with bourgeois society. "Selflessness and courage" were also required.

Kautsky thus added moral qualities to the rationalistic account of the conversion of intellectuals presented in the *Communist Manifesto*. Without such qualities, or what he called "character," the Social Democratic appeal "was useless."[43] In the absence of "character" the fundamental differences between the true socialist and the mere social reformer might be effaced: "If we stop being critical with respect to their inadequacy and impotence then we simply strengthen illusions which we want to destroy and we enable them to remain as social reformers when otherwise they would come to us unconditionally. . . . The sharper we maintain the dividing wall between social reform and true socialism the clearer we show the impotence of the former and hence push the courageous, honest, and insightful elements away from them."

Again Kautsky's conception of socialist development included motives, or psychological dispositions, which were not easy to reconcile with his economic determinism. What one modern philosopher has described as the "invisible background" or "unavowed moral sources" in Marxism remained integral to Kautsky's position.[44] The blend of rational insight and moral qualities required of the true socialist was again evident when he fixed on students as that element among the educated which was "easiest for us to reach."[45] Because they did not yet belong to any profession, "their views were not clouded over by material interests." It was not surprising that nine-tenths of the "proven . . . party men who have come to us" out of academic circles came as students. In the inevitable conflict between their socialist convictions and their professional interests they had, through strength of character, remained faithful to the movement.

The Social Democrats should, therefore, seek converts among the students. But Kautsky cautioned against attempts to bring these recruits directly into the party's political activity. Not only were they too immature for such work, but it was not wise for them to "burn their bridges" before completing their education.[46] Rather, their desire for action should be met by propaganda work among their fellow students. Indeed,

Kautsky saw no danger to the party in the prospect of students forming their own organization and even holding congresses. Given the strength of the proletarian party, there was no danger, as the Jungen affair indicated, that the young intellectuals would "take over leadership."

Kautsky's articles concentrated on the potential points of contact between the Social Democrats and disaffected bourgeois intellectuals. He did not deal with the role which the educated recruits would play in the party. He simply assumed that the newcomers were entering a movement with "unassailable foundations." They came, therefore, as "learners" who could then "advance our theoretical work." There was no suggestion that the disaffected middle-class intellectuals might bring fresh perspectives on the ideological or tactical questions arising within the party.

Kautsky had reaffirmed the view, expressed by Marx and Engels in the *Communist Manifesto,* that intellectuals were capable of freeing themselves from the determinants of their social backgrounds and assuming a special place in the party. He restated that view clearly in responding to an article which Rosa Luxemburg published in the *Neue Zeit.*[47] She had dismissed the intellectuals in her own country, Poland, as of no importance for the movement. "They hang in the air," she wrote, "powerless to give life to their ideals." Kautsky disagreed. As long as the class struggle was "merely instinctual in nature," he replied, intellectuals functioned as "guides to the lower classes," giving them "decisiveness and force" through their "greater clarity."[48] That the German movement still required the guidance of theorists was obvious.

The need for such guidance was becoming urgent during 1895. Even as Kautsky attempted to clarify the party's relationship to the "free intellectuals," several of the educated recruits were challenging the orthodox Marxist doctrines. The controversy over the agrarian question, the policy of the Social Democrats toward the workers on the land, also "laid bare the deepest roots of the party structure."[49]

The Agrarian Question

The growing crisis of German agriculture, faced with intense competition from abroad during the eighties and nineties, presented the Social Democrats with both opportunities and dilemmas.[50] Here were sections of the population being victimized by economic developments and seemingly ready to respond to the socialist attack on capitalism. Yet the Marxist ideology placed narrow limits on the party's capacity to appeal to the workers on the land. According to Marxist theory, agrarian developments paralleled those in the industrial realm—toward the concentration of property in ever fewer hands. The middling possessors of the land, peasants who had not yet been reduced to landless laborers, were, like their bourgeois counterparts, destined to be proletarianized in the process of capitalistic consolidation. Could the Social Democrats offer the rural workers anything more than a judgment of doom?

Marx and Engels had, nonetheless, viewed the peasants and the landless laborers as potential allies in the proletarian struggle for political power.[51] Engels had emphasized the importance of the landless workers east of the Elbe. To convert these elements to socialism, he argued, would deprive the Junkers of the docile recruits who provided the basis for their domination of the German army. Kautsky, too, had urged the party to develop an agrarian policy. While it would be foolish, he wrote late in 1888, to entertain any illusions about the ability of the peasants to enter the "thought processes" of the Social Democrats, they might be neutralized politically and thus hasten the party's march toward power.[52] Moreover, Kautsky, like Engels, had come to believe that the rapid political advance of the Social Democrats required the support of non-proletarian sections of society. The party, he wrote early in 1894, needed to adapt its agitation to "the forms of thought and feeling" of other groups, but only insofar as this did not "lead to the weakening of our principles."[53] He thus stated the problem rather than offering a solution.

The problem of applying the Marxist ideology to the plight of the agricultural workers had already occupied several of the young intellectuals. Schippel, Kampffmeyer, and Schmidt had addressed the issue from differing perspectives.[54] And Ernst had turned to the agrarian world to test his wavering Marxist beliefs. When, during 1894 and 1895, the relationship of the Social Democrats to the rural population became a central concern of the party, the younger intellectuals initiated and dominated the discussion.

A new call on the party to pay attention to the plight of the rural population came from Calwer in the fall of 1893. He criticized the Social Democratic speakers and agitators for their indifference to the cause of the small landholders in southern Germany.[55] Calwer soon retreated to the rigid Marxism expressed a year later in his pamphlet *The Communist Manifesto and Modern Social Democracy.* There he denounced the "wonder doctors" within the party who "proposed ways of winning the peasants."[56] The wonder doctors were young intellectuals who had begun to explore ways in which Social Democrats might appeal outside the industrial areas.

The main forum for their efforts was the *Sozialdemokrat,* the weekly paper begun in February 1894 out of the belief of Bebel and others that the party needed an organ capable of dealing with pressing political issues. As editor of the paper, Schippel was determined, he told his readers, to help the Social Democrats "adjust their tactics to changing circumstances."[57] He soon published the first in a series of articles dealing with the advantages of a "land agitation." In his own "weekly review," Schippel began to comment more or less regularly on agrarian problems.

One of the earliest contributions to the discussion came from Ernst, fresh from his experience in agricultural administration. He urged Social Democrats to recognize the peculiar "psychology of the peasants."[58] Their religious outlook, in particular, needed to be acknowledged. From his work with Meyer, moreover, Ernst had concluded that the concentration of the means of production, central to Marx's economic forecast, did not apply to agriculture.[59] The optimum unit of production on the land was between seventy-five and a hundred acres. The appropriate Social Democratic policy, therefore, was a demand for a redistribution of land which would promote such units. Ernst thus sought a middle way between the Marxist prediction of agricultural consolidation and the existing system, in which the overwhelming majority of German peasants possessed property of five acres or less. Drawing on the ideas of Meyer, Ernst argued that the party should also favor the nationalization of mortgages, an increasing burden on the small landholders, and propose other aid by the state. Such a policy, he declared, would make the peasants Social Democrats in the "shortest conceivable time." It would also anticipate the suitable form of agriculture in a socialist society.

Ernst's general approach was supported by one of the ablest of the party's new educated recruits. Simon Katzenstein was a native of Hesse who even before he joined the Social Democrats had been involved in efforts to help the small farmers.[60] After studying law and history at the universities of Giessen, Leipzig, and Zurich, he took a position with the judicial service. When that work proved incompatible with his socialist convictions, he served the party as a speaker and journalist. Like Ernst he urged Social Democrats to accept the peasants as they were.[61] Given their commitment to private property and their limited outlook, the peasants could not, however, become genuine Social Democrats in the immediate future. The party should simply view them as potential political supporters, attracted through appeals to their immediate interests. Katzenstein recommended that the party propose cooperative marketing arrangements, promoted by the state and designed to provide greater economic security for small landholders.

Ernst and Katzenstein anticipated the views of the figure who made the most important attempt to develop a Social Democratic agrarian policy—Eduard David.[62] David was a close friend of Katzenstein's at the University of Giessen, where the two worked together on behalf of the small farmers. His adherence to Marxism was, at most, loose, and he ranged freely beyond the confines of the party's ideology. But he was not hesitant, as his spirited defense of the intellectuals at the Frankfurt conference indicated, to plunge into the controversies of the party. In a series of eight articles, published in the *Sozialdemokrat* during August and September 1894, David argued that the way to socialism for rural workers lay through cooperative institutions, promoted by the state and building on existing peasant associations.[63] Like Ernst, he also defended the economic viability of the smaller or middling peasants, particularly in the production of meat, fruit, and vegetables.

David had diverged even more sharply than Ernst and Katzenstein from the characteristic Social Democratic view of the peasantry. Instead of viewing them simply as allies in the proletarian struggle for political power, he had accepted them "as they are" and urged the party to adopt measures to meet their immediate grievances and, indeed, to perpetuate their way of life. David rejected the notion of a social revolution in favor of a gradual development of socialist institutions within the present political structure. His proposals, a Marxist critic later observed, implied the "quantitative extension of existing social relations by means of the existing state" rather than any "qualitative change."[64]

Ernst, Katzenstein, and David were developing an approach to the agrarian question which corresponded to the outlook of the Social Democratic politicians in the southern states. The main pressure for a new agrarian policy came from party leaders in Bavaria, Württemberg, Baden, and Hesse. Much less industrialized, yet more liberal in their traditions than other areas of Germany, these states presented different challenges to the Social Democrats.[65] In a party which remained decentralized, the southern leaders had assumed considerable autonomy in adapting their political tactics to the special conditions of their region. During the nineties, as they gained representation in the parliamentary bodies of these states, they began to cooperate with other parties and, in violation of the general Social Democratic policy, they supported state budgets. The pragmatism or, what seemed to their critics the extreme opportunism of their practices, aroused a growing anger within the party.

Much of the anger was directed against Vollmar, the leading Social Democrat in Bavaria.[66] His declaration on behalf of reformism in the summer of 1891 had been followed by other deviations from the Erfurt program and by an explicit commitment to state socialism. Moreover, he had gained, by virtue of his skill in developing a propaganda suited to the special conditions of the region, strong support from other Social Democratic leaders in the south. At the Frankfurt conference in October 1894, Vollmar and the Bavarian representatives were the target of resolutions of censure for their recent vote in favor of the state budget.[67] But Vollmar's strong support among the delegates, inflated somewhat because of the location of the conference at Frankfurt, ensured that the debate over the issue would end in a compromise.

Vollmar had, however, helped to set in motion machinery for reexamining the party's relationship to the workers on the land. With little opposition the delegates approved a resolution to appoint a committee to study the problem and report at the next conference. The Agrarian Commission named by the party Executive was carefully balanced in order to represent regional interests as well as the different viewpoints which had emerged in the course of the year. Included in its membership of fifteen were five of the academically educated—Schippel, Katzenstein, David, and two others who had begun to play important parts in the discussion, Bruno Schönlank and Max Quarck.

Schönlank, born in Bavaria and now one of the party's leading journalists, combined wide-ranging cultural interests with a capacity for the historical investigation of social and economic issues.[68] In 1893 he was elected to the Reichstag from a district in Breslau. Appointed editor of the new *Leipziger Volkszeitung* in September 1894, he proceeded to make it one of the party's most influential organs. At the Frankfurt conference he joined Vollmar in sponsoring the motion to appoint an Agrarian Commission.

Quarck, like a number of the younger intellectuals, had come to socialism by way of Rodbertus, publishing his first article on that thinker in 1883 at the age of twenty-three.[69] During the same year he undertook a close study of Marxist writings—the *Poverty of Philosophy* and *Capital.* Although he contributed to the *Neue Zeit* and other socialist papers during the mid-eighties, he did not join the party. Trained in the law, he worked in the judicial system until 1886, when he was dismissed, presumably because of his radical views. Subsequently he took a position with a bourgeois paper, the *Frankfurter Zeitung,* losing that post in 1891 after a quarrel with the publisher. At that point he joined the party, becoming editor, in 1894, of the Social Democratic paper in Frankfurt. What seemed to some a questionable past made Quarck the target of Social Democrats who feared that the party was becoming a haven for individuals who had been "shipwrecked" in their bourgeois careers.[70] Nevertheless, he was appointed secretary of the Agrarian Commission.

The readiness of the delegates at Frankfurt to approve, overwhelmingly, the resolution of Vollmar and Schönlank was surprising in view of the fact that the Erfurt program virtually consigned the independent peasant to oblivion. But practical political considerations dominated the short discussion.[71] The delegates were influenced too by reports that party agitators were adopting varied and contradictory appeals to the peasants.[72] Hence the need for a consistent policy. Party leaders had also become worried about the growing effectiveness of the conservative parties in mobilizing the rural voters. Theoretical considerations did not figure in the discussion.

Shortly after the conference Engels sounded the alarm. He saw in the party's efforts to reach out to the peasants, together with a parallel move on the part of the French socialists, a threat to Marxist principles. There were "certain limits," he wrote to the French leader Paul Lafargue, a party could not pass "without betraying itself."[73] French socialists were in danger of sacrificing "the future of the party for the success of the day." He expressed similar concerns to Bebel who, already troubled by the proceedings at Frankfurt, urged Engels to state his objections publicly.[74] Engels did so in a letter, published in *Vorwärts*.[75] It was one of his rare public interventions in the affairs of the German Social Democrats. A short time later Engels developed his views in an article, "The Peasant Questions in France and Germany," published in the *Neue Zeit*.[76]

Here Engels reaffirmed his long-held belief that the Social Democrats might strengthen their drive for political power by gaining support from the workers on the land. He rejected any appeal to the small landholders in southern Germany and elsewhere. The peasants there were doomed. Social Democrats were bound to make clear the "absolute hopelessness of their condition" under capitalism. East of the Elbe, however, where a mass of landless workers were employed on large estates, the party could make headway. Confident that economic considerations outweighed all other influences, Engels predicted that the Social Democrats could win over the agricultural laborers in the east by the end of the decade.

Engels helped to awaken Kautsky to the gravity of the situation. Despite his misgivings about the action at Frankfurt, Kautsky had not taken up the issue in the *Neue Zeit*. But after Engels' intervention he entered the discussion with a ringing denunciation of any appeal to the peasantry.[77] It would mean a "fundamental reconsideration of our program and tactics." He reaffirmed the orthodox Marxist view that the decline of the peasants was inevitable. Concessions to nonproletarian groups, moreover, would endanger the solidarity of conviction which was already being imperiled by the party's rapid growth.

> Since 1890 a mass of new elements has streamed to us, so that the old comrades are not sufficient to educate and enlighten them, all the less since the practical tasks grow so enormously and absorb our schooled forces. The deficiency from which we suffer is not followers, but clear, thoroughly educated party members. And their number becomes relatively smaller. To remedy this defect is today . . . perhaps the most important of our next tasks. Its solution will not be advanced through the attraction of elements which want to know nothing of our ultimate aims.

Bebel also spoke out. Goaded by Engels and driven in part by his long-standing quarrel with Vollmar, he delivered a harsh attack on the southern leader and his supporters, first in a speech in Berlin in mid-November and then in a series of articles in *Vorwärts*.[78] The "effort to win followers at any price" he declared, threatened to undermine the "proletarian nature" of the party. He warned against the dilution of the Social Democratic outlook through the infiltration of a petty-bourgeois spirit. In its "intellectual development," Bebel maintained, the party was gaining "more in breadth than in depth." A "small party" was to "be preferred to one which is large yet without clear minds."

Bebel's denunciation of the agrarian reformers and his reaffirmation of proletarian exclusiveness opened "one of the bitterest polemics in the history of the party."[79] Angered by the attack, his opponents charged that Bebel was following in the "footsteps of the Jungen" and challenging the will of the party as expressed at Frankfurt. For several weeks the Social Democratic press was dominated by the polemic, until the Executive, nervous about a new move by the government to seek repressive legislation against the party, secured an armistice.[80] Engels, meanwhile, was pleased with Bebel's campaign. The party leader, he wrote to a friend in America, "is by far the clearest, most farsighted head of them all."[81] Recalling their fifteen years of regular correspondence, Engels added, "we almost always agree."

In the controversy which followed the Frankfurt conference, ideological issues assumed a new prominence in the life of the party. The politicians, one historican has written, had "been chased from the stage."[82] But only temporarily. Political considerations gained the upper hand during the first six months of 1895 as the Agrarian Commission, divided into three regional subcommittees and meeting secretly, developed a policy designed to connect the Social Democrats with the many-layered agricultural world. The report, published in June, was a compromise; it satisfied neither the reformers nor the orthodox Marxists. Since the proposals, which included various forms of state aid, would enhance the power of the state and preserve the peasant way of life, the report clashed directly with the party's Marxist principles.

In a letter to Engels early in July, Bebel expressed his hope that the shock produced by the report had not been too great.[83] Engels, now fatally ill, did not respond. But the limits, beyond which the party could not go, according to Engels, without undermining its Marxist integrity, had clearly been crossed by the authors of the report.[84] Kautsky was quick to take up the challenge. In a series of articles on "our newest program" he restated the orthodox Marxist position.[85] A "Social Democratic agrarian policy under the capitalistic mode of production was a nothing." The peasants were a doomed class. Only among those sections of the landed population which had been proletarianized was there a possibility for effective agitation. Even here the prospects were dim. As for the peasants generally, the Social Democratic message was clear. The "situation is hopeless." Their problems could be solved "only through joining the class struggle of the proletariat." The party rested on "the firm ground of science," and it alone knew "the direction in which modern society will move."

The report had, as Kautsky recognized, raised the question of the adequacy of the party's Marxist ideology. Even before the report was published, David had begun to present a theoretical justification for its recommendations.[86] What had been implied in his earlier articles now became an explicit challenge to the Marxist doctrines. The smaller farmers were not, he argued, being swallowed up by the larger producers; they were competitive. To reach the peasants, the Social Democrats would have to acknowledge their immediate interests as property owners. As for the principles contained in the Erfurt program, David wrote Vollmar, it was a matter of whether or not the Social Democrats were willing to discard their fallacies or "ossify."[87] Ernst agreed. The Marxist doctrines, he declared, bore little relationship to agricultural realities; it was time for party members to recognize the facts.[88] Thus the theoretical issue had been joined. Throughout the summer and early fall of 1895 the debate continued in the party press.

What mattered most to Bebel and the other supporters of the report was the prospect of strengthening the party's political appeal. Here was the key to the party leader's dramatic reversal during the first half of the year.[89] Persuaded that the way was open for electoral gains in the rural population, ideological considerations had little force. But the hope for a broader electoral base led, ironically, to a rare political miscalculation on Bebel's part; he misjudged the attitudes and feelings of the Social Democratic rank and file.

Schippel was more realistic. As editor of the *Sozialdemokrat* he had encouraged the reexamination of the agrarian question and then participated in the work of the commission. But his initial editorial, responding to the report, was cautious and expressed the fear that the party might, in its zeal to reach the peasants, "get stuck in a dead end."[90] A week later he declared outright that the commission's proposals did not belong in the party's program. What a later critic of Schippel's turnabout described as a "fine feeling for the weather" in the party was also a recognition that an appeal to the peasantry clashed with deep feelings in the Social Democratic membership.[91] The meetings held at the local level to discuss the report expressed a "rising storm of protest."[92] Recognizing that the party members were delivering an overwhelmingly negative judgment, Schippel announced early in August that the "agrarian report was already a corpse."[93]

The failure of the report to evoke from the workers "any feeling of solidarity with the peasantry" throws light on the nature of the Social Democratic party at this time.[94] The resistance of the rank and file was partly economic. They recognized that proposals designed to enhance the party's appeal to the small landholders were likely to hurt their own interests as consumers of foodstuffs. But there was, as Lehmann observed, an "instinctive, unconscious disinclination" on the part of Social Democrats, living in an urban and industrial setting, to "adapt 'their' party to the wishes" of another class. The episode suggested the extent to which the Social Democratic party expressed the interests and the class-consciousness of the industrial workers.

Bebel was not willing to give up on the peasantry. He resisted the inclination of his southern allies to retreat in the face of rank-and-file opposition. And he disregarded the advice of the party's co-chairman, Paul Singer, who conceded that the "agrarians had been slaughtered."[95] Bebel decided to push on with the debate at the party conference. Not only was he convinced of the political importance of the issue, but he was confident of his ability to bring the delegates around. The agrarian question dominated the proceedings at Breslau.

The debate at the conference reflected the curious alignments which had developed during the previous months. Intellectuals who favored a new agrarian policy found themselves in a rare and, as it turned out, brief alliance with the older party leaders, Bebel and Liebknecht. On the other side, Kautsky joined forces with an intellectual, Schippel, with whom he had already had sharp differences and would quarrel bitterly in the years just ahead. Beneath the ostensible agreements there was, in fact, an array of cross purposes.

The debate took up more than half of the six-day meeting, recapitulating the arguments aired earlier in the press. Intellectuals who favored a new policy attempted to play down its theoretical or ideological implications. Thus Quarck, the official reporter for the proposals of the Agrarian Commission, argued that the issue was essentially political.[96] And David, who had emerged as the chief spokesman of the agrarians, denied that questions of theory could be dealt with at a party conference. These were matters for experts; with respect to the question of the economic vitality of the peasants, the judgment was not in yet. What the delegates had to decide was "a political question of the first rank."[97] Bebel took the same position. The party needed to formulate its policy "according to circumstances." What really mattered was "clarity for purposes of agitation" at all political levels.[98] Schönlank also emphasized the need for Social Democrats to adjust to changing political possibilities. But he also questioned the class basis of the party. It was ceasing to represent merely the industrial proletariat and becoming a party for all those who suffered under capitalism. Schönlank threw down the ideological gauntlet. The "revision" of the Social Democratic program, he declared, was inevitable, notwithstanding the "bitter fanaticism of the party dogmatists."[99]

The ideological problem was inescapable. Each of the intellectuals made some attempt to justify his position in Marxist terms. It "would be sad for socialism as a world view," Quarck observed, if it could not be creative with respect to the workers on the land. Indeed, the greatness of the party had come from its capacity to "reconcile practical politics with theoretical aims." This had been "the great achievement of Marx and Engels."[100] Even David, who showed little attachment to the Marxist doctrines, attempted to turn them against his opponents. The "revolutionizing of the masses," he said, "goes not from the head but from the stomach." And he maintained, in an obvious reference to Kautsky, that excessive concern with the mind would simply produce "a small sect of scientific socialists."[101] Bebel, however, cautioned against a strict adherence to Marxist doctrine. Responding to charges that the agrarian proposals were at odds with the *Communist Manifesto,* he simply observed that its "practical demands" were "to a considerable degree obsolete today."[102]

Kautsky led the attack on the agrarians. His abandonment of his customary reticence in public indicated the importance he attached to the issue. The terms of the debate were largely set by his resolution calling for a clear repudiation of the commission's proposals. Once more he defended his conception of a party, firmly united ideologically and enrolling only those who were willing to "fight the great battle" as Marx had defined it.[103] "It is not our task to draw in hangers-on who are unclear about our principles." Social Democrats must have the "courage to tell people unpleasant truths," that the condition of the peasants under capitalism was hopeless. The Agrarian Commission had attempted to "solve a problem which cannot be solved" in the existing order. Kautsky denied that an appeal to the peasants was likely to aid the workers in achieving political power.

Kautsky's chief supporters at Breslau—Schippel and Klara Zetkin—employed very different arguments. Schippel concentrated on the political consequences of the party's adoption of the commission's proposals. "Would this strengthen or weaken us as a working-class party"?[104] His answer was clearly no. The agrarian program, he declared, was "a piece of political charlatanry." The only way to win the small property owners was to "convince them that they had no future save as followers of the proletariat." In a pointed reference to his academically educated opponents, he warned the "younger comrades" that the workers would show them the right path "if they did not mend their ways." Indeed, Bebel, noting the applause which greeted Schippel's put-down of the academics, accused him of appealing to the "calloused hands" against the "so-called intellectuals."[105]

Zetkin was the party's leading female figure, editor of *Gleichheit,* its weekly designed for women, and a zealous adherent of the established Marxist doctrines. At Breslau she defended the party's theorists, that is to say, Kautsky. Answering the accusation that the theorists were mere "bookworms," who viewed life "in terms of the narrow circle of light coming from their study lamps," she asserted that they provided "the most penetrating knowledge of reality," that they provided "exact knowledge" of the "deeper connections . . . of social phenomena."[106] Noting the spontaneous opposition of the local branches to the agrarian report, she claimed that Kautsky's position was being confirmed by the "healthy revolutionary instincts of the rank and file." Zetkin's declaration that the party's chief task was to organize the "proletarian class struggle" evoked the most prolonged and stormiest applause during the proceedings.

One of the party's veteran working-class leaders, Hermann Molkenbuhr, caught something of the dilemma which ideological claims were creating for a party committed to electoral politics. As a political party, he observed, "we must take a position on all pressing national issues, such as the deepening crisis in agriculture."[107] "We cannot, if the nut seems too hard, disregard the difficulties . . . of everyday life." The theoretician, however, unlike the politician, "can choose what issue to deal with." And Molkenbuhr noted, in an obvious reference to Kautsky and his supporters, the temptation to resort to "noble philosophical-sounding speeches."

Molkenbuhr recognized the growing difficulty of keeping the party's Marxist ideology tightly linked to its political practices. But the passage of Kautsky's resolution, rejecting the agrarian program, permitted Social Democrats to continue to believe that their principles and their tactics were in harmony. Kautsky, in particular, could view the outcome as a victory for his conception of the party and its mission. Since the delegates had rejected the utopian belief that the capitalistic state might serve the socialist cause, the party had "no need to undertake a revision" of its program.[108] The Social Democrats remained "the party of the struggling proletariat." Mehring reinforced Kautsky's views. When, after the conference, Kautsky's critics attacked him for dogmatism, Mehring defended "dogma" as simply "knowledge of those laws," gained through "historical materialism," through which "the emancipation of the proletariat is realized."[109]

At Breslau Kautsky had appeared, so Lehmann concluded, as a "grand inquisitor," determined to protect the party's "sacred principles" from "heretical assault."[110] In that role he had maneuvered the party into a "blind alley" and prevented it from responding creatively to the challenge which the agrarian question presented to a Marxist thinker. While the judgment captures the intensity of Kautsky's allegiance to the central Marxist doctrines, it exaggerates his influence on the life of the party. Ideological considerations were much less important than the pressures, material and psychological, which influenced the Social Democratic rank and file. The party's working-class supporters were determined to prevent any dilution of their proletarian identity and interests.

Bebel, viewing the outcome of the Breslau conference in terms of the party's political prospects, was depressed. The delegates had erected "a barrier to our passage" to the peasantry which might delay the party's access to political power for a decade or more.[111] The Marxist principles, he observed sarcastically," had been "saved" by the strange alliance between the "men at the study table" and the industrial workers in the large cities. Ignoring his own strange alliance with the young reforming intellectuals, Bebel recognized, however, the incongruent nature of the relationship between the party's chief ideologist, Kautsky, and the rank and file.

Bebel also recognized that the ideological rigidity expressed in Kautsky's resolution would have little effect on the political activities of the party leaders in the south. He had seen the agrarian proposals as a way of strengthening party discipline and overcoming the inconsistencies which had marked its rural agitation. Now, lacking any clear guidance from the party, the southern Social Democrats would continue to respond as they saw fit to local circumstances. Acceptance of Kautsky's resolution, Bebel observed, had "left the field to the opportunists."[112] Indeed, Social Democrats in the south remained confident, as David wrote Vollmar, that "healthier views" were "bound to win out."[113] In fact, the continued pragmatism of Vollmar and like-minded Social Democrats clashed periodically with general party policies. But the limited success of the southern Social Democrats in winning support from the peasantry in the years ahead also indicated that Bebel had miscalculated both the potential for political growth there and the magnitude of the setback at Breslau. The decision of the delegates has, however, been seen as a turning point in the life of the party. It became much more difficult, Gerhard Ritter has observed, for the Social Democrats to reach sections of society outside the industrial workers.[114]

This issue was addressed by Schippel in the *Sozialdemokrat* during the weeks following the conference. The central issue in the controversy, he observed, had been "tactical."[115] Would the party be strengthened or weakened by redrawing its social boundaries? At Breslau, the Social Democrats had decided—correctly, according to Schippel—that they would "move forward more rapidly" by "limiting the circle" of their agitation "to the interests and demands of the wage workers." But to mark off the "proletarian army" in this way was not to deny the possibility of "peaceful steady development." Nor would it fix the party in an unchanging tactic or theory. Both were in the process of development. The agrarian debate, Schippel believed, had helped the party to recognize the problem of relating theory and practice. Although the Erfurt program had attempted to unite the two sides of the party's work, Social Democrats still needed to discover the ways in which method and goal penetrated each other. How, Schippel asked, could "principles" and "tactics" be related dialectically?

Schippel's editorship of the *Sozialdemokrat* was nearly over. No doubt he had weakened his position by turning against Bebel in the summer, but the weekly had never gained the readership hoped for. Hence the decision to terminate the paper at the end of December. In a final editorial, "a look at our party,"[116] Schippel examined once more the relationship between ideology and politics, or what he called the "inner and the outer." How could the Social Democrats reconcile the proletarian mission, the "deepening of our ideas," with the tendency to become simply "a party of the dissatisfied"? The Social Democrats were winning many who had not yet been prepared by economic developments to be socialists. This process would hasten their conquest of political power, but it "would lead to great disillusionment" if the workers did not understand their role. Having restated the dilemma, Schippel simply expressed the hope that the party would develop an "organ of criticism" which would have "better success than the *Sozialdemokrat.*"

Early in 1895 a group of Social Democrats in Berlin had started a new "organ of criticism." In the columns of the *Sozialistische Akademiker* the younger Marxist intellectuals attempted not only to define their place in the movement but to develop the cultural implications of the new socialist mentality.

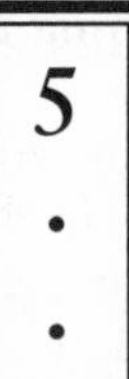

The Cultural Meaning of Marxism

THE appearance of the *Sozialistische Akademiker* in January 1895 indicated that the hopes expressed in the Jungen rebellion were still alive among the educated recruits coming into the party. Those who started the paper—students and other Social Democrats in Berlin—accepted the policies of the party. But the Marxist promise of a radically new way of life remained central to their outlook. Before long the tension between the promise and the increasingly pragmatic policies of the Social Democratic politicians was again evident.

Contributors to the *Sozialistische Akademiker,* like the Jungen intellectuals, were eager to nurture the new values and attitudes with which they identified socialism. Unless institutional changes were accompanied by a new culture—a transformed consciousness—the promise of socialism could not be realized. During 1895 and 1896 the *Sozialistische Akademiker* drew back together the political and aesthetic aspirations which had for a time united the young intellectuals gathered around the *Berliner Volks-Tribüne.*

Orthodox Marxists believed that socialism would bring a new culture. Cultural questions could, in the light of economic determinism, be granted only secondary significance. But they remained, for most of the Marxist intellectuals, matters of interest and speculation. Social Democrats had responded enthusiastically to the formation of the Free People's Theater and, following the departure of Wille, turned to Mehring for leadership. During the mid-nineties, moreover, a leading party editor, Edgar Steiger, set out to alter the aesthetic sensibilities of the Social Democratic rank and file. At the Gotha party conference in 1896 the delegates confronted the question: did their ideology entail new artistic tastes?

The *Sozialistische Akademiker,* 1895–1896

An editorial in the first issue of the new bimonthly journal reminded its readers of the important role which students and intellectuals had played in earlier movements for political liberation in Germany—in the struggle against Napoleon and during the revolutionary upheavals of 1848. But following the defeat at mid-century, the writer observed, students, like the educated classes in general, had made their peace with the emerging Bismarckian order and betrayed the cause of freedom. Now the socialist movement called them to renew the struggle. There were two natural points of contact between the socialists and the academically educated—the tendency for intellectuals under capitalism to "sink into the proletariat" and the "power of logic." Socialism was the only form of the modern struggle for freedom which "rests on a scientific foundation."[1]

The editors of the *Sozialistische Akademiker* appealed, therefore, to the "representatives of the future intellectuals" and particularly to those who were attempting to overcome the "presumption and arrogance of the educated world."[2] For such an appeal, however, existing socialist literature was inadequate; those in the universities required a "different fare" than that suited to the "simple understanding" of the workers. The new paper did not claim a leading role for the intellectuals; the workers were, as Engels had stated, the "true bearers of modern culture." And Bernstein, in a cautious endorsement of the *Sozialistische Akademiker,* published in its first issue, noted that the "academics" had "more to learn from the workers" than they could teach them.[3]

Initiative for the paper came from a group of students at the University of Berlin. They were aided by Johann Sassenbach, a local trade union leader who provided facilities for publication and served as the chief editor. Many of the articles during the first year were unsigned or had authors identified only by means of pseudonymns such as "Catilina," "Gracchus," and "Junius." Three contributors were especially prominent: Joseph Bloch, writing as "Catilina," Heinz Starkenburg, and Georg Zepler, a Berlin doctor. But other young socialist intellectuals, including Katzenstein, wrote for the paper. In 1896 they were joined by Schmidt, Kampffmeyer, and Ernst, who found in the *Sozialistische Akademiker* a new outlet for their growing doubts about the adequacy of Marxist theory and the policies of the Social Democrats.

Much of the paper's attention was directed toward the difficulties of young men seeking to enter the professions. Several writers described the frustrations and the despair of unsuccessful candidates, employing Marxist ideas to explain their plight. Mental labor, like physical labor, was being reduced to a commodity subject to the laws of supply and demand; intellectuals were also being relegated to a "reserve army" exploited by the capitalists.[4]

Contributors to the *Sozialistische Akademiker* conceded that the "intellectual proletariat" did not easily find its way to socialism. Thus Katzenstein, drawing on personal experience, emphasized the hold of petty-bourgeois notions of self-reliance and ambition.[5] Educated young men who were attracted to the socialist world view, he observed, experienced a painful struggle of conscience, intensified by the prospect of leaving their old circle of friends. No wonder they usually remained "trapped within a petty-bourgeois world." How different, he added, from the condition of the workers, whose "inner essence" and "life habits" impelled them to "think, feel, and act socialist." Katzenstein argued that the "power of logic" was not sufficient to attract the educated recruits; "idealism and courage" were necessary to break through to the socialist world view.

For those who did break through and join the movement, however, there were new barriers. An anonymous contributor noted the tendency for some party members to view the educated recruits as "office-grabbers."[6] Hence the "violence . . . almost hate" which had been expressed in the academic debate at Frankfurt in 1894. Some Social Democrats, he suggested, were seeking to "cut the academics off from party posts." Instead of welcoming the "educated proletarians who . . . have found their way through science," the party was in danger of retreating into a narrow, sectarian outlook.

Sensitive to the charge that they were "feeding at the socialist trough," writers for the *Sozialistische Akademiker* set out to build a case for their special role in the movement. Thus Zepler questioned the extent to which the Social Democrats could count on "that simple operation of economic necessity."[7] He maintained that the manual workers and the self-educated could not provide what was needed to reach the final goal; the workers required the academics as "teachers and leaders." To gain the intellectual resources needed, he urged the Social Democrats to extend their agitation into the middle classes. He argued, moreover, that the educated converts need not identify themselves completely with the immediate interests of the workers. Zepler saw the workers and the academic socialists as two army corps, each permeated with the new spirit, but marching separately: "So, allied, brotherly, and well instructed, each class will for the time being go its own way, each performing its own . . . tasks, corresponding to its own nature . . . and in the end both army corps will find themselves together and grasp hands as victors."

Zepler's argument was accompanied by disclaimers on the part of the editors, for he had departed from the orthodox Marxist point of view which characterized the *Sozialistische Akademiker* during its first year. Most of its contributors accepted the materialistic conception of history, the class struggle, and the decisive role of the proletariat. They also supported the policies of the Social Democratic party. Nowhere was this more apparent than in their view of the agrarian controversy. Starkenburg, noting the contradiction between the proposals of the Agrarian Commission and the Erfurt program, concluded that "land agitation was premature."[8] Zepler, too, despite his deviant view of the intellectuals, denied the need for a special appeal to the peasants.[9] Indeed, he held that a split might be less dangerous to the party than the dilution of principles resulting from the acceptance of the agrarian proposals. A split, at least, would mean a "cleansing" of the party; it would find new strength in a "firm, goal-conscious core." After the agrarian proposals had been rejected at Breslau, a contributor commended the delegates for holding fast to the party's "only duty, the class struggle."[10] "Nothing less than the principles of the party" had been at stake. Given their strong support of the party's policies, the editors of the paper were disappointed when their request that the *Sozialistische Akademiker* be considered an official part of the Social Democratic press was turned down by the party executive.

Within their orthodox Marxist framework, however, several of the writers for the paper were raising once more the questions which had engaged the Jungen intellectuals. Preoccupation with the inner meaning of socialism, its bearing on personal values, was most evident in the articles of the figure who became the guiding spirit of the journal, Joseph Bloch.[11] In the midst of the Jungen dispute he had elicited from Engels the acknowledgment, so important to the young intellectuals, that ideas, or consciousness, might influence social development. Since that time Bloch had moved from Königsberg to Berlin to continue his study of mathematics and then participate in the founding of the *Sozialistische Akademiker*. That he had not set aside his earlier concerns was apparent in his contribution to the paper's first issue.

The Jungen protest, Bloch argued, should be viewed as a split within Marxism.[12] To explain the nature of that split, he distinguished between the "communist school of thought" and the "free socialists." While the former represented the genuine Marxist point of view, the "free" or "youthful academic socialists" who had broken away to form the Independent party, had recognized that socialism was not "a mere question of food" as "some over-zealous propagators of the 'materialistic conception of history' seemed to think." The dissenting intellectuals had also seen that the "ultimate goal" of socialism was being neglected "through the absorption in daily work." Misled by their petty-bourgeois backgrounds, however, they had turned away from "the system of communism" as propagated by Marx. They had viewed the teachings of Marx mainly in abstract terms and had lost touch with the interests of the working class.

Now, according to Bloch, it was time to heal the rift between the two forms of socialism. The two groups shared the same goal—a society in which "the free development of each is the free development of all." What was needed was "systematic agitation" designed to impart "scientific knowledge" to the party rank and file.

Not until the following summer did Bloch address the problem he had identified—the need to reintegrate the elements in Marxism which had broken apart during the Jungen rebellion. In the meantime his contributions to the paper indicated his commitment to the class struggle and to economic determinism, qualified, however, by an emphasis on the special role of the intellectuals and their "freedom drive."[13]

During August Bloch published the first of a five-part article on the relationship between "communism" and "anarchism."[14] There could be no doubt, he wrote, that "capitalist society more and more shows its true face . . . and nears its end." Its executioner, the international proletariat, "stands before the door." All the more urgent, therefore, the need to correct the mistakes which had led to the divergence between the "communistic" and "individualistic" conceptions of socialism. Bloch traced the divergence to the imprecision and "striking misunderstanding of logical principles" found in Engels' *Anti-Dühring.*[15] The confusion had been increased by the "superficiality of his followers."

In his attempt to reconcile the Social Democrats and the anarchists, viewed as two sides of Marxism, Bloch proceeded deductively. He sought, like a mathematician, the "indispensable axioms" underlying the two approaches to socialism. The "laws of logic," he insisted, were "absolutely valid" and "indissolubly tied to our thought."[16] Bloch claimed, in fact, that a simple axiom—the utilitarian principle of the pursuit of pleasure and the avoidance of pain—was assumed by the main anarchist thinkers, Proudhon, Stirner, and Mackay, as well as by the Marxists. Having demonstrated to his own satisfaction that the two viewpoints were "the same in the final analysis," that they converged in the goal expressed at the end of the *Communist Manifesto,* Bloch claimed for his reasoning the force of a "mathematical proof."[17]

What had divided the two sides, apart from defective reasoning, was a difference in tactics. The communists counted on "historical necessity" to bring socialism; the anarchists had relied on "rational men."[18] But the tactical issue was not an "either/or." The Social Democratic leaders at Erfurt had erred in thinking that they could overcome the disagreement by "throwing out the spokesmen of the opposition." Here too reconciliation was possible. Bloch attempted to show how the two tactics might develop dialectically. While it was unlikely that the anarchists could be persuaded to view the state with favor, the "two sides might work together in trade unions and consumer cooperatives." The anarchists should acknowledge, however, that most workers "belonged to the Social Democratic party."[19] It was time for them to recognize "the common struggle" and rejoin the working-class movement.

In seeking to persuade the anarchists to return to the party, Bloch was conceding the validity of much of their criticism of Social Democratic development. Through their insistence on the subjective qualities in socialism, on the power of reason and the "freedom drive," the anarchists had corrected the excessive emphasis on economic determinism by the orthodox Marxists. To support this interpretation of the movement Bloch used the letter he had received from Engels. A few weeks after the latter's death in August 1895, the letter was published in the *Sozialistische Akademiker.* The "deadly schematic materialism" against which it was directed, Bloch observed, still "holds many today."[20]

Bloch's rejection of the rigid materialism and economic determinism of the orthodox Marxists was supported by Starkenburg. In October he published a second letter from Engels, written the previous year to W. Borgius in Breslau, who had also sought a more precise statement about the "causal role of economic conditions."[21] And Starkenburg's contributions to the *Sozialistische Akademiker* indicated his own dissatisfaction with the Marxist ideology. In a review of a study of Marxism by Achille Loria, he maintained that much work still needed to be done before the materialistic conception of history could be established as a "triumphant hypothesis."[22] It was especially important for materialists to "investigate moral judgments as psychological phenomena" and show "why we cannot accept any other motivations than the economic."

Fears that the Social Democrats were becoming imprisoned in a "stereotyped materialist" outlook at the expense of "inner conviction" were increasingly evident in the columns of the *Sozialistische Akademiker.* Thus an unsigned article, published in July, complained of the exhaustion of the old phrases and their failure to touch the feelings.[23] The author contrasted the existing state of the Social Democratic press with the picture of socialism presented by the *Volks-Tribüne* a few years earlier. Contributors to that paper had covered the whole range of intellectual life, and did not "leave one cold"; they offered a conception of socialism which, at once "joyful and creative," was now difficult to find in the movement. Still, there was no point in withdrawing, as the Independents had. The stagnation could only be overcome through self-criticism and an effort to convince the majority of the true meaning of socialism.

That meaning and the role of intellectuals in advancing it was expressed most passionately by a foreign contributor, the young Spanish philosopher Miguel de Unamuno.[24] Warning against the preoccupation with objective social and economic facts, or "dead statistics," he reaffirmed the interdependence of the workers and the intellectuals: "Only out of the inner binding of the socialist intellectuals with the whole people can the socialist idea, the idea of humanity, unfold. The people, without the intellectuals, will live in a more or less deep unclarity, which will delay its deliberations without gaining a clear consciousness of their goals; the socialist intellectual will, without a close connection with the people, fall into an intellectualism which leads to a self destructive Jacobinism."

Reviewing the first year of the *Sozialistische Akademiker,* an editorial conceded that it had found little support within the party, that its efforts had been met with misunderstanding and even "outspoken hostility."[25] But those associated with the paper had discovered that "much in the teachings of our master needs to be reinterpreted and clarified." "Obsolete parts" would have to be cut out, mistakes corrected, if Marx's heirs were to prevent his work from becoming "petrified." The paper would, according to the editorial, have to "pay more attention to theory" in the future. And while it would continue to address the special problems of the academic socialists, the *Sozialistische Akademiker* would also seek to "reach into the ranks of the proletariat."

The critical edge of the paper became sharper during the early months of 1896. This was mainly the work of three intellectuals who had been closely associated with the *Volks-Tribüne* and the Jungen protest—Schmidt, Kampffmeyer, and Ernst. Each was attempting, moreover, to go beyond the economic and political difficulties posed by orthodox Marxist theory and to look more closely at the cultural implications of socialism.

Schmidt had, in his exchanges with Engels, raised ethical and epistemological questions. His first contribution to the *Sozialistische Akademiker,* "Egoism and Socialism," addressed once more the failure of Marxist theory to account for the self-sacrifice and altruism which seemed to him to be inescapable features of the socialist movement.[26] The answer, according to Schmidt, seemed to lie in the "educating power of social relationships," which taught the workers to identify themselves with the "wider egoism of class." But the epistemological issue remained a stumbling block. He restated the Kantian objection to the orthodox position in a long review of a new book on the materialistic conception of history by Georgi Plekhanov.[27] Although Schmidt found much to admire in the book, he denied that the Russian Marxist had answered Kant's insistence that "there is no direct perception of nature or reality without a mixture of mind." Indeed, Schmidt now claimed that Marx and Engels had never "taken the bull by the horns" with respect to philosophical questions. And Plekhanov had simply repeated Engels' argument that Kant's inaccessible "thing-in-itself" had been "put an end to" by "what we can do to nature" through experimentation and industry. Schmidt's break with the materialism of orthodox Marxism was expressed in his assertion that "feelings, thoughts, and purposes" were "co-determinants in history."

Kampffmeyer indicated his continuing preoccupation with the apparent contradiction between the "priority of economics accorded in the theory" of Marx and "the centrality of political interests in the party."[28] He now conceded that he had been mistaken in joining the Independents in repudiating parliamentary politics. "Calmer, clear considerations" had shown that his simple confidence in the economic associations of the workers had been unrealistic. But the Independents had been correct in emphasizing the "inner connections of economics and politics" and the limitations of political action. Kampffmeyer still believed that the Social Democrats were too concerned with the "conquest of political power."[29] The key to the socialist future lay in the trade unions and cooperatives, "permeated with the spirit of socialism" and engaged in the "step-by-step appropriation of capitalism."

For Kampffmeyer, however, the economic and social categories of orthodox Marxism were no longer adequate for understanding the task facing socialists. By introducing the concept of the "social," he attempted to deal with wider aspects of life.[30] The "social" was a vague and elastic concept, covering matters such as education, public opinion, and cultural trends. Kampffmeyer justified his use of the concept by referring to British experience where, he argued, the respect accorded the workers by the public was quite disproportionate to their small parliamentary representation or even to their economic power. Indeed, the "best barometer" for measuring "social attitudes" was the theater. The "stench of corruption" emanating from the portrayals of the bourgeoisie on the stage indicated that "we are on the verge of great changes."

Ernst also used the columns of the *Sozialistische Akademiker* to restate his view, expressed in the agrarian debate, that "economic developments had taken a turn that Marx did not foresee."[31] His experiences in agriculture and the administration of welfare had given him a new sense of the general interests of society. He now saw "dangers for the whole society," for example, in the impact of falling grain prices on the Junker class. The ruin of that class, he warned, might mean a "general catastrophe . . . which would hit the workers hardest."[32] And he criticized the Social Democrats for their failure "to see the economic life of the nation as a whole."

The disenchantment with Marxism implied in such remarks was also a reflection of a deeper disappointment—the fading of the socialist promise of a rejuvenated cultural sensibility. That need was evident, according to Ernst, in the condition of lyrical poetry. The feelings which inspired such poetry were "no longer real" in Germany.[33] He suggested that the literature of Japan and China provided a possible corrective to the "frozen, conventional perceptions" of the present.

Ernst thus expressed his belief that the socialist movement was losing its capacity to transform the inner lives of its followers. His experiences had convinced him, moreover, that the intellectuals could not attain genuine solidarity with the workers. The "educated always find themselves part of another class."[34] Ernst had, in short, concluded that the attempt to transform the mentality of the working class by means of orthodox Marxism was hopeless.

Other contributors to the *Sozialistische Akademiker* were reaching a similar conclusion. Zepler, for example, maintained that the Marxist materialists had failed to demonstrate that they could replace the older religious values.[35] And he suggested that socialism and Christianity might, after all, be compatible. Katzenstein, writing in the *Neue Zeit*, criticized Bebel's *Women under Socialism* for its excessive emphasis on the "influence of outer circumstances" and his neglect of the "inner essence of the human spirit."[36] Bebel ignored the question of "what will happen to the religious yearnings after material satisfactions are realized."

For the editors of the *Sozialistische Akademiker*, however, the answer to the problems posed by Ernst, Zepler, and Katzenstein lay in the realm of culture. It was the task of modern art and literature to provide values and meanings to replace the traditional belief systems. To develop the cultural meaning of socialism the editors turned mainly to the creative writers of the Friedrichshagen circle. Holz, Schlaf, the Hart brothers, Wille, and Hartleben contributed articles and poetry, and Bölsche explored the relationship between socialism and Darwinism. The *Socialistische Akademiker* served, as Herbert Scherer has observed, to bring back together the young Marxist intellectuals and the new generation of creative writers in Germany.[37]

Collaboration between the two groups indicated, however, the difficulty of establishing a clear direction for a socialist culture. The Naturalism which had united the writers in earlier years was now in decline.[38] It had given way to a new period of artistic experimentation and eclecticism. The relationship between the socialist movement and the literary or artistic tendencies of the period was increasingly ambiguous.

The difficulty of identifying any clear connection between the historical process as explained by Marx and cultural renewal was acknowledged by Ria Claasen.[39] "Who has found the thread," she wrote, "which leads with certainty through the labyrinth of the human soul . . . back to the final economic cause?" The web of causal relationships was simply "too fine to unravel." Still, the significance of art was inescapable. Art provided what "no age up to now has been without"—religion. In a time of profound transition like the present, however, the artist faced a special challenge. Art had lost its roots in the "soil of the people." The "bourgeoisie no longer had time for it"; the "proletariat still no time for it." Hence the isolation of the artist who "follows his deepest bent" and explores life in its "depth and complexity." Claasen claimed, nevertheless, that artists were anticipating the "life-feeling" which would grow in the "soil of the future wonder-garden of socialism." Despite the diverse trends in contemporary art—Naturalism, Symbolism, Impressionism—she assured her readers that the "empty dead time" of the present would be followed by a cultural renewal.

During its first two years the *Sozialistische Akademiker,* renamed the *Sozialistische Monatshefte* in January 1897, had developed a clearer sense of its mission. It provided, as Katzenstein observed, both a defense of the "claims of the academically educated comrades . . . for equal treatment in the party" and a new awareness of their role as critics.[40] In that role they had become convinced that, as Bloch put it, the Social Democrats were stagnating intellectually.[41] Indeed, some members of the party were ready "to throw all ideology overboard." The editors of the *Sozialistische Akademiker* had responded by seeking to broaden and deepen the cultural significance of Marxism.

They were not alone in that effort. A few years earlier Mehring had set out to develop the cultural implications of orthodox Marxism. And Edgar Steiger, editor of the party's weekly entertainment supplement, the *Neue Welt,* had undertaken that task from another perspective. His campaign to transform the literary tastes of the Social Democratic rank and file would bring the problem of culture onto the floor of the party conference.

The Question of a Socialist Culture: Franz Mehring, Edgar Steiger, and the Gotha Conference

Confident that the socialist movement held the seeds of a new culture, several of the young intellectuals, including Schmidt and Kampffmeyer, had taken an active part in the Free People's Theater founded by Wille in the summer of 1890. The theater's sponsors hoped to nurture the aesthetic tastes of the workers, contribute to their "moral elevation," and stimulate them to "reflect on the great issues of the time."[42] Under Wille's leadership the theater proved highly popular, gaining several thousand subscribers during its first two years and introducing its largely working-class audiences to plays by Ibsen, Sudermann, Tolstoy, Hauptmann, and others on Sunday afternoons. But Wille's role in the Jungen rebellion and his attempt to impose his aesthetic views on the workers antagonized his Social Democratic colleagues. In the fall of 1892 Wille and the literary figures he had drawn into the venture departed to form a New Free People's Theater.[43]

Social Democrats who assumed control of the Free People's Theater soon found, in Mehring, an individual well equipped by virtue of his academic training and his broad cultural background to provide new leadership. Determined to make the theater an instrument of the class struggle, Mehring initially viewed Naturalist drama as a contribution to this goal.[44] The "artistic rebellion" of the Naturalists represented an attempt to break free from the "stifling bonds of a declining society." But the courage and love of truth with which they were describing social conditions, Mehring argued, had taken them only halfway toward "a new art and world view." Preoccupied with the misery of the lower classes, they needed to overcome their pessimism and recognize the creative energies within the proletarian movement.

Despite his Marxism, Mehring remained attached to classical aesthetic norms, according to which political or ideological considerations should not intrude on the work of art. "Politics and poetry," he wrote not long after assuming the leadership of the theater, were "separate realms; their boundaries should not be blurred."[45] The contribution of art to the development of the proletariat was indirect. Along with aesthetic pleasure, art could contribute to workers' spiritual edification and social understanding. To enhance the latter Mehring provided commentaries designed to clarify the social meaning of the plays to be performed. He attempted to train the "proletarian eye" by applying the materialistic conception of history to the plays.

There was an obvious tension between Mehring's view of the theater as an instrument to train the proletarian eye and his defense of the autonomy of art. Initially he ignored that tension, confident that the workers were naturally making their way into "the world of beautiful appearances" as the movement gained in depth and breadth.[46] Although there was no possibility of a "new era of dramatic art on bourgeois soil," it would be foolish to ignore the upsurge of interest in art and literature among the workers. Mehring saw himself as a servant of a developing proletarian consciousness. His Social Democratic colleagues and the working-class subscribers could be relied on to select the plays which would contribute most to the class struggle. In contrast to the authoritarian policy of Wille—an aesthetic pedagogy imposed on the workers—

Mehring held that the policies of the theater should be decided democratically.

Within a year after accepting its leadership Mehring realized that he had been too optimistic in viewing the theater as a vehicle for an emerging proletarian consciousness. There were several difficulties. The theater remained dependent for its repertoire on plays already performed on the bourgeois stage. And the contemporary dramatists who offered critical treatments of society were soon used up. The hope of finding new dramatic talent capable of dealing creatively with the lives of the workers was not realized.[47] The plays submitted which treated the class struggle lacked artistic merit. Nor did the Naturalist writers, apart from Hauptmann's play "The Weavers" (performed in October 1893), present the workers in a positive way. Only Paul Bader's "Other Times," also staged during 1893 and one of the theater's two premiere performances, seemed to Mehring to bring "the actual proletariat onto the stage."[48] Unlike the Naturalists, who usually portrayed a "lumpenproletariat" found in the bordello or tavern, Bader described workers who were "not eaten up by dreary pessimism or deadened by unsavory pleasures." They exuded a "cheerful optimism." Here was the "living man as capitalistic development had created him."

The responses of the working-class audiences also disappointed Mehring. Their capacity to judge plays with a "proletarian eye" proved to be limited. A "whole set of additional factors" had entered in.[49] The Social Democratic subscribers tended to favor the type of drama popular among bourgeois audiences—entertaining rather than socially illuminating. When Mehring attempted to check the rapid growth of the theater on the ground that its aesthetic and social aims were being diluted by the influx of members who were merely seeking cheap seats, he was overruled by the executive.

Mehring's hopes for the theater led, as Scherer observed, to an impasse.[50] There was a growing contradiction between the "spontaneous requirements" of the working-class subscribers, conditioned as they were by "various influences out of the bourgeoisie," and the goal of proletarian self-education. To resolve the problem Mehring gradually assumed a pedagogical role analogous to that which he had condemned when exercised by Wille.

During the fall of 1893 Mehring, convinced that the plays of Lessing, Goethe, and Schiller combined the aesthetic force and the social insights lacking in contemporary drama, began to shift the theater's repertoire toward the German classics.[51] The older plays, he argued, mirrored the struggles of the new middle class against the aristocracy in the late eighteenth century. Although the middle class had been defeated in that struggle, its dramatists had carried its revolutionary spirit into the compensatory realm of art. From this art the proletariat could gain social understanding and moral inspiration helpful to its own struggle. The enthusiasm with which the audiences of the theater responded to productions such as Schiller's "Kabale und Liebe" (Intrigue and Love) was evidence, Mehring claimed, of the "subjective will" of the proletariat to "seize its own prehistory."[52] Eager to identify "his own motives with those of the workers," Mehring was deceiving himself.[53]

By falling back on the German classics Mehring could recover something of the theater's aim of educating the workers artistically. Reliance on the older drama supported the Marxist claim that the modern bourgeoisie had exhausted its creative possibilities, that a renewal of culture would await the transformation of economic conditions. The new policy also enabled Mehring to reconcile his Marxism with his deep love for a German literature which, according to his ideology, was passé. He could view the proletariat as the true heir of the German cultural tradition.

The return to the classics did not solve Mehring's dilemma. The accommodation of the theater to conventional tastes, at the expense of its proletarian aims, continued. In the end the Prussian authorities provided a way out. The growth of the theater's membership exceeded, in the eyes of the authorities, the limited number necessary to justify its claim to be a private club, exempt from the censorship laws. During 1896, after a lengthy judicial process, the theater lost its legal status.[54] Unwilling to submit to the censors, Mehring and his associates closed the theater. It was, he wrote later, an "honorable ending."[55] It was also an escape from the impasse to which his expectations for the theater had led.

Judged in terms of Mehring's belief that the proletariat was conquering the "world of beautiful appearances" with its own ways of thinking and feeling, the theater had clearly failed. He had exaggerated the readiness of the workers to go beyond conventional or "pre-ideological" tastes. To account for that failure Mehring could fall back on economic determinism. The theater's lack of success was due to circumstances rather than persons. Any significant impact on culture by the working class would have to await the destruction of the capitalistic mode of production.

One leading Social Democratic editor, Steiger, was not ready to surrender the belief that a cultural renewal was an integral part of the existing socialist movement. And he still hoped that Naturalist literature would, in Schmidt's words, "find entrance into the hearts of the proletariat."[56] Naturalism provided, according to Steiger, a common ground for the Marxism of the Social Democrats and modern art.

The son of a Swiss parson, Steiger had studied theology until his "thirst for beauty" and the influence of Jacob Burckhardt at the University of Basel altered his course in life.[57] Moving to Germany, he was caught up in the social and cultural ferment of the late eighties and entered the Friedrichshagen circle. In 1889 he published a study of contemporary drama in which he expressed the hope that the new literary movement and the socialist movement would join forces.[58] During the early nineties he became active as a socialist speaker and writer in Leipzig. When the local paper was taken over by Schönlank and renamed the *Leipziger Volkszeitung,* Steiger became its literary editor, helping it to reach a level of cultural sophistication unmatched by any party daily. He introduced his readers to major contemporary writers—Zola, Tolstoy, Ibsen—as well as to the German Naturalists.

Early in 1896 Steiger was appointed editor of the *Neue Welt,* the party's entertainment supplement. Distributed to nearly 200,000 subscribers of the party's newspapers each week, the *Neue Welt* was by far the most widely read of the Social Democratic publications.[59] Steiger was thus well placed to influence the literary tastes of the party rank and file. He soon began to publish, in serial form, two novels by the Naturalists—Hans Land's *Der Neue Gott* and Wilhelm Hegeler's *Mutter Bertha.*[60] In two articles published in the *Leipziger Volkszeitung* in the fall of 1896, Steiger made his case for the aesthetic education of the workers.[61] Given their limited access to art and the "stepmotherly fashion" with which art had been treated by the Social Democrats, the task would, he acknowledged, be difficult. It would require an effort comparable to the party's attempt to instruct the workers in the "most important teachings of scientific socialism." But the "socialist movement was the greatest cultural movement of all time." It was crucial, therefore, that the Social Democrats "solve the task" of helping the workers become "full men." To do that they should concentrate initially on "the most progressive element among the workers" and familiarize them with the "living art of the present" which, according to Steiger, was emerging with "a natural necessity."

Steiger's promotion of Naturalist writings aroused strong opposition in the party. The sharpest criticism came from Hamburg, where the editor of the local Social Democratic paper, R. Berard, denounced the fiction being published in the *Neue Welt* as "absolutely indigestible."[62] The workers, he declared, were accustomed each day to see "misery in its naked form." What they needed was reading material which would help them to bear the "new horrors" ahead. Sunday was, after all, the only day in the week when they could relax; the proper function of the *Neue Welt* was to "fan the idealism" the workers needed for the class struggle. It should "advance the good impulses in man . . . the love of freedom, charity, feelings of solidarity and self-sacrifice in the struggle and the self-consciousness of individuals and the class." Referring to the "ugly, disgusting, and shocking scenes" presented by the Naturalist writers, Berard charged that they killed the "indispensable idealism" within the party.

Steiger countered by claiming that Berard wanted Social Democratic tracts rather than genuine art.[63] He cited the success of the *Leipziger Volkszeitung* in cultivating the literary tastes of its readers. In a subsequent article, Steiger argued that Social Democrats who "marched at the head" of mankind in "politics and social science" could not lag "far behind the bourgeoisie in aesthetic matters."[64] Naturalism represented "a living example" of the Marxist method. Like Marx, the modern writers were tearing aside the masks of present-day vices and hypocrisies. Did his critics really express, Steiger asked, "the proletarian spirit"?

> No. The mass of the workers have long since broken with these philistine judgments. . . . However, I know who again makes himself the spokesman for the workers' wishes to muzzle free art. It is the ghost which has long haunted us, the narrow-hearted, limited—petty bourgeoisie.

Steiger's critics were not impressed by his attempt to "open the eyes and ears of the workers."[65] They denounced his "tone of absolute intellectual superiority" and his suggestion that only a small, younger group of party members could be taught to enjoy true art initially. And they defended the "healthy natural feelings of the people." An art which contradicted these feelings could not be a means of education. Indeed, the critics maintained that the ordinary perceptions of the workers were superior to those of the Naturalist writers who were entangled in the corruptions of bourgeois society.

The dispute was projected into the party's conference at Gotha in October 1896. Several resolutions, including a sharply worded complaint from Hamburg, called on the delegates to condemn Steiger's policy of making the *Neue Welt* a "playground for literary experiments."[66] The debate over the issue took up a day and a half of the six-day meeting.

Steiger defended his effort to guide Social Democrats "on the path of modern art."[67] Amid the "decadence and self-disintegration of bourgeois society," he declared, the Naturalists were employing the techniques of modern science to illuminate the "most secret motives of the human breast."[68] Social Democrats need not fear the objective treatment of social realities. The "sacred affair" for which they struggled could not be damaged by the unflattering portrayals of the workers. Could the socialist cause have advanced, he asked the delegates, if Lassalle had pulled back from his beliefs in the face of the views of the majority? At the same time Steiger reaffirmed his own commitment to the practical side of their struggle: "Art is for me the second thing for which I live and want to die. In the first place lies . . . the great liberation of working people from economic need. In the second place, however, lies the raising up of the people so that it can participate in the joys of culture. For we must not forget the goals we struggle for. We want the working people to take over the leadership in all areas of life."[69] In matters of culture, he added, it was not possible for the proletariat to "create something out of nothing." Workers would have to come to terms, therefore, with the changes under way in art and literature.

But the issue which was central for Steiger, the relationship between socialism and culture, was set aside as the delegates concentrated on the question of "decency." The discussion focused mainly on the desirability of the *Neue Welt* presenting to Social Democratic families matters which offended their sense of propriety. Much was made of an episode in *Mutter Bertha* in which the author reported that the heroine had gone behind a bush to relieve herself. To several of the speakers at Gotha this could only be viewed as "smut." The course of the debate suggested the utter conventionality of the tastes of those who represented the Social Democratic rank and file.[70]

The paradox—the co-existence within the party of a revolutionary ideology and conventional tastes—was noted by Bebel. Again he played the role of peacemaker, seeking to reconcile the opposing views. Although Bebel conceded that "a party such as ours" could not remain backward in the areas of art and literature, he expressed his confidence that the editor of the *Neue Welt* would take to heart the lesson emerging from the discussion.[71] Bebel persuaded the Hamburg representatives to withdraw their resolution.

A lead editorial in *Vorwärts* after the conference praised the delegates for their treatment of the issue.[72] Gotha demonstrated that the Social Democrats, "alone among the parties," did not "stop before any question of life"; the debate demonstrated that socialism was the "bearer of a new world view." In reality the episode demonstrated the opposite—the resistance of the party's rank and file, or their representatives, to any serious attempt to connect the Marxist ideology to changes in aesthetic sensibility. It showed, as a later Marxist critic of the Gotha discussion declared, that the cultural tastes of the Social Democrats were still narrowly circumscribed.[73]

Mehring was pleased with the debate at Gotha; it confirmed his own view of the relationship of the working classes to modern art.[74] The "complete unanimity" with which Naturalist literature had been rejected expressed the refusal of the proletariat to accept an art in such "clear opposition to all its thoughts and feelings." And Mehring again pointed to the deep pessimism of the Naturalists, their inability to see any way out of the misery they depicted. They failed to recognize the "rebirth under way within the proletariat," and the "joyful spirit of struggle," in a class which was convinced that it "could transform the world." The writings of the Naturalists simply reflected the inevitable decline of the bourgeois class. The "alleged conservatism" of the workers, the claim that they lacked artistic sensibility, was disproved, according to Mehring, by "their enthusiasm for the classics."

The Gotha conference had also shown the danger, Mehring declared, of "exaggerating the significance of art for the proletarian struggle."[75] Unlike the bourgeoisie at the time of Goethe and Schiller, the modern proletariat lacked the resources for developing a new drama. Hence the futility of attempts, like those of Steiger, to educate the workers artistically. Such efforts were bound to end in "bitter disillusionment." It was unrealistic, Mehring argued, to expect the emergence of a new aesthetic sensibility in a proletariat still caught up in the class struggle.

In a series of essays published during 1897 and 1898 Mehring argued that the gulf between the proletariat and an art growing out of a class doomed by the "iron laws of history . . . could not be bridged."[76] Since art, like religion, philosophy, and all other intellectual disciplines, had its "roots in . . . material conditions," its renewal would require the transformation of the means of production. "In other words, if the declining bourgeois class can *no longer* create any great art, so the rising working class *still* cannot create a great art, though in the depths of its soul a warm yearning after art can still live."[77] Only the full victory of the proletariat would bring "a world turning point in art." And it would mean, Mehring predicted, an art "nobler, greater, more glorious than human eyes have ever seen."

Steiger, too, concluded that his efforts to alter the literary tastes of the party rank and file had been premature. During the summer of 1897, while he sat in the the Zwickau prison in Saxony after being convicted of charges arising from his editorial activity, he reflected anew on the relationship between Marxism and culture. His book *The Rise of Modern Drama*, published the following year, dealt with the problem of cultural renewal.[78] He noted that the struggle of the "slaves and proletariat" in the ancient world had been paralleled by the rise of a "new great culture." But there had been no clear link between "proletarian feelings" and the new art. So, too, in the modern world. The "tired pessimism" of contemporary writers bore no clear relationship to the sense of "rebirth" and the "joyful strivings" of the workers.[79] Although the latter embodied the hope for cultural regeneration, that process still lay in the distant future.

Toward the end of the final essay in his series of literary essays, Mehring noted the efforts under way to revive the Free People's Theater, even though the "exuberant illusion" with which it had begun had "long since been shattered on hard facts."[80] And when, in the spring of 1897, a legal basis was found for a fresh start, Mehring allowed himself to be elected to its executive body. Within a year he resigned, convinced that the theater was, under its new leader, Schmidt, on a "downward path." Two years later he attacked the theater for falling back on "the plays which charmed our grandfathers."[81] Schmidt claimed, however, that he and his colleagues were, in their efforts to give the workers "a new appreciation of dramatic art," simply carrying forward the development that had begun under Mehring.[82] He was correct. At the same time he was conceding that the theater had ceased to have any clear connection to the Marxist ideology, that it was, in short, being "depoliticized."[83]

Despite the efforts of Mehring and Steiger, the Social Democratic party had maintained throughout the nineties a policy of neutrality toward cultural developments; its press was open to various literary and artistic perspectives.[84] In refusing to identify the socialist movement with new tendencies in art or literature the party leaders were, ironically, contributing to the process through which the workers were being integrated "into the bourgeois idea world."[85] At times they even emphasized the role of the party in protecting what was most valuable in German cultural life.[86]

As the hope for a distinctive socialist culture faded or was put off until the postrevolutionary period, one young intellectual concluded that Marxism itself was an obstacle to a genuinely new consciousness. Paul Ernst's disenchantment with orthodox Marxism has already been noted. A number of his essays in the late nineties took aim at the central Marxist doctrines, including the materialistic conception of history, the notion of a homogenous working class, and, indeed, the idea of class.[87] But he also continued to struggle with the problem which had drawn him to the movement—the spiritual emptiness of the modern world.[88] In resuming his career as a creative writer, abandoned when he adopted Marxism, Ernst focused on the moral struggles of the individual. He had become convinced that the Marxists, like the Naturalists, had reduced the human being to a "will-less product of the environment," or social conditions, and thus had cut themselves off from "all that was most valuable" in the personality—the "extraordinary" and the "exception," indeed, the "I" itself.[89] It is not suprising that Ernst found fresh inspiration in the writings of Nietzsche. For Nietzsche had "dared to show" that the "progressive ennoblement of the human race" could only come from a "fearful internal struggle" and an "ethical goal which had nothing to do with happiness."[90]

Ernst recorded his gradual liberation from what he called the abstractions of Marxism in an autobiographical novel published in 1902, *The Narrow Path to Happiness.* Here he portrayed the social setting in Berlin that he had entered in the late eighties. He described the search of educated young men like himself, estranged from their middle-class backgrounds, for new social ties and meaning in life. The novel was, for the most part, an account of their failures. Toward the end of the story, the hero, Hans, observed that his friends were "falling like leaves," having suffered from broken relationships, betrayals, and disillusionment with the working class.[91]

In an assessment of the Social Democratic party in 1902, Ernst explained the failure of the project to which he and other young Marxist intellectuals had been dedicated.[92] There was a touch of melancholy in his review of the party's history as he recalled the spell which it had cast over young intellectuals. They had been convinced that the development of the proletariat transcended class interests and represented the "highest and ultimate goals of mankind." They were persuaded that the workers were gaining "a theoretical sense" no longer found in the educated classes. Then came the disappointments and doubts. The preoccupation of the Social Democrats with "political tasks" demonstrated that the hopes of the intellectuals had been misplaced. The "enthusiasm and good conscience" which came from their belief that the workers would build "a new order for mankind" had also produced "blindness." The intellectuals failed to recognize, according to Ernst, that the Social Democratic rank and file had never gained any genuine understanding of the socialist goals; they had only been persuaded that they possessed it. The Marxist doctrines soon became, as a result, "mere phrases" which lost all meaning and functioned simply as "illusions" useful for political agitation. Ernst concluded that the workers were even more deficient in the qualities of morality, courage, and enthusiasm than were the classes above them. What the upper sections of the working class really wanted was a petty-bourgeois existence.

Having left the movement, Ernst renewed the search for a new way of life which he had, for a time, identified with the development of the working class.[93] But the other young socialist intellectuals who shared in that quest remained, with few exceptions, within the Social Democratic party. They had, however, as the columns of the *Sozialistische Akademiker* indicated, begun to reconsider the nature of the socialist vision.

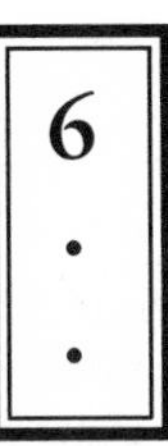

Revising Marxism

THE revisionist controversy which erupted within the party during the late nineties has been identified mainly with Eduard Bernstein.[1] Expelled from Germany under the antisocialist laws, Bernstein had lived in Zurich and then London, where his close ties with Engels had helped him to become, next to his close friend Kautsky, the chief authority on Marxist theory among the Social Democrats. When, in a series of articles in the *Neue Zeit* during 1897 and 1898, Bernstein abandoned the central Marxist doctrines, the disturbance within the party was immense.

Bernstein was not academically educated. His significance here is twofold. His criticisms of the party's official ideology exposed the tension between the visionary and the apologetic elements within the Marxist synthesis. And Bernstein gave fresh stimulus to the process of socialist self-criticism which had been unfolding among the younger intellectuals. "Bernstein," Kampffmeyer declared, "showed us what we were" but "had not dared" to admit.[2]

The revisions which followed took a variety of forms. Kampffmeyer and Schmidt, building on their earlier criticisms, developed a gradualist approach to socialist growth. Schippel, Calwer, and Heine, members of the party's parliamentary group after 1898, began to put aside ideological claims and emphasize practical political possibilities. Other Revisionists, the Neo-Kantians, attempted to reconstruct the philosophical basis of Marxism. And two remarkable women, Lily Braun and Rosa Luxemburg, revealed hitherto hidden potentialities within Marxist theory. Viewed as a whole, the Revisionists demonstrated both the instability of Marx's synthesis and its capacity to open new paths for the Social Democrats.

Bernstein's Challenge and the Response of Kautsky and Bebel

Writing from his exile in London in the fall of 1898, Bernstein recalled the moment when, after a lecture before the Fabian Society in London, he realized that his attempt to defend the Marxist doctrines was an "injustice to Marx."[3] The best service to Marx's memory, Bernstein decided, was to "be clear as to where Marx is still right and where he is not" and to abandon the effort "to stretch his theory until it will prove anything." Bernstein began his criticism of Marxist theory in a series of articles in the *Neue Zeit* in 1896.[4] There he suggested that the Social Democrats were avoiding "theoretical difficulties" and counting on a "sudden leap from capitalism to socialist society" to solve all their problems. In subsequent articles during 1897 and 1898 he went on to question, on the basis of statistics, the Marxist forecast of economic concentration, social polarization, and the growing misery of the workers. Along the way he denied that Marxist theory was scientific, at least in the sense claimed by its orthodox adherents. It was, rather, a mixture of the scientific, defined by Bernstein as an impartial, provisional investigation of empirical data, and what he called "ideological" elements—"ideal impulses" born of the imagination or derived from moral, religious, or legal traditions.

Much of Bernstein's criticism of the party's ideology was directed at its "almost mystical belief" in the proletariat.[5] The "proletariat as a class acting with conscious purpose and outlook," he argued, was "largely a figment of the imagination."[6] He took issue with the orthodox view that the minds of the workers were shaped in a mechanical manner by economic conditions. "Why," he asked, "do workers in exactly the same class situation often behave in diametrically opposite ways?"[7] Their actions, he maintained, were often "influenced by historical memories and traditions" and "other ideological factors," the most important of which was the "concept of justice." Indeed, without the ideal influences Marxism would lose much of its power to motivate its followers.

Bernstein had, in short, rejected the belief that socialism entailed a radically new mentality. On the contrary, the vitality of the movement presupposed the persistence of older values and moral feelings. To seek to transform the mentality of the workers in a fundamental way was no more realistic than the desire for an imminent and catastrophic collapse of capitalism.

Initially Kautsky had welcomed Bernstein's proposal to discuss problems in Marxist theory. Despite his rigid defense of the orthodox doctrines in the agrarian debate, Kautsky had never viewed Marxism as a finished system of thought.[8] Although he followed Bernstein's articles with growing uneasiness, he did not awaken to the full import of the critique until the spring of 1898. "Ede," he wrote Adler, "has become uncommonly skeptical."[9] By the late summer, as the "unbelievable theoretical retreat" continued, Kautsky concluded that he could no longer work with Bernstein.[10] At the Stuttgart conference in September, after Bebel had read a statement from Bernstein summarizing his views, Kautsky attacked the man "who for eighteen years has been one of my closest companions in arms."[11]

At stake was the work to which Kautsky had devoted himself for nearly twenty years. "If the materialistic conception of history and the concept of the proletariat as the motor force of the coming revolution are erroneous," he told Bernstein, "then must I state that my life no longer has meaning."[12] The struggle to propagate a "unified world view" had been the chief aim of his editorship of the *Neue Zeit*. When Bernstein compared the paper to a "church magazine," Kautsky conceded that the term could be applied to his effort to make the *Neue Zeit* a "fighting journal for Marxist theory."[13]

Given the "cleft between us," Kautsky attempted to persuade Bernstein to give up his editorial position with the *Neue Zeit*.[14] Much to Kautsky's dismay, Bernstein refused. To resign, he held, would be an "admission that he was in the wrong," that he "no longer belonged in the party."[15] Early in 1899 he published a systematic statement of his views. It was, he wrote Adler, an attempt to adjust Marxist theory to the practices of the party and to actual social and economic developments in Germany.[16]

For Kautsky the war with Bernstein, conducted through letters and the party press, meant anguish and frustration. Bernstein, he complained, lacked the courage to do what was appropriate. If Bernstein had come to view his life's work "as a folly"—and that, Kautsky believed, was "basically Ede's position"—then he should leave the movement.[17] And while he was convinced that Bernstein's ideas would find little support in the party, Kautsky feared that they would spread "confusion and unrest . . . in our ranks."[18]

Bebel, too, worried about the impact of Bernstein's criticism on the Social Democrats. But he was mainly concerned with its effect on those qualities from which the party derived its unity and morale. "Only the mystic aura of a grand mission," Bebel's biographer notes, could "instill dedication and impart unity of purpose to a revolutionary movement."[19] To say that the party's ideology served chiefly as an instrument for Bebel is not to deny the strength of his Marxist convictions. His role in the ensuing controversy brought out more clearly, however, the apologetic function of his Marxism.

As the full extent of Bernstein's apostasy became clear, Bebel continued to worry about its impact on party solidarity and discipline. Bernstein had given new life to the "heterogeneous elements" which had long been "concealed in the womb of the party."[20] Early in 1899 Bebel suggested that a break might be necessary for the health of the party: "If we had only one Bernstein it would not be a matter of concern, but we have quite a number of them and most, to be sure, in respected party positions. Those do not have the courage to say what they think but they offer passive resistance and work under cover. . . . Essential to our progress is the solidarity and decisiveness of our advance, both of which, however, are lost as soon as a number of people are present who engage in criticism and fault finding."[21]

Bernstein recognized that he had challenged Kautsky and Bebel in quite different ways. Kautsky, as one of the "Calvinists of doctrine," was defending the Marxist world view.[22] For Bebel, the Marxist ideology was primarily a "source of desirable slogans." Bebel, worried primarily about party morale, was even less willing than Kautsky to submit Marxist theory to rational scrutiny; hence Bebel's attack was the sharper.

And yet Bebel could not, as the party's leader, join those who wished to expel Bernstein and his followers. For Bebel now presided over an increasingly diverse membership, drawing electoral support from outside the working class and reaching sections of the German population which did not share the views of the Prussian and Saxon Social Democrats who dominated the party. To force a showdown would risk alienating significant sections of the party, especially in the south. Hence Bebel's mediating role at the Hanover party conference in 1899, where the delegates were presented with resolutions calling for the expulsion of leading Revisionists. Bebel's compromise resolution, which simply reaffirmed the principles and tactics of the party, passed overwhelmingly.[23] An armistice had been declared.

An Alternative Path for Social Democrats: Kampffmeyer and Schmidt

Even before Bernstein took aim at the orthodox Marxist doctrines, Kampffmeyer had posed a question which puzzled several of the younger intellectuals. How, he asked, could Marxists claim that the workers, who were condemned to increasing misery under capitalism, would also experience a "moral and physical rebirth"?[24] This paradoxical mixture of gloom and optimism, contained within the Erfurt program, had, according to Kampffmeyer, led Social Democrats to quite different views of the state. The Jungen and the Independents had dismissed the state as a "tool of the dominant class"; Vollmar and the party's right wing viewed the state as a lever for advancing working-class interests.

Kampffmeyer hoped to "ignite a lively discussion of . . . fundamental issues of theory."[25] No one within the party took up the challenge. But the editor of the *Sozialistische Monatshefte* now drew on the criticism of Marxist theory being developed by the French socialist Georges Sorel.[26] Convinced that the orthodox Marxists had become captive to abstractions, Sorel focused on the materialistic conception of history and argued that it failed to do justice to the moral and religious aspects of human experience or to account for the role of great individuals. Sorel also began to familiarize the readers of the *Sozialistische Monatshefte* with the growing current of Marxist self-criticism in Italy and elsewhere.

Only after the significance of Bernstein's revisionism became clear did the *Sozialistische Monatshefte* renew the effort to promote critical reflection among the Social Democrats. It was time, Kampffmeyer wrote in the spring of 1898, to "begin again."[27] In taking up the critical task Kampffmeyer fixed once more on economic associations—trade unions and cooperatives—as the most promising vehicles for the "inner development of the workers." He did not reject the political activity of the party, but he reminded his readers that politics still stood, according to Marx, "in complete dependence on the economic." Here lay the "living formative force" for change.

Kampffmeyer had moved from the radical wing of the movement, expressed in his association with the Independents, to the party's right. A fellow participant in the Jungen rebellion, Ladislaus Gumplowicz, explained the shift.[28] The "mental disposition" which had fixed on the "mystical enlightenment of the proletariat, the chosen people of the revolution," had led intellectuals like Kampffmeyer to identify themselves more closely with the immediate economic struggle. In doing so, however, they had gained a new respect for the "fruitful activity of the workers," expressed in the trade unions and cooperatives. Here was the "germ of an about-face" on the part of Kampffmeyer and others who had traveled for a time with the Independents.

Kampffmeyer presented his new vision of the movement in a pamphlet, *More Power,* published in the fall of 1898.[29] It was an attempt to deal with the paradox he had noted earlier—the "major gap" in the Erfurt program between the "depressing, paralyzing mood" resulting from the immiserisation thesis, on the one hand, and the belief in the "growing economic and social power of the workers," on the other.[30] Even though the capitalist enemy had shown a "surprising agility," Kampffmeyer now claimed that the workers were gaining power "step by step" by means of the trade unions and cooperatives. He found support for his optimism in British experience. In Great Britain, he argued, the workers had entered the "constitutional fabric" of the nation and demonstrated that "radical reform" was "possible on the soil of bourgeois society."[31] Capitalism, he declared, "flows into socialism."

Although Kampffmeyer held that the barriers between the proletariat and the bourgeoisie were breaking down, he had not abandoned his belief that socialism would mean "a fundamental alteration of the whole way of life."[32] Machines would take away the "cross of work" and free individuals, including women, from a single vocation and "make all-around development possible." Having given a highly utopian turn to his Marxism, Kampffmeyer declared that the new society, driven by "elementary forces," was "within sight."[33]

Schmidt, meanwhile, had undertaken a similar revision of Marxism. During 1897 and 1898 he restated his doubts about the Marxist theory of value and his skepticism about "theoretical deductions."[34] By freeing themselves from doctrinal claims, Social Democrats would be liberated "from the notion that any powerful natural law" stood in the way of the efforts of the workers to improve their position through legislative or trade union activity. Indeed, from the "basic idea of Marxism," the recognition that progress to a higher society depended on economic conditions, Schmidt concluded that a "sudden leap" into socialism was unthinkable. And he joined Bernstein in emphasizing the importance of the movement rather than the final goal. What mattered was the capacity of the movement to incorporate the final goal as a "vitalizing and energizing principle."[35]

For Schmidt, however, the philosophical underpinnings of Marxism were still suspect. Although he retained the materialistic conception of history, he had rejected economic determinism. He continued his efforts to reconcile, by means of Kantian philosophy, historical materialism and ideal motives. That effort now led to a sharp clash with Georgi Plekhanov, the leading philosophical defender of orthodox Marxism. The orthodox view, that men gained through "praxis" a direct knowledge of reality, was, according to Plekhanov, "as clear and irrefutable as the proof of a mathematical theory."[36] But Schmidt dismissed as metaphysical the claim that practical activity provided direct access to the "thing in itself."[37] It was, he added, an example of the tendency for orthodox Marxists to dispose of the "most difficult questions" by means of "a final and fixed dogma." Kant, in contrast, had drawn back before the "mysterious depths" of the human psyche.

An outside observer, Chajm Schitlowsky, sympathetic to Schmidt, recognized the significance of the dispute between the two thinkers. Plekhanov, "the strictest orthodox Marxist of them all," was holding on tenaciously to the view that socialism represented a "religious world view."[38] But the "metaphysical period in socialist thought" was, according to Schitlowsky, coming to an end. "Progressives," like Schmidt, were seeking to free the Social Democrats from churchlike dogmas while preserving the "kernel of Marxism." The gulf between the two socialist thinkers was evident when Plekhanov abandoned philosophical argument to ask: "What wicked spirit has moved Konrad Schmidt to hold forth on matters which . . . are unfamiliar to him?"[39] To Plekhanov the answer was clear. The bourgeoisie were using Kant to "combat materialism." Kant's philosophy was an "opium through which the proletariat . . . might be lulled to sleep." For Schmidt, however, Plekhanov's "psychological analysis of my humble self" was simply another expression of a dogmatic way of thinking in which the slightest criticism of Marxism was seen as "intellectual immaturity" or "cowardice."[40]

But Schmidt and Kampffmeyer had altered the Marxist ideology in a fundamental way. They had rejected, in Schmidt's words, the belief that the Marxist conception of history provided socialists with "fixed propositions valid for all time" in favor of the demand that Social Democrats constantly test their ideas in economic and social circumstances that Marx and Engels had not foreseen.[41] Schmidt and Kampffmeyer had retained the vision of a radical transformation of life. But they had softened their opposition to the bourgeois world and modified their belief that the future society required a radically new working-class mentality. This process of social and cultural accommodation was carried much further by three of the younger intellectuals who were involved in parliamentary politics.

The Intellectual as "Praktiker": Schippel, Calwer, and Wolfgang Heine

One of the most perceptive students of German Social Democracy has observed that the decisive influence on the party by the turn of the century was being exercised by the "local trade union leaders and officials, the municipal politicians and 'landtag' representatives . . . the irreplaceable carriers of its immediate practical work."[42] As for the "revisionist academicians around the *Sozialistische Monatshefte,*" they were "merely a weak reflex" of the party's "many-sided reformist practices," of its "thousands of single activities in ever new areas of practical possibility."

Some of the revisionist intellectuals would probably have accepted the judgment. Their efforts to alter the party's ideology were stimulated mainly by a recognition that Social Democratic practice was, notwithstanding its revolutionary rhetoric, increasingly reformist. The gradualist ideology of Kampffmeyer and Schmidt was, in part at least, a reflection of the rapid growth of the trade unions which, during the second half of the nineties, doubled their membership.[43] The trade union leaders were demanding greater autonomy and rejecting the role assigned to them in orthodox Marxism—as simply recruiting agencies for the movement and condemned, through the inner workings of capitalism, to transitory significance on the road to socialism.

The clash between the party's Marxism and its practices was felt most keenly by the younger intellectuals in the party's Fraktion. They confronted in their parliamentary activity pressures and choices which did not mesh easily with their ideological commitments.

Schippel was especially bold in addressing the dilemmas facing the Marxist politicians. He was continuing the journey, begun in the early nineties, through which the central Marxist doctrines were being set aside in the face of immediate legislative issues. When, at the Hamburg party conference in 1897, Schippel reported on the activities of the Fraktion during the preceding year, he pointed to the "dilemma in which we find ourselves" with respect to the government's proposed military budget.[44] The party's goal, stated in the Erfurt program, of "an armed nation instead of a standing army," was not realistic: "For the . . . abolition of all standing armies there is no majority at present and one is not likely to be created in the foreseeable future. . . . Should we, therefore, because the bourgeois parties do not do our will in this connection, penalize the German workers . . . who are placed in danger, [and] atone in blood for the folly of the enemy? That would be madness and acting against the interests of the working class. We can find better opportunities for the struggle against militarism." What was the party's responsibility in a world where war was possible, even likely? Should it deny the workers, who made up the bulk of the German army, the "best weapons available"? Schippel simply stated the dilemma; he did not recommend that the party alter its firm opposition to military expenditures.

Several delegates, however, recognized the danger in Schippel's comments. A working-class speaker from Berlin voiced their suspicions: "Visualize what Comrade Schippel was earlier and how he stands today. When he came into the Fraktion the comrades believed that he entered . . . with heels of iron. [He who was] so radical that he was in danger of being counted among the Independents has now developed in a way that I can, like most Berliners, say—Max, I shudder at the sight of you."[45] Bebel and Liebknecht sought to dispel the fears of opportunism. Schippel, they suggested, had simply expressed himself in an unfortunate way. After all, they reminded the delegates, "he voted like the rest of us."[46] But Ignaz Auer, the least ideological of the veteran party leaders, was more candid. Responding to a resolution introduced to censure Schippel, he warned the delegates that if they wished "to settle accounts with Schippel," they would have to deal with himself and with Bebel and Liebknecht as well, both of whom had at times acknowledged the party's obligation to the German soldier.[47] Auer noted the possibility of an invasion by "an enemy out of the east," in the face of which the whole Fraktion would accept measures proposed by the government with "a storm of approval."

In his report at Hamburg Schippel also suggested that the party's traditional endorsement of free trade did not provide adequate guidance in dealing with the nation's trade policy. "I was not elected as an internationalist free trader," he declared, "but as a representative of the interests of the German industrial workers."[48] Should the party's Fraktion adhere to a doctrine which, given fierce international economic competition, would favor the bourgeoisie in other nations at the expense of "our own workers"? The workers were not simply consumers, concerned with the price of foodstuffs, but producers whose interests might not be served by a policy of free trade.

At the Stuttgart conference a year later Schippel expressed his pragmatic approach to the question of protectionism by introducing a resolution calling for a gradual reduction of tariffs rather than the total rejection traditionally favored by the party. The choice between protectionism and free trade, he argued, was "a practical question which must be decided in each individual case."[49] He was quickly answered by Kautsky, who viewed free trade as a matter of principle, and one which indicated the integral relationship between the party's Marxist theory and its political tactics. In the ensuing debate Schippel prevailed, thanks to a compromise resolution introduced by Bebel. Kautsky's tendency, as Vollmar put it, to turn everything "into a world view" had been rejected in favor of the realities facing the politician.

It proved more difficult for Schippel to loosen the hold of principle on the Social Democratic view of military policy. He had reopened the issue in a series of articles, published under a pseudonym, in the *Sozialistische Monatshefte.*[50] "Was Engels," he asked, "a believer in a militia?" After arguing that Engels had a realistic grasp of the nature of modern armies, he compared those Social Democrats who believed in a citizen militia to the "strange enthusiasts" who held that "the wild, brutal meat eaters of the past" could suddenly be turned into vegetarians. Again Kautsky took up the challenge, maintaining that Schippel had tacitly abandoned the Marxist point of view.[51] Kautsky's view prevailed at the Hanover party conference in 1899. Schippel had failed, in Ritter's words, to adjust the party's view of military affairs to "existing circumstances."[52]

Calwer, too, was setting the party's doctrines aside. The firm adherence to orthodox Marxism which had marked his earlier years weakened as he became one of the party's experts on current economic issues and, after his election to the Reichstag in 1898, a spokesman on trade policy.[53] By 1896 he had concluded that "it would be wrong" to identify socialism with any "particular philosophical or ethical premises" or to see it as a "world view."[54] And he joined other Revisionists in emphasizing immediate reforms, arguing like Kampffmeyer and Schmidt that "capitalism grows into socialism." Confident in that process, he organized an "economic bureau" which gathered statistical data on such issues as unemployment, the working-class standard of living, and profit rates. In concentrating on matters relating to the immediate well-being of the working class, Calwer lost interest, as his biographer has observed, in theory. "Circumstances" rather than "ideological principles" became decisive; "statistics took the place of Marxism."[55]

Wolfgang Heine did not go that far. But as one of the most active Social Democrats in the Reichstag, he also exemplified the process through which political practice was eroding the party's Marxist doctrines. No other socialist intellectual recognized so clearly the nature of that process or the way in which orthodox Marxism functioned as an apologetic for working-class interests.

Heine was one of the few socialist intellectuals who came out of the upper middle class.[56] After completing his legal training at the University of Berlin in 1883, he took a position in the judicial service in Oranienberg, just outside Berlin. During the late eighties he found, through a close reading of *Capital* and the *Anti-Dühring,* "a universal and imposing structure of teachings."[57] But even as he accepted Marxism, Heine was eager to reconcile socialism with "a new national feeling."

Disgust with the political and class biases he experienced in the legal profession led Heine to leave the state service in 1889 and start a private law practice. In the years ahead he represented Social Democrats and trade unionists in various legal difficulties. His friendship with Leo Arons, a wealthy Social Democrat and a generous supporter of socialist publications, drew Heine into a more active relationship to the party. In 1894 he began to take part in a "red salon" over which Arons presided—more or less regular evening meetings of Social Democratic intellectuals, trade union leaders, and others.[58] But not until 1897 did Heine "step forth as a Social Democrat." The occasion was an invitation to speak, in place of the ill Liebknecht, before a student social science association in Berlin. Here he demonstrated both his intellectual independence and his revisionist outlook.[59] Marxism, like any scientific method, he told the students, provided "only hypotheses," subject to continual testing and alteration. Later that year Heine was urged by Arons, Braun, and Auer to stand as a Social Democratic candidate in a Berlin district. Troubled by the attacks on Schippel at the Hamburg conference, they hoped, as Braun put it, to increase the "practical reform element" in the party's Fraktion.[60] "I had just read the report of the party conference," Heine recalled, when a delegation from the constituency arrived. The "silliness of the attack on national defense" at Hamburg overcame his reluctance to be a candidate.

In the electoral campaign in the spring of 1898 Heine shocked a number of Social Democrats by proposing that the party support the government's military budget in return for concessions in the area of civil rights.[61] His "compensation policy" made him, alongside Schippel, a target for those Social Democrats who feared the growth of opportunism. Heine was forced to defend his views at the Stuttgart conference in the fall.[62] But he had also begun to reflect on the relationship of the party's Marxist theory to the experiences of the politician. Late in 1898 he entered the controversy generated by Bernstein's revisionism.

Heine denied that the disputes over theory had much "practical significance."[63] "Even if he [Bernstein] shattered the Marxist structure of teachings," this would not alter the party's political conduct "in the slightest." The "peculiar character of practical politics" derived, he wrote, from considerations which had little to do with theory. The politician was called on to make judgments in a setting where complex circumstances, including the "unreasonableness of the enemy," the immediate interests of the workers, and the play of personalities limited the range of possibilities and made the outcome of any decision uncertain. Heine denounced the "priestly dogmatists" and the "academic arrogance" of those who insisted that party membership required the "acceptance of definite doctrines." Even Bernstein, he added, overvalued "the significance of science for practical politics."

And yet Heine did not want the party to soften its Marxist rhetoric. To do as Bernstein and other Revisionists urged would deny that "we lay our hands to the root of the evils."[64] Moreover, the militant phrases used in the party's propaganda were vital for "practical politics." "Pregnant slogans," notions of exploitation and the final socialist goal, need not "stand up to a strict scientific test," for they stimulated "the will to act." Heine thus emphasized the apologetic functions of the party's ideology.

The three "Praktiker" intellectuals had rejected the claim of the orthodox Marxists that theory provided guidance for the party's political practices in favor of a pragmatic approach to legislative issues. To adopt a more constructive role in the Reichstag debates was also to assume the existence of a wider community of interests. A nationalistic spirit was increasingly evident in the outlook of Schippel, Calwer, and Heine. But it was left to one of the party's most recent recruits to develop the logical implications of the retreat from orthodox Marxism.

Paul Göhre was the party's most celebrated convert from the ranks of the academically educated during the late nineties.[65] In 1890, as indicated earlier, Göhre, a young Lutheran minister, had sought insight into the "dark unknown world" of the working class by securing employment, under an assumed name, in a machine tool factory in Chemnitz. From his experience, recorded in his widely read book, *Three Months in a Workshop,* he emerged with a deep respect for the moral and intellectual qualities of his fellow workers together with a strong sense of the threat which the Marxist ideology of the Social Democrats posed to Christianity.[66] During the early nineties he and other Protestant clergymen attempted to apply Christian teachings to the problems of the workers. And in 1894 he joined Friedrich Naumann in forming the National Social Union, with the aim of drawing workers away from the Social Democrats by means of a program of social reform based on Christianity.[67] The "chiliastic enthusiasm" of the Social Democrats could only be countered, according to Naumann, by a comparable blend of social and spiritual forces. By the late nineties, however, Göhre had given up on the venture. The "plan for the creation of a genuine party of proletarian socialism," he wrote later, had been replaced by "love for the fatherland" and "bourgeois liberalism."[68]

Göhre did not go over to the Social Democrats until 1899, but conversations two years earlier with Schönlank indicated that he would enter the movement only on his own terms. He was "prepared to join," Schönlank wrote in his diary, if he could be assured of the "right to freedom of expression."[69] In his talk *How a Parson Became a Social Democrat,* which also became one of the party's most effective tracts, Göhre declared that he could identify himself with the socialists because Marxism was perfectly compatible with his religious convictions.[70] He cited the "fourth clause" of the Erfurt program, which stated that religious beliefs were private affairs, to support his claim that his Christian faith had not been compromised by entering the movement. Much of his early propaganda work for the party was designed to answer Social Democratic attacks on Christianity and what he regarded as distortions of the teachings of Jesus. At the same time he attempted to develop the logic of the "fourth clause" and limit the scope of Marxism.

Replying to the argument that there was "an unbridgeable gulf" between the "principles of proletarian socialism" and Christianity, Göhre maintained that socialism simply presented a "political and economic program."[71] As such it rested on the "theory of surplus value and the class struggle" as well as the "teaching of a final goal." These beliefs constituted the "unshakeable, firm basis of Marxist socialism." Toward the other parts of Marxism, particularly the materialistic conception of history, however, "we must adopt a critical position." To accept "the whole of Marxism" would lead to the "same dogmatism in Social Democracy as in the church." Hence the need for "absolute toleration" within the party.

In denying that Marxism constituted a world view or an ultimate grounding for life, Göhre had carried further the revisions of the gradualist and Praktiker intellectuals. He had, at the same time, called into question the project to which Marxist intellectuals had been committed—the cultivation of a distinct consciousness among the workers.

The Neo-Kantian Revisionists

Some of the revisionist intellectuals were unwilling to abandon the effort to create a new working-class mentality. During the late nineties they attempted to reconstruct the socialist world view through a philosophical revision of Marxism. Schmidt had led the way by drawing on Kantian ideas to remedy the philosophical deficiencies of Marxism.[72] But Kant, according to Schmidt, provided only a critique of materialism. Since Kant's philosophical system incorporated many traditional moral, religious, and metaphysical views, it offered little to Marxists who were committed to a strictly naturalistic position. Several Social Democratic intellectuals believed, however, that Kant provided more than a critique. They were influenced by the Neo-Kantian revival in Germany which had been under way since the sixties.[73] The leading representatives of the Marburg school of that revival, Hermann Cohen and Paul Natorp, had employed Kantian philosophy to formulate an ethical socialism as an alternative to Marxism.

The defenders of Marxist orthodoxy were ill prepared for such a challenge. Kautsky recognized that philosophy was not his "strong suit."[74] One sign of his philosophical uncertainty was his willingness to assign responsibility for dealing with philosophical issues in the *Neue Zeit* to a Neo-Kantian, Franz Staudinger.[75] Writing under a pseudonym, "Sadi Gunter," Staudinger did not hide his differences with the orthodox Marxists. Convinced that the problem of ethics had been "foreign to Engels," he attempted to reconcile the Kantian position—that ethics could only be understood deductively, as the necessary logical consequence of human freedom and rationality—with the Marxist view of history.[76] He argued that Marx had disclosed the economic and social developments by means of which Kant's abstract conception of justice could be realized. Ethical ideals, according to Staudinger, were powerless without the right historical conditions. Marxism and Neo-Kantianism were complementary. But Staudinger's synthesis, and his adoption of a gradualist form of socialism, proved incompatible with Kautsky's views. Staudinger soon moved to the *Sozialistische Monatshefte,* where he joined those Revisionists who looked to cooperatives as the most promising vehicle for bringing a new society.[77]

Karl Vorlander, a teacher in a gymnasium, also sought to "complete Marxism" by means of Kant. He argued that the value-laden terminology employed by Marx and Engels expressed their preoccupation with ethical questions. Without its implicit ethical drive Marxism could not generate the enthusiasm and the spirit of self-sacrifice required for its struggle against capitalism. Vorlander's *Kant and Socialism,* published in 1900, was an attempt to clarify what he viewed as the "newest theoretical movement within Marxism."[78]

The most ambitious figure in that movement was Ludwig Woltmann, who set out to reconstruct the Marxist world view with the help of Kant.[79] He had become a socialist at the University of Freiburg while studying medicine and philosophy. In 1896, at the age of twenty-five, he published the first of three books which he viewed as efforts to save the Social Democrats from "intellectual rigidity."[80] The most important of these, *Historical Materialism,* published in 1899, presented a reinterpretation, influenced by Kant and Darwin, of Marx's view of history. Woltmann believed that Kautsky was open to the kind of revision made possible by Kant.[81] An article in the *Neue Zeit* expressed his hope of completing the work which Marx had been "unable to finish."[82] Marx, he argued, was a "greater philosopher than an economist." The "innermost drive" in Marxist theory was "self-criticism and self understanding." And though Marx had not lived long enough to "review critically his own intellectual development," he had presented, in his materialistic conception of history, the "middle point" for a "comprehensive world view." Drawing on the early writings, Woltmann went on to claim that Marx had, in his critique of Hegel, "returned to Kant . . . without being conscious of it." Implicit in Marx's dialectic was "the spirit of Kant's critical analysis of consciousness." Failing to see this, Engels had devalued "psychological and ideological factors." Engels' later attempt to modify his determinism by describing economic conditions as simply the "last instance" had not altered his "dogmatism and unclarity."

Woltmann reaffirmed the importance of ideal motives within Marxism. Before long he joined those Revisionists who looked to the trade unions and the cooperatives as instruments for the "great moral transformation" demanded by socialism.[83] "Moral feelings," he insisted, were the "necessary grounding" of the movement. Socialism was still a "necessity arising from the inner laws of the development of mankind," but it was a "moral necessity."

Still, Woltmann did not believe that ethical idealism would be sufficient to revitalize the socialist ideology. In *The Position of Social Democracy toward Religion,* a pamphlet published in 1901, he declared that the "metaphysical problem was inescapable."[84] The Marxist attempt to "unravel the religious puzzle" had failed. In predicting the "natural death of religion," Marx, Engels, and Kautsky had ignored those aspects of human consciousness which could not be explained by natural science or simply in terms of social developments. If the Social

Democratic party was still a "vehicle for a new world view," it must also be "the carrier of religious progress." Woltmann attacked those propagandists who, faithful to their Marxist convictions, were hostile to Christianity. The party needed to acknowledge the "close ties between Christianity and socialism" and the debt of socialism to the teachings of Jesus. Apart from his assertion that man was "a metaphysical animal," however, Woltmann offered no deeper grounding for socialism save references to a "religion of nature." During 1902 he abandoned his effort to synthesize Marx and Kant and, by means of a new journal, the *Politische-Anthropologische Revue,* attempted to promote, outside of any philosophical doctrine or political party, the investigation of the relationship between social and biological developments. Before his early death in 1907, Woltmann's thinking had taken a racist direction.[85]

What Woltmann described as the "inner crisis of Social Democracy" had found expression in a variety of theoretical and tactical turns. It had shown, too, how the breakdown of orthodox Marxism could give rise to new ways of viewing the socialist project.

Female Revisionists: Lily Braun and Rosa Luxemburg

The academic element among the Social Democrats did not include women, apart from Luxemburg. University education was not a normal option for females in late nineteenth-century Germany. The middle-class women who entered the movement had been trained as teachers or had joined their husbands in working for the cause. A number of these women—Klara Zetkin, Mathilde Wurm, Gertrud David, Wally Zepler, and Kate Duncker—played prominent roles as writers and speakers. The female section of the party was, like the male, overwhelmingly working class.[86]

By the early nineties women formed a distinct and self-conscious force within the party. Barred by the laws of the Prussian state from direct participation in politics, the women had been encouraged by the Social Democratic leaders to form their own organization, and they were given representation at the party conferences. Yet the women in the party were "reluctant feminists," for they were torn between the "twin pulls of class and sex," between their distinctive problems as women and the proletarian struggle.[87] In dealing with this tension they found a strong and able leader in Klara Zetkin.

Born in 1857, Zetkin had turned away from a promising career in teaching to work with the Social Democrats in Leipzig, and then followed her lover, Ossip Zetkin, a Russian Marxist, to Paris.[88] Through her contacts with revolutionary intellectuals in Paris, further study of Marxist theory, and her writing for the movement, she had become by the end of the eighties one of the leading women in the newly formed Second International. When she returned to Germany after the death of Ossip in 1889, she was appointed editor of the Social Democratic weekly for women, *Gleichheit,* and set out to give clarity and direction to the inchoate feminist wing of the party. Clarity for Zetkin came from the Marxism of Engels and Kautsky. What mattered most was the class struggle and the need to educate the workers, male and female alike, in Marxist ideas.[89] Her orthodoxy left little room for distinctly feminist issues—the special disabilities of women in the workplace, in the legal system, and in marriage and family life. Her attachment to the conventional view of women as wives and mothers reinforced her belief that the socialist movement contained no "woman's question" as such. The liberation of women could only come through "a struggle of proletarian women with the men of their class against the capitalistic class."[90]

Zetkin's views were challenged by Lily Braun, who expressed, in Jean Quataert's words, "a new feminist consciousness" among Social Democrats.[91] Born into a Prussian aristocratic family in 1865, Lily von Kretschmann had moved until her mid-twenties along the path prescribed for young women of her class.[92] But two events—the fall of her father, an army general, from imperial favor, and her rejection by the man she had hoped to marry—weakened her ties to her social class and awakened her to the plight of women in Wilhelmine society. Her marriage in 1893 to Georg von Gizyki, a crippled university professor and one of the founders of the German branch of the Ethical Culture movement, reflected both her spirit of independence and her search for new values and social relationships. As an "ethical socialist" she attempted to draw middle-class and working-class women together in a common struggle. But after being rebuffed by Zetkin, who was determined to avoid any embrace by the "dressed up, perfumed, and mannered socialism" of the educated,[93] Lily concluded that the gulf between the classes was too wide to be bridged. Following the death of her husband in 1895 she joined the Social Democrats.

Later she compared her adoption of Marxism to a religious conversion.[94] She had laid "aside the old Adam of bourgeois ideas" and entered a new community of believers. She was now convinced, as she told the delegates at a feminist congress in Berlin in 1895, that "the liberation of women from their material and moral dependence, from wage-slavery and prostitution," could only be achieved through the "transformation of the class state" and its "capitalistic economic order."[95]

During 1895 Lily had fallen in love with Heinrich Braun, to whom she had gone for advice in setting up an agency to study the working conditions of women. But there were obstacles to their union. After divorcing his first wife, Heinrich had married his housekeeper, mainly out of concern for the well-being of his two small sons. His separation from his second wife, pregnant at the time, to marry Lily, was viewed by most Social Democrats, firmly attached to conventional notions of the family, as scandalous. Her willingness to marry under such circumstances increased the suspicion within the party toward the aristocratic recruit.

Marriage to Heinrich no doubt strengthened Lily's desire to develop practical proposals on behalf of women. But her efforts led to clashes with Zetkin, who opposed activities that might disperse energies from the task of raising class consciousness.[96] Lily's relationship to the movement was also altered by the revisionist controversy. The Marxist faith, from which she had "drawn all my energies," was undermined by the "cool clarity," the "facts and figures," presented by Bernstein.[97] "Intellectual honesty" demanded that she sacrifice the orthodox Marxist beliefs. Her move toward revisionism was hastened by her disillusionment with proletarian women. Initially she had accepted Zetkin's claim that the "logic of facts and living conditions cram into the proletariat a way of understanding which a bourgeois idealist can only acquire with great effort" if at all.[98] But now, when working-class women dismissed Bernstein's ideas with contempt and asserted that their own experience gave them a knowledge superior to "long years of study," she was repelled. Their captivity to crude class interests was reinforced by Zetkin's appeals to "proletarian vanity." Nor did Lily find among the Social Democratic leaders the enlightened views she had anticipated. "They are all philistines," she told her husband after a dinner at the Bebels'.[99] The men had remained at the table to discuss the problems facing the party while the wives withdrew to talk about the "price of meat and recipes." "They do not talk about questions of general interest."

Like a number of the Revisionists, Lily began to consider ways in which capitalism might be transformed from within. In a pamphlet published shortly after the turn of the century, she presented a plan for communal living in which household duties and child rearing would be handled collectively.[100] She also attempted, by employing the Marxist interpretation of history, to gain a broader perspective on the plight of women under capitalism. The outcome was a pioneering and influential contribution to the woman's movement, *The Woman's Question,* published in 1901.[101] The book dealt mainly with the exploitation of working-class women in modern society. Although she did not ignore the problems of bourgeois women, she argued that they, unlike proletarian women, tended to seek work as a liberation from the confines of marriage and family life. The interests of women in the two classes remained, therefore, distinct.

Publication of *The Woman's Question* completed Lily's rupture with the orthodox Marxist circle around Zetkin.[102] Zetkin was able to isolate Lily within the party. Later Lily would complain that she had been unable to form any close friendships with working-class women. But her style—elegant and cultured—made it difficult for her to bridge class differences. "Simply for your appearance," a veteran party leader told her, "the women will never forgive you."[103] Lily's imperious nature and her egoism contributed to her isolation.[104]

She remained a member of the party and took an active part in her husband's campaign to alter its outlook. But in the years ahead she moved beyond the narrow boundaries within which the orthodox Marxists had viewed the problems of women. As her faith in the proletariat weakened, distinctly feminist concerns became more prominent. Although she continued, like Zetkin, to hold that woman's highest duty was motherhood, she increasingly emphasized the need to free human sexuality from the repressions of traditional morality as well as from the tendency for a woman's sexuality to become, under capitalism, a commodity. "We now stand," she wrote in 1905, "at a turning point in the history of love."[105] More and more, marriage seemed to her an obstacle to love and to the capacity of women to fulfill their natural sexual desires. She ruled out "free love" as long as existing economic arrangements prevented women from gaining economic independence, but she ceased to feel bound by her own marriage ties. Her readiness to enter into "liaisons" was perhaps one outcome of her revision of Marxism.[106]

Rosa Luxemburg also discovered new meaning for socialists out of the crisis of Marxist thought. Indeed, the inadequacies of the defenses of orthodox Marxism by Kautsky and others provided an opportunity for her to make her mark on the party. She exploited that opportunity brilliantly and was soon acknowledged as one of the leading Social Democratic thinkers. At the same time she began her own revision of Marxism. Her revision contained a new conception of the way in which the working class acquired a socialist mentality.

When Luxemburg entered the German movement in the spring of 1898 she came, like the young socialist intellectuals a few years earlier, as a "stranger," little touched by the "habit, piety, and precedent" of the party. She proceeded to judge the Social Democrats in the light of their Marxist doctrines. The features which characterized her subsequent role in the movement—a fierce independence and a rather scornful attitude toward the veteran leaders—were already evident.

Born in a Poland ruled by Russia, she became involved in the revolutionary movement while still in her teens and then went to Switzerland to continue her education.[107] In contrast to the older exiled Polish Marxists there, who wished to connect the socialist goal with the cause of national independence, Luxemburg emphasized the international solidarity of the workers. Much the same outlook marked her initial activity in the German party; it centered in upper Silesia, where she helped local Social Democrats combat the tendency for the Polish workers to stress nationalistic aims at the expense of working-class unity.[108]

Luxemburg's scorn for the quality of intellectual activity in the German party was expressed early in a letter to a friend. The articles in the Social Democratic press, she wrote, were all "so conventional, so wooden, so stereotyped," comparable to wheels revolving in a machine.[109] The revisionist controversy challenged her to correct those defects and provide a more effective answer to Bernstein than any presented thus far. Her articles on the subject, published in the *Leipziger Volkszeitung* during 1898 and 1899, established her as a new intellectual force in the party.[110]

She centered her attack on the revisionist argument, developed by Bernstein, Kampffmeyer, and Schmidt, that capitalism was overcoming its contradictions and could be transformed peacefully into socialism. To the contrary, she wrote, the economic process making for the collapse of capitalism, the "cornerstone" of Marx's theory, was unfolding as an "objective necessity."[111] The "beginning of . . . the final crisis of capitalism" was near at hand. It followed that the party's ultimate goal, the conquest of political power by the workers, must be kept to the forefront. The revolutionary class struggle remained the "soul" of the movement.

What distinguished Luxemburg's reply to the Revisionists was her insistence on the totalistic character of Marxist theory.[112] Marx, she held, had "deciphered the hieroglyphics" of capitalism and produced "one solidly constructed edifice."[113] The chief fallacy of her opponents lay in their attempt to deal with specific economic, social, or political questions in isolation; they had lost sight of capitalism as an organic system of interrelationships in which everything must be referred to the whole. The whole was more important than the parts. Failing to see this, the Revisionists had fallen into a "vulgar empiricism."

Although Luxemburg reaffirmed the decisive role of economic factors and the objective laws of capitalistic development, there was in her Marxism a new stress on subjective elements, on the "moral rebirth" and the new will being created within the proletariat. Class consciousness was, as J. P. Nettl has observed, the "lynch-pin" of her Marxist theory.[114] She was particularly concerned with the way in which the "mental vacuum" in the proletariat was being filled with new content.[115] She argued that the new consciousness was generated by the social frictions resulting from the economic and political struggle. She was convinced, in fact, that the dialectical way of thinking, developed by Marx, came naturally to the industrial workers; it provided a "sword with which to pierce the darkness of its historical future" and perceive the "inevitability of the proletarian society." The workers, she insisted, needed to "become acquainted actively and in detail" with theory. There could be "no coarser insult, no baser defamation of the workers" than the suggestion that "theoretical controversies are only for the intellectuals."

In contrast to Kautsky, who had assigned to intellectuals the task of bringing a theoretical understanding to the workers, Luxemburg relied mainly on the working-class struggle to generate a new consciousness. But she did not explain the crucial transition from class consciousness to socialist consciousness, from the growing sense of class solidarity to the kind of understanding required for the proletariat to play its historical role. She failed to make clear, one commentator on her thought has noted, "the actual concrete process" through which the daily struggles of the workers and the knowledge directed toward the final goal were combined.[116] The gap was simply covered over by a "sleight of hand"; logical deduction took the place of any attempt to deal with the psychological and cognitive processes involved.

Luxemburg did not discuss the role of the intellectuals directly. But she viewed that role, exemplified in her own activity, as the articulation and interpretation of the experiences of the workers themselves. She worried lest the theoretical understanding provided by Marx be confined to the intellectuals: "As long as theoretical knowledge remains the privilege of a handful of 'intellectuals' in the party, it will face the danger of going astray. Only when the great mass of workers take into their own hands the keen and dependable weapon of scientific socialism will . . . all the opportunistic currents come to naught."[117]

Luxemburg's faith in Marxism was absolute; she questioned neither the foundations of Marxist theory nor the nature of her own commitment. She expressed an "aversion and contempt toward all personal inner emotions," in order to concentrate "all attention on the visible results of acts."[118] And yet she also confessed to a strong sense of a "calling," noting the power of the poet Helmut Borne to "recall me to my vows." She recognized that any vital socialist faith tapped elemental feelings. Only speakers and writers who "went deeply into themselves," so as "to feel and live through the cause," could find the words which "go from heart to heart." With her belief that she could, "by the power of conviction," act on people "like a thunderclap," went a sense that she was capable of stating the Marxist truths in a new way.[119] "I feel within me there is maturing a completely new and original form which dispenses with the usual formulas and patterns and breaks them down, and which will convince people naturally through force of mind and conviction." She believed that her reply to the Revisionists constituted "nothing less than a brief argument for a new form of scientific socialism."[120]

Luxemburg's articles against the Revisionists restated concerns which had been central to the Jungen protest.[121] There was the same charge that the party was being taken over by a "petty-bourgeois element" together with the belief that the proletariat would "throw aside" that element "when it sees it in a fuller light." Luxemburg also echoed the Jungen distrust of parliamentary activity, arguing that its chief value lay in its educational function; it demonstrated that fundamental change could not be achieved within a bourgeois state. She worried, too, about the seductive power of the Reichstag. "Forced to maneuver on the slippery floor of the bourgeois parliament," Social Democrats might "unconsciously and involuntarily" take on many of its mores.[122] Luxemburg also resembled the Jungen in judging Social Democratic practices strictly in terms of the Marxist doctrines. At times, for all of her insistence on the dialectic, her concern with doctrinal rectitude gave an idealistic cast to her thought. The "principles of scientific socialism," she wrote, "impose clearly marked limits on practical activity, its aims as well as its methods."[123] She viewed the Erfurt program as a model against which the party's policies should be measured.

> If our program is the formulation of the historical development of society from capitalism to socialism, obviously it must formulate, in all its fundamental lines, all the transitory phases of this development, and consequently at *every* moment it should be able to indicate to the proletariat what ought to be its correct behavior in order to move toward socialism. It follows generally that there can be *no time* when the proletariat will be obliged to abandon its program or be abandoned by it.[124]

The Revisionists, she maintained, had abandoned the party's program. "We stand on a very different terrain."[125] "Now the same words no longer express the same concepts and the concepts no longer express the same facts for both sides." The discussion with Bernstein had become "an argument of two world views."

Luxemburg urged Bebel to acknowledge that Bernstein was "lost to the party."[126] But she saw an even greater threat to its integrity in the "practical opportunism" of Schippel and Heine.[127] Schippel's approach to military and trade issues and Heine's "compensation policy" represented more dangerous retreats into bourgeois ways of thinking. In the face of Schippel's denial that he had abandoned any aspect of the party's program, she argued that his statements had "their own logic" even though he failed to recognize it. She sought to extract a "wholly consistent sociopolitical world view" from the position of her opponents.

The full meaning of Luxemburg's revision of Marxist orthodoxy did not emerge for several years. In the meantime she closed ranks with the party leaders in their battle against Bernstein and his supporters. But she did not hesitate to scold Bebel and Kautsky for failing to press the case against the heretics more vigorously. While the party leaders hoped to "settle things behind the scenes," she was determined to bring "new life" to an "oral and written agitation" which, in the "old form was petrified and scarcely affected anyone any longer."[128]

Bebel and Kautsky welcomed her brilliant critique of the Revisionists, but they were troubled by her uncompromising spirit and her tendency to resort to personal invective. The attitude of the party leaders was probably expressed by Adler, who denounced her as a "doctrinaire goose . . . trying to do our thinking for us."[129] But Luxemburg, dedicated to her version of Marxism and lacking any feeling, as Nettl has observed, for the "organized structural fellowship of the party," was incapable of assuming roles in which she was required to work closely with others.[130] Her attempts to serve as chief editor—for the *Sächsische Arbeiterzeitung* in the fall of 1898 after the previous editor had been expelled and, later, for the *Leipziger Volkszeitung* following the death of Schönlank—soon ended with her resignation. She refused to accept limitations on her editorial freedom, either from the staffs of the papers or from local party committees. No doubt her relative youth, her sex, and her Jewishness made her a target for prejudice and private resentment. But her intellectual certitude and her extraordinary personal force ensured that she would remain a "stranger" in the movement, "quite without regard for her surroundings or the views of others."[131]

The various currents of revisionism gave new visibility to the party's educated recruits. The Akademikerproblem had been increasingly evident at the Social Democratic conferences. At Gotha, in 1896, the delegates heard charges that the party was providing jobs for individuals who had been "shipwrecked" in their bourgeois careers.[132] A year later, at Hamburg, a working-class delegate from Berlin complained that Social Democrats were relying on writers who did not understand the "language and sufferings" of the workers.[133] Soon, he warned, they would cease to be a "proletarian party" and be "led only by academics." At subsequent party conferences, at Stuttgart and Hanover, the mounting criticism of the intellectuals was directed mainly against their support for revisionism.[134]

In the early years of the new century the Akademikerproblem assumed an important place in the life of the party. Until the question of the proper role of the intellectuals was settled, the nature of the new working-class consciousness remained uncertain. For orthodox Marxists, in particular, the problem had become critical.

The Akademikerproblem, 1901–1903

TEN years after the antisocialist laws had been lifted the Social Democrats could look back on a period of steady growth in membership, electoral support, and representation in the Reichstag. Their vote in general elections had increased from just under 9 to 14 percent of the total, and their parliamentary Fraktion had grown from thirty-five to fifty-six. A surge of trade union membership after 1895 was further evidence of a labor movement marked by an ever-greater sense of class interests.

The increasing solidarity of the working class was one sign of a changing economic structure, marked by large-scale factory production and the consolidation of major industrial, commercial, and financial enterprises. An economic upturn after 1895 resulted in some improvement in the living standards of the workers, but their share of the new wealth lagged far behind that of the propertied classes.[1] And despite a social security system superior to that of the other industrial societies, the German workers were still highly vulnerable to the uncertainties associated with a dynamic capitalism. The political system established by Bismarck, designed to maintain the power of the preindustrial ruling class—the Junker landholders in Prussia and their counterparts in the other German states—only increased the vulnerability of the working class.

Historians have debated about the extent to which there was significant political participation in Germany.[2] What is not in doubt is that the system was essentially authoritarian, with strong internal resistance against constitutional reform. Moreover, the German leaders were, through an aggressive foreign policy, the "Weltpolitik," seeking to direct the nation's energies outward. Here was the political context within which the Social Democrats attempted to advance their program.

Throughout the nineties the Social Democratic leaders continued to fear the reimposition of repressive measures against the party. And while its representatives played vigorous roles in the Reichstag debates, they remained in a state of quarantine, a result in part of the party's revolutionary ideology but even more of its ostracism by the other parties. Given its political isolation, it is not surprising that the party turned inward, that its press and annual conferences were much occupied with questions of unity and ideological agreement. One reflection of this self-absorption was the prominence of the Akademikerproblem in the early years of the new century.

Kautsky: Defending Orthodoxy

The nomination of Göhre as a candidate for the Reichstag little more than a year after he had joined the Social Democrats brought new complaints that bourgeois intellectuals were taking over the party. Calwer conceded that the charges were to some extent justified.[3] But he noted the tendency for local party members to overvalue "educated men." The basic problem, however, arose out of the party's development. It now faced tasks which exceeded the capacities of the "simple practical men" who had dominated the earlier years. Hence the growing dependence on academics, for the "advantages of fifteen years of education" could not be denied. It was futile to resist the trend. Calwer urged party leaders to eliminate the "academic debate" from meetings lest it become "an attack on science and knowledge itself."

Kautsky agreed.[4] Without judging the merits of the Göhre case, he pointed to the limitations of the workers: "If socialism is not to remain naive and is to represent insight into the interrelationships of society, it requires systematic investigation. . . . Science is still a privilege of the possessing classes. A vital socialism, therefore, cannot be created by the proletariat; it must be brought to them by thinkers who are armed with the tools of bourgeois science, who place themselves on a proletarian standpoint and from it develop a new proletarian position."

Kautsky acknowledged the "widespread suspicion toward the academic elements in our ranks." He went on to differentiate more clearly than previously the respective functions of the intellectuals and the workers. The function of the intellectuals was limited. They were needed to lift the workers above "momentary interests" and provide "knowledge of the whole movement and the goal," but intellectuals were not equipped to play leading roles in the practical struggle.[5] In such matters as proposing legislation, organizing strikes, or forming cooperatives, the workers knew "better than the academics." Indeed, for everyday work academics were "superfluous"; in practical affairs they "learned from the workers."

Left to their own resources, however, the workers would lose their way. Kautsky pointed to the English working class as an example of the weakness of a "proletarian movement free of academics." By concentrating on immediate material gains, the English workers expressed the danger "in its purest form." But the Göhre case, according to Kautsky, provided a warning to the Social Democrats; it indicated the "remarkable ways" in which the "English model" had taken hold of "a section of our young academics." The praise of "day-to-day work" by a number of the Revisionists had meant a "growing neglect of theory" and an attempt to "kill the scientific impulse which is so strongly developed in the German movement." No wonder the academics were coming into disfavor among the workers; they had begun to "appear superfluous." Intellectuals, Kautsky concluded, should learn from the anger over Göhre's candidacy: "The 'intellectuals' in the party are called on to develop and establish scientifically the ideals which come out of class conditions. That is their historical task. . . . If, in contrast to this deepening and sharpening of the ideals, they bring only tired skepticism and trivialities, then they deny the branch on which they sit."

The threat to the integrity of Marxist theory—Kautsky's chief worry—was being renewed by Bernstein. In February 1901 his long exile ended.[6] Chancellor von Bülow, who rescinded the order for his expulsion, was influenced in part by liberal political leaders who viewed Bernstein as a potentially moderating, perhaps disruptive, force within the Social Democratic party. Their hopes were realized. In March Bernstein delivered a lecture, "How Is a Scientific Socialism Possible?," before a student social science association in Berlin.[7] There was little that was new in the talk. But he developed more fully one of his central claims—that the ultimate goal of socialism and the will to achieve it could only be viewed as idealistic or "utopian" additions to Marx's scientific analysis of economic and social developments. Bernstein's public restatement of his views and his choice of "bourgeois territory" to present them evoked widespread protests within the party.

Kautsky welcomed the opportunity to get the debate "out into the open" once more.[8] The "silent war" that had been under way was "more poisonous than the bitterest polemic." During the previous year he had, with the aid of Adler, persuaded Bernstein to sever his ties with the *Neue Zeit.* The close friendship between the two men, forged in the struggles of earlier years, was giving way on Kautsky's part to exasperation and bitterness: "He professes . . . to play the old party comrade as if nothing had happened. . . . I have lost the last bit of my sentimentality toward him, hate him as our worst enemy, for our worst enemy is confusion. [I] despise him because of his lack of character [for he] clings to a party to which he no longer belongs. . . . So long as Bernstein remains in the party there is no peace." Kautsky now asserted that Bernstein had "never understood" Marx, that "his Marxism was only varnish" which soon disappeared after the death of Engels. Bernstein did not represent a "right wing within the party," but "a new party" which is "too cowardly or uncertain or too weak to cut loose from us."

Bernstein's return to Germany and his lecture gave fresh impetus to the intellectuals who identified themselves with the "new party." During the months which followed Kampffmeyer developed, in a series of exchanges with Kautsky, the gradualist position he had advanced earlier.[9] And Bernstein's talk prompted Heine to insist once more that practical activity was more important than theory.[10] But at the same time, he rejected Bernstein's suggestion that Marxists drop the term "scientific" in favor of "critical" as a prefix to their socialism. By defining science as "simply an honest striving after truth," however, Heine set virtually no limits to the "self-criticism of Marxism."

During the summer of 1901 Kautsky attempted to "accelerate the crisis"; the differences within the party should be made as clear as possible.[11] The defenders of orthodoxy must act while they could still draw on the prestige of Bebel. The revisionist intellectuals, Kautsky wrote Adler, were simply waiting until Bebel, the "last great representative of the old party traditions," was gone before they moved to take over. In the meantime, "Heine and his people" were "occupying one post after another." Not that Kautsky was sanguine about any rapid elimination of "this thorn in our flesh." But the threat of "confusion and corruption" in the "coming generation" needed to be battled at all costs.

In a remarkably candid article, Kautsky reflected, somewhat ruefully, on his initial encouragement of Bernstein's exercise in Marxist self-criticism.[12] He recalled his expectations when Bernstein began his "Problems of Socialism" series in 1896. At that time, Kautsky wrote, there had been a need to "cut out the obsolete parts" in Marx's teachings and "take new facts into consideration." Doubt, after all, was an "indispensable preparation for progress." But Kautsky had assumed, he told his readers, that Bernstein had "solutions in his pocket" when he identified difficulties in Marxist theory, that his criticisms would mean "a decisive step forward in our knowledge." Only when Kautsky saw the lack of "positive results" did he join Bernstein's opponents. It had become clear that "only empty doubts lay behind Bernstein's Problems," that the outcome would be "rising confusion, endless discords and growing bitterness." His great mistake, Kautsky admitted, was to encourage Bernstein in a task he could not pull off.

Most striking about Kautsky's reflections was the claim that Bernstein erred in placing his doubts "before the public." Doubts, particularly in matters of principle, he now insisted, were only fruitful in the study. "In politics" they were likely to lead to paralysis. In suggesting that the party rank and file should be protected from the critical activities of the intellectuals, Kautsky implied that ideology functioned mainly as dogma, as a source of integrating ideas and symbols. His "confession" was at odds with his commitment to a higher level of understanding among the workers.

During the weeks before the 1901 annual conference, scheduled for Lübeck in late September, revisionist intellectuals and the practical reformers within the party were targets for new attacks in the *Neue Zeit.* In a series of articles, "Parvus" focused on the several forms of "opportunism" which, he claimed, were jeopardizing the party's final goal.[13] Luxemburg singled out the trade unionists, who were seeking greater autonomy, for special criticism.[14] She also condemned Social Democrats in Baden for their willingness to support state budgets. The polemics troubled Bebel, for they threatened to raise feelings to a danger point on the eve of the conference. "You have no idea," he wrote Kautsky, of the antagonism which many Social Democrats felt toward the two radical intellectuals.[15] Keen on addressing immediate political issues—the housing problem and the government's proposals for higher tariffs—Bebel was not eager for a new "Bernstein debate."

But the Bernstein debate dominated the Lübeck conference.[16] Beneath the surface of the heated exchanges there was, as David observed, a persistent "opposition between the manual workers and the brain workers."[17] It was expressed in the charges that the intellectuals were engaged in "theoretical hairsplitting," providing weapons for the enemy and creating confusion in the rank and file. Although David, Bernstein, and others defended the role of the theorists and the need to "take off the coat of party" in dealing with scientific questions, revisionist intellectuals denied that such issues could be dealt with at a party conference. They sought to shift the debate onto practical or tactical grounds. After all, as David put it, one who believed with Marx in the "historical necessity of the emancipation of the proletariat" should not be nervous about differing interpretations of certain passages in *Capital.*[18] The truly valuable knowledge came from those who were "directly involved in agitation." Heine made the same point.[19] Although he assured the delegates that he stood "on the firm soil of Marx," he discounted the importance of theory. Theoretical questions "separate people," he said; "practical work brings them together."

Bebel joined the retreat to the less controversial ground of party tactics, but not before he denounced Bernstein for his "Talmudic sophistries."[20] It was time, Bebel added, for Bernstein to stop his "nit-picking" and apply himself to the "urgent issues of the day." After rejecting resolutions to expel Bernstein or at least to repudiate the views of his supporters, the delegates gave overwhelming approval to Bebel's motion simply reaffirming the Erfurt program. The resolution was, as Bebel's biographer has observed, "toothless."[21]

Those speaking for Marxist orthodoxy were thus denied a clear victory at Lübeck. Moreover, they were placed on the defensive when the *Neue Zeit*, the chief instrument through which Kautsky hoped to educate Social Democrats, was strongly criticized. Fischer, who managed the party's publications, charged that Kautsky had made the journal an "organ for . . . the purity of a definite point of view" and alienated "almost all who were literarily active in the party."[22] He denounced Mehring for his polemical style and blamed the invectives of "Parvus" and Luxemburg for the refusal of a growing number of Social Democrats "to sit at the same table with a pair of literary rowdies." Other speakers noted that the *Neue Zeit* made "no progress" while the *Sozialistische Monatshefte* "wins more readers daily."[23]

Kautsky saw the attack as simply an "echo of the Bernstein debate."[24] And while he dissociated himself from the tone of the "Parvus" articles, much to the author's dismay, he defended his own editorial policy. "If you demand that the *Neue Zeit* stand above the debate you demand something beyond my power." "No man of character," he added, could play a neutral role in the disputes within the party.

After the conference Kautsky attempted to put a good face on the proceedings.[25] They had demonstrated, he told his readers, that Bernstein's challenge was "a thing of the past." In letters to Adler, however, Kautsky expressed his discouragement and his sense of isolation.[26] A visit to Vienna reminded him of "how much a stranger I remain in Germany" and his lack of close friends. "Even with August [Bebel] who is dearest to me . . . understanding is often difficult." He contrasted the tendencies toward "procrastination and bogging down" in the party with the decisiveness and enthusiasm of earlier times.[27]

In November Kautsky again found himself on the defensive. Doubts about the adequacy of the orthodox Marxist doctrines had emerged within the Austrian party. Proposals for its coming conference sought changes in its program similar to those favored by revisionist intellectuals in Germany.[28] Reformers in the Austrian party rejected the orthodox Marxist notion that capitalism meant the inevitable impoverishment of the masses, and they called for a greater emphasis on the immediate interests of the workers. Such a change meant, according to Kautsky, the eclipse of theory. He reminded Adler that the workers, left to their own resources, simply developed "socialist instincts or dispositions."[29] A "scientific knowledge" could only "be carried into" the masses from outside.

In a long article in the *Neue Zeit* Kautsky reasserted the need for the

Austrians to adhere to the orthodox Marxist doctrines.[30] A program "which cannot recognize that capitalism produces with natural necessity mass poverty and mass misery . . . conceals the decisive side of the working-class movement and thus contains a serious gap." Kautsky conceded that the party's old program, adopted at Hainfeld in 1889 with his help, was excessively deterministic and pessimistic. But the proposed revision erred in the opposite direction. It suggested that a socialist consciousness could be "the direct outcome of the proletarian class struggle."

> That is false. . . . The modern socialist consciousness can only develop on the basis of deeper scientific insight. . . . The carrier of science is not the proletariat but the bourgeois intellectuals—a few members of that section which has developed modern socialism and communicated it to the intellectually advanced element in the proletariat who then carry it into the class struggle . . . where the circumstances permit it.

The program subsequently adopted by the Austrian Social Democrats satisfied Kautsky.[31] But it still represented, according to one historian of the party, a "greater readiness to acknowledge its reformist practices" than was evident in the German party.[32]

Despite Kautsky's reaffirmation of the indispensable role of the intellectuals, he was increasingly troubled by the unreliability of the educated recruits. In the early years of the century he placed a new emphasis on the natural growth of a revolutionary consciousness among the workers. The "intellectual moulting" expressed in the speeches of the Revisionists at Lübeck, he insisted, did not correspond to the "actual mind of the masses."[33] Revolutionary feeling in the "circle of intellectuals" was "less strong than in the proletariat itself."

There was evidence to support his claim. Many Social Democrats at the local level were angered by the "hairsplitting" of the intellectuals. Even in those areas where party members favored a reformist policy, there was little sympathy for the discussions of theory.[34] The discussions were dismissed as "literary spectacles" or viewed as "superfluous spinning mills," remote from the real business of the party. After each "Bernstein debate" at the party conferences there were protests that the intellectuals, both revisionist and orthodox, were wasting valuable time. At the Munich conference in 1902 one delegate even suggested that the academics meet separately a few days before the other delegates arrived. Perhaps, he added, they might devour each other.[35]

But rank-and-file hostility toward the intellectuals did not indicate the growth of consciousness Kautsky was seeking. Indeed, much of the revisionist criticism had been directed against the extravagant hopes with which orthodox Marxists intellectuals viewed the mental development of the workers. When Ernst cited the proceedings at Lübeck to justify his own claim that the party's rank and file had failed to grasp the teachings of Marx,[36] Bernstein argued that Ernst was a victim of the "excessive expectations" characteristic of Marxists during the nineties.[37] Belatedly Ernst had discovered that "there is no theoretical sense among the workers." Bernstein confessed that he too had been pained by the discovery, until he realized that the struggle of the workers was "ever more concrete" and less abstract.

For Kautsky the growth of a Marxist understanding among the workers was essential to the development of socialism, and the intellectuals remained crucial to that process. But the problem of integrating these two sides of the movement was becoming more difficult. Kautsky noted the problem in two lectures he delivered in Holland during the spring of 1902.[38] He still insisted that capitalistic development produced "bourgeois intellectuals" who were free from "special class interests" and could, by virtue of their "scientific point of view," be won "more easily by our party."[39] But he conceded that Social Democrats could no longer be confident in the soundness of those intellectuals who turned to the party. In earlier years the intellectuals "came only through a complete break with the whole capitalistic world"; they "had need of great energy and revolutionary passion and strong proletarian convictions" and constituted the "most radical wing of the movement." It was "wholly different today." Socialism had become something of a fad; it required "no break with capitalistic society to assume the name of socialist." No wonder more and more of the newcomers remained entangled in their previous ways of thinking. By disavowing the idea of revolution and preaching the possibility that socialism would evolve out of capitalism, these intellectuals were dividing and weakening the proletariat.

Kautsky still maintained that the genuine acceptance of Marxism entailed a radical break with "previous modes of thought and feeling." Conversion to Marxism put an end to the notion of a realm of knowledge beyond class. There was "no greater self-deception," he declared at this time, "than the talk about a science above class antagonisms."[40] For Kautsky the bridge over which intellectuals crossed to the proletariat separated them once and for all from the old ways of thinking.

During 1902 the Akademikerproblem was largely set aside as the Social Democratic leaders emphasized the need for party solidarity in the face of an approaching general election. The party conference at Munich in September was spared the acrimony displayed at Lübeck. Only a new "press debate" marred the harmony of the meeting and expressed the antagonism between the two groups of intellectuals.[41] In the course of that debate, critics of the *Neue Zeit* contrasted the policy of its editor with the open-mindedness of the *Sozialistische Monatshefte*. Several defenders of orthodox Marxism now demanded that Social Democratic journalists write only for official party publications. Aimed at the *Sozialistische Monatshefte,* which did not have official status in the party, the proposal was denounced by revisionist intellectuals as a "grotesque" attack on freedom of expression.[42] Both Kautsky and Bebel dissociated themselves from the motion.

During the early months of 1903 the party leaders confronted the Akademikerproblem in a new form. At the center of the next stage in the controversy was Braun, who sought to provide new leadership for those intellectuals who wished to alter the party's ideology and tactics.

Braun's Attempt to Mobilize Revisionist Intellectuals

From the beginning of his association with the socialist movement Braun had held, much like Kautsky, that intellectuals and scientific knowledge would play crucial roles in the transformation of German social and political life. "In his mind," Braun's biographer has written, "was a platonic conception of the state ruled by philosophers."[43] But through his efforts to bring his Marxism closer to the practical problems of the day Braun had diverged sharply from Kautsky. Between Kautsky's Marxist or proletarian exclusiveness and Braun's attempt to open a dialogue with bourgeois social thinkers there was a deep gulf.

During the nineties Braun had attempted to raise the intellectual level of the Social Democrats. Without greater social understanding in the party's rank and file, he believed, gaining political power could only be a "pyrrhic victory."[44] As editor of his *Archiv* and the *Centralblatt,* he remained outside the party but urged other intellectuals to play active roles. He helped to bring Göhre into the party and joined others in persuading Heine to become a parliamentary candidate. He also tried to persuade his close friend, Sombart, to commit himself to the Social Democrats. "You would probably become," he wrote Sombart, "the leader the party needs."[45]

Braun welcomed Bernstein's challenge to orthodox Marxism. The efforts of revisionist intellectuals to loosen the hold of the received doctrines confirmed views he had held for a decade or more. He saw in the new criticism an opportunity to bring socialist theory closer to pressing social and political problems. "The path to an inner transformation of the party," he told Sombart in December 1900, had opened.[46]

Earlier in that year Braun set out to give greater clarity and coherence to the new forces within the party. His efforts centered on Bernstein and a plan for a new paper. A letter to Bernstein in May outlined the project: "It is not only important that you personally speak but that a whole current of scientific expression and practical influence be presented. It must also take positions on the problems of the day. . . . [Hence] the idea of a new journal, in which all the adherents of the new direction come together."[47] During the summer and fall Braun sought funds for the venture, turning to wealthy figures who had contributed to the *Archiv* and the *Centralblatt*. Financial support was not forthcoming, but at the end of the year he was still determined to go ahead. In an exchange of letters with Bernstein he explored several options.[48] Braun invited Bernstein to become a regular contributor to the *Archiv* and thus give it a clearer socialist orientation. He also discussed the possibility of a socialist daily in Berlin. Finally he settled on the plan for a weekly. He hoped to create an "organ of battle" for socialism but one which would—in an obvious reference to the *Neue Zeit*—avoid the "prevailing cant and the method of personal insults in which . . . an influential part of our party literature" engages.[49] Freeing the party from its "rigid forms and stereotypes" would mean no loss of Social Democratic energy; on the contrary, an "organ . . . of criticism, even against its own party," would mean a "great expansion and deepening of socialist ideas."

In January 1901 Braun discussed the plan, in secret, with two leading liberal intellectuals, Paul Nathan and Theodor Barth. He had begun to see his weekly as a bridge between progressive elements among the liberals and Social Democratic Revisionists and reformers. At the end of the month he was convinced, he told Bernstein, that they stood before "a great historic task"—that of raising the Social Democrats from their "stagnant condition."[50] The party leaders, Bebel and Singer, had been cool toward his project, but the response of several of the Revisionists, including Heine and Göhre, was encouraging. Meanwhile he received a promise of financial support from a wealthy sympathizer, Charles Hallgarten.[51]

All depended on Bernstein. But after Bernstein returned to Berlin in February 1901, ending his exile, he lost any enthusiasm he had felt for Braun's project. For all his doubts about the Marxist doctrines, he was intensely loyal to the party, firmly committed to its political policies, and wary of any action that might divide it. Braun's plan was likely to do just that. Although Braun soon concluded that Bernstein lacked "character and insight," he recognized that the attempt to draw socialists and liberals together was premature.[52] He also concluded that his hope of unifying revisionist intellectuals could best be realized inside the party.

Braun joined the party and during the summer of 1901 revived the idea of a new weekly. He now saw it as a Social Democratic paper, providing a forum for all points of view within the movement. In a letter to his wife in August, however, he expressed his hope of drawing on the wider German educated community.[53] There was, he believed, a "wealth of intellectual forces" in the country, still irresolute and wavering, repelled by the rawness and disdain for learning in the party, and hence unwilling to avow it publicly. "I want to win the German intellectuals, insofar as they have the capacity to develop, toward socialism . . . in order to raise [the party] from its sad level . . . and strengthen its intellectual and political effectiveness."

Bebel and Kautsky viewed Braun's return to the party with suspicion.[54] But he appeared as a delegate at the Lübeck conference, where he introduced a resolution calling on Social Democrats to recognize the need for self-criticism. And he indicated his new commitment to the party by accepting a request to be its candidate for the Reichstag in the unpromising constituency of Frankfurt-Lebus. "Filled with the idea of reforming the party," he was also prepared, against the advice of Sombart and others, to give up the *Archiv,* on which his livelihood now depended.[55] He delayed such a step, however, as he sought financial support for the new weekly.

In the early years of the century Braun participated in a group of socialist intellectuals who were meeting Thursday evenings in the Café des Westens in Berlin. The gatherings were described later by Willy Hellpach, a young man who had recently completed a medical degree at the University of Leipzig and had been contributing to the *Sozialistische Monatshefte.*[56] The circle, he recalled, included Bloch and several of the chief writers for the journal—Eduard David and his wife Gertrud and, less frequently, Kampffmeyer and Schmidt. The Brauns were regular attenders—Heinrich, cold and reserved, Lily, who "drew all eyes when she entered," self-centered and argumentative. Bernstein was often there as well as two younger men who later made their marks in the party, Friedrich Stampfer, a journalist newly arrived from Austria, and Hugo Haase, a lawyer from Königsberg. There were nonsocialists as well—Sombart and Maximillian Harden, editor of the widely read weekly, *Zukunft.* But Hellpach noted that the leaders of the party and the trade unionists "stayed far from this coffee-house chatter."[57] It seemed to him that these intellectuals lacked "genuine feeling for the masses" and "avoided close contact with them."

Discussions at the Café des Westens often dealt with the discrepancies between the party's Marxist doctrines and its political practices. To a number of the intellectuals it even seemed as though the leading Social Democrats "no longer believed what they said or wrote" and yet "could find no way of resolving their dilemma."[58] The party's political leaders were caught between their perceptions of practical possibilities and the "ossified phrases" with which they appealed to the rank and file.

But the renewed effort of the revisionist intellectuals to deal with the discrepancies between Marxist theory and the party's practices now took a strange turn. When a young Social Democrat, Georg Bernhard, attempted to deal with the dilemma, he generated a storm of protest within the party. Bernhard also initiated a new and critical stage in the dispute over the Akademikerproblem.

Bernhard did not have an academic background. While working as a bank clerk, however, he had become an effective speaker for the party in Berlin and had educated himself sufficiently to write articles on trade and financial matters for the *Sozialistische Monatschefte* and *Zukunft.*[59] His article "Marxism and the Class Struggle," published in the *Sozialistsiche Monatshefte* in 1898, indicated both his attachment to Marxism and his belief that Bernstein was helping Social Democrats to see more clearly the obstacles in their path.[60] It is not certain that Bernhard participated in the group at the Café des Westens, but it seems likely, since he was contributing to both the *Sozialistische Monatshefte* and *Zukunft.* His article in Harden's weekly in January 1903 was a natural outgrowth of the discussions in the group.[61]

Bernhard's essay "Party Morale" started from the "indisputable fact" that the leaders of a political party often spoke quite differently in public than they did in private. It was, he observed, a problem which was particularly difficult for intellectuals, who in their efforts to clarify theoretical questions constantly ran ahead of the masses. The latter remained for the most part prey to "old life habits and herd instincts."[62] What then was the responsibility of those whose ideas might "shake the confidence of the rank and file" if expressed openly?

Bernhard's answer was much like that which Kautsky had given eighteen months earlier in discussing Bernstein's critique of Marxism. The doubts of the theorist were not matters for public discussion. But Bernhard was disarmingly, indeed, brutally frank. He defended the tendency for party leaders and intellectuals to dissemble in public, to keep their "mental reservations" to themselves, and to resort to "silences and evasions."[63] Since the masses "could not be dispensed with in the struggle" for a "new community," and since they were still burdened by the primitive ideas with which they had entered the movement, they could only be treated as "immature children." Although "no thinking man" could give himself completely to a party, only a misguided egoism would lead the educated recruits to place considerations of intellectual integrity over the welfare of the movement. The spirit, after all, was "higher than the word"; the goal "sanctified the method."

Bernhard's article, with its mixture of condescension, candor, and cynicism, outraged Kautsky and Mehring. It struck at the core of their conception of a party in which the workers were gaining the knowledge of history and social relations provided by Marx. Mehring immediately denounced the article as a "slap in the face" of the party.[64] To suggest that the masses were animated by "dark impulses" and, therefore, needed to be led or even fooled by the leaders, was comparable to the "Jesuitical morality" of the bourgeois enemy. Mehring directed his anger mainly at Harden. The editor's coup in getting a Social Democrat to express his "infectious morality" was, he asserted, the latest in a series of efforts by Harden to damage the party. The episode raised once more, according to Mehring, the question posed at the Lübeck conference—the propriety of Social Democratic writers' discussing party matters in bourgeois papers. *Zukunft,* he maintained, was especially insidious, because it pretended to be neutral in politics. But the very pretense of impartiality was a sham, a means of spreading the "poison of capitalism."

Bernhard protested that Mehring had deliberately misrepresented his views.[65] He claimed, rather lamely, that the article did not "deal with the Social Democratic party as such" but only with parties in general. Mehring had, moreover, ignored his motive in writing the article, for it was aimed at individuals who refused to subordinate their personal freedom to the "needs of a struggling party."[66]

In an editorial note attached to Bernhard's reply, Kautsky entered the debate.[67] "Whoever speaks to the masses in ways other than he thinks" violated Social Democratic principles. The "education of the proletariat" could only take place by presenting things openly as they are, without any regard for "the prejudices of the masses" and without employing any "statesmanlike subterfuges." No method was acceptable which was not in harmony with the growing self-consciousness of the working class. Here lay the only sound basis for the party's morale. Kautsky then declared that the Social Democrats needed to "set firm norms" regarding contributions by party members to bourgeois papers. Although Bernhard's article could be dismissed as the "gushings of youth," the cases in which Social Democratic writers were allowing themselves to be used by the enemy were multiplying. Delegates at the next party conference should confront the issue. Kautsky proposed, as a guideline, the principle that no party member contribute to a paper in which the Social Democrats had been maligned. Those members of the party who had contributed to *Zukunft,* he added, served the enemy.

Angered by the charge, several of the Social Democrats who had written for Harden's paper, including Göhre and Lily Braun, and joined by Heinrich Braun and Heine, protested to the party Executive.[68] They demanded a "speedy remedy" for the attack on the honor of the contributors and the threat to "freedom of expression within the party." Not only did the Executive reject the complaint, but it denounced the practice of writing for papers which engaged in a "malicious and scornful criticism of the party."[69] This language, drawn directly from Kautsky's reply to Bernhard, was incorporated into a resolution prepared by the Executive for the party conference in the fall.

The dispute strengthened Braun's determination to mobilize revisionist intellectuals. During the spring he secured a promise of financial support from a wealthy young man and made plans to start publication of a new weekly in the summer. His part in the protest to the Executive, however, had increased the distrust of the party leaders. Nor did they welcome a rival to the *Neue Zeit,* which already required a substantial subsidy. Auer informed Braun that he should not expect a friendly reception within the party.[70] A request that the publishing facilities of *Vorwärts* be made available for Braun's weekly was turned down.

In the spring of 1903 Braun also campaigned as a Social Democratic candidate for the Reichstag in the coming general election. Prospects for his success in the election, scheduled for June, were not good. Moreover, Braun was not an effective political speaker. "My husband sought to persuade," Lily recalled, "while I appealed to the feelings."[71] But her eloquence on the platform, together with widespread discontent over the government's new protectionist measures, brought victory to Braun. The party scored major gains as it increased its parliamentary representation from fifty-three to eighty-one.

With this electoral triumph the party had reached, in the eyes of Braun and other revisionist intellectuals, a critical point in its development. Unless the party exploited the victory which had "fallen into its lap," Braun wrote Vollmar, its success might be changed into "an irreversible defeat."[72] The time had come for the Social Democrats to develop a more constructive approach to the political process.

But just as Braun was prepared to help guide the party onto a different path by means of his new weekly, the promise of financial support was withdrawn. The potential benefactor seems to have been scared off in part by Braun's imperious personality, in part by divisions among the Revisionists. He had also been courted by Bloch, who hoped to turn the *Sozialistische Monatshefte* into a weekly. Göhre, who attempted to mediate between the two editors, worried about preserving the "unity of the Revisionist movement."[73] The outcome was mutual recrimination between Bloch and Braun.

Braun was nevertheless determined to go ahead, convinced that the crucial moment for "building up a new future for the party" had arrived.[74] To finance the weekly, the *Neue Gesellschaft,* he sold the *Archiv.* Late in July it was purchased by Edgar Jaffé, who with Sombart and Max Weber continued its work under a new title, *Archiv für Sozialwissenschaft und Sozialpolitik.*

It proved impossible to start publication of the new weekly before October. And before it appeared the position of Braun, together with his most important allies, Göhre and Heine, had changed dramatically. Developments during the first six months of 1903 had convinced the main defenders of orthodox Marxism that it was time to "clear the table" once and for all. In the weeks before the Dresden conference, scheduled for late September, they prepared to deal with the revisionist intellectuals.

Preparing for a Showdown: Kautsky, Bebel, and Mehring

During the spring of 1903, following the protests of the revisionist intellectuals over the treatment of Bernhard, Kautsky turned once more to the Akademikerproblem. He was especially angry over Bernstein's continuing claim that the Revisionists were "truer students of the master" than the defenders of orthodoxy. In a letter to Adler in April, he restated his exasperation with the intellectuals in the party:

> I am prepared to grant far-reaching concessions to the masses who are not completely clear, in order for them to fight in our ranks. But tolerance toward the intellectuals who are confused I hold to be harmful. . . . These people have only one task with us—to spread clarity. . . . To the unclear proletariat the right direction will be accessible through class instinct. The confused intellectual has no such compass. He gropes helplessly in the dark and does all the more damage to us the more talented he is for more adherents join him in his wanderings.[75]

The intellectual, he added, could not be allowed to turn upside down that which had "taken us a generation to learn." If it were possible, he would throw "Göhre, David and their associates out of the party."

Kautsky's distress over the intellectuals was coupled with a new emphasis on the learning capacity of the workers. He now stressed the ability of the workers to transcend old class interests. The proletariat was developing the "social impulses—helpfulness, sympathy, devotion to the community"—which had declined in the middle class, captive as it was to an individualistic and competitive outlook.[76] As the workers gained a new awareness of their condition, they naturally accepted the "ideal of social property and the social control of production." The Social Democrats were also exercising a growing appeal to those members of the bourgeoisie who possessed "courage and clarity"; the latter had "only one place to turn" if they wished to struggle "against the sources of need and misery."

Several of the revisionist intellectuals, meanwhile, were urging the Social Democrats to reach out to the middle classes. In March Göhre suggested that the party might soften its opposition to the monarchy without weakening its attack on capitalism.[77] And shortly after the general election in June Heine and Kampffmeyer declared that the Social Democrats, by working toward a fuller citizenship for all, had become the heirs of a declining liberalism. The party represented the "future of the whole nation."[78]

Bernstein also favored a course of political accommodation. Earlier in the year, winning a by-election, he had entered the party's Reichstag Fraktion. Following the general election he called on the Social Democratic leaders to accept parliamentary precedence and claim, as the second largest party, the vice-presidency of the Reichstag.[79] To take such a step meant abandoning the party's traditional refusal to make the customary obeisance to the Emperor. Bernstein was recommending a significant shift in tactics. Not all of the Revisionists were happy with the idea. It seemed to Heine, for example, to demonstrate Bernstein's "political incapacity."[80] Instead of making a public statement, Heine observed, the idea should have been tried out on the Fraktion itself. Bernstein's proposal became, however—alongside the contributor issue—a second major source of controversy among the Social Democrats.

During the summer two able recruits joined the ranks of the revisionist intellectuals. The crushing defeat suffered by Naumann's National Socialists in the June election convinced two of their leaders—Max Maurenbrecher and Gerhard Hildebrand—that the future lay with the Social Democrats, and they joined the party.[81] Conceding that he had failed to develop an alternative political path for the workers, Naumann gave his former colleagues his blessing. He also expressed the hope that they would strengthen the revisionist element among the Social Democrats.[82]

Kautsky, however, could only view Maurenbrecher and Hildebrand as "political wanderers" who had simply been stranded by the collapse of the National Socialists.[83] He complained again about the "preponderance of academics in party offices." They threatened to "darken the proletarian character" of the party. He suggested that the economic associations of the workers offered the best counter against that danger. The parliamentary candidates, administrators, and "journalistically schooled proletarians" needed by the party could best be found in the trade unions. Indeed, one of the most encouraging features of the election, according to Kautsky, was the increased number of trade union officials in the Fraktion. That Kautsky could place his faith in these working class leaders was evidence of both his disenchantment with the educated recruits and his ability to overlook the indifference of most trade unionists to theoretical considerations.

Kautsky looked forward to the Dresden conference as an opportunity to correct the "lack of clarity and decisiveness" of previous conferences.[84] He appealed to the Revisionists to resist the temptation to play down the disagreement within the party and "bring it out into the open." "Nothing can be more pernicious, nothing can be more degrading to the proceedings of the party conference than maintaining the fiction that there are no great tactical and theoretical differences among us." The delegates needed to deal firmly with the contributor and vice-president issues. Dresden, he predicted, would be "filled with passionate debate."

Bebel, too, was determined to bring the internal discord to an end. He viewed the efforts of the revisionist intellectuals to combine "freedom of thinking" with "unity of action" as an invitation to anarchy.[85] "Is it possible to have unity of action without unity of principle and basic views?" Bernstein's proposal to seek the vice-presidency would be the first step in a process which would make it "impossible to maintain the former tactics of the party." What worried Bebel most was the attempt within the party to "weaken the opposition between bourgeois society and the class-conscious proletariat." Heine's claim that the Social Democrats should "now fulfill the liberal heritage" ignored class differences. It was all the more important to assert the proletarian character of the party because it was attracting more nonworkers. There were, Bebel observed, a growing number of "flatterers" of the revisionists in the bourgeois camp. Seeing a "process of disintegration" within the party, they were like "jackals going after carrion."

> Many of these elements come into the party still strongly burdened with the eggshell of bourgeois prejudices and views. Even those who have grasped theoretically the standpoint of the class struggle . . . frequently fall back into . . . bourgeois methods of battle. . . . And so these elements become a party within the party.

Bebel even suggested that the bourgeois enemy might command its intellectuals to join the Social Democrats "in order to accelerate the crisis in the party."

It was time, Bebel declared, to put a stop to the internal disputes which had, for six years, been the source of so much "irritation and exasperation."[86] But Bernstein was not the "genuinely dangerous" figure; he was relatively harmless compared with those of strongly practical bent—intellectuals like Heine and Braun and reformists like Auer and Vollmar. Here lay the main corruption within the party and the "betrayal of its interests." The delegates at the conference needed to act decisively. There must be no "hushing up, no evasion." Bebel assured Kautsky that he had prepared a "battle plan."[87] "At Dresden I will preach the most intensive distrust of all those who come to us as academics and intellectuals."

On the eve of the conference there were efforts within the party to lower the temperature of the polemic. After all, Auer observed, the contributor question was hardly a "burning issue."[88] He urged the delegates to concentrate on the problem of how to use the party's new parliamentary strength to advance the interests of the workers. The party's organ, *Vorwärts,* which after the death of Liebknecht in 1900 had been directed collegially by the staff, also attempted to play down the controversies. But the determination of Kautsky and Bebel to establish a "clear line of march" made it impossible for *Vorwärts* to exercise a conciliatory role. When the paper rejected two pieces by Bebel that were aimed against Heine and other Revisionists, on the ground that they would exacerbate tensions, the editors earned the party leader's animosity and, as it turned out, retaliation.[89]

Mehring was the most zealous among the orthodox Marxists in demanding a showdown with revisionist intellectuals. They threatened the conception of a party tightly bound together by doctrines to which he, like Kautsky, was committed. Mehring had worried for some time about the lack of interest in theory among the party rank and file. A review of the first twenty years of the *Neue Zeit,* written late in 1902, expressed the hope that the paper's third decade would witness a greater appreciation for theory on the part of Social Democrats.[90] In defense of his conception of the party Mehring had denounced Bernhard and strongly supported the Executive in the contributor dispute. "Whoever joins a party," he declared, "renounces the right of free expression of opinion, insofar as it conflicts with its discipline and program."[91]

Mehring denied the possibility, advocated by Heine and Göhre, of a "peaceful relationship between the Social Democrats and the monarchy." Bernstein's proposal that party leaders "visit the court" and seek the vice-presidency was completely unacceptable; it could only lead to an "inner disintegration" of the movement.[92] Nor did he welcome the recruits from the National Socialists. They were simply entering the party in order to change it.[93]

Following the death of Schönlank in 1901 Mehring had taken over the editorship of the *Leipziger Volkszeitung,* which continued to be the most radical of the party's newspapers. He still wrote lead articles for the *Neue Zeit,* but he delivered his harshest attacks on the revisionist intellectuals in the Leipzig paper. As the Dresden conference approached he warned the delegates that they would "poison the inner life" of the party if they failed to choose between the "old revolutionary tactic" and the "policy of alliances and compromises."[94] German socialists, he announced, faced their "greatest battle" since the conflict between the Eisenachers and the Lassalleans, the two groups which had come together at Gotha almost thirty years earlier to form the united party.

Mehring's polemical skill and invective had made him the chief target of the revisionist intellectuals. For several years Braun had seen him as a baleful influence on Kautsky.[95] And now, in the days before Dresden, the group around Braun came to view Mehring as a sinister force within the party, who "from the seclusion of his study fanned the flames of hatred" against all Social Democrats who were not "literal believers."[96] To free the party from him, Lily Braun recalled, would be a major step toward saving it. "No task seemed more important at the moment." Her husband seized on the idea and made plans to discredit Mehring before the delegates.

Many of the Social Democrats who traveled to Dresden in September 1903 arrived with a sense of excitement and foreboding. The escalating polemics of the previous weeks, coming after the elation of the electoral victory, indicated that the party had reached a crossroads. The Dresden conference was a crucial moment in the party's relationship to its educated recruits.

The Rout of the Revisionist Intellectuals

Two and a half days of the party conference at Dresden were devoted to the question of the propriety of Social Democrats' contributing to bourgeois papers. To outside observers and, indeed, to many within the party it was, to say the least, a strange use of the annual meeting. Given the party's electoral gains in June, it was expected that the delegates would be concerned mainly with the political implications of the increased Social Democratic representation in the Reichstag. The internal explosion which occurred at Dresden indicated the extent to which the party, denied significant parliamentary influence, had been driven in on itself.

In this new clash between the orthodox Marxists and revisionist intellectuals, the latter suffered a crushing defeat. Other defeats followed over the next two years as the Social Democratic leaders sought greater ideological conformity within the party. The new demand for discipline culminated in the purge of the staff of *Vorwärts*. But while the overt challenge to orthodox Marxism was repulsed, the retreat of the Social Democrats into the "ghetto of fixed principles" meant an ever-widening gulf between the party's ideology and its political practices.[1]

The Contributor Debate

At Dresden the delegates accepted the proposal of the chairman, Paul Singer, that they deal first with the resolution of the Executive, which grew out of the Bernhard article in January. The resolution was supported by several branches of the party. A motion to remove the time limit on speeches, in view of the "deep and important" differences on the issue, was also accepted.[2] What seemed to many delegates the more significant issue—the proposal to seek the vice-presidency of the Reichstag—was scheduled for later. Party leaders believed that the contributor question would be disposed of quickly—in fifteen minutes, according to Bebel.[3] The hosts of the conference, the Dresden Social Democrats, had arranged for an all-day outing for the delegates in mid-week, having assumed that the proceedings would permit such a break. The length of the initial debate scotched the plan.

Braun led off.[4] He claimed later that he had not been ready to begin the discussion, despite the preparations he and other Revisionists had made. But he started off well. "I am a writer," he declared, and he went on to affirm the "dignity and the significance" of such a vocation. The present controversy, he maintained, was largely a squabble among writers. Braun scolded the Executive for making it a public issue. Now, however, it had to be dealt with at the highest level. He then defended the freedom of the party's intellectuals, noting that for many years their "tact and sense of responsibility" had been sufficient to prevent any damage to the cause. Was the Executive about to establish an "index" of publications, off limits to both contributors and readers?

During his opening remarks Braun referred to "Herr Doktor Franz Mehring" in a manner which brought an angry response from Bebel and a rebuke from the chairman.[5] It was not the custom, Singer reminded Braun, to employ such titles among comrades. But it was soon clear that Mehring was Braun's main target, as he turned to what he called the "personal side of the whole affair." He attacked Mehring for his treatment of Bernhard and his general role in the party. Braun reviewed Mehring's career, noting his support for the Social Democrats in the seventies, his denunciation of the party after it was outlawed, and his return to the movement. Braun recalled, ironically, that he himself had arranged the meeting with Bebel and Singer in 1888 which led to Mehring's reconciliation with the Social Democrats. But Mehring, according to Braun, remained a "chameleon," who frequently changed his friends as well as his political colors. His rage against Bernhard was simply the latest example. Addressing Mehring directly, Braun accused him of "literary terrorism," of inciting comrades against each other and poisoning the party. "You will cease to be dangerous to us," Braun concluded, "when you are again our enemy."

Braun had blundered. He had misjudged the mood of the meeting. His remarks brought angry interruptions from Bebel. Despite the efforts of the chairman to restrain the two men, sarcastic and insulting exchanges continued. It was clear, too, that the majority sided with Bebel and resented Braun's mode of attack. Braun's tactic made him and other revisionist intellectuals vulnerable to what his wife described as the "secret hate against the academics."[6] Much of the subsequent discussion centered on the "academic question."

The speaker who followed Braun addressed the issue. "We are getting more and more people" from outside the working class, a delegate from Hamburg declared.[7] "Salon socialists" were assuming the leading roles in the party. Amid expressions of approval from the delegates he demanded that those who came from the middle class "burn their bridges to bourgeois society." Other speakers echoed his distrust of the educated recruits. Several noted the tendency for local branches to favor them as candidates. One delegate charged that the intellectuals were much more interested in complicating matters for party members than they were in criticizing the enemy.[8] To believe that one could continue to contribute to papers which maligned the party and still be a true Social Democrat was, according to another speaker, to accept a "two-soul theory."[9] These remarks were received with prolonged applause.

Kautsky also entered the debate.[10] After reviewing his own role in the events following the publication of Bernhard's article, he contrasted his attitude toward the academically educated with Braun's: "I am not one of those who greets with hosannas any doctor who comes to us and prefers him to old experienced comrades. . . . I believe that the academics who come to us ought to experience a waiting period. . . . A healthy mistrust against the academics would be in place." Kautsky went on to defend Mehring as an unsurpassed "representative of scientific socialism," for whom the party program was a "living truth."

Revisionist intellectuals were on the defensive. Bernhard conceded that his article had been a mistake,[11] but he charged that Kautsky and the party executive had exaggerated its significance. He then produced the sensation of the conference—a postcard written by Mehring to Harden in the early nineties, in which he promised to expose a member of the party. Referring to Schönlank, Mehring told the editor of *Zukunft:* "I will tame the lout." The disclosure shocked the delegates. It also provided the backdrop for a speech from Bebel which took up the entire afternoon of the second day of the conference and completed the rout of the offending intellectuals.[12] Among Bebel's many and lengthy addresses at party conferences, none matched his performance at Dresden. It was a remarkable example of his skill in using words to obscure ideological or tactical issues while appealing to the feelings which made for party loyalty and solidarity.

Bebel dealt first with those who dismissed the contributor issue as simply a "literary squabble" and who, in the face of the practical tasks facing the party, were reluctant to take up the "bitter cup" of internal debate once more.[13] At stake, he declared, was the very soul of the party. Bernhard's article was symptomatic. Bebel likened the contributor problem to an abscess. "Just as little as the doctor finds it pleasant to operate on an abscess . . . and perhaps must guard against [revulsion], so it also happens with us, that similar operations will be felt to be unpleasant, but nevertheless must be undertaken." A diatribe against *Zukunft* and its editor followed, during which Bebel called attention to Harden's Jewish background, his admiration for Bismarck, and his criticisms of the Social Democrats. How could one, Bebel asked, keep one's honor and still write for the paper?

Bebel then reviewed Mehring's relationship with the Social Democrats in a long digression punctuated by angry exchanges with Braun. There was no excuse, the party leader acknowledged, for Mehring's treatment of Schönlank. Even Bebel's defense of Mehring was half-hearted. The party leader attempted to balance Mehring's brilliance as a journalist with his propensity to quarrel with other socialist writers and editors. Mehring, he conceded, was a "psychological riddle."[14]

For Bebel, the contributor issue provided an opportunity to launch his planned attack on the academics. "There are marauders among us," he declared, who had fallen on "the back of the party."[15] He urged the delegates to be suspicious of the educated recruits: "Consider each party comrade but if he is an academic or intellectual look at him two or three times. . . . I do not say that these comrades are dishonest, that they wish to hurt the party. . . . [But] they have the damned duty, in all their activity, to consider doubly and triply that they are in the right party, and inform themselves . . . how the masses think, how they feel, and what they want; these masses who know better than the academics what concerns the proletariat." Bebel granted the party's need for the academics. But he appealed directly to feelings which had, in the course of the debate, been aroused against the intellectuals. To drive home his demand that the offending intellectuals fall in step with the party rank and file Bebel publicly humiliated Bernhard. Although the latter had already admitted that he had erred in writing the article, the party leader asked Bernhard to promise that he would never again write for *Zukunft.* Intimidated by Bebel and the hostility around him, Bernhard submitted, much to his subsequent regret.

The fever pitch to which Bebel had aroused the delegates was described later by the young intellectual who followed him to the rostrum.[16] Robert Michels had come to Dresden as the leader of a small group of academics in Marburg who were angry about Heine's endorsement of a local liberal candidate in the recent election and were committed to Bebel's position.[17] Drawing on his diary account, Michels recalled that Bebel had rendered the delegates "incapable of reflection." Sensing the danger, fearing a split in the party, and conscious of his youth and his responsibility, Michels abandoned his plan to continue the attack on the Revisionists. Instead, he offered conciliatory words. The present mistrust, he remarked, was "unworthy of a great party."[18]

The revisionist intellectuals retreated in the face of the storm they had generated. Each of the principals in the controversy—Heine, Göhre, Bernhard, and Braun—repudiated Harden and announced that they would henceforth have nothing to do with *Zukunft*. At the same time they answered the charges which in the course of the debate had been directed against them.

Heine put the blame for the "disgusting academic debate" on Bebel and the other party leaders.[19] And he reaffirmed the need for freedom in matters of "principle and thought" within the party. The contributor resolution, as presented, was, according to Heine, impractical. Still, he indicated his readiness to support a resolution which referred only to Harden's weekly.

Göhre, hurt and angered by what he saw as Bebel's attack on his honor, reviewed the process which had led him to the party.[20] His turn to the proletariat, he observed, had meant the sacrifice of his vocation, his income, his social position, and his family ties. "But until yesterday," he said, his honor had not been questioned. Now Bebel had reviled him before the whole world as a "vagabond academic" who had no feeling for the class struggle. After all, he had only agreed to become a candidate for the Reichstag when three constituencies sought him. To have refused, Göhre told the delegates, would have invited the complaint—"see the academic, he is in the party but he does not work." But now, out of envy, his critics charged—"see the academic . . . how he pushes forward." Why, Göhre asked, had Bebel not warned him that contributions to *Zukunft* damaged the party? In the end Göhre too bowed before the fury loosed against Harden and agreed not to write for the paper.

Braun joined in the denunciation of Harden.[21] He also assured the delegates that his wife would no longer contribute to *Zukunft*. Although he repeated his accusations against Mehring and scolded Kautsky for failing to check the excesses of his fellow editor, Braun was conciliatory. Lost from sight now was his plan to challenge the policies of the Social Democratic leaders. He denied that there were serious differences between the two sides. "The artificially constructed opposition between Revisionists and Radicals," he insisted, were "nothing more than superficial ripples." Party members had a common basis. "Resting on the ground of the materialistic conception of history, they see in the class struggle the forward driving means and in the socialist order of society the final goal that gives it direction." Lily Braun, who had remained in Berlin to care for her sick child, was dismayed when she read, in the newspaper accounts of the conference, of her husband's "abject surrender."[22] The Revisionists, she concluded, "had gone back on everything they had stood for earlier."

Before the vote on the Executive's resolution, Bebel repeated his warning against the intellectuals.[23] Noting that he had often been criticized for "flirting with the academics," he expressed his admiration for recruits who had laid "aside their class prejudices." But too many of them had "failed to fulfill what was expected of them," and had fallen back into "the old conceptions." There was a continuing need to scrutinize the intellectuals with special care. Bebel had largely succeeded in directing against the Revisionists the deep-seated hostility toward intellectuals that had developed within the party. Protests that educated recruits were to be found on both sides of the theoretical issues—that they constituted, in fact, the main speakers in the debate—were ignored. The resolution condemning contributions to papers which engaged in "hateful and malicious criticisms" of the party passed by a vote of 283 to 24.

The second major debate at Dresden—dealing with the vice-presidency issue—was an anticlimax.[24] It repeated the triumph of the party leaders and reaffirmed their traditional tactic. It did bring a confrontation between Bebel and Vollmar to which one young intellectual, at least, had looked forward to with "breathless anticipation."[25] Some Social Democrats believed that Vollmar might, in view of the party's altered political situation, challenge Bebel's leadership. The Bavarian Social Democrat had no intention of doing so. He recognized Bebel's overwhelming support in those areas of the north—Prussia and Saxony—which dominated the party. Vollmar realized, moreover, that he could not match the skills to which Bebel owed his leadership. But Vollmar also saw in those skills a danger to the party. In his remarks on the vice-presidency issue he pointed to the hazards associated with Bebel's kind of leadership.

Bebel's leadership came, according to Vollmar, mainly from his "apocalyptic passion" and his "poetic force";[26] imagination and emotion had given him an unchallenged position. But there lay the danger. These qualities prevented calm and rational consideration of actual developments. Confident that he was in gear with "unerring class instincts," Bebel was incapable of recognizing that the masses were as "prone to deception and self-deception" as any individual. Vollmar criticized the party leader for his dictatorial ways and his habit of scolding all who disagreed with him. Bebel was too ready to accuse academics who had been in the party a decade or more of being stuck in "bourgeois ways of thinking."

Vollmar also attacked Kautsky—the "fanaticist of theory."[27] Rather than "let one span be pulled out of his beautiful building of thought," the theorist would allow the party "to fall into ruins." Now, according to Vollmar, those Social Democrats who thought like Kautsky saw an opportunity to impose their views on the party and drive out all who refused to conform. The outcome, he warned, would be ossification and an inability to attract "warm-blooded, gifted men." "Absolute freedom of thought" was essential to the life of the party.

The debate on the vice-presidency question ended with the adoption of a resolution which "condemned in the most decisive way the revisionist struggle to alter our present, well tested, and victory-crowned tactic of the class struggle." Only eleven delegates voted against it. With the exception of David, revisionist intellectuals supported the resolution. "After all," Braun told his wife, the "phraseology could be interpreted in a way that was acceptable to the Revisionists."[28] The party remained, despite "all the commotion," united on tactics.

Bernstein suggested later that the major debate at Dresden was a "prearranged comedy," staged by the leaders in order to keep the party members in line.[29] And one historian of the party has concluded that the scenes at the conference were mere "theatrics," a "tempest in a teapot."[30] For revisionist intellectuals, however, Dresden was a disaster. It dashed the hope of Braun and the group around him that orthodox Marxism might give way to a new openness in questions of theory and attract a growing number of educated individuals. Heine claimed that the Social Democrats suddenly lost their appeal to the new generation of academics.[31] Many "young academics who had been turning to the party now turned their backs"; recruits from this social stratum "ceased completely . . . much to the damage of the intellectual level of the party press." A young academic on the edge of the party agreed. It was at this point, Willy Hellpach recalled, that many in the younger generation of the educated were "scared away from the working-class movement."[32] For Bebel and Kautsky, however, the party's soul had been preserved.

Naumann, who sat at the press table during the conference, attempted to grasp the significance of this moment in the party's history. Bebel, he claimed, sensed the "secularization of his church."[33] The members still "sang the old words, but only perhaps in the way a religious synod sang the stormy songs of Luther." The party leader was desperately seeking to sustain the old beliefs, for they provided the enthusiasm, the spirit of self-sacrifice, which energized the movement. But the "disenchantment" of the Marxist faith, Naumann concluded, was under way.

The attack on the intellectuals was, in Naumann's view, ironic. It was conducted on behalf of ideas, defended most strongly by Kautsky, which earlier intellectuals had created. The "content of party history" was derived, after all, from "brain processes which were not of direct proletarian origin."[34] The masses simply thought "what the previous generation of the academics thought." According to Naumann, the academics among the orthodox Marxists had achieved a "dangerous importance." "Who controls them? Who criticizes them?" The wage earners, who made up the bulk of the party, were "even more helpless" in relationship to such "literary types" than they were before their capitalist employers. What intellectual, Naumann asked, would now be willing "to make the leap into the party"?

In his analysis of the party conference Naumann raised a further question. Would Bebel seek "to pull off what he could not achieve at Dresden" and attempt "to ruin" the offending intellectuals?[35] Shortly after the conference, Bebel renewed the attack. "This unpleasant business," he declared, needed to "be burned out with fire."[36] The party leader, sensitive to the danger to party unity, soon pulled back, however. Nevertheless Dresden proved to be the first step in a more or less concerted drive against revisionist intellectuals which continued over the next two years.

After Dresden

During the weeks following the conference charges and countercharges arising out of the proceedings dominated the party press. For a month or more the columns of *Vorwärts* were filled with excerpts from Social Democratic newspapers, letters from the principals in the debate, and editorial comments. Most of the local papers supported the party leaders and blamed the intellectuals on both sides for "the hateful tone of the proceedings."[37] There were new complaints about "theoretical hairsplitting" and the tendency for the educated recruits to waste valuable time at the conference with their petty concerns. But Bebel also came under fire for his "immoderate tone." And an editorial in *Vorwärts* criticized the party leaders for their failure to address the practical significance of the electoral victory. "You have given us stones," the writer declared, "rather than bread."[38]

Kautsky, however, was pleased with the outcome. Dresden had witnessed a "passionate struggle for the moral purity of the party."[39] The delegates, he claimed, had buried "theoretical revision" as a "political factor" and "brought greater clarification."[40] The decision at Dresden had shown, moreover, that the infectious morality of the bourgeoisie, found in the sensation-seeking journalists of the Berlin coffee houses, was no match for proletarian morality. The delegates had demonstrated, too, that an intellectual who lacked "firm theoretical foundation" was "like a dry leaf in the wind," at the mercy of personal moods or circumstances. Kautsky also attempted to explain this new clash with the intellectuals in Marxist terms.

"Nothing could be more erroneous," he wrote, than attributing the disagreements at Dresden to personal differences.[41] "Theoretical revisionism" was a product of a brief period of prosperity in Germany.

Revisionist intellectuals, still influenced by their class background, had generalized on the basis of temporary economic conditions.

Kautsky now drew a sharp line between the worker and the intellectual: "The proletariat is never an isolated individual. He feels great and strong as part of a strong organization. . . . His individuality counts little beside it. He struggles with full devotion as a part of an anonymous mass, without prospect of personal gain or personal fame, fulfills his duty in the post in which he is placed, in voluntary discipline which fills his whole feeling and thought."[42] The intellectual, however, "comes to account" only through his individual personality. His tools are personal knowledge, argument, ability, and personal conviction. It is natural for him to demand complete freedom for his work. He is naturally attracted to Nietzsche and his "cult of the superman." The intellectual usually comes to the proletariat as a superior; only with great difficulty can he serve the whole movement. Hence the conflicts between the writers and the party. "And it is often the best element of the writers who come over to the party who suffer shipwreck, that is, those who are full of character and true to conviction. So each writer should test himself before he turns to the party and ask if he can be a simple soldier without feeling himself narrowed and forced down."[43] Kautsky cited Marx and Liebknecht as men who had entered completely "into the feeling life of the proletariat." He thus left room for intellectuals like himself who had adopted Marxist theory and were, therefore, in harmony with the working class outlook.

Kautsky's reflections on Dresden brought him close to a dialectical conception of the relationship between theory and practice. The "true object of study" for the party theorist, he wrote, was "the practice of the proletariat itself."[44] Only a knowledge drawn "out of praxis" could "fruitfully play back" on the practical struggles of the workers. Such an understanding was very different from "that gained in the lecture hall by the academics." But Kautsky only claimed that a "scientific based self-knowledge" needed to originate in "proletarian circles." His concept of the dialectic remained abstract, a mere possibility. His Marxism was still strongly deterministic. And he continued to warn that the "theoretical sense" was dwindling in the party.[45] Social Democratic writers needed to renew, through "systematic study," their efforts to transmit the "meaning of Marxist theory."

Luxemburg was also heartened by the outcome of Dresden; it reinforced her confidence in the workers. But the conference led her to reflect on the nature of leadership in the movement.[46] She argued that the prominence of recruits from the bourgeoisie and, indeed, the "dictatorship" of Bebel, were signs of the "immaturity of the masses." The "so-called 'leader' among the Social Democrats" should, she argued, merely explain to the masses their historic task. The workers could then dispense with leadership; the leader became simply "the instrument of conscious mass action." The "dominant tendency" in the movement was, in short, the "abolition of the 'leader.'"[47] That the revisionist intellectuals continued to treat the masses "as children who must be educated . . . even deceived for their own good" indicated their attachment to an obsolete political ethic. Dresden demonstrated the determination of the workers to "block off the supply of academics" and cleanse the party of the demoralizing influence which had entered during the previous five years. Luxemburg was elated by the "painful withdrawal of the outstretched hands of the bourgeois interlopers." Once again an "unbridgeable gulf" yawned between the "proletariat and the bourgeois world."

The gulf was not as wide as Kautsky and Luxemburg desired. By November Kautsky recognized that Bebel's determination to put down the revisionist intellectuals was wavering as his primary concern—party unity and its political advance—once more gained the upper hand. The party leader, Kautsky complained, was putting the brakes on and delaying any settlement of the internal party opposition "until the state elections were over."[48] A few weeks later one of the younger Marxist intellectuals in the Reichstag, Albert Südekum, described Bebel as "the most stalwart Revisionist in the Fraktion."[49]

Nor was it clear that the Revisionists viewed Dresden as a decisive defeat. One of their supporters, Adolph von Elm, a leader in the cooperative movement, claimed that Bebel and others had exaggerated the importance of the contributor and vice-presidency issues and had produced "pain, sadness and shame in many proletarian hearts."[50] Bebel he added, misunderstood the "party's soul." Intoxicated by the spirit of great meetings, the party leader knew little of the daily realities of the working-class struggle. Other observers noted the one-sidedness of the attack on the intellectuals. "Out of understandable psychological grounds," Bernstein argued, the academic recruits were more likely to stand with "the so-called radical wing of the party."[51] An Austrian Social Democrat agreed. The Social Democratic leaders who had directed the "accumulated grudges" against the academics and Revisionists had ignored the prominence of educated recruits—Kautsky, Mehring, Luxemburg, and others—on the opposite side.[52]

The revisionist current of thought continued with little interruption after Dresden. Indeed, it was strengthened by a new "press service" created by a young intellectual recruit from Austria, Friedrich Stampfer. At Dresden he completed arrangements with several Social Democratic editors to supply articles of general socialist interest to party newspapers. Although Stampfer denied that this "Pressekorrespondenz" favored any point of view within the party, it became, a later critic has claimed, a means for the infiltration of "bourgeois ideology" into the Social Democratic press.[53] Luxemburg described the enterprise as a "factory for the pasting of opinions on the brains of the proletariat."[54]

The main vehicle for the revisionist intellectuals was still the *Sozialistische Monatshefte.* Its writers remained convinced, as David put it, that the "logic of facts" would prove "stronger than the revolutionary tradition."[55] Social Democrats were freeing themselves from the narrow boundaries of class and becoming a "people's party" in which the intellectuals would play an important role.

Yet the period following Dresden was a painful one for revisionist intellectuals. "We have delivered ourselves into the hands of the enemy," Calwer declared.[56] The figures who had been the main targets of attack at Dresden were in for a difficult time. They were now caught in a vicious cross fire between Harden, who felt they had betrayed him, and Mehring, whom they had sought to destroy. Braun, Bernhard, Heine, and Göhre also faced party hearings to determine whether they should be expelled.

Harden was indignant. Despite his attempts over the years to "give full freedom to Social Democrats" to express their views in *Zukunft,* members of the party had spent three days reviling him.[57] The editor now described Bebel as an "Asiatic despot" whose demagoguery indicated the "depth of the corruption" within the party. The abject surrender of Braun, Bernhard, Heine, and Göhre "before the rage of the incited mass" was further evidence of the corruption. Harden attempted to show, by means of quotations from his correspondence with the four men, that they had "acted dishonestly and cowardly" and had "lied to the party conference" in order to save themselves. A flurry of letters in *Vorwärts* between Harden and his former friends damaged the reputation of the four Revisionists. Meanwhile they faced a counterattack from Mehring.

Following the disclosures at Dresden, Mehring's position in the party, as Kautsky recalled, "hung by a thread."[58] Only the intervention of Kautsky and Bebel saved him. But he immediately resigned the editorship of the *Leipziger Volkszeitung* and stopped writing lead articles for the *Neue Zeit.* Mehring also answered his critics in a pamphlet, *My Vindication: An Additional Word on the Dresden Party Conference.*[59] It was a typical display of Mehring's polemical style, in which the major issues were frequently obscured by personal invective. He dismissed Bernhard as one who worked freely during the day under the yoke of "capitalist business" while playing the role of a revolutionary socialist in the evening. He denounced Heine as one who had been a "miserable anti-Semitic philistine" during his school days. He accused the Brauns of holding a "war council" with Harden to "consider how I might be killed." Mehring attempted to explain away the incriminating postcard by describing the circumstances in which it was written.

Mehring also used *Vindication* to comment on the condition of the party. The "moral assassination" at Dresden was evidence of the "diminishing of the great theoretical sense" among Social Democrats.[60] He again urged party writers "to cultivate theory more zealously" and to avoid excessive concern with practical issues. The theorist saw developments more clearly and more broadly than the "Praktiker." "Without a general staff" informed by theory, Mehring declared, the workers could not free themselves from the hold of capitalist culture.

Embarrassed by Harden and placed on the defensive by Mehring's assault, Bernhard, Braun, Heine, and Göhre were also subject to party tribunals. Disclosures at the conference and in the correspondence published in *Vorwärts* suggested that the four men had "seriously violated the principles of the party program" and "engaged in dishonorable acts" which justified their expulsion.[61] To deal with the charges the Executive set up "courts of arbitration." Party statutes permitted the defendants to choose half of the eight-man panels appointed to hear the complaints. The presence of other revisionist intellectuals—Schmidt, Calwer, Bloch, and David—on one or more of the panels ensured some sympathy for the accused.

The charges were vague. They included the uttering of dishonest or deceitful statements at the conference and claims that one or more of the defendants had conspired to make Mehring's continued "literary activity impossible." Each of the hearings ended with a decision not to expel, much to the disgust of Mehring.[62] Both Bernhard and Braun, however, were reprimanded. The courts were, in fact, mainly exercises in conciliation. Afterward the Executive urged both sides to "let the matter rest" and concentrate on fighting the enemy.[63]

But the judgments were not reached until the late spring of 1904, and none of the four defendants emerged from the strife without wounds. Each was forced to reexamine his relationship to the party.

Bernhard had reasserted his independence after Dresden. Appearing before the party court, he repudiated "only the form, not the content" of his article on "party morale."[64] His work as a Social Democratic journalist, however, had been damaged beyond repair. He virtually ceased to write for the party press and, in the spring of 1904, started his own weekly paper, *Plutus,* which was dedicated to the "independent presentation" of financial and commercial issues.[65] The new paper published articles by Calwer, Göhre, David, and Schippel. But Bernhard soon left the party altogether to pursue a journalistic career which took him to the editorship of one of Germany's leading newspapers, the *Vossische Zeitung.*

Braun had, as Adler observed, committed "political suicide" at Dresden.[66] But despite the disaster at the conference he went ahead with the plan for a new weekly. The first issue of the *Neue Gesellschaft* appeared in October 1903. While the weekly was soon "swept away" by the hostilities generated at Dresden, Braun continued to believe that the time for a more "rational and fruitful policy" for the party had arrived.[67] Some months later he resumed its publication. In the meantime his parliamentary mandate had been revoked by the authorities because of an electoral technicality. When he ran again, in the spring of 1904, strong opposition from within his own party ensured his defeat. Braun did not quit the party, but his "lack of feeling for the masses" had destroyed any chance of influencing the Social Democrats from within.[68]

Göhre resigned his parliamentary seat shortly after Dresden.[69] Although he had received a vote of confidence from his constituents, he concluded that his credibility had been destroyed at the conference. He soon reconsidered his position. When another Saxon constituency asked him to stand, he accepted. The "agitation committee" of the party in Saxony and the Social Democratic Executive then challenged his candidacy on the grounds that he had failed to consult his constituents before giving up his previous mandate. During the bitter dispute that ensued Göhre withdrew, though he loyally supported the candidate chosen in his place. He remained in the party and, in 1912, again served it in the Reichstag.

The veto of Göhre's nomination by the party Executive prompted a heated discussion over the right, unquestioned up to this time, of local Social Democrats to choose their candidates. To Heine it was an ominous sign of a tendency toward "oligarchy" in the party.[70] Behind the episode, he asserted, lay the animus of Bebel against Göhre and other Revisionists. The new demand for "discipline in intellectual matters" portended, according to Heine, the "surrender of our best forces" and the "death of intellectual life in the party."

Heine also reassessed his place in the party. He came away from Dresden with the "deepest disgust," determined, as he wrote Vollmar, "to lay down my mandate."[71] But in the face of Bebel's apparent desire "to throw them out" he decided to fight. The decision of the Executive to institute proceedings against the four men was a challenge to both Heine's integrity and his skills as a lawyer. His demand for clear evidence to back up the charges of conspiracy and dishonesty probably contributed to the conciliatory outcome of the hearings. By the spring of 1904, Heine had, as his sharp criticism of the Göhre decision indicated, resumed his role as a spokesman for the Revisionists. Yet his parliamentary work, he wrote later, had "lost much of its charm" and he reduced his "personal contact with his colleagues."[72]

What Heine saw as a new demand for "discipline in intellectual matters" came to bear on Schippel in 1904. After questioning the party's military and commercial policies during the late nineties, Schippel continued his efforts to persuade Social Democrats to reconsider their absolute opposition to protective tariffs. A speech in Berlin early in 1904 called into question the party's slavish devotion to the "free-trade argument of the bourgeoisie."[73] Following protests in the Social Democratic press and demands by other members of the Fraktion that he clarify his views, Schippel discussed the problem in a series of articles in the *Chemnitzer Volkstimme.* Social Democrats, he argued, needed to look at the interests of the working classes in terms of the health of the whole economy, from the standpoint of industrial production as well as consumption. Yet, as Ritter has observed, Schippel presented the issues in such a way as to encourage his readers to draw their own conclusions.[74] He did not take a clear stand himself.

Bebel was furious at Schippel's latest "breach of discipline." His old antagonist had again "revealed himself to be a scoundrel" and should immediately be thrown out of the party.[75] But how, Bebel asked Kautsky, could this be done? In order to set up a court of arbitration for the purpose they needed a bill of particulars. And while Schippel had clearly deviated from party policy, he had presented only "theoretical objections."[76] He still joined other members of the Fraktion in voting against tariffs. To Bebel it appeared as though Schippel was guilty of the worst kind of "double dealing." The party leader hoped for a time that Schippel's constituents in Chemnitz might force him to lay down his mandate. Otherwise the matter could only be addressed at the next party conference, scheduled for Bremen in September 1904.

At Bremen party leaders were determined to avoid any repetition of the ugly scenes a year earlier, and the proceedings were relatively peaceful. Only the debate over Schippel's views, which took up a full day of the conference, marred the general calm.[77] The debate was occasioned by Bebel's resolution calling on the delegates to express their disapproval of Schippel's treatment of the tariff question. Amid the assault on Schippel which followed there were charges that he had "broken with the basic views of the party" but lacked "the courage to express it openly."[78] Others attacked him as "double souled." Could a man who identified himself with "the standpoint of our enemies remain" in their ranks?[79] Several delegates demanded that Schippel declare his unequivocal support for the party's program.

Bebel reviewed Schippel's career—his movement from the "extreme left of the party . . . to the extreme right."[80] For eighteen years there had been "a Schippel case every other year": "It is time we put a stop to it. A great number of comrades diverge on many points. But no one acts continually like Schippel . . . always looking down from above with absolute certainty and infallibility and scorn for those who do not think like him. What would we do if we had ten like Schippel? That would necessarily lead to the complete dissolution of the party." Bebel was, as so often, indulging in hyperbole. Although he denied any wish to expel Schippel or curtail freedom of speech, he urged the party to deal with this case of "a man of intelligence" who was misusing the "trust of comrades." Much of Bebel's attack, and that of others, was directed toward Schippel's scornful tone, his tendency, as Kautsky put it, "to put the whole party down as a herd."[81] Perhaps, Bebel observed, "he wants to be thrown out of the party."

Schippel gave his critics little satisfaction.[82] The issue of protectionism, he told the delegates, was, as socialists in other countries recognized, very complicated. He reaffirmed his commitment to the fundamentals of the party. But he also deplored the poisonous tendency to turn "differences of opinion into great oppositions." He denied that he was a protectionist, but he refused to provide the clear statement demanded of him. Bebel's resolution was adopted by an overwhelming majority, and an amendment, which declared that Schippel would have "to suffer the consequences" if he "continued in his ways," passed by a narrow margin.[83] To some of the delegates the consequences meant expulsion; to others, simply the loss of his parliamentary mandate.

Less than a year later Schippel resigned his seat in the Reichstag.[84] He had retained strong, though diminished, support in his Chemnitz constituency. But apparently he had found it necessary to choose between his continuing social and economic investigations and his political role. According to Bernhard, who now viewed party affairs from the sidelines, Schippel "saw himself condemned to silence and inaction" in the "area of his specialized knowledge."[85] He did not leave the party. And he soon found work with the General Commission of the trade unions, where his capacity for detailed investigation of economic problems could be utilized. But the Fraktion had lost, as Heine recalled, "one of its best minds" and "its only researcher of significance."[86]

Schippel was a victim of the new drive for discipline which followed the Dresden conference. During 1905 the effort to secure greater ideological conformity was directed against the staff of *Vorwärts.*

The Purge of *Vorwärts*

The editorial policy of the party's central organ, *Vorwärts,* had troubled Bebel and Kautsky throughout the nineties. Liebknecht's insistence that the paper provide a forum for all views in the party was at odds with Bebel's belief that it should express the views of the leadership on theoretical and tactical matters.[87] Kautsky saw the chief function of *Vorwärts* as educational; it should show the party rank and file how Marxist principles illuminated day-to-day issues. Although Liebknecht's influence steadily declined during the nineties, his prestige, as one of the founders of the party, made his policy unassailable before his death in 1900.

In the period that followed the staff of *Vorwärts,* now numbering ten or more, maintained the policy of editorial independence and openness to all party views. But the chief influence on the paper was exercised by two academically educated men who joined the staff in the late nineties, Georg Gradnauer and Kurt Eisner. The dissatisfaction of Bebel, Kautsky, and Mehring was directed mainly at them.

Gradnauer had studied philosophy and history at the universities of Geneva, Berlin, Marburg, and Halle before joining the party in 1890.[88] In the same year he became an editor of the party paper in Dresden and, in 1896, moved to *Vorwärts.* Two years later he was elected to the Reichstag as one of the party's representatives from Saxony. He continued to be the main commentator on foreign affairs in *Vorwärts.*

Eisner joined the staff in 1898, replacing Adolf Braun who, as an alien, had been ordered out of Prussia by the authorities. Born into a prosperous Jewish family in 1867, Eisner had studied philosophy and literature at the University of Berlin and then had worked as a journalist.[89] He did not join the Social Democrats until 1898, but his writings during the nineties, which included a study of Nietzsche, expressed socialist convictions. His parody of Emperor William II, written in 1897, brought a nine-month prison sentence. Although he accepted the central Marxist doctrines he had been deeply influenced, while working for a paper in Marburg, by the Neo-Kantianism of Cohen. Like a number of young socialist intellectuals in the late nineties, he viewed the ideas of Kant and Marx as complementary. In contrast to the other Neo-Kantian Social Democrats, however, he was critical of Bernstein's views. As a member of the *Vorwärts* staff he soon became the leading figure; even before Liebknecht's death, Eisner was, in effect, the editor-in-chief.

Bebel had viewed Eisner's appointment with misgivings; the young editor's lack of theoretical knowledge and his unfamiliarity with the party's history made it unlikely that he would counter the opportunistic tendencies which worried the party leader.[90] But initially Eisner looked to Kautsky for guidance and saw *Vorwärts* and the *Neue Zeit* playing complementary roles in the party.[91] The latter addressed theoretical issues; the former dealt with day-to-day events. Still, Eisner and Gradnauer were determined to follow an independent course. A plan floated by Bebel—to add Luxemburg to the staff in 1899—was called off when it became clear that it would mean the resignation of the two editors.[92]

Kautsky shared Bebel's doubts about Eisner.[93] His confidence in the

Vorwärts staff was no doubt shaken when, at the Lübeck party conference in 1901, Gradnauer joined the critics of the *Neue Zeit.* At the same conference Bebel scolded the editors of *Vorwärts* for failing to take a strong stand against the Revisionists.[94]

Not until the summer of 1903 did the policies of *Vorwärts* come under serious fire. Attempts by the editors to play down the importance of the contributor and vice-presidency issues angered Bebel and Mehring. "How little has *Vorwärts* been fulfilling the . . . functions of a central party organ," Mehring wrote.[95] Instead of clarifying problems on the basis of first principles, it was "hushing them up." A few weeks before the conference Eisner antagonized Bebel when he refused to publish his reply to charges by Heine that the party leader was spending too much of his time at his villa in Switzerland. Claiming that his freedom of speech had been denied, Bebel told the editor that he would "demand satisfaction at Dresden."[96]

Bebel carried out his threat. After criticizing the way in which *Vorwärts* had dealt with Bernhard's article, Bebel lamented Eisner's ignorance of the party's history and policies.[97] Although he praised Eisner for his intellectual brilliance and his value as a political commentator, Bebel remarked that the editor occasionally wrote things which caused veterans in the party to hold their heads in dismay. He again suggested that *Vorwärts* was soft on revisionism.

Eisner was so upset by Bebel's comments that he decided to resign, only to be dissuaded by Adler.[98] He and Gradnauer continued, moreover, their independent course, criticizing the party leaders for their handling of the issues at Dresden and their failure to give priority to practical political questions. The attempt to maintain editorial independence soon made them targets of renewed attacks. In *Vindication,* Mehring singled out Eisner and Gradnauer for special attention.[99] The central party organ, he declared, had withdrawn from its main task—the dissemination of revolutionary ideas to the rank and file. His own exchanges with Eisner, Mehring wrote, had always ended with the sense that the two spoke different languages. In response, Eisner and Gradnauer recalled Mehring's inability to work with Liebknecht and suggested that his appeal to principle often expressed purely personal motives and a "guilt-laden past."[100]

The *Vorwärts* controversy was complicated by the desire of Social Democrats in Berlin, who lacked a local organ, to gain control of the paper.[101] Their special stake in *Vorwärts* had been recognized by the appointment to its staff of two figures of radical bent—Heinrich Ströbel and Heinrich Cunow. Ströbel had become a speaker for the party in 1889 after studying literature, history, and national economy.[102] He then served on party papers in Kassel and Kiel and wrote on cultural matters for the *Neue Zeit* before accepting a position at *Vorwärts* in 1900. Cunow was one of the few self-educated workers who had mastered Marxist theory sufficiently to make significant contributions to the party's literature.[103] By 1904, however, there was growing tension between Ströbel and Cunow on the one hand and Eisner and Gradnauer on the other. An article by Ströbel a few days after the Dresden conference suggested that *Vorwärts* was speaking with two distinct voices.[104]

For a year or more the conflicts involving *Vorwärts* were kept under control. But in December 1904 Mehring initiated a new and, as it turned out, decisive stage in the criticism of its chief editors. He again accused them of vacillation in matters of principle and a failure to provide readers with "the background . . . for a scientific understanding of political developments."[105] Mehring's new attack backfired. The "extremely hateful personal nature" of his remarks brought a reprimand from the party executive.[106] Even Bebel was indignant over Mehring's "loutish and mean attack."[107] It was, he wrote Adler, the "last straw." Mehring was "done for" if he continued such behavior.

A few months later, however, Bebel concluded that the conflicts among the editors of *Vorwärts* had become unbearable. He considered a move to alter the balance on the staff by adding two more members who had the support of the Berlin Social Democrats. A meeting early in June 1905 between the Executive and the local Press Commission, which was responsible for overseeing the paper, failed to resolve the problem. A few days later Kautsky attacked Eisner in what proved to be the opening salvo in an increasingly bitter debate about the nature of the party's ideology.[108] The debate also indicated that the drive to achieve ideological conformity extended to the philosophical basis of Marxism.

Kautsky was angered by Eisner's hostile review of an examination of the general strike by a Dutch socialist, Henriette Roland-Holst.[109] For her, as for a growing number of Social Democrats during 1905, the value of the strike had been demonstrated by its effectiveness in extracting reforms from the Russian authorities earlier in the year. Kautsky, who wrote the foreword to the Roland-Holst volume, welcomed it as a means of stimulating discussion of tactics within the party.[110] Eisner disagreed. He conceded that the general strike might serve as a means of protecting the political rights of the workers, but he warned that it might also be used to discredit the party's parliamentary activity. It could lead to "hopeless confusion" over the question of tactics.[111]

Kautsky seized on his differences with Eisner over tactics to shift the dispute to questions of the philosophical grounding of Marxism and the nature of its scientific method. Having contrasted the indifference of *Vorwärts* with the lively discussion of the general strike under way in the Social Democratic press generally, he expressed doubt about the ability of Eisner to deal with "internal party questions."[112] Eisner, in turn, complained that Kautsky had made no attempt to "represent our position objectively"; he was resorting to "disparagement and denunciation."[113] How could they carry on a fruitful discussion, Eisner asked, if Kautsky failed to recognize the "duty of comradeship"?

What followed was a series of exchanges between the two editors which lasted over the next two months and degenerated at times into name calling.[114] But the debate laid bare fundamental theoretical and philosophical differences between the two men. It was also a new encounter between orthodox Marxism and Neo-Kantian socialism.

Kautsky contended that *Vorwärts* had ceased to interpret daily events by means of the materialistic conception of history and the "economic modes of thought" characteristic of the paper during the nineties.[115] *Vorwärts* no longer provided insight into the "underlying connections and the whole social process." Rather, he argued, the paper had adopted an "ethical-aesthetic point of view." By aiming at "moralistic and aesthetic effects"—the indignation and abhorrence of readers toward existing social conditions—the writers in *Vorwärts* tended to dwell on the "superficial, the striking, and the sensational." Their "feeling socialism" meant, according to Kautsky, an indifference to theory. In view of the "increasing influence of uneducated elements within the party" and the emphasis on practical tasks, *Vorwärts* needed to stress the theoretical education of the workers more than ever.

Eisner denied that the economic and ethical points of view were opposed; they "inevitably go together."[116] He argued that Kautsky had become wedded to the mere "letter of the great teacher." Like "all epigoni," he had lost the spirit of the master. If Marx were alive, Eisner added, "he would struggle enthusiastically for an economic-ethical view." Not only had orthodox Marxists failed to grasp the nature of "revolutionary idealism," but they did not realize that the "kindling of enthusiasm" was the most important educational task facing the party.[117]

Kautsky concluded that nothing could "bridge their difference," that he and Eisner spoke "different languages," and meant "different things with the same words."[118] The "ethicists" on the staff of *Vorwärts,* he claimed, were the "epigoni of Heine, David," and other Revisionists. But Eisner could only view many of Kautsky's statements as "oracular." The exchanges convinced him that the party's leading theorist had "lost the capacity to conduct a useful, factual, and fruitful debate."[119]

Local Social Democratic papers joined the debate. Several editors attacked Kautsky, but a larger number were critical of *Vorwärts*. Mehring provided strong support for the *Neue Zeit*. As chief editor of the *Leipziger Volkszeitung,* he devoted a series of articles to the "*Vorwärts* Question." No party paper, Mehring asserted, could be "edited according to the old principles" without "colliding with the central organ."[120] The present dispute, he maintained, could only be resolved by giving *Vorwärts* back "to the Berlin comrades."

Kautsky called on the party leaders to settle the dispute. The "deep opposition" between *Vorwärts* and the *Neue Zeit* was creating serious damage.[121] It was necessary "to decide for the materialistic or the ethical method." At the same time he reaffirmed the mission of the *Neue Zeit;* it was not "an organ of propaganda for the masses," but it sought to stimulate and inform "those who speak to the masses—our editors, representatives, local leaders, and agitators."

Kautsky's campaign against *Vorwärts* was criticized by Adler.[122] Was it really necessary, Adler asked, to discredit the paper and "put down its editor as an idiot"? But Kautsky justified his polemic by contrasting it with his failure to speak out early against Bernstein.[123] Had he not delayed at that time, he told Adler, he would have saved the party a great deal of unpleasantness. "You see my attack on *Vorwärts* as a breach of solidarity. . . . I do not do it with a light heart. . . . But if the most important party organ is at the mercy of a band of ignoramuses and intriguers . . . and all reform efforts fail . . . then nothing remains but to go public. . . . The present staff is cancerous . . . so nothing remains but to discredit it."

Although Bebel also felt that Kautsky had gone too far, he recognized that the *Vorwärts* problem had become intolerable.[124] Disagreements within the staff had grown sharper after Ströbel suggested that Eisner had gone over to the Revisionists. The Berlin Social Democrats meanwhile continued to demand control of the paper. Eisner and Gradnauer, however, stuck to their independent course and renewed their criticism of the party leaders for the failure to address the tactical implications of their own electoral victory. Determined to keep *Vorwärts* as a general party paper, Bebel attempted to solve the crisis.

Early in September the Executive, the Berlin Press Commission, and members of the *Vorwärts* staff met to discuss their differences. The meeting was acrimonious. At one point Eisner and Strobel nearly came to blows.[125] There was no resolution, and the problem was passed on to the party conference, held a few weeks later in Jena. There the delegates received a series of resolutions directed either against *Vorwärts* or against the *Neue Zeit* and the *Leipziger Volkszeitung.*

During the Jena conference a fifteen-man committee, appointed to consider the problem, rejected the claim that the party faced a mere "literary quarrel" and reported that a "serious dispute over principle" was involved which required "public discussion."[126] The subsequent debate veered away from the issues which divided Eisner and Kautsky and centered instead on a proposal from the Berlin Social Democrats that they be given control of *Vorwärts.* Although Bebel persuaded the delegates to reject the proposal, he acknowledged the justice of the complaints coming from Berlin and promised that the "present intolerable situation" would be remedied.[127]

Shortly after the conference, at a secret meeting of the Executive and the Press Commission, those attending decided to alter the balance on the staff by replacing two of its members with individuals whose views were in closer harmony with the Executive and the Berlin Social Democrats.[128] Having learned of the plan, Eisner, Gradnauer, and four other members of the staff announced that they would cease to work for *Vorwärts* on April first of the following year. A few days later the Executive responded by firing the six editors outright and reconstituting the staff.

The abrupt dismissal of the editors was a bombshell. The reaction in the party press nearly matched the uproar that had followed the Dresden conference. Much of the criticism was directed against the Executive for its secret proceedings and its refusal to give the discharged editors an opportunity to state their case. Some Social Democrats likened the dismissals to the conduct of the capitalists.[129] Many of the harshest criticisms came from trade union leaders, who were especially sensitive to arbitrary acts by employers. The Executive had also refused, moreover, to consider an offer of mediation by the Association of Labor Editors, formed a few years earlier by Social Democratic journalists to protect their interests in the party.[130]

In his attempt to appease the Berlin Social Democrats and, at the same time, bring the policies of *Vorwärts* into closer conformity with the views of the party leaders, Bebel had joined Kautsky and Mehring in claiming that the paper had been taken over by Revisionists. But this claim, which Kautsky based on Eisner's Neo-Kantian deviations, had little substance for Bebel.[131] Hence Eisner's protest to the party leader: "I would confess to being a Revisionist if I cherished such views . . . but you know very well, Comrade Bebel, that I have always gone along with you, and where I have diverged with respect to tactics, my place has generally been to the left of yours. I have nothing to do with the Revisionist group."[132] When Bebel also charged that Eisner was associated with the intellectuals who, as he put it, gathered at the Café des Westens in order to conspire with bourgeois journalists, he drew an angry letter from Bloch.[133] A leader of the cooperatives, Elm, caught the irony of the situation when he suggested that the Revisionists could take pleasure in seeing Eisner, "the ablest writer of the Radicals, being put on the shelf."[134]

Bebel did move to strengthen the radical bent of *Vorwärts.* Using Kautsky as a go-between, he invited Luxemburg to join the staff and contribute at least two articles each week.[135] Assured that she would not be subject to editorial restraints, she eagerly accepted the proposal; it promised to make her once more, as she wrote a friend, the "leading spirit of the left" by giving her an "influential political position directly in the center of the party." Ströbel and Cunow, she declared, were rubbing their hands at the prospect of giving the paper a truly radical voice. Her enthusiasm was short-lived. After the staff was reconstituted in November she found herself limited to writing on developments in Russia. By early December she had become disillusioned. The staff, she reported, consisted of "oxen," none of whom was capable of answering effectively the criticisms which Eisner and others were now directing against *Vorwärts* in the party press.[136] Later in the month she left for Poland to take part in the upsurge of revolutionary action there.

The dismissal of the six editors evoked strong opposition from most Social Democratic editors.[137] While no one, including the discharged editors, denied the right of the Executive or the Press Commission to hire and fire, the case raised serious questions about the independence and the integrity of party journalists. The ensuing controversy was fueled by the publication in late November of the *Vorwärts Konflikt,* a collection of documents—letters and statements—compiled by the six editors and designed to expose the "secret courts, dark intrigue, blind caprice, and demagoguery" to which they had fallen victim.[138] "We feel," they declared in the preface, "like the proletariat" in the face of the bourgeoisie. The "whole inner health" of the party was at stake.

The discharged editors claimed that the Executive had "conjured up" the "revisionist danger" in order to put a "pair of intellectuals" in their place.[139] There was no attempt to show that "we had anything to do with revisionism." Revisionist intellectuals, however, were quick to take up the cause of the editors. Braun moved back into the battle. He had resumed publication of the *Neue Gesellschaft* in the spring of 1905. Initially he had avoided issues which might lead to a clash with party leaders, but the *Vorwärts* conflict convinced him that he should resume his criticism of the Executive. Bebel, he wrote Vollmar, "is a megalomaniac."[140] It was of the "highest importance" that they put a stop to the authoritarianism of the Social Democratic leaders. "How can we wave the flag of democracy," a writer in the *Neue Gesellschaft* asked, "when we use the same weapons as monarchical absolutism" and members of the party are "accused of heresy" for "any difference of belief"?[141] Heine denounced the changes at *Vorwärts* as a "triumph of the Leipzig clique" with its constant cry for "theoretical deepening."[142]

Braun also published Eisner's article of self-defense after it had been rejected by the *Neue Zeit*'s editor.[143] The six editors, Eisner wrote, had given up their positions because it was their duty not to condone "the degradation of intellectual work." While he again denied that he was a Revisionist, Eisner contrasted his views with those intellectuals in the party who "cultivated a kind of empty hurrah Marxism in which . . . no breath of the spirit of Marxism" was present. By robbing its writers of their self-confidence, the Executive had damaged a party which was already "defective in talent and experts."

To one revisionist intellectual, Georg Zepler, the *Vorwärts* affair offered another example of the "distrust which for years has been directed against the academics."[144] He maintained that the "laughable distinction" which Kautsky had made between the "historic-economic" and the "ethical-aesthetic" meant nothing to the party rank and file. Zepler charged that the "free intellectual development" of the party's journalists was being thwarted by "radical dogmatism" and "personal rancor." Calwer took a somewhat different view, conceding that the party could, out of its need for discipline, require its journalists to "subordinate . . . their personal convictions."[145] But given their fundamental agreement about tactics, Social Democrats need not fear, according to Calwer, that "complete freedom of opinion was damaging the party."

To Bebel and Kautsky the damage was obvious. The journalists, Bebel contended, were seeking to take over the party.[146] Kautsky charged that they were attempting to free themselves from party control.[147] He renewed his warning against intellectuals. "There is nothing in the world more individualistic than the products of the mind"; the natural inclination of the brain worker was toward anarchism, the rejection of "discipline and organization." The party demanded that a Social Democratic journalist "surrender one's personality to the requirements of a great organism."

The clash with Eisner also demonstrated, according to Kautsky, the multiple forms of revisionism. Along with the theoretical and political or practical variants which, he believed, were bankrupt, he had identified a third form—the political neutralism of the trade unionists. But now Kautsky also saw a fourth type of revisionism: "the unexpressed, consisting of comrades who do not intend to transform the proletarian movement and give it new direction, but who do not feel comfortable in the party as it is, who cannot get into proletarian feelings and thoughts or be narrowed by proletarian discipline. And so they seek to enlarge the freedom of opinion."[148] Kautsky also claimed that the Revisionists, whatever the form, were "a general staff without an army." They were recruited "almost exclusively out of the intellectuals, be they academics or autodidacts." Because of their special needs as intellectuals or their class background this element could not triumph, but it would not die out either. It needed to be constantly "disciplined by the proletariat."

Eisner and Gradnauer had been disciplined. But the end of their work at *Vorwärts* did not mean separation from the Social Democrats. Indeed, one sign of the decentralized nature of the party—the relative autonomy of local branches or regions—was the readiness of other Social Democratic papers to hire the men who had been discharged. Gradnauer continued to serve in the Reichstag and returned to his earlier paper in Dresden, where he became its chief editor. Eisner, after engaging in freelance journalism in Berlin for a year, became chief editor of the *Fränkischer Tagespost* in Nuremberg. There he continued an independent course, not easily identified with the Revisionists or the orthodox Marxists.

In the period after Dresden the orthodox Marxists had strengthened the hold of their views on the party. With the Akademikerproblem apparently resolved, Kautsky and his supporters could concentrate once more on their essential task—the inculcation of a Marxist understanding and a revolutionary will into the party's rank and file. But the turmoil of these years had raised new doubts about the capacity of the Social Democrats to transform the consciousness of the workers. It had become evident that the party's "inner development," as Mehring put it, had "failed to keep up with its outer growth."[149] For a number of the intellectuals the effort to renew the revolutionary drive and instruct the rank and file in Marxist ideas now became the most pressing task facing the party.

9

The Making of a Socialist Mentality

How did the proletariat advance from a simple awareness of class ties to a genuinely socialist mentality? In the period after Dresden, this question again became urgent for Marxist intellectuals. Their responses recalled the ambivalence in early Marxism. Marx had wavered between the belief that the struggle of the workers themselves was the main source of a new socialist consciousness and the conviction that they could only gain the knowledge they needed from bourgeois intellectuals. Only after the failure of the revolution of 1848 had Marx fixed on the decisive role of the intellectuals. But Engels' later tendency to emphasize the inner development of the proletariat indicated that the ambivalence remained. Even Kautsky, despite his insistence on the indispensable function of intellectuals, declared in 1904 that the proletariat "would be forced by the logic of facts" to develop socialist institutions.[1]

During 1904 and 1905 several of the Social Democratic party's intellectuals, disenchanted with the results of parliamentary politics, began to see in the spontaneous development of the workers a more promising source of socialist consciousness. Convinced that the party's preoccupation with elections was eroding its revolutionary spirit, these intellectuals turned to the general strike as an alternative tactic. The new approach to the problem of consciousness found its most forceful champion in Luxemburg, who now developed the radical implications of her earlier revision of Marxism.

A second group of intellectuals still held, like Kautsky, that it was the responsibility of the educated recruits to bring a socialist understanding to the workers. But in the early years of the century these orthodox Marxists were becoming aware that their ideas had not penetrated very far into the working class. "Scarcely ten percent of the workers," one Social Democrat declared in 1906, possessed some "knowledge of the Marxist way of reasoning."[2] There was, he added, a widespread distrust of intellectuals and an "absolute skepticism toward theory." The educational campaign which orthodox Marxists undertook in these years was a new attempt to instruct the party rank and file in the Marxist ideas. It was largely the work of Social Democrats who had been trained as public schoolteachers.

The Problem of "Enthusiasm": Raphael Friedeberg, Robert Michels, and Luxemburg

Intellectuals who looked to the immediate struggles of the workers as the primary source of a socialist consciousness were less concerned with theory in any formal sense than with the need to cultivate new qualities of will and spirit. German Marxists had, in fact, frequently acknowledged the role of "enthusiasm" in the growth of a socialist mentality. The Jungen intellectuals cited the words of Saint-Simon to a disciple: "Remember my son, that a man must be filled with enthusiasm to accomplish great things."[3] Kautsky, despite his resolute rationalism, declared in the early nineties that "revolutionary enthusiasm" was the "great lever of our success."[4] But the failure of orthodox Marxists to recognize the importance of moral, religious, and aesthetic feelings had troubled a number of the younger intellectuals. The question arose again during the debate between Kautsky and Eisner in the summer of 1905. Eisner claimed that the "kindling of enthusiasm" had become the "most important educational problem facing the party."[5] Alongside their efforts to alter the system of production, Social Democrats needed to consider "the structure of human motivation."

In his reply to Eisner Kautsky assured his readers that "sufficient enthusiasm" would "stream out of the class struggle."[6] The "new insights, the glorious view of the future, the elevating goals," he maintained, would generate the necessary motivation. "Nothing more is required." Forms of enthusiasm which were not "called forth by material circumstances and study" were momentary and shallow.[7]

Kautsky soon decided, however, that the problem required closer examination. His small book *Ethics and the Materialistic Conception of History* was a direct outgrowth of his exchanges with Eisner. Written "in a fever" during October and November of 1905,[8] the work explained the idealistic drives within the proletariat in terms of the Darwinian conceptions which had been influential in Kautsky's earlier development. The ability of the workers to transcend the narrow pursuit of material interests could be traced to "social instincts," to biological drives which in human beings, as in other animals, served the well-being of the species. The proletariat was, by virtue of its place in the productive process and the class struggle, the main bearer of the "social instincts" in modern history. It alone was capable of overcoming the egoistic, acquisitive, and competitive values nurtured by capitalism. For Kautsky, then, the will to achieve socialism was a natural outcome of biological evolution.

His answer was not, for a number of the intellectuals, satisfactory. For Raphael Friedeberg, the materialistic conception of history itself had become an obstacle to the growth of a revolutionary spirit. Friedeberg was a medical doctor who had served for a time as publisher of the *Sozialistische Monatshefte* and had represented the party on one of the municipal bodies in Berlin. Having become disillusioned with politics, he called on the delegates at the Dresden conference to endorse the general strike as a way of bringing the "class struggle movement onto fresh ground."[9] In a talk in August 1904, distributed as a pamphlet, *Parliamentarianism and the General Strike,* he argued that the appeal to voters had led to a "flattening out of the revolutionary movement."[10] Socialism had ceased to be a "great, all-encompassing cultural movement" and had been reduced to a "purely economic, even a pure stomach question." Friedeberg placed most of the blame for this outcome on Marx's claim that "social being determines consciousness." This statement had meant indifference to the "inner life of the proletariat." The general strike would renew the workers' sense that they were engaged in an "ethical battle" and a larger social mission.

To combat the "historical dogmatism" of orthodox Marxism Friedeberg formed a Free Association of German Trade Unions.[11] Its program, which he labeled "anarcho-socialism," was twofold—psychical and economic. Through the renewed struggle against traditional religion and the reaffirmation of a proletarian world view, the new program would aim at the "psychological transformation of man." The general strike would unite "historical psychism" with an economic strategy and guide the workers back onto the revolutionary path.

Friedeberg had, as Kampffmeyer was quick to point out, reasserted central features of the Jungen rebellion—the claim that parliamentarianism was corrupting the movement, the belief that the trade unions represented a more effective vehicle for the revolutionary spirit, and the commitment to a socialist world view.[12] For Kampffmeyer, however, the protests of the "anarcho-socialists" demonstrated once more the deficiencies of "theoretical schooling" within the party. He noted that Friedeberg's followers were drawn from those who were "most carefully drilled" in Marxist ideas. Their leaders had "devoured whole tubs of socialist theory"; they were "models of clear revolutionary thought and feeling." In following Friedeberg they had shown the tendency for Marxists to lose "touch with reality."

For one of the ablest of the educated recruits in these years, Robert Michels, however, Friedeberg had displayed "a rare clairvoyance and courage."[13] Michels welcomed anarcho-socialism as a way out of the "disastrous sterility" which had followed the party's electoral victory in 1903. The reliance on parliamentarianism had meant a loss of "will and energy": "Parliamentarianism kills socialism in its most profound aspects. Men of heart and thought within our ranks see with sadness the disappearance of the idealistic side of our system of ideas. Formerly socialism was a faith, a sentiment, which seized the whole man and determined all the acts of his life." Michels, like Friedeberg, charged that the party was "no longer occupied with creating socialist personalities."

In his efforts to renew the Marxist goal of transformed personalities, Michels was influenced by the French syndicalists—Georges Sorel, Hubert Lagardelle, and Edouard Berth.[14] But he did not share their hostility to intellectuals. Class action alone, the "brutal egoism" of a "blind proletariat," would not, according to Michels, generate the necessary "willpower and energy."[15] The movement could not advance without "a troop of intellectuals to serve it as guides." Their present role, however, was to correct an "ill-understood historical materialism" and show the workers that "the economic factor was powerless without the coefficient of a moral pedagogy."

For a time Michels joined Friedeberg in the attempt to push the tactic of the general strike within the German party. By 1907, however, he had concluded that the party's "hegemony in international socialism" had ended.[16] The behavior of the German Social Democrats at international meetings had become "equivocal, its resolutions negative or ambiguous, its actions erratic or inconsequential." Only a "pseudo-radicalism" veiled its stagnant condition.

The party had, according to Michels, abandoned the task of educating the workers in favor of an attempt to "pour its members as parts into a complicated machinery."[17] This was the reason, he observed later, why so many of the educated converts like himself had given up on the party. Bebel, through his dogged devotion to parliamentarianism and party unity at all costs, was largely responsible.[18] It was never clear to the leader "how great a part of the blame" he bore for the defections of so many of the "young intellectuals coming out of academic circles."

Revisionist intellectuals were not oblivious to the problem of enthusiasm. At times they worried about the loss of emotional intensity resulting from a more peaceful and "reasonable" approach to socialism. To be "impelled more by reason and understanding than by heart and feeling" might lead to "lukewarmness."[19] But the solution to the "present crisis of Marxism," as one of their spokesmen put it, lay in a renewal of ethical idealism. The "day of ethics," he declared, "has come for socialism."[20]

But the hope, expressed for a time by Friedeberg and Michels, that new enthusiasm and energy might be found in the immediate struggles of the proletariat was being rekindled by Luxemburg. She, too, had by 1904 concluded that the party was stagnating. She blamed Kautsky for drawing back into the "safe domestic fold of old principles" and "failing to address the burning need—to increase the revolutionary aspect of the movement."[21] Impressed by the recent use of the general strike in Belgium and Holland, and then elated by its seeming success in Russia early in 1905, she saw in the strike a way of releasing dormant energies in the masses. The general strike represented a solution to the flagging spirit in the German party. During the spring and summer of 1905 she campaigned, by means of articles in the party press and talks to local branches, on behalf of the new tactic.

At the Jena conference in the fall the delegates endorsed the proposal that the general strike be viewed as an important weapon in the party's armory. Bebel and the other leaders still saw it as a defensive weapon, a means of resisting efforts by the government to curtail political rights. But Luxemburg regarded the vote of the delegates as evidence of a new revolutionary will. She was convinced that the "whole party conference" was on her side.[22] Her optimism was reinforced by the outcome of the *Vorwärts* dispute, for her new place on the party's central organ seemed to indicate a shift of Social Democratic policy to the left. The Revisionists—Heine, David, and others—"could only grind their teeth" over their impotence.[23] By December, however, she was frustrated; her efforts to give a more radical impulse to the paper had failed. Late in the month she left Berlin, determined to take part in the surge of revolutionary activity in Poland and Russia.

The next six months were crucial in Luxemburg's development. Immersed in the work of agitation and organization, then imprisoned for three months, she emerged from the experience with a new view of the revolutionary process. Letters to friends back in Germany early in the summer of 1906 expressed her sense of discovery. "Here, the time in which one lives, is glorious."[24] Poland had revealed a "fruitful, pregnant time, which gives birth hourly and out of each birth becomes pregnant again." She "trembled with anticipation" over the prospect of describing to the German comrades "the tremendous events" she had experienced. Luxemburg had found an answer to the problem of enthusiasm and clarified her view of the way in which a new socialist mentality would arise within the working class.

In July 1906 Luxemburg withdrew to Finland, where, in daily contact with Bolshevik leaders, including Lenin, she interpreted the experiences of the previous months. The outcome was a pamphlet, comissioned by Social Democrats in Hamburg, in which she discussed the nature of the mass strike and its implications for the German party.[25] The pamphlet was also aimed at the delegates to the coming Social Democratic conference at Mannheim, where Luxemburg planned to resume her work for the party.

Luxemburg denied that the mass strike entailed any change in Marxist theory; it was not even a new tactic. It simply expressed the economic and social forces disclosed by Marx: "The mass strike is merely the form of the revolutionary struggle . . . the living pulse beat of the revolution, and at the same time its most powerful driving wheel. . . . [It] is not a crafty method discovered by subtle reasoning for the purpose of making the revolutionary struggle more effective *but the method* of motion of the proletarian mass."[26] The mass strike was a "natural historical phenomenon," a product of the social frictions created by economic development. A spontaneous expression of class feeling, the mass strike acted back on the workers like an "electric shock." Its "most precious, because lasting" effect, was a "mental sediment, the invincible guarantee of further irresistible progress."[27]

Revolutionary energy, or enthusiasm, was beyond the control of party leaders. Their task was to remain in the "closest possible contact with the mood of the mass."[28] Nor could the theorist or the "scientific investigator" influence the character of the movement's "revolutionary energy." "Logical dissections" or "lifeless theoretical plans" were likely to be damaging.[29] "In the advent of the revolutionary mass strike," she maintained, "history has found the solution" to the political struggle.[30] The economic and social process was generating a "mass idealism" among the workers which would set aside all considerations of material well-being and even "life itself."

Luxemburg was moving, on the basis of her experience in Poland, toward a concept of a dialectical relationship between Marxist theory and the practical struggle. Between her dogmatic attachment to economic determinism and her revolutionary activism, however, there remained a crucial gap. She did not clarify the process through which the new socialist consciousness developed. Despite her own role as an agitator and a teacher and her frequent references to the need to educate the workers, she did not discuss the function of the theorist. Confident that Marx had disclosed the laws of economic and social development, she expressed a mystical faith in the proletariat. Her vivid imagination covered over the difficulties, theoretical and psychological, presented by the problem of working-class consciousness. Indeed, the metaphors, biological or physical, with which she described the energies at work often took on a lyrical quality. "After every foaming wave of political action," she wrote, "a fructifying deposit remains from which a thousand stalks of economic struggle shoot forth."[31]

From her belief in irresistible historical forces Luxemburg drew two central and controversial propositions. She claimed that the unorganized workers were more important than the organized workers in the march toward socialism. Luxemburg also insisted that the Russian masses were at the forefront of the international revolutionary struggle. Both propositions followed from her conviction that the mass strikes which had taken place in Russia and Poland had universal validity. They were the natural expression of the "proletarian class struggle" at the "present stage of capitalistic development."[32]

Luxemburg's interpretation of the mass strike held, therefore, important lessons for the German Social Democrats. Although the German party contained the "most enlightened and the most class-conscious vanguard of the proletariat," any attempt to rely on the organized workers for a mass strike was "absolutely hopeless."[33] Luxemburg criticized the Social Democrats for underestimating the "political maturity . . . of the unorganized proletarian mass." A revolutionary situation would draw this "deeper-lying layer" into the struggle. Its very backwardness would make it "the most radical, the most impetuous element," in action. Without the unorganized workers a mass strike would be a "miserable fiasco."[34]

Luxemburg also argued that the German Social Democrats were inferior to the Russian proletariat. The "class instinct of the youngest, least trained, badly educated, and still worse-organized" workers in Russia gave them advantages over the other European movements.[35] The advanced character of the German party inhibited its spontaneity.

> In the case of the German workers the class consciousness implanted by the Social Democrats is *theoretical and latent;* in the period ruled by bourgeois parliamentarianism it cannot, as a rule, actively participate in a direct mass action. . . . In the revolution, when the masses themselves appear upon the political battlefield, this class consciousness becomes practical and active. A year of revolution has, therefore, given the Russian proletariat training which thirty years of parliamentary and trade union struggle cannot artificially give the German proletariat.

Only through the "actual school of experience," "by the fight and in the fight," could the German movement be revitalized.[36] "Six months of a revolutionary period" would not only complete the education of the organized workers but mobilize the unorganized workers, still unmoved by "ten years of public demonstrations and distribution of leaflets."[37] Luxemburg's goal, when she returned to Germany in September 1906, was to convince the German Social Democrats that there were revolutionary energies latent in the workers, organized and unorganized alike, which could be set into motion by means of the mass strike.

Luxemburg's task had become more difficult since her departure for

Poland. In February 1906, at a secret meeting of the Social Democratic Executive and trade union leaders, Bebel and his colleagues had retreated from their endorsement of the general strike.[38] They were responding to pressure from trade union leaders who were determined to control the policies of their own organizations and to exercise an influence within the party commensurate with their growing strength. When news of the secret pact became public, Luxemburg, along with Kautsky, began to attack the trade unions. It had become clear that the unions were obstacles to any renewal of the party's revolutionary will.

At the Mannheim party conference in the fall Luxemburg failed to persuade the delegates of the significance of the mass strike. The conference ratified the new understanding with the trade unions. Some weeks later Luxemburg shared her feeling of frustration with Zetkin: "I am conscious as never before of the timidity and pettiness of our party. . . . The situation is simply this—August and all the others have given themselves over completely to parliamentarianism. They deny completely any turn that goes beyond [its] limits."[39] She was still convinced that the party's rank and file was "inwardly finished with parliamentarianism" and would "greet with jubilation" any fresh approach to revolutionary practice. But she conceded that it might take years to overcome the "general stagnation."

Although the delegates at Mannheim turned deaf ears to the claim that the key to revolutionary enthusiasm lay in the mass strike, they welcomed a set of proposals designed to revitalize the party's educational mission. What followed was a new concerted effort to instruct the rank and file in Marxist ideas.

Renewal through Education: Otto Rühle and Heinrich Schulz

During the nineties the task of instilling Marxist ideas into the party's rank and file had been assigned mainly to the Social Democratic press—its newspapers, pamphlets, electoral leaflets, and other publications. There was a "relative stagnation of the oral agitation" which had been a vital part of the propaganda activity.[40] Bebel's confidence in the power of the written word, heightened by the remarkable success of his own popularization of Marxism, *Women under Socialism,* amounted to a "publicity euphoria." He and the other party leaders assumed that the revolutionary energy needed to drive the movement forward would be generated by disseminating knowledge of socialism through the printed word.

That confidence had weakened by the turn of the century. Signs that the Social Democrats were failing in their educational mission were numerous. Two of the party's most widely circulated papers, the *Neue*

Welt and *Gleichheit,* had begun to deemphasize that mission in order to appeal to wider readerships. After Steiger's abortive effort to alter the aesthetic tastes of the party's members, his editorial successors were less inclined to challenge conventional or popular expectations. Zetkin, too, was turning away from her initial goal—educating a cadre in Marxist theory—to appeal to the unconverted and to address the special interests of women. Both papers were undergoing a process of "depoliticization"; ideological considerations were giving way to entertainment, practical questions, and matters of broader interest.[41]

The limited reach of the *Neue Zeit,* intended by Kautsky to be the primary instrument for Marxist enlightenment, was another sign of the educational failure. So, too, from the orthodox Marxist point of view, was the growing circulation and influence of the *Sozialistische Monatshefte.* Few of the local Social Democratic newspapers, moreover, gained the percentage of readers among the party's members necessary for them to play their appointed role.[42] The widespread sense that the press was not doing its job, a feeling which had surfaced in the *Vorwärts* conflict, was expressed in frequent complaints about the need for a "theoretical deepening" in the rank and file.

Against this background and a growing recognition of the obstacles which the public schools presented to efforts to transform the mentality of the workers, a number of Social Democrats reconsidered the educational problem. The party had never defined a distinct approach to public education, falling back instead on the views of bourgeois reformers who hoped to secularize the schools and make more room for scientific subjects.[43] At the turn of the century several Social Democratic writers also joined middle-class critics of trashy literature aimed at the young. "We must save our children," an article in the *Neue Zeit* declared, "from the poisonous influence of capitalistic literature."[44] Greater concern for the younger generation was an important aspect of the new interest in the educational issue. The problem of the next generation took on increased significance as the party's prospect of gaining political power in the near future faded. "Whoever has youth," one Social Democrat declared, "to them belongs the future."[45] The party, he added, should "turn attention away from the showplace of the political and social struggle" and concentrate on the needs of youth.

Lacking any distinct pedagogy of their own, Social Democrats looked to educational reformers of the past or to contemporary bourgeois thinkers for progressive ideas. But the whole question was complicated by doubts about the desirability of indoctrinating the young. For one party intellectual, Julian Borchardt, it was absolutely necessary to free children from the prejudices implanted by the public schools and to bring them into "the feeling and thought world of socialism."[46] But even orthodox

Marxists, including Kautsky, disagreed. Political or "tendentious" materials should not invade the learning process. Children most needed training in character and the ability to think clearly. After all, "one who sees clearly and thinks logically will become a Social Democrat or our world view is false."[47]

The efforts of Social Democrats to reach the younger generation led to the creation of two new organizations in the fall of 1904. At the Bremen party conference in September, William Liebknecht's son, Karl, a lawyer, called on the delegates to develop a "sharper and more systematic agitation among the young."[48] He was particularly keen on countering militarism in German society. A few weeks after the conference Liebknecht helped form an "association of young workers and apprentices" in Berlin.[49] Prevented from engaging in direct political activity by Prussian laws governing associations, the new organization concentrated on economic issues. It also provided lectures and courses of instruction in socialism. A monthly paper, the *Arbeitende Jugend,* founded early in 1905, strengthened this educational work. It represented, according to its editors, a means of "awakening to new life" a spirit in the movement which was threatened by everyday work.[50]

Similar considerations lay behind the formation of a youth organization in Baden during the fall of 1904.[51] Here the leader was Ludwig Frank, a young lawyer and one of the ablest of the party's educated recruits in these years.[52] Frank was troubled, as he wrote Kautsky, by the deepening "gulf between socialist science" and the struggles of the workers.[53] Within a few years, he feared, Marxist theory would "exist not inside the working-class movement but outside the working-class movement." His new "association for young working-class men and women," he explained, would combat the tendency for Social Democrats to rely simply on economic developments, to "lay our hands in our laps" and neglect the work of education. To fulfill its aim of "initiating and grounding the young in the thought world of socialism," Frank also founded a monthly paper, the *Junge Garde.*[54] Other Social Democratic branches soon followed the examples of Berlin and Baden in forming associations designed specifically for the young.

A number of orthodox Marxists believed that the most urgent need was systematic instruction in socialist theory for the party as a whole. That need had long been recognized in those Social Democratic centers where social and cultural associations had grown up alongside the party's electoral organizations.[55] Leipzig, with a network of such associations, by the late nineties provided a model for the attempt to instruct the rank and file in Marxist ideas and to develop a socialist subculture.[56] The effort was guided to some extent by the party's most radical newspaper, the *Leipziger Volkszeitung.* Leipzig became, for some socialists, the "mecca of the new religion."[57] Much of the inspiration for the nationwide campaign to revitalize the party through a more systematic education came out of the Leipzig experience.

Five individuals were especially important in pushing the cause of education. Four were former schoolteachers who were keen on applying their pedagogical training and skills to the movement. Zetkin, the oldest of the group, had taught school in Leipzig before her conversion to Marxism. As editor of *Gleichheit* and a strong voice for orthodox Marxism, she was a leading advocate of a new educational effort.[58] The Dunckers, Kate and Hermann, had met in the party in Leipzig. Both devoted their lives to educational work for socialism. Kate had arrived in the city in 1890 to continue her training as a teacher.[59] Moved by a lecture by Zetkin in 1893, she became active in one of the party's educational associations. When, in 1896, she joined the party and placed herself "outwardly as well as inwardly on the ground of the proletariat," she was forced to resign her teaching position.[60] Two years later she married Hermann Duncker. The son of a merchant who had gone bankrupt, he had come to Leipzig to study music at the Conservatory.[61] Involvement in the socialist movement led him to change his course of study, and subsequently he completed a doctoral dissertation on the medieval village economy. During the late nineties Duncker organized Sunday classes for the study of socialism. Not only was he convinced, as a Marxist, that "economic science" was the foundation for the education of the proletariat, but he held that the workers, by virtue of their social and economic position, were able to think more freely and more clearly than other classes.[62] He saw his Sunday-morning classes as a means, much like those in the Protestant churches, of propagating a world view.[63]

The key figures in the emerging educational campaign were Otto Rühle and Heinrich Schulz. Both had given up careers as schoolteachers to work for the party. Rühle, born in 1874, the son of a railroad official, began writing for Social Democratic papers in the mid-nineties.[64] In the years ahead he lectured widely for the party in the north, placing special emphasis on the place of science in the socialist view of the world. After the turn of the century he began to examine, on the basis of his experiences within the movement, the problem of educating socialists. His article in the *Neue Zeit* in the spring of 1904 initiated a new stage in the party's concern with the problem.[65]

Rühle had been struck during his lecture tours by the difficulties which the oral and written use of the German language presented not only to the party's rank and file but to its agitators and organizers. He became convinced that a serious educational effort should begin, therefore, with basic instruction in grammar and logic. To implement this approach

Rühle proposed that those Social Democrats who were eager for self-improvement be provided with a series of twenty monthly exercises in the proper use of language.[66] The lessons would then be corrected at a central party office and returned to the student. Only by "teaching the comrades to read, write, and speak" well, according to Rühle, could they be prepared for "fruitful occupation with science." In time the new "circle of learning" within the party would create an "intellectual elite" capable of rising "to the higher levels of knowledge."

Rühle's "New Way" was promptly criticized by Schulz, the figure who proved to be the most influential and energetic in developing a new educational program for the party.[67] Schulz had also become convinced that the decline of revolutionary zeal could only be corrected through a new effort to instill Marxist ideas into the rank and file. In taking up this task he frequently cited Kautsky's warning in 1894 that the party's rapid growth had meant a relative lack of the "schooled forces" necessary for "theory-educated party members." The "need to penetrate the masses with principled clarity and unshakeable true convictions," Schulz told the delegates at Jena in 1905, was "even greater today."[68]

Schulz was well seasoned in the party's propaganda activity. Born in Bremen in 1872, he "came out of a typical petty-bourgeois family."[69] He was teaching in Hamburg in 1893 when he crossed his Rubicon and joined the Social Democrats. For a time he served a journalistic apprenticeship with Schönlank in Leipzig. Moving to Berlin in 1894, he was drawn into Liebknecht's school for workers. Schulz was largely responsible for shifting the school away from its tendency to cater to the vocational interests of its students and restoring its initial goal of "awakening proletarian class consciousness."[70] Subsequently he worked for party papers in Erfurt and Magdeburg before returning to Bremen in 1902 as chief editor of the local Social Democratic organ. Along the way Schulz was imprisoned several times, narrowly missed gaining a seat in the Reichstag, and became the main contributor to the *Neue Zeit* on educational issues. Having been given freedom to express his views on questions facing the party, he soon aligned the Bremen paper with an "intransigent Marxism" against the local forms of revisionism and reformism.[71]

Schulz rejected Rühle's plan for correspondence courses and proposed instead that the Social Democrats create a central party school to which "talented young comrades . . . can come for long or short periods."[72] There they would receive instruction in the subjects most relevant to the class struggle—economics, history, and philosophy—viewed from the standpoint of the materialistic conception of history. The school would not only send its students back to the local parties or trade unions with renewed vigor and social insight but would help the party develop another agency for educating the rank and file—a "special body of traveling lecturers," who would present "cycles of lectures" and address "the core questions of socialism" in the major centers of Social Democratic activity.

To Rühle the proposals of Schulz seemed like an attempt "to build the upper story of the house first."[73] He argued that the plan was designed to "breed ten Social Democratic supermen" while leaving "the great masses in ignorance and intellectual impotence until we have conquered political power." Rühle also argued that the trade unions, not the party, offered the best vehicle for "bringing a deeper understanding . . . to the mass of the working classes." Still, he acknowledged that he and Schulz were "simply traveling a different way to the same goal." It was Schulz, however, who charted the new educational course for the party.

Schulz, like other orthodox Marxists, held that only a party thoroughly informed by theory could carry out its mission. His dedication to this view led to a bitter dispute among the Bremen Social Democrats early in 1905. It arose over the question of participation in the Goethe League, a cultural association which reached across class lines, was pledged to political neutrality, and sponsored evening lectures, concerts, theatrical performances, and art exhibits.[74] Local party leaders had been active in the formation of the association. But late in 1904, when the Goethe League scheduled a lecture by Sombart entitled "Economics and Art," Schulz charged that the policy of neutrality had been violated. The lecture demonstrated the impossibility of cooperation between the classes: "A working together of class-conscious workers and their bourgeois enemies in order to contribute to the clarification of all the great questions of the world is a complete impossibility. Such a going together is only thinkable in the form of a battle against one another. From that I draw the conclusion: the class-conscious workers of Bremen must turn their backs on the Goethe League and develop their artistic interests by means of their own organized force."[75] Schulz's views divided the local party, but after two months of highly charged meetings his viewpoint prevailed. The debate ended with the adoption of a declaration that "the thirst for knowledge and the artistic interests of the workers could only be satisfied by their own organization and energies." What one historian has described as the "isolation and self-encapsulation" of the Bremen Social Democrats was expressed in their formation, in cooperation with the local trade unionists, of a new committee to sponsor lectures and cultural events.[76]

Having freed the educational aspirations of the local Social Democrats from the embrace of the middle class, Schulz confronted anew the dilemma which Mehring and Steiger had faced in their efforts to develop a distinctly proletarian point of view toward culture. Could one find in the development of the workers, in the party or in Marxist theory, the resources for a distinctly socialist education? Both Schulz and Rühle attempted to develop new Marxist pedagogies "oriented to the world of work."[77] Schulz pointed to the ruinous consequences of the division of labor and the ways in which the public schools under capitalism discriminated on the basis of class and sex.[78] Rühle published a series of pamphlets which dealt with the educational needs of children while stressing the significance of work.[79]

Despite their claims that socialism represented a new world view, Schulz and Rühle relied mainly on a pre-Marxist tradition of educational reformers that reached back to Johann Pestalozzi and Friedrich Froebel.[80] The ideas of these reformers—the belief in the spontaneous growth of the child, the importance of play, close contact with the natural world—became part of the developing Social Democratic views about education. But Schulz and Rühle also owed much to contemporary thinkers—to the Neo-Kantian educational theorist Paul Natorp, to the feminist Ellen Key, and to Heinrich Wolgast, a leader in the movement to provide edifying literature for the young.[81] The two Social Democrats became "trustees of a progressive pedagogical inheritance" still bound to the ideals of bourgeois humanism. In these years there was, as Norbert Schwarte has observed of Schulz, "no critical or analytical advance" in Marxist thinking about education.[82]

The turmoil following Dresden provided new opportunities to push the cause of education within the party. At the Bremen and Jena conferences Zetkin and Schulz urged the delegates to pay more attention to the need to instruct the rank and file in Marxist ideas.[83] Systematic instruction in theory, Schulz declared at Jena in 1905, would "take away the ground for the unpleasant debates of recent years."[84] Meanwhile, the challenge of the anarcho-socialists and the stimulus of the Russian Revolution made the Social Democratic leaders more receptive to the claim that a greater educational effort would serve party unity.[85] Although Zetkin and Schulz failed in their efforts to place the educational issue on the agenda of the Jena conference, the party leaders asked them to prepare a set of proposals for the annual meeting in 1906.

During the spring and summer of 1906 a lively discussion of the educational problem was under way in the party press. It was initiated by a pessimistic diagnosis of the intellectual condition of the rank and file by Alexander Kosiol, a leader in a working-class cultural association in Berlin.[86] Scarcely 10 percent of the members of the party, he declared, possessed "some knowledge of Marxist reasoning." The figure was arbitrary; there is no indication of how he arrived at it. But he voiced the sense of urgency felt by many orthodox Marxists: "The question of whether the party is going to . . . advance the socialist enlightenment of the mass or hold back from that is more important than all the theoretical problems which have created such heated feelings in recent years. The question of the deepening of the socialist spirit touches the life-nerve of the party." Kosiol blamed the party leadership for the absence of any concerted attempt to raise the workers from "class-feeling to class-consciousness." Lacking such an effort, the workers were as helpless in dealing with the writings of Marx or the flood of ideas presented by the party's lecturers as the "Australian aborigines confronted with firearms."

In the discussion in the press which followed, Schulz played a prominent role. Again he urged party leaders to create a central school in Berlin and appoint "scientifically educated traveling lecturers."[87] Several of the contributors to the discussion questioned the effectiveness of lectures and emphasized the need to carry Marxist ideas into the "workshops and families and circles of friends."[88] But most agreed that Schulz had "pointed a way out of the dilemma" and had shown how the "mass of underlying revolutionary energies" could be mobilized.[89]

By the summer of 1906 the party Executive was convinced of the need for a central school. Although the leaders were influenced by Schulz's ideas, they were moved mainly by practical considerations.[90] With the growth of the party came an increasing need to train functionaries to assume positions as editors, local party secretaries, and organizers. But the Executive accepted Schulz's conception of a school which would emphasize instruction in economics, history, and theory. In July *Vorwärts* announced plans to start such a school in November. A month later *Vorwärts* published the "six theses" dealing with educational policy which Zetkin and Schulz had prepared for the Mannheim conference in September.

At Mannheim the education issue appeared on the conference agenda for the first time. Discussion of the issue was curtailed by Zetkin's illness and by the attention given to the mass strike. But the delegates accepted the six theses as guidelines for the party's new educational effort.[91] The guidelines expressed the Marxist insistence on the centrality of economic activity and the need to reconsider the place of work in the educational process. Making work a "source of happiness and joy" would overcome the deficiencies of public education under capitalism—"the distinction between hand and head work" and discriminations based on class and sex. A socialist education would be secular, free, compulsory to the age of eighteen, and provide instruction which was both specialized and liberal. It would also strengthen the role of the parents—so important to Zetkin—in nurturing "their children in the spirit of socialism."

The fifth of the theses declared that "the proletariat" was the "bearer of a self-contained world view."[92] It was the responsibility of the party, therefore, to fill its members, especially the young, with the "basic principles of scientific socialism." To advance that goal the delegates accepted the plan for a central party school and traveling lecturers as well as a proposal that the Executive establish a central educational committee to oversee these activities. In December Schulz moved to Berlin to administer the school and serve as secretary of the newly appointed committee.

Revisionist intellectuals observed these developments with misgivings. Maurenbrecher expressed the fear that the new school might simply drill the orthodox Marxist doctrines into the students rather than encouraging independent thought.[93] His remarks led Berlin Social Democrats to veto his appointment to the staff of the school.[94] David, too, questioned the principles which underlay the new educational program. In a commentary on the Mannheim theses he criticized the claim that the proletariat was the "bearer of a self-contained world view" opposed to that of the bourgeoisie.[95] He noted the narrowness of Schulz's "experiment in Bremen," the inability of the new education committee there to provide a rich cultural program and thus to carry out its aim of an exclusive "proletarian educational movement." The party, David charged, was adopting the model of the Catholic church, determined to "protect its members against dangerous influences." It was hardly surprising, in view of the doubts of Maurenbrecher and David, that the party's educational program became a new battlefield for orthodox Marxists and revisionist intellectuals.

In mid November 1906, the party school opened in Berlin. Thirty students, selected by local parties and trade unions, arrived for six months of study. The control of the orthodox Marxists over the curriculum was apparent in the declaration that "a solid theoretical basis" provided the "indispensable foundation for any practical work in the service of the working class."[96] For instruction in historical materialism and social theory, the Executive appointed the Dutch Marxist Anton Pannekoek, a frequent contributor to the *Neue Zeit*. A young Austrian intellectual, Rudolf Hilferding, taught economic theory. There was also a class in oral and writing skills, presumably inspired by Rühle's ideas, and taught by Schulz himself.

In July 1907, after the completion of the school's first semester, the Prussian authorities banned Pannekoek and Hilferding, as aliens, from teaching at the school. They were replaced by Mehring and Luxemburg. Despite her initial doubts about the school and a learning process separated from the struggles of the workers, Luxemburg became the school's most dynamic and influential teacher.[97]

The party leaders made concessions to the Revisionists and reformists by appointing David and Vollmar to the central educational committee. Its early meetings were marked by heated arguments between the two and the orthodox Marxist members—Schulz, Zetkin, Bebel, and Mehring—over the question of whether the committee was bound by the Mannheim theses.[98] But the domination of the orthodox Marxists was evident both in the appointments to the teaching staff and in the selection of Rühle and Duncker as full-time traveling lecturers.

Between 1906 and 1910 more than two hundred students attended the school in Berlin.[99] In most cases they returned to the localities from which they came to serve as editors, party secretaries, or in other roles. Periodic reports by Schulz expressed satisfaction with the development of the school.[100] His favorable assessment was supported by testimonies from the students.[101] What "once seemed incomprehensible to me . . . Marx's *Capital* and the writings of Engels and Lassalle," one student commented, were "now quite clear."[102] Others who attended the school gave it credit for their continuing study of socialist theory and for their greater confidence as speakers. A few started their own courses in Marxism at the local level.

Meanwhile, Rühle and Duncker attempted, through their cycles of lectures which began in the fall of 1907, to develop a fuller understanding of socialism in the party rank and file. During the first eight months of their activity they presented two hundred and thirty-two lectures in twenty-nine centers of Social Democratic support.[103] Between 1907 and 1910 they reached, according to one estimate, forty thousand party members.[104] Educational committees, formed in several hundred branches of the party, assisted them in their work.

The traveling lecturers combined instruction in Marxist doctrines with the claim, expressed in talks with titles such as "The New and the Old World View," that socialism contained a total view of life. Rühle, in particular, attempted to engage the minds of those who attended.[105] He did not allow his listeners to take notes, urging them to restate the main points of the lecture at home afterward. His pedagogy encouraged a critical spirit; he began with immediate facts or experiences and worked up to the "more difficult scientific" conceptions.

Still, the educational campaign fell far short of the goals of those who promoted it. Despite the zeal of the traveling lecturers, they could reach only a small percentage of a party membership approaching one million by 1912. The limitations of the educational effort were most evident in the development of the party school. The cause was partly quantitative. To provide formal instruction to a few hundred of the party activists was, as Rühle observed, like "a drop on a hot stove."[106] Although the benefit to these individuals was clear, there was little indication that the school made a significant impact on the life of the party.[107]

One measure of the limited reach of the Berlin school was its failure to attract the trade unionists, whose influence was growing steadily in these years. Few of the ten or twelve spaces initially reserved for trade union nominees each year were filled.[108] Trade union leaders showed little interest in the kind of education favored by the orthodox Marxists.[109] Even before the central school had opened, the trade union leaders formed their own school—oriented toward the practical problems faced by their functionaries. That the staff, which included Schippel, Calwer, Katzenstein, and Bernstein, was selected from "the ranks of the Revisionists" seemed to Joseph Bloch an encouraging "sign of the times."[110]

Luxemburg maintained that the divergence between the two schools could only be temporary.[111] They were, after all, simply "two branches of the modern working-class movement," two expressions of the development forecast in Marx's "scientific socialism." In time, she predicted, the trade union leaders would recognize that those whom they called "dogmatists and doctrinaires" were "much more practical" than the so-called Praktiker. But the divergence between the two schools reflected a growing divorce between the practical and the ideological drives within the movement. It also indicated, ironically, the idealistic turn of those orthodox Marxists who emphasized the need for education in theory.[112]

The policies of the Social Democratic leaders reinforced the idealistic tendency of the school—its emphasis on theory. The Executive directed the teaching staff to avoid discussions of the practical issues facing the party.[113] The injunction, which seems to have applied to the traveling lecturers as well, reflected the concern of the leaders for party unity. But they were, in fact, separating Marxist theory from the immediate working-class struggle. Luxemburg could boast that the students knew "more about Marx and scientific socialism" than did the entire Executive.[114] The knowledge she praised, however, remained abstract; it lacked any clear relationship to the practices of the party and the trade unions.

The educational campaign represented a further stage in the process through which the apologetic and the visionary elements in the Marxist synthesis were breaking apart. Socialist intellectuals increasingly confronted, therefore, a choice of either accepting the tendency toward political accommodation—and of tacitly using Marxism to rationalize that process—or renewing the search for ways of realizing the Marxist promise of a fundamental transformation of human existence. The alternatives can be illustrated by the subsequent courses of Schulz and Rühle.

Schulz's work in the educational campaign raised him to a leading position in the party. During his administration of the party school and the other educational activities, however, he gradually "surrendered those aims which had carried him to a high post."[115] He ceased to be an orthodox Marxist, moved toward the Revisionists, and played a mediating role in the disputes arising over educational policy. He abandoned his own efforts to formulate a distinctly socialist pedagogy in favor of a reaffirmation of the "classical humanistic ideals" of the German tradition; education was to serve the general needs of society rather than those of a class.[116] By 1912, when Schulz was elected to the Reichstag, he had gone over to the Revisionists.

Rühle's course was more complicated. He, too, felt the growing pressures which the party's practical aims exerted on the educational mission. By 1910 his lecture cycles no longer concentrated on the "principles of scientific socialism" and the effort to build a new community based on a world view.[117] Educational issues gave way to political considerations. Insofar as he continued to occupy himself with pedagogical questions, they ceased to bear any close relationship to orthodox Marxist doctrines.

Rühle's later development testified, however, to the continuing hold of the Marxist vision. Although he was elected to the Reichstag in 1912, he moved during the war years to the left of the party, joining those who broke away from the Social Democratic majority and its support of the war effort.[118] In 1917 Rühle served, alongside Luxemburg, on the first executive of the Spartacists, the forerunner of the German Communist party. But in the postwar years he rejected both the Communists and the Social Democrats, taking part in several ill-fated efforts to find a new revolutionary tactic. Convinced, as a student of his later thought has observed, that the prewar socialist movement had "landed on the dust heap of history," Rühle renewed the quest for a pedagogy which would nurture the "new man" promised by Marx.[119] What was needed, he believed, was deeper psychological insight into the "powerlessness of the proletariat." Increasingly he placed his hopes on the next generation. Rühle spent his last years seeking, with the aid of Adlerian psychology, forms of education which would prepare the young for "a coming socialist society."

The twofold effort—to "rekindle enthusiasm" and to deepen the theoretical understanding of the party rank and file—repeated the earlier failure of the Marxist intellectuals to transform the mentality of the workers. Given that failure, the revolutionary enterprise, as understood by orthodox Marxists, was imperiled.[120] The Revisionists, meanwhile, were abandoning the project of creating a new working-class mentality, at least as envisioned earlier. They were increasingly occupied with the problem of reintegrating the workers into the life of the nation.

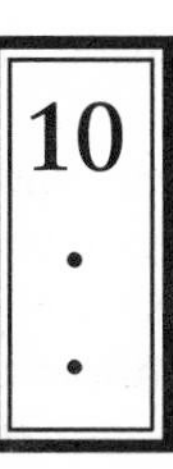

Revisionists, Nationalism, and Accommodation

EVEN as the educational campaign got under way, the Social Democrats experienced a major political setback. In the general election early in 1907 the party lost nearly half of its seats in parliament, and its percentage of the total vote declined.[1] By demonstrating the vulnerability of the Social Democrats to patriotic appeals by the government, the election results forced the leaders of the party to reconsider its relationship to German society as a whole.

The intellectuals drew different lessons from the election. Kautsky could see in the apparent loss of middle-class support evidence that the party was becoming "almost exclusively proletarian, not only in its conception and goals, but in its composition."[2] Marx's prediction of growing class polarization was being borne out. Revisionist intellectuals, in contrast, argued that the party had paid a heavy price for its tactic of "self-isolation." "We talked," Bernstein commented, "only to ourselves."[3]

Having broken with orthodox Marxism, the Revisionists had not developed a systematic theory or even a coherent point of view. There were only individual Revisionists, who sought to correct what they saw as flaws in Marxist theory and adapt it to unanticipated economic and social changes. During the period after the election revisionist intellectuals sought further alterations in Marxist theory and in the tactics of the party as they attempted to guide it down the road of political accommodation. Central to their policy was the hope for cooperation with the liberal parties. For intellectuals who favored such a course the *Sozialistische Monatshefte* was now, more than ever, the main vehicle for their views.

Leading Revisionists could look back over twenty years of experience in the movement. From their exercises in retrospection—a common feature of these years—they concluded that the party had changed in fundamental ways. The sectarianism and class orientation of the earlier years had been superseded by an outlook which considered the interests of the whole nation. No wonder questions of foreign policy assumed a new prominence in the life of the party. Social Democrats were also responding more directly to the course of "Weltpolitik" being pursued by the German leaders.

Revisionist intellectuals were encouraged by the policies adopted by the party leaders following the election. Chastened by their defeat at the polls, Bebel and his colleagues attempted to alter the party's antipatriotic image in order to secure broader electoral support. They were largely successful. Their policies seemed to be vindicated by the party's dramatic gains in the general election of 1912.

The *Sozialistische Monatshefte:* Reexamining the Party's History

Under Bloch's editorship the *Sozialistische Monatshefte* had attracted most of the party's leading intellectuals, surpassing the *Neue Zeit* in both the range and the quality of its articles. By 1908 the contents of the *Sozialistische Monatshefte* were differentiated by twenty or more categories, each subject edited by a figure well equipped by training or experience for the task. Thus Schippel headed the political section, Kampffmeyer supervised a department called "social history," and Schmidt handled "social science." Calwer was in charge of "economics," Heine edited "legal practices," Wally Zepler dealt with the "woman's movement," and Staudinger was responsible for "philosophy." Although something of the pluralism of earlier years remained, Bloch now emerged from the relative obscurity of his previous editorial role to give a more distinct orientation to the paper. Early in 1908 it began to appear twice a month, evidence of its success in attracting subscribers and wealthy financial supporters.[4]

A number of the postmortems on the 1907 election emphasized the party's diminished appeal to middle-class intellectuals. The "stream out of academic circles," one Revisionist observed, "has completely ceased."[5] For writers in the *Sozialistische Monatsheft* there was no doubt about the cause. Those who "were on the way to us" had been repelled by Dresden and its aftermath. Indeed, the party had "created enemies in those places where sympathy for socialism had been present."[6] Hence the ability of the government to mobilize many intellectuals against the party. Even students, largely indifferent to politics, had appeared as "touts" for the enemy.[7] It was essential for the party, Bloch declared, to win back this "lost terrain."[8]

But intellectuals were only a small part of the lost terrain. Revisionists were now convinced that the Social Democrats could not resume their march toward political power if they did not gain substantial support in the "new middle class."[9] The social structure was changing, they argued, in ways not anticipated by Marx. Rising between the workers and the capitalists were growing numbers in the liberal professions—lawyers, doctors, teachers, the clergy, and lower civil servants. Moreover, the middle sections of society were being augmented by various technicians and specialists associated with industrial and commercial growth. The "new middle class" also embraced clerks and assistants in commercial establishments. These groups often felt, as one Social Democrat conceded, an "instinctive aversion to our ideas."[10] But the intermediate social layers included many individuals who, by virtue of their vulnerability to capitalistic exploitation, were potential supporters of the Social Democrats. The election had demonstrated that the party could not conquer political power unless it won many of the nonworkers.

This view was pressed most vigorously by the editor of the *Magdeburger Volksstimme,* August Müller. Born in 1873, the son of a gardener, Müller had earned a doctorate at the University of Zurich before going to work for the party as a journalist.[11] A year before the 1907 election he had called attention to the sharp decline in local electoral support for the party after 1903.[12] For the retreat of the voters, he wrote, "we can thank Dresden" and the "self-laceration" of the party. Shortly after the election Müller undertook a detailed analysis of the electorate in Magdeburg, an industrial city.[13] He used his findings to refute those Social Democrats committed to a "pure working-class party." In Magdeburg, he argued, the workers were "not strong enough to conquer power by themselves, even if they were all Social Democrats." The same was true, he contended, of other industrial centers. Drawing on a study of the 1903 election, in which the investigator maintained that nearly a quarter of the party's vote came from nonworkers, Müller maintained that the Social Democrats could only advance politically if they played down the class struggle and viewed themselves as a "people's party."[14] It was necessary for socialists to "come out of their tower" and recognize their minority status, not only in terms of numbers but in "economic strength and intelligence."[15]

To view the Social Democrats as a "people's party" was also a clear rejection of the project to which Marxist intellectuals had been committed—the nurturing of a new mentality in the working class. Writers in the *Sozialistische Monatshefte* now took aim at what Bernstein called the myth of "the infallible intelligence of the proletariat" and its "appointed role in history."[16]

It was time, Wally Zepler declared, to recognize the naiveté of the belief that the workers possessed, "by virtue of an instinctive knowledge of their own interest," the capacity to serve as the "path finders of socialism" and to "decide difficult theoretical questions."[17] The workers, she added, were as little able to judge the complicated questions of economic life and as little interested in doing so as the members of any other class. As long as there were inequalities in aptitude and motivation, established by nature, the number of individuals who were willing to immerse themselves in abstract ideas would be limited. Social Democrats needed to recognize that the "truths perceived by Marx" would still "wander for a long time" before they became the "self-understanding of the great majority."

The orthodox Marxist confidence in the reliability of proletarian instincts was attacked most sharply by Ludwig Quessel, one of the few academically educated Social Democrats who had come out of the working class. Until his mid-twenties he had worked at several trades and taken an active part in the labor movement in Königsberg.[18] He then went to Zurich to study law, before returning to Germany to work as a Social Democratic journalist and becoming a frequent contributor to the *Sozialistische Monatshefte.* Quessel wrote out of personal experience, when, in a review of a study of the socialist movement by Sombart, he discussed "the psychology of the modern proletariat."[19] As a working man, he recalled, he had seen little sign of the socialist sentiments which, according to orthodox Marxists, grew naturally among the factory workers. "Quite the contrary, . . . the proletarian milieu can be seen rather as the school for a narrow individualism." Left to himself, the proletarian man was "as little likely to become a socialist" as the member of any other occupational group. Socialist ideas could only "flow into" the worker from outside. Orthodox Marxists might have agreed with this statement, but they would have objected vigorously to Quessel's claims about the nature of the outside influences. Receptivity to socialist ideas, he argued, was prepared by pre-ideological factors—especially the moral and religious education in the primary schools. For most members of the proletariat, socialism initially assumed the form of a "moral religious postulate."

Other Revisionists pointed to the failure of the party's educational effort. The masses, Maurenbrecher observed, had "simply rejected" the Social Democratic attempt to provide "historical-economic education."[20] No wonder, he added, that so many of the "lower officers" of the party and the trade unions were "bitterly demoralized and disappointed" over the indifference of the workers to the Marxist doctrines. It was not, according to Maurenbrecher, the "popularization of the first fifty pages of *Capital*" that shaped the mentality of the workers but the "yearning after a better life." Instruction in theory, as a means of mass education, was like "smiting the waters." Kampffmeyer agreed. Social Democrats had not translated such concepts as "productive forces" and "productive relations" into terms which were meaningful to the workers.[21]

Having concluded that the rank and file lacked interest in theoretical issues, writers in the *Sozialistische Monatshefte* emphasized the need to educate party functionaries and activists. What Bernstein referred to as the "upper ten thousand"—party and trade union secretaries, and other local officials and leaders—should become the objects of "systematic political and economic education."[22] They constituted, in Maurenbrecher's words, the "life or death of the working-class movement." To make wise decisions at the local level, however, the functionaries required not "a whole system of theoretical education" but, rather, a "knowledge of political history over the past fifty years" and a detailed grasp of contemporary economic problems.

Revisionist intellectuals were critical of the party school. Control of the curriculum by the orthodox Marxists threatened to perpetuate the "monstrosities of Marxist scholasticism" and the "unbelievable assurance" with which some Social Democrats made judgments about society.[23]

> They have heard of historical materialism or taken a course at the party school and believe that they have found the magic key to solve all the world's riddles. . . . The superficiality of their whole conduct carries over unfortunately to the . . . ten thousand worthy men who, out of lack of opportunity for further education, allow themselves to be persuaded that class-consciousness and discipline are sufficient to make good politics or policy.[24]

At the Nuremberg party conference in 1908 Eisner, now editor of the party paper there, attacked the Berlin school for its excessive concern with abstract theory.[25]

Revisionists accepted the growing bureaucratization of the party in these years as indicative of its maturity as a political organization. The *Sozialistische Monatschefte* displayed little sympathy for the argument of Michels, presented during 1908, that the Social Democrats were surrendering to the "iron law of oligarchy," to increasing control of the party from the top.[26] Quessel suggested that Bebel was using plebiscites to consolidate his own authority.[27] Other Revisionists worried about the "Prussification of the party."[28] They agreed, however, that the Social Democrats had left their "sectarian" or "utopian" stage behind and adopted a more realistic view of the world. But this did not necessarily mean the abandonment of Marxist theory. Several of the Revisionist intellectuals continued to see their task as the working out of Marx's "theoretical inheritance."[29] That task was viewed from different perspectives by three of the intellectuals who had first questioned the orthodox doctrines nearly twenty years earlier—Schippel, Kampffmeyer, and Schmidt.

What mattered for the true Marxist, Schippel argued, was the interest of the working class.[30] And he saw in the party's increasingly pragmatic policies a vindication of the course he had followed as a Social Democratic politician. The party, he wrote in the summer of 1908, was freeing itself from the "either/or" outlook and the "inescapable hollowness" of the fear that it might win approval, even praise, from its political opponents. The "rigid outlook" and the "illusory simplicities" of the past were "dead or dying in the party." The new socialist politician adapted his principles to "unforeseen or completely new circumstances."[31]

Kampffmeyer also wished to rescue that which was "lasting" in Marxist theory.[32] And he reaffirmed the role of "academically educated intellectuals" who, having "first opened the eyes of the proletariat," were still "building up theory." But many of Marx's ideas, particularly his view of the proletariat, had been "overtaken by historical changes." "What distinguishes the proletariat of today" from that of Marx's time was "its greater security," its greater capacity for resistance to "capitalistic exploitation."[33] Kampffmeyer was convinced that a working-class consciousness, most visible in the development of cooperatives, was becoming the decisive force in economic and social life.[34]

Schmidt, too, maintained that the "living in Marxism" could only be saved by cutting away the obsolete parts of the theory.[35] Only then could its essential element—the materialistic conception of history—be applied to changing conditions. Although Schmidt still saw *Capital* as an "incomparable analysis of exploitation," he had not ceased to struggle with those economic issues—the law of value and the profit rate—which, he believed, had led to "inescapable contradictions" in Marxist theory.[36] Schmidt was also still seeking ways of reconciling the Kantian view of ethics with Marx's explanation of economic and social development.[37] To Kampffmeyer, who shared Schmidt's evolutionary approach to socialism, the latter seemed a "brilliant exception" to the decline of serious theoretical activity within the party.[38]

Other revisionist intellectuals, meanwhile, argued that the party had now freed itself from the naive outlook of earlier years. They used various terms to describe that outlook—"chiliastic," "messianic," and "childlike" as well as "utopian" and "sectarian." But they agreed that the Social Democrats were coming to term with the realities of human nature and society.

After all, Maurenbrecher declared, Marx was essentially a prophet.[39] His most important ideas had come not from "observation of reality" but out of the feelings of a great idealist. His fantasy, "his false conception of the workers," and his declaration of the inevitability of socialism had generated the "enthusiasm and the willingness to sacrifice for the cause." But now, through "better knowledge of historical development, we are forced to think differently." Having lost the belief in a "natural necessity" and a "sudden upheaval of society," Social Democrats recognized that the victory of the workers could come only through the exercise of conventional virtues—"sacrifice, tenacity, steadiness" in the pursuit of their goal.

The "gates of paradise" had closed for Social Democrats.[40] So wrote Karl Leuther, an Austrian intellectual who became in these years one of the main contributors to the *Sozialistische Monatshefte.* The eighteen nineties and the decade which followed, he maintained, were "two human ages." Young intellectuals who now came into the party were less likely to be "led astray by illusions," less likely to allow themselves to be damned up inside a "dead orthodoxy." They no longer viewed Marxism as a source of "ultimate truths" and solutions to all puzzles. Leuther maintained that the "new man" envisioned by the early socialists was being realized, albeit in realistic ways, within the party's actual struggles.

Wally Zepler struck a similar note. "The naive hope for earthly perfection," she wrote, had been "cast off."[41] But she also called attention to what had been lost. The psychological consequences of the change had not been happy. It had left behind "a certain spiritual emptiness"; the yearning after a new world view and "inner personal cultivation" had not been fulfilled. Zepler believed that the "question of the proletarian world view" still confronted the Social Democrats. Could socialism provide a "substitute for the sinking religious ideal"?

In raising the religious issue, Zepler indicated that even among the revisionist intellectuals the earlier commitment to radically new ways of thinking within the working class had not been completely eclipsed. The concern with religion was prompted, in part, by the resistance which Catholicism presented to the party's efforts to win some sections of the working class.[42] But it also reflected a continuing tendency to identify socialism with a new world view. Thus Maurenbrecher, formerly a member of the clergy, noted the failure of the party to deal with the spiritual condition of the workers.[43] Not only had the "old religious teachings" lost their hold, but the "materialistic philosophy" which had for a time replaced them had also "lost its power." Maurenbrecher went on to argue that the "inner essence" of Marxism was a faith that history was moving from "nature to freedom." It was time for Social Democrats to "bring out the religious" element more fully; the movement required a "deeper grounding." Maurenbrecher saw, in Nietzsche's notion of the superman and his affirmation of this world, religious meanings which complemented the Marxist doctrines. Hans Müller, too, who had viewed the German movement from Switzerland since his ill-fated participation in the Jungen rebellion, held that Social Democrats needed to address the religious question.[44] The loss of the religious-like commitment of the earlier years had meant a "flattening out" of the socialist consciousness.

Most Revisionists rejected the attempt to "distill a new religious teaching" out of Marxism.[45] The party, Kampffmeyer observed, was now concerned with immediate economic and political problems; it would be a mistake to identify it with a new world view.[46] Staudinger agreed. Although the decline of religion had resulted in a widespread desire "to fill the gap," it was not the function of the Social Democrats to provide a "metaphysical completion of reality."[47]

Revisionist intellectuals were discovering in the rising spirit of German nationalism a new emotional anchorage for a socialist ideology which had lost its earlier intensity. Their patriotic turn was a further sign that the hope for a new mentality in the working class had been abandoned in favor of an accommodation with conventional attitudes and interests.

The Nationalism of the Revisionists

During the late nineties revisionist intellectuals had begun to reconsider the relationship of the Social Democrats to the nation and its foreign policy.[48] Schippel and Calwer, two of the party's most pragmatic politicians, took aim, in particular, at its commitment to free trade.[49] It was time, Schippel declared in 1900, for Social Democrats to judge working-class interests not simply from the standpoint of the consumer but in terms of production and employment, the vitality of the nation's industry, and its capacity to compete for international markets.[50] After the turn of the century, as the leaders of Germany advanced their new and aggressive view of the nation's place in the world, Schippel and Calwer continued to reexamine the party's trade policy. In the light of his study of commercial treaties in the nineteenth century, Schippel urged party leaders to deal with questions of trade policy on a "case-by-case" basis.[51] It was clear to at least one outside observer, Naumann, that Schippel was seeking to modify the dogmatic opposition of the Social Democrats to any form of protectionism.[52]

Schippel's efforts cost him his seat in the Reichstag. According to Bernhard, writing in his new economic review, *Plutus*, the insights Schippel had acquired through scientific investigation had proved incompatible with his role as a Social Democratic politician.[53] Bernhard went on to ask if the party could develop clear principles on matters of trade if "the two commercial policy experts of scholarly reputation, Schippel and Calwer," were forced into the position of disappointed spectators.

Calwer had been even bolder in proposing a new trade policy and a fresh Social Democratic approach to international relations. In 1897, drawing on the ideas of Naumann and others, he had advanced the idea of a "middle European customs union" as the best means of guaranteeing the economic future of Germany in a world dominated by the British, the Americans, and the Russians.[54] Such a scheme, he argued, would be necessary to sustain the economic progress on which the working-class movement depended. And yet until the workers had access to political power through a genuinely parliamentary system, they could not support those measures—the naval buildup, the pursuit of colonies, and the general policy of Weltpolitik—by means of which the nation's leaders were seeking to advance German interests.

In Calwer's claim that the working classes were "equally interested in a rapid and widening development of capitalism" lay the basis, as Naumann recognized, for a new Social Democratic view of such related issues as national defense and colonies.[55] And by 1905 Calwer had endorsed Germany's new course in international affairs. Given Germany's disadvantages, compared with those of the British and the Americans, he argued, the nation could not "renounce economic expansion," because it would mean its abdication as "a decisive political power."[56] Moreover, the resulting "stagnation of production" would undermine the capacity of the working class to move forward economically. What was needed, according to Calwer, was a new economic order on the continent, a customs union in which the Germans and the French could cooperate. The attempt to confine the socialist movement to a "narrow nationalist framework" would kill it.

Calwer's commitment to a customs union on the continent did not interfere with his growing nationalism. He favored the German military buildup. Although the naval program under way in the early years of the century was "bound up with the interests of capitalism," it also served the nation's general economic and political needs.[57] He supported as well the search for new colonies.

For both Calwer and Schippel the key to a sound German foreign policy was friendship with France; any provocation of this most important neighbor must be avoided. Hence their concern when the two nations clashed in the first Moroccan crisis in 1905. But after the Germans had suffered a diplomatic defeat at the Algeciras conference, Calwer vented his nationalistic feelings. He attacked the Social Democratic leaders for criticizing their own government.[58] They were opposing policies which were necessary for the "socialization of our economy." As a German socialist, he declared, "I want Germany to march at the head of economic progress." Economic advance required the "growth of German political power."

The party's defeat in the election of 1907 demonstrated, according to Schippel and Calwer, the price it had paid for its failure to identify itself with the real interests of the nation. The fate of the workers and, indeed, the future of socialism depended, Calwer maintained, on the "rapid, energetic, and general unfolding of German capitalism"—all the more so because the "germ of the socialist order" was increasingly visible "within the capitalistic economy."[59] "We must as socialists push the capitalistic economy forward." Schippel agreed. The party had suffered from its inability to deal realistically with such issues as protectionism and colonialism. Schippel now believed that colonies were crucial to Germany's future; here lay "the most powerful unfolding of the general productive forces of mankind."[60]

The nationalistic spirit exemplified by Schippel and Calwer was increasingly characteristic of revisionist intellectuals. They were intent on refuting the orthodox Marxist claim that the worker had no fatherland. But the approaches of the Revisionists to this issue differed markedly. David, for example, displayed little of the militant patriotism of Calwer. In a series of "letters concerning the love of fatherland," published in the *Neue Gesellschaft* during 1905, David simply argued that the Social Democrats represented a healthy nationalism, which was compatible with their commitment to internationalism.[61] Heine, too, had never allowed his socialist beliefs to interfere with what he saw as the legitimate needs of national defense. At the party conference in 1907 he spoke eloquently of his own patriotism: "Our fatherland is not the unfreedom and the injustice of our political institutions but it is our people . . . with whom we suffer and strive . . . our cities, villages, fields and woods, over which the sun shines, even if largely it shines on private property. The love for this no one can take away from us. Fatherland is above all the cultural community, in which we grow up, in which our spirit . . . has become what it is."[62] Social Democratic efforts to make German culture available to all members of society demonstrated that they were the true nationalists. Heine dismissed as nonsense the suggestion that the workers would not support Germany in the event of war.[63] Not only would such a policy "sacrifice many of our sons," it would "forfeit the sympathy of the nation."

Through their efforts to connect Social Democrats more closely with the policies of the German leaders, Schippel and Calwer separated themselves from the mainstream of the party. And as politicians they suffered the consequences. Calwer's failure to win reelection to the Reichstag in 1903 and again in 1907 made him vulnerable to his critics. In September 1907 the Social Democrats in his Braunschweig electoral district dropped him as their candidate. To his fellow Revisionists the action seemed to be one more blow to freedom of opinion within the party.[64] But Calwer, having discarded his earlier Marxism, had ceased to believe that the policies of the Social Democrats represented the interests of the workers.[65] Before long he left the party.

Schippel, having resigned his seat in the Reichstag, remained an active Social Democrat and continued to see himself as a Marxist. But he kept up his criticism of the orthodox Marxists; their views of trade policy, he wrote in 1908, were "not worth the paper they were written on."[66] He took particular exception to the tendency of "our noble Marxists" to deplore, on humanitarian grounds, the plight of native populations—the Zulus in Africa and the Indians in North America. While Social Democrats should do what they could to moderate the "birth pangs of capitalism" in the colonial areas and train the natives for leadership, the intervention of the Europeans, he insisted, corresponded to "our entire Marxist conception." Schippel cited Engels to support the view that working for the development of the European economies was a "historical duty." He had become an apologist for German imperialism.

In the period following the election of 1907, however, Schippel and Calwer were no longer the chief advocates of a socialistic nationalism among the Revisionists. That role had been taken over in part by the editor of the *Sozialistische Monatshefte,* Joseph Bloch. As late as August 1904 he still expressed the radical bent evident earlier in his sympathy for the anarchists.[67] But by early 1906 he had identified with Calwer's views.[68] Shortly after the election he urged Social Democrats to overcome the negative attitudes which had been so costly and to reconsider Germany's "world and colonial policy."[69] The tendency for the party to follow "exclusively liberal doctrines . . . contradicted the essense of socialism" and "ignored the true interests of the workers."

Bloch accepted Schippel's treatment of colonial questions "from the standpoint of Marx" as "splendid and convincing."[70] But he also believed that Schippel remained "too much the politician," limiting himself to discussing "definite resolvable cases" in "specific circumstances." The task of the *Sozialistische Monatshefte,* Bloch believed, was to rescue the party from its "false path."[71] To do so meant not only a change in tactics—cooperation with the liberal parties—but a new socialist theory, distinguished both from orthodox Marxism and from the views of those Social Democrats who concentrated on immediate practical possibilities. Schmidt, he held, was showing "the true significance of Marx for us" and providing an escape from "dogmatic narrowness" as well as from "mere practicality."[72] But socialists also needed a new, bold vision of Germany's place in the world. Bloch found such a vision in the Austrian Social Democratic journalist, Karl Leuther.

Like several of his German contemporaries, Leuther had moved from the state socialism of Lassalle and Rodbertus to Marxism before joining the Austrian party in the early nineties.[73] His subsequent development paralleled that of Schippel and Calwer as he gradually discarded the liberal approach to international relations in favor of a "new realism." But unlike Schippel and Calwer, he had not participated directly in parliamentary politics. Committed to German culture, an admirer of

Nietzsche, Leuther viewed the German Social Democrats from a distance. His contributions to the *Sozialistische Monatshefte* displayed an abstract character and a strident tone unmatched by other Revisionists. In the Austrian intellectual, however, Bloch had discovered, in Roger Fletcher's words, his "favorite and most voluble spokesman."[74]

In the articles of Leuther the socialist nationalism emerging in the *Sozialistische Monatshefte* took on a more aggressive spirit and comprehensive form. The repudiation of liberal notions of international relations and the conviction that Germany was caught up in a life-and-death struggle with other imperialistic powers led to his insistence on the need for German hegemony on the Continent and a world empire comparable to that of the British. For Leuther such policies also provided a way of overcoming the class struggle and integrating the workers into the nation.

A similar point of view was expressed by Maurenbrecher and Hildebrand, who joined the Social Democratic party because they viewed it as a more promising vehicle for realizing the goal formulated by Naumann—integrating the workers into a powerful German empire.[75] They began to write regularly for the *Sozialistische Monatshefte* during 1909. Maurenbrecher took over the editorship of the political section, vacated by Calwer, while Hildebrand began to comment regularly on colonial issues. The two believed they were filling a major gap in the Social Democratic party—the absence of "a proletarian foreign policy."[76] To fill that need meant, first of all, a recognition of the foolishness of the party's constantly opposing its own government. Such a practice simply strengthened the dominant classes in the neighboring states. The "softness of the Social Democratic press" toward France in the Moroccan affair seemed to Maurenbrecher an example of the party's "blind opposition" to German interests. The real threat to international harmony, Maurenbrecher added, was British imperialism. "A Marxist," he wrote, "should recognize the cloven hoof behind England's liberal tradition and her push for the limitation of armaments."[77]

Hildebrand, too, attacked the "limitless doctrinairism" of Social Democratic "colonial thinking."[78] The party should acknowledge Germany's need for raw materials and new markets. Expansion in Africa and elsewhere was necessary for the nation's continued economic development. Colonization was justified by its "release of economic forces," and its promotion of the most advantageous utilization of the soil and other resources.[79] To the dominant economic forces Hildebrand added a "natural human drive," the "impulse of a people" to expand.[80] While he held that moral checks on the exploitation of the natives were desirable, he associated colonization with moral and cultural progress. The fruitful energies of the Europeans remedied the "incapacities of the black race."[81]

Hildebrand had attempted, as editor of the party's paper in Solingen, to educate the local Social Democrats along the new nationalistic line. It proved to be a frustrating task. He expressed his disappointment over the "cultural backwardness" of the party members in a conversation with a local leader, Wilhelm Dittmann.[82] After Dittmann suggested that he had not yet cast off the "eggshell of the bourgeois mentality," Hildebrand admitted some truth to the charge. But the Social Democrats, he insisted, would have to "come around to his standpoint." In the spring of 1909, however, he resigned the editorship, conceding that the local workers did not "wish to learn" what he, as a "brain worker," had attempted to provide.[83] Since he was "completely superfluous" for them, his "energy and knowledge" could best be spent on "those who actually want to hear me." He also indicated a desire to undertake the "scientific study" for which his editorial duties had left little time. For a year or more he immersed himself in economic data, seeking to grasp the main trends in German commerce. The outcome of his investigation was a book, *The Shaking of Industrial Society and Industrial Socialism,* published in the fall of 1910.[84] It presented a bold and disturbing picture of the nation's economic future, with profound implications for Social Democratic policy.

Capitalistic imperialism was, in Hildebrand's scenario, self-defeating, but not in the way anticipated by orthodox Marxists. Imperialism was doomed, he argued, by its impact on colonial peoples. Colonialization would gradually free the natives from economic and political tutelage and enable them to meet their own needs for industrial goods. As they became economically self-sufficient, they would cease to serve as markets and sources of raw materials or food for the European societies, which in turn would face economic stagnation and impoverishment. Factory workers, superfluous and helpless, would be especially hard hit; "a sharp fall in the standard of living" would follow.[85] Only a new economic and political order in Germany would avert in the long run an industrial Götterdämmerung. To restore the balance between industry and agriculture, Hildebrand proposed "colonies" which would bring people back to the land in Germany.[86] But in the face of the growing power of the Americans, the Russians, and the emerging states of the Far East, the Germans could not compete as a single nation. Hildebrand took up the idea, advanced by Calwer and others, for a "United States of Europe," a customs union reaching from Hungary to France and, in time, including Britain.[87] It would be based on democracy but only if the workers gave up the "communist utopias."[88]

Hildebrand's picture of the future was inspired in part by the *Communist Manifesto* and its claim that the transformation of the world by capitalism was inevitable. But the chief inspiration for the book, and the figure to whom it was dedicated, was Friedrich List, champion of a

German customs union eighty years earlier.[89] Now that vision was enlarged to embrace all of western and central Europe. The present moment in history offered, according to Hildebrand, a unique opportunity for Europeans to overcome the barriers of nationalism, class antagonisms, and religious distinctions and to provide a model for the technical, scientific, and economic advance of the whole world.[90]

Hildebrand had presented, according to his friend Maurenbrecher, "a new post-Marxist agrarian-industrial theory for the working-class movement."[91] Although basic ideas had come from the *Communist Manifesto,* Hildebrand had applied them to a world very different from that analyzed by Marx. The book was, in fact, the outcome of a "dialogue between Marx and Naumann." It also represented, Maurenbrecher argued, a fuller working out of Marx's teachings than that offered by "the epigoni who filled the party" with their interpretations.

Hildebrand had gone much further than any other Revisionist beyond the ideological and tactical boundaries of the party. His continuing commitment to democracy and to the special mission of the proletariat checked any final accommodation with the policies of Germany's leaders. But he had abandoned central elements in the Social Democratic program. The socialization of the means of production had been relegated to secondary importance in the face of the coming crisis of industrial capitalism. The class struggle lost much of its significance in view of the problems confronting the nation as a whole. And he had reopened the agrarian question, which had disappeared from the party's agenda fifteen years earlier. Like earlier advocates of a Social Democratic agrarian policy, Hildebrand denied that the peasants were being proletarianized.

A year before Hildebrand published his book, Wally Zepler observed that the "bold structure" of Marxism had "broken into many pieces."[92] The disappearance of any "unified scientific socialist structure" within the party had meant a tendency for each Social Democrat to "possess his own Marxism." The loss of a common ideology posed, according to Zepler, a new question: "Where, then, is the point at which we cease to be party members?" Since it could no longer be found in theory, she suggested, Social Democrats could only be united through action, as decided by the majority of the party. "Reality," Zepler concluded, was now "the great regulator." Hildebrand's views provided a test for the question posed by Zepler. Could an individual who had gone so far in embracing imperialism and who diverged so sharply from the Erfurt program still be considered a member of the party? By the time the Social Democrats confronted the question—at the Chemnitz conference in 1912—the party leaders themselves had moved a long way down the road of political accommodation.

Accommodation by the Social Democratic Politicians

The party's electoral defeat in 1907 brought, in the words of one Social Democrat, a "sobering up."[93] Over the next several years the party leaders followed a course much like that favored by the Revisionists. Bebel and his colleagues were especially keen on overcoming the perceptions of the party which had proved so costly during the election and on demonstrating its reliability in such matters as national defense and foreign policy. In the spring of 1907, when the successor to Schippel's seat in Chemnitz, Gustav Noske, delivered an impassioned speech in the Reichstag on behalf of the fatherland, he was roundly applauded by other members of the Fraktion and congratulated by Bebel.[94] Later in the year, at the International Socialist Congress in Stuttgart, the German Social Democrats resisted, though with only partial success, the strong stand which the other socialist parties wished to take on questions of militarism and imperialism. The congress, as Carl Schorske has observed, indicated the extent to which the party had, under the impact of the election, adjusted "to the facts of life in an era of imperialism."[95] Not only had it "revealed itself as the leader of the conservative forces in the International," but it had reversed a long-standing policy and "pressed for a fuller acceptance of colonialism." At the end of the year Bloch could look back on the party's development and claim that the election had strengthened its "political sense."[96]

Revisionist hopes for accommodation rested largely on the possibility of reforming the Prussian electoral system. Here, all elements in the party agreed, was the major obstacle to a genuinely parliamentary order in Germany. Given Prussia's dominant place in the nation, the whole German situation depended on the alteration of voting laws which virtually disenfranchised the lower classes. But political conditions in Prussia indicated, according to Revisionists, the futility of waging the struggle in terms of "the class opposition between the bourgeoisie and the proletariat."[97] Only by allying with the middle class, also denied real access to political power, could the Social Democrats secure reform. The Prussian state elections scheduled for June 1908 provided, therefore, a test for the tactic of cooperating with other parties—the Progressives, National Liberals, and the Catholic Center—to change the system. The results of the election were disheartening. Although they polled 24 percent of the vote—the most of any party—the Social Democrats gained only 2 percent of the seats. The party's candidates received virtually no support from liberal voters. Bloch conceded that the "prospects for electoral reform" were "worse than ever."[98] The "utter failure of the liberals" to cooperate with the Social Democrats meant that a long period of "political schooling" lay ahead.

Later in 1908 Revisionists were reminded of the strong opposition within the party to political alliances by the angry outcry against the Baden Social Democrats, who joined liberals there in support of the state budget. The ensuing controversy demonstrated the deep differences between party leaders in the southern states, where equal voting rights prevailed, and those in the north. At the Nuremberg party conference in September the policies of the Baden Social Democrats were defended by Frank, the young lawyer who had organized the socialist youth in the south and more recently had worked for an alliance with the liberals in the state diet. His debate with Bebel at Nuremberg indicated his willingness to risk a split in the party in order to increase the autonomy of Social Democrats in the south.[99] Bebel himself opposed attempts to punish the southerners; he chose to view their policies as a "breach of discipline" rather than as a clear violation of party principles. He thus placed himself, in Frank's words, "on the ground where comradely discussion is possible."[100] The young intellectual from Baden could see that the mild rebuke which followed was a retreat from the demand of the "Berlin movement" for uniformity. Bloch, too, was pleased with the outcome of the conference. It marked the end of a "period of reaction within the party" which had begun at Lübeck in 1901.[101] The Baden Social Democrats were showing the way for the whole party.

Despite the Prussian election, developments inside and outside the party after 1907 reinforced tendencies toward political accommodation. The steady increase of trade union influence helped to check the spirit of militance among Social Democrats, while the increasing bureaucratization of the party in these years also made for more cautious policies.[102] A series of victories in by-elections between 1907 and 1912 indicated that the party was again attracting voters from outside the working class.[103]

Political trends in Germany provided encouragement for the Revisionists. A fiscal crisis, brought on by the naval buildup, led the Chancellor, von Bülow, to propose, late in 1908, direct federal taxation for the first time. Although this traditional Social Democratic demand was bound up with the military expenditures which the party had always opposed, the tax proposal suggested new possibilities for political cooperation across class lines. The prospect for cooperation with the liberals improved the following summer when conservative resistance to the tax reform measure led to the collapse of the Bülow bloc, the coalition of Conservatives, National Liberals, and Progressives which had governed Germany since 1907.[104] With the breakup of the government, Revisionists could hope for the formation of a "left bloc," stretching from "Bebel to Bassermann," the leader of the National Liberals.[105]

At the Leipzig conference in 1909, when Social Democrats debated the question, now hypothetical, of whether their Fraktion should support government proposals for a direct tax, Revisionists could again applaud the good sense of the delegates. Kautsky's demand that the party's representatives in the Reichstag use a tactic of obstructionism to fight budgetary proposals was "scarcely taken seriously."[106] While the outcome of the debate was inconclusive, the growing willingness of party members to be guided by "practical considerations" was apparent. In a letter to Bloch discussing the triumph of the revisionist point of view, Heine cautioned against boasting about their victory. It might encourage the radicals to "pick a new quarrel" and again pose as "saviors of the party."[107]

A formidable agitation against the Prussian electoral system during the early weeks of 1910 again seemed to create a common ground for Social Democrats and liberals. While the prospect proved to be short-lived, Revisionists remained optimistic. Hence the assessment of Quessel in the summer. What could be designated as the "Dresden spirit," he wrote, was "noiselessly passing" out of the party.[108] It was unrealistic, he added, to expect the Social Democrats to gain a majority in parliament in the foreseeable future. He attempted to dispel "romantic revolutionary illusions" by means of an analysis of the social structure which emphasized the growth of the "new middle class." To break the hold of reaction, cooperation with the liberals would be necessary. Maurenbrecher was more optimistic. A new "left bloc," he believed, was "at hand."[109] He cited Marx to support his claim that cooperation with the middle class, given its failure to conquer political power in Germany, was crucial.

However, renewed protests within the party against the budgetary policies of the Baden Social Democrats indicated, according to Bloch, how easy it was for "many comrades to forget the lessons of 1907."[110] But over the next eighteen months, as the party prepared for a new general election, collaboration with the liberals assumed the central place in revisionist hopes for accommodation. Not all Revisionists believed that the liberals would reach out to the Social Democrats. Heine, ever the skeptic, as he described himself, did not believe that the main body of the Progressives, let alone the National Liberals, wished to cooperate.[111] Schippel shared Heine's skepticism.[112] Even Quessel, for all his optimism, conceded that an alliance presupposed the "inner transformation" of the liberals.[113]

The second Moroccan crisis, in July 1911, indicated once more the difficulty of finding a common ground for Social Democrats and liberals in matters of foreign policy. The decision of the German leaders to send a warship into the port of Agadir in order to assert the nation's interests in North Africa was firmly supported by the liberals. The Social Democratic leaders, however, equivocated. They were caught between their traditional opposition to the government's policies and their fear that outright criticism would make them vulnerable to charges of antipatriotism in the coming election.[114] Their hesitations exposed them to renewed attacks from the party left. At the Jena conference in the fall, however, the party leaders succeeded in focusing the attention on domestic issues and the coming election. The discussion of electoral tactics demonstrated the extent to which the party had moved down the road of accommodation. Virtually all the delegates agreed that the chief task at the moment was to defeat the governing coalition of Conservatives and Catholics. For this task cooperation with the liberals in the run-off elections was essential. The electoral strategy adopted at Jena was, as Schorske has observed, "a victory for the Revisionists. . . . Social Democrats thus resolved to try to break the stalemate in German politics with the help of the liberals."[115]

The general election early in 1912 seemed to justify the hopes of the Revisionists.[116] On the first ballot the party gained nearly a million votes over the total received five years earlier, and it increased its percentage of the poll from 28.9 to 34.8. Having gained sixty-four seats from the initial ballot, the Social Democratic leaders entered into an agreement with the Progressives, kept secret lest it arouse the radicals, which was designed to maximize the strength of the two parties in the run-off elections. For the most part the Social Democrats in the designated constituencies kept their end of the bargain even though it required that they dampen their campaigns. By providing crucial votes in thirty-five of the forty-two districts won by the Progressives, the socialists enabled them to survive as a party. Social Democratic candidates, in contrast, received scant support from rank-and-file Progressives. Middle-class voters were unwilling to reach out to the working-class party.

The "unreliability of the bourgeois left," as Schippel put it, did not diminish the enthusiasm with which Revisionists greeted the results of the election.[117] Having gained a fourth of the seats in the Reichstag, more than any other party, the Social Democrats seemed ready for a new political role. Schippel observed that the party's deep differences with the liberals on the "big issues"—colonialism and national defense—would make cooperation difficult, but he saw a "wide and rich field" of activity opening up for the Fraktion. Other Revisionists shared his expectations and drew lessons from the electoral success. The "brilliant outcome" could, according to Bernstein, be attributed to the party's escape from its doctrinaire past.[118] Another writer concluded that the party would now once again attract "bourgeois intellectuals."[119]

The election demonstrated to Kampffmeyer that the party had made a critical transition. The "acts and words of the masses" had finally displaced the "ideas of individual theoreticians and leaders" in forming "the actual nature of the Social Democratic movement."[120] Referring to the orthodox Marxist attempt to free proletarian consciousness from the "remnants of bourgeois ideology," he reviewed the process through which the workers had gained a new self-awareness. But the new proletarian consciousness had assumed, according to Kampffmeyer, a form very different from that expected by the orthodox Marxists. It had come not from abstract theory but through the practical political and economic struggle. Although Revisionists were still "students of Marx," they recognized, unlike the orthodox Marxists, the influence of practical experience.

While Revisionists celebrated the success of the policy of accommodation, Social Democrats in parliament were confronting the realities of German political life. After dropping their effort to secure the presidency of the Reichstag, a traditional perogative of the largest party, the Fraktion attempted to win one of the vice-presidencies.[121] Negotiations with the liberals, whose support was necessary, broke down. Faced with the choice of cooperation with the Social Democrats and pushing toward democratization, on the one hand, and an alliance with the authoritarian parties, Conservative and Catholic, on the other, the National Liberals moved to the right. But the negotiations also indicated, to some Revisionists at least, that the Social Democrats were still held back by their own "traditions and feelings."[122] Party leaders, Heine claimed, were unwilling to dismantle the barriers of language and obsolete principles and become "revolutionaries against" themselves. Quessel also criticized the members of the Fraktion for their failure to make the concessions to monarchical institutions necessary to play a new role in parliament.[123]

By the late spring of 1912 revisionist hopes for rapid progress toward accommodation were fading. The limited results of the electoral agreements with the Progressives, together with the rebuffs in parliament, engendered new protests from the party left. As early as March Schippel could see within the party the "advanced riders" of a "second Dresden" whose "war cry" was the class struggle.[124] There were complaints that the "battle enthusiasm of the masses" was being destroyed by the political policies of the leaders.

This was the setting for the Hildebrand affair. At a time of growing uncertainty among the Social Democrats, Hildebrand's ideas called into question the social and ideological foundations of the party.

The Hildebrand Affair: The Limits of Revisionism

Hildebrand's book, *The Shaking of Industrial Society and Industrial Socialism,* had found little favor in the party press. The *Neue Zeit* ignored it. Social Democratic papers which reviewed it were critical. Even the reviewer in the *Sozialistische Monatshefte* was guarded. Hildebrand, he wrote, had "raised issues which socialists had tended to dismiss," but his gloomy forecast, together with his solutions—the strengthening of agriculture and a "United States of Europe"—were as one-sided as the views he challenged.[125]

Undeterred by the response, Hildebrand continued his efforts to "nationalize the Social Democratic mind." In a pamphlet published in the fall of 1911, *Socialist Foreign Policy,* he presented a popular version of his ideas.[126] Written in the aftermath of the second Moroccan crisis, the pamphlet defended the government's policies and German rights to colonies in those areas where the people were incapable of developing their own resources. Hildebrand also attacked the anti-imperialistic stance of his party.

To support his views Hildebrand cited passages from the *Communist Manifesto* that described the process through which capitalism forced "all nations to adopt bourgeois modes of production" and "create a world after its own image."[127] This process, he argued, was still not complete; it included, moreover, a development not recognized by Marx and Engels or their "epigoni"—the tendency for colonial peoples to take control of their own economies. Hildebrand went on to restate the argument presented earlier in his book. The industrial societies in Europe could only avert the catastrophe of reduced markets and shrinking sources of food and raw materials by uniting. Since this "world-historical formation" would take time, however, the immediate need was to insist on Germany's right to colonies. It was necessary to put an end to the attempts of the British and the French, which reached back a quarter of a century, to stifle Germany's economic life. The workers had a deep stake in a vigorous colonial policy, not only economically but politically. Moreover, such a policy would enable the Social Democrats to reconnect the workers with "wide sections of the German population" which had been antagonistic to the party.[128] Hildebrand was pointing the way for collaboration between the Social Democrats and the National Liberals.

Hildebrand and his close ally, Maurenbrecher, pressed their case at the Jena conference. They introduced a resolution calling for support of the government's colonial policy. In a letter to Naumann, Maurenbrecher explained their decision not to mobilize support for the motion before the meeting.[129] They wanted to find out "how many other Revisionists are sufficiently determined to accept our standpoint." They found out. Apart from the sponsors "not a hand was raised" for the motion.[130]

Hildebrand was already in trouble at the local level.[131] A lecture before a meeting of trade unionists in Solingen early in August 1911, in which he discussed Germany's dependence on foreign markets, had angered local party leaders. His talk had also drawn sharp protests and an extended critique from the *Leipziger Volkszeitung*. Later in the month, at a meeting of the Solingen Social Democrats, a motion to expel Hildebrand, on the grounds that he had abandoned the party program, passed by a vote of 118 to 58. A hearing before the agitation committee of the region followed, at which Hildebrand defended his views. The party court voted four to three to expel him. At this point his chief offense was his denial that the peasantry was doomed to proletarianization.

In keeping with party statutes Hildebrand appealed the decision to the party conference in 1912. In April a grievance committee, appointed to hear his case and report to the conference, upheld the earlier judgment by a vote of five to four. The case was then taken up by other Revisionists.

Discussion of the affair in the *Sozialistische Monatshefte* began with an article by Hildebrand himself. Was he guilty, Hildebrand asked, of "gross offenses against the principles of the party program," the charges justifying his expulsion?[132] The issue, he argued, was of fundamental importance for Social Democrats. What were the limits of freedom of opinion within the party? Although he shared the party's view of the relationship between capital and labor, he was being punished for exploring problems "not addressed by party thinkers up to now." Hildebrand conceded that he had rejected the view of agricultural development presented in the Erfurt program. But his ideas were the outcome of "scientific investigation." As such, they were subject only to "scientific judgment," especially in a party which claimed to "stand on the ground of science."

Other Revisionists were quick to defend Hildebrand. Heine denied his own competence to evaluate the economic issues involved and fixed on the procedures used to expel Hildebrand.[133] They amounted to an "auto-da-fé" designed to protect "pure teachings." The party courts had simply pronounced an "anathema. He is damned." According to Heine the courts had misunderstood the party statutes, which referred to "actions," not "opinions," as grounds for expulsion. He agreed that freedom of opinion, the right to scientific investigation in the party, was at stake.

Kampffmeyer also claimed that the party courts had exceeded their competence.[134] Only a "scientific forum" could deal with the issues raised by Hildebrand. To attempt to set limits to free inquiry within the party violated the spirit of Marx and Engels. It killed "fruitful criticism." One of the leading intellectuals among the southern Social Democrats, August Erdmann, agreed. He praised Hildebrand for reviving the "long-neglected agrarian question."[135] He worried lest the action taken against Hildebrand hinder the "influx of intellectuals." Another writer in the *Sozialistische Monatshefte* noted the uncertainty within the party over the issues addressed by Hildebrand. What strict Marxist could claim that Social Democrats had a "scientifically, indispensable basis on questions of trade, agriculture, colonizations, and world politics"?[136] Bernstein claimed that the treatment of Hildebrand was not only unjust to an individual but jeopardized the party's ability to represent the interests and rights of all members of society.[137]

On the eve of the Chemnitz conference Maurenbrecher explained why, in the face of so much hostility and misrepresentation, he and Hildebrand were still Social Democrats.[138] The greatest problem of the age, he wrote, was the economic and social condition of the industrial masses. Until this problem was solved, all other questions—educational, religious, the development of a "new will" in the nation—were "only wind." "We are Marxists," he declared. And he claimed that Hildebrand, following Marx, had seen "more clearly than anyone else" that the "uninterrupted progress of industrial production" was the presupposition for a "worthy human life in the future."

The "real danger to the party," Maurenbrecher argued, lay in the educational deficiencies of "our agitators."[139] They were overworked, lacked time for serious reading, and their tendencies toward arrogance were often increased by attendance at the party school. Given the lack of appreciation for genuine "intellectual work" among the local functionaries, could they, as delegates to the conference, recognize that they were "not competent to decide" the questions raised by Hildebrand? Yet Maurenbrecher's sense of defeat was plain. He recognized that the issue facing the party was deeper than that of freedom of opinion and scientific inquiry; Social Democrats had failed to "create the conditions" through which workers or their representatives could "learn different views" and judge them.

The proceedings at the Chemnitz conference gave little comfort to the Revisionists. Speakers for the party courts recapitulated the reasons for Hildebrand's expulsion.[140] Citations from his book and statements during the hearings had shown that he was "no Social Democrat." He had denied that the "socialization of the means of production" was the primary solution to the problems facing the workers, reduced the differences between socialists and liberals to mere "differences in tendency," rejected the view of the peasantry laid down in the Erfurt program, and adopted views on protectionism, colonies, and foreign policy which diverged from those of the party. In defending himself, Hildebrand again declared that he stood "on the ground of the class struggle."[141] He insisted that his "cursed duty" as a scientific investigator had been to present the catastrophic possibilities which had "come quite unexpectedly out of my studies." He had not, after all, claimed infallibility; his book was an effort to stimulate discussion.

Revisionists, hampered by time limits on the debate, provided only weak support for Hildebrand. Gradnauer observed that this was the first time in the history of the party that a member had been "excluded because of scientific convictions."[142] Heine again complained that the courts had based their decisions on opinions rather than actions as prescribed in the party statutes.[143] He was answered by Zetkin, who maintained that Hildebrand's disruptive behavior at meetings constituted "practical activity" which threatened to damage the party.[144] At stake was the "living interest of the party . . . the foundation on which we stand and fight together." She was seconded by Heinrich Laufenberg, an orthodox Marxist intellectual, who had, as a leader of the party in Düsseldorf, tangled with Hildebrand some years earlier. "We are not a scientific but a political congress," he declared.[145] For Zetkin, Laufenberg, and the overwhelming majority of the delegates who voted to uphold the expulsion of Hildebrand, the issue raised by the Revisionists—freedom of opinion—was irrelevant. Hildebrand had questioned the very nature of the party.

Bernstein recognized that the delegates had "no intention of disparaging science."[146] They voted, he observed, simply on political grounds. If, by "political," Bernstein in this context meant the determination to preserve those characteristics which had made the Social Democrats a party, he was surely correct. Hildebrand had dismissed the resentments, the aspirations, the sense of common interests which bound the Social Democrats together. He had questioned the basis of the party most directly by suggesting that the peasantry, not the industrial workers, constituted the most urgent problem facing society in the immediate future. In "giving priority to the peasantry over the industrial worker," Laufenberg observed, Hildebrand had denied the proletarian character of the party.[147] Chemnitz was, in this respect, a replay of the Breslau conference seventeen years earlier; the delegates refused to tolerate views which denied the primacy of working-class interests. Hildebrand's expulsion indicated the limits which the working-class character of the party placed on the Revisionists.

While the Hildebrand affair demonstrated the determination of the Social Democrats to preserve the identity of their party, it also pointed to their deepening political dilemma. There was considerable evidence by 1912 that the party had exhausted its capacity to grow insofar as it relied on the industrial workers.[148] Given the reluctance of the liberal parties to cooperate, and given the formidable powers—military, economic, and political—which they confronted in the Wilhelmine order, the Social Democrats had reached an impasse. The election of 1912 was deceptive; it was not a victory which opened the way to further growth; it was the climax of a process, reaching back several decades, through which the working class had found, in the Social Democratic party, a vehicle for expressing its interests and aspirations within the German nation.

A year after his expulsion Hildebrand reflected on the outcome of the project to which he and the other intellectuals had been dedicated—the remaking of the working-class mentality.[149] How could one explain, he asked, the failure of the "socialism of the educated" to connect with the working-class movement? Time and time again the young academics who responded to the call of history emanating from the Social Democrats had, after their initial enthusiasm, suffered disillusionment. Hildebrand noted the "internal resistance" which the educated recruits often experienced when they encountered the coarseness, impetuosity, and one-sidedness of the working-class socialists. He blamed economic and social conditions for the inability of the Social Democratic rank and file to rise to "larger conceptions" of socialism. The Chemnitz conference had demonstrated the gulf between the classes; it had shown that the "socialism of the masses" was confined within "ever narrower horizons."

Although he was now outside the movement, Hildebrand continued to view the "intellectual and moral fertilization" of the workers as a fundamental task for socialist intellectuals.[150] He urged them to address the "deep inner strife and dissatisfactions in the proletariat" and "crystallize a post-Christian religion."[151] But most Revisionists, having abandoned the view that socialism required an "ultimate grounding," were now committed to the path of political and cultural accommodation.

For Kautsky and the orthodox Marxists, meanwhile, the period after 1907 presented a new set of problems. The party's political course was creating new obstacles to the growth of the Marxist consciousness among the workers on which the socialist revolution depended. The orthodox view of proletarian development was being challenged, moreover, by a younger group of Marxist intellectuals.

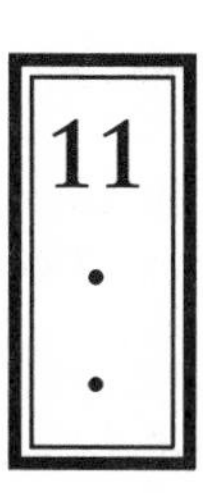

The Exhaustion of Orthodox Marxism

KAUTSKY remained faithful to the orthodox Marxist claim that the proletariat was a unique class, steadily growing in numbers, solidarity, and social understanding. It would be foolish, he wrote shortly after the electoral defeat in 1907, to "veil the proletarian character of the party" in order to win the support of other groups.[1] His forceful restatement of this view early in 1909, however, collided with the policies of the Social Democratic political leaders. The result was a crisis in Kautsky's relationship to the party. That crisis brought to the surface once more the dual function of Marxist theory—as a guide to the party's historical mission and as an apologetic for working-class interests.

A younger group of Marxist intellectuals—they can be designated the Radicals—recognized that orthodox Marxism was leading to a theoretical and tactical impasse. To escape that predicament they followed the alternative path Luxemburg had earlier opened in her response to the Revisionists and then elaborated on the basis of her experience in the Polish and Russian uprisings. By 1910 she believed that German developments were catching up with the revolutionary process she had analyzed in the *Mass Strike.* Both the Radicals and the orthodox Marxists were again confronting, however, the problem of inculcating in the proletariat the socialist understanding necessary for it to play its revolutionary role.

Kautsky: The Dilemmas of Orthodox Marxism

Kautsky had been surprised by the success of the government's nationalistic appeal during the election of 1907. In the spring and summer he attempted to explain the surge of patriotism in the middle class, building on his earlier analyses of the militaristic and imperialistic tendencies within capitalism.[2] Bourgeois patriotism, he argued, was the result of imperialistic rivalries and actually foreshadowed the ruin of the existing order. The Social Democrats should continue, therefore, to combat the chauvinistic spirit and attack policies which were leading toward military conflict, but they should also prepare for the "great successes" which would come at "the end of a war." Above all, the party must avoid compromises with a social order which was doomed.

Kautsky had little sympathy for the efforts of the party leaders to soften criticism of the government's defense and foreign policies. Social Democrats who applauded Noske's speech in the Reichstag during the spring, he charged, were capitulating to nationalistic feelings. Kautsky also opposed the efforts of the party's delegation at the International Socialist Congress in Stuttgart to moderate proposals for mass action in the event of war.[3] At the Essen party conference in the fall of 1907, he clashed with Bebel over the question of Social Democratic policy in case of a conflict with the Russians.[4] Against the party leader's argument that working-class support of the government would be justified if Germany were on the defensive, Kautsky maintained that the distinction between aggression and defensive action would provide no guidance amid the confusion which would attend the outbreak of hostilities. The only guide for the party should be the interests of the proletariat.

During 1907 and 1908 Kautsky found more time for historical inquiry. One result of his studies, *The Foundations of Christianity,* published in 1908, indicated his continuing effort "to bring the proletariat to social insight, to self-consciousness and political maturity."[5] To enlighten the workers and strengthen their organization remained the most important task for the party.

For Kautsky that task was becoming more and more defensive, a struggle to preserve the traditions of the party. Revisionists now claimed that he was simply "defending the true church," that orthodox Marxism had stiffened into a determination to hold fast to a scripture.[6] In countering such claims Kautsky could only refer to the "basic socialist writings," including his own commentary on the Erfurt program, as expressions of the party's commitment to scientific method.

Determined to protect the proletarian character of the party, Kautsky again attacked the Baden Social Democrats for cooperating with the liberals in supporting their state budget.[7] Such a policy, he argued, meant complicity with a bourgeois state which could only be viewed as an instrument of capitalism. What mattered most was still the "spreading of theoretical knowledge" among the workers. Similar considerations lay behind his attack, at the Nuremberg conference in 1908, against Social Democrats who saw in the proposals of the Chancellor for direct taxes the possibility of cooperation with the liberals.

Late in 1908 Maurenbrecher denounced Kautsky's proletarian purism.

In an open letter published in the *Neue Zeit*, the Revisionist declared that Kautsky's position could only be justified if Germany stood "before the door of a proletarian victory."[8] But no revolutionary development "could be expected in the foreseeable future." What occupied Kautsky, therefore, was a "question for our children." In the meantime, Maurenbrecher argued, Social Democrats should concentrate on winning a majority at the polls.

In the spirited exchange which followed, Kautsky applied his orthodox Marxist doctrines to contemporary developments. Now, in his eagerness to refute Maurenbrecher and the Revisionists, he abandoned his customary scruples against forecasting the future course of events. His pamphlet *The Road to Power* was published in January 1909. Here Kautsky declared that European societies were entering the revolutionary era predicted by Marx.[9] He envisioned a decisive shift in power in favor of the proletariat. In Kautsky's new analysis the revolution ceased to be a vague event on the historical horizon and became an imminent possibility.

The Road to Power dealt in large part with the efforts of capitalists to overcome the contradictions in the economic system by means of monopolistic practices and the pursuit of colonial markets. Kautsky argued that the growing competition for colonies was inescapably tied up with an armaments race and the likelihood of war. For capitalists there was no escape from the coming disaster. German society faced, therefore, the alternatives of imperialism or socialism.

Kautsky's pamphlet was concerned mainly with the proletariat's "road to power." He claimed that the road was now opening through the workings of objective economic and social forces. Capitalism had lost its capacity for growth within Germany; the upswing of the economy which had marked the period after 1895 was over. The future held only economic stagnation, growing misery for the working class, and an intensification of class conflict. The increasing polarization of social classes, Kautsky argued, now meant that the proletariat—defined as those who did not possess the means of production—constituted a majority of the electorate. The "new middle class," to which the Revisionists attached such importance, was thus absorbed into an increasingly homogeneous proletariat. The nonproletarians could now be viewed as "one reactionary mass."[10]

It followed that the main work of the party was still to prepare the proletariat to take power when the crisis of capitalism became acute. Kautsky again insisted on the indispensable role of consciousness—the growth of theoretical knowledge among the still-unaware sections of the proletariat. But he had little to say about the way in which the educational process might be accelerated.[11] The intellectuals, so important in his earlier explanations of that process, had little place in the analysis in the *Road to Power.* Indeed, he now suggested that the decisive influence on the workers might come from the struggle itself. In a revolutionary situation the masses would learn the nature of their interests with "unbelievable rapidity."[12] A political education which otherwise might take generations would be reduced to a few years.

The opening of a revolutionary era required, according to Kautsky, a change of tactics. The deepening crisis of capitalism had ended the possibility of the workers' gaining significant reforms through parliament or by means of trade union activity. It was time for the party to attack the foundations of the state and especially its cornerstone—the Prussian electoral system. To change that system and achieve the next step on the road to revolution—the democratization of German political life—demanded new methods. Social Democrats must overcome the separation of the economic and political struggles of the workers and politicize the trade unions.[13] The political mass strike, hitherto viewed by Kautsky and the party leaders as a defensive tactic, now became an offensive weapon. Kautsky had set aside his characteristic caution in deriving lessons from theory for the immediate practices of the party.

Kautsky's analysis in the *Road to Power* ruled out any cooperation with the liberals in a "left bloc."[14] It also meant that Social Democrats should not take part in any coalition government. To do so would be to participate in the corruption of the ruling class. Kautsky had reaffirmed the principle of proletarian exclusiveness. Only a "dictatorship of the proletariat" could make the transition to a socialist society.

In the *Road to Power* Kautsky made his divergence from the policies of the party clear. The result was a crisis in his relationship with the Social Democratic leaders. Publication of the "scandalous pamphlet" evoked strong protests from trade unionists, Revisionists, and reformist members of the party who, in an increasingly fluid political situation, saw new tactical possibilities.[15] The *Road to Power* also alarmed the Social Democratic Executive. Its members worried lest Kautsky's assertions about the inevitability and imminence of revolution invite persecution by the government. Bebel and his colleagues refused to authorize republication and further distribution of the pamphlet.[16]

Kautsky was shocked by the decision of the Executive. He suddenly faced the possibility that his life's work lay in ruins; his "position in Germany," he confessed, "could become untenable overnight."[17] He considered resigning from the editorship of the *Neue Zeit,* and then he rushed off to Vienna to consult with Adler. The Social Democrats, he believed, were on the edge of an "enormous scandal." The decision of the Executive indicated that "a secret program" existed alongside the party's "public program." To accept the suppression of the *Road to Power* would be suicidal for the Social Democrats.

Kautsky appealed to the Control Commission, the body within the party which considered complaints against the Executive. There he could count on the support of Zetkin. The Control Commission instructed the Executive to authorize republication. The Executive refused to do so.

Bebel could only view Kautsky's obstinancy in the matter as stupid. His behavior, the party leader told Adler, showed Kautsky's lack of "all feeling of solidarity"; he was "hypnotized by ends" and unable to grasp "tactical questions."[18] Here, as on a number of occasions, Bebel was unwilling to allow ideological claims to interfere with the party's political advance. But to one of Kautsky's supporters, Hugo Haase, a lawyer from Königsberg who was becoming an influential figure in the party, Bebel had "struck out his whole past" by supporting the decision of the Executive.[19]

Kautsky was now in a position comparable to that in which several of the revisionist intellectuals had found themselves in the period after Dresden. Like them, he protested on behalf of the freedom of Social Democratic journalists. At stake for Kautsky, however, were more fundamental issues.[20] What was his status as the party's leading theorist? What was the relationship of orthodox Marxism to the party's policies? In rejecting his attempt to point the way ahead, the Executive had suggested that Marxist theory was irrelevant, even antagonistic, to the considerations which influenced the leaders. Kautsky saw in their action a scorn for the "impractical theoretician." "The louts," he complained to Haase, "wished to show the intellectual" that he was "merely a coolie who has to knuckle under when they command."[21]

The dispute ended in a compromise which simply confirmed the differences between Kautsky and the party leaders. A new edition of the *Road to Power* was published by the party's press after Kautsky agreed to tone down the passages referring to revolution and to write a new foreword in which he acknowledged that the views expressed were his own.[22] The Executive thus distanced itself from his analysis of the social and political situation.

To Zetkin the compromise meant a "complete capitulation" by Kautsky.[23] The Executive had, in effect, repudiated the notion that "we must conquer political power in a revolutionary struggle." Such a view had become no more than a personal opinion. She berated Kautsky for his unwillingness to bring the issue before the whole party; his submission was a "cruel, cowardly mockery of himself." Indeed, Kautsky's decision not to press the issue can be seen as a defeat, not only of his "claims as a theorist," but for the orthodox Marxism he represented.[24] Not surprisingly, the *Road to Power* has been described as "the swansong of doctrinaire Marxism."[25]

Kautsky's defeat no doubt contributed to his pessimistic assessment of the party a few months later. In September 1909 he conceded that the German Social Democrats had lost the leadership of the International. The party was going backward.[26] He attributed its condition in part to bureaucratization; the party's "enormous apparatus" was absorbing its best energies and producing an "idiocy of specialization." Occupied with administrative details, even the ablest of the party leaders were losing their capacity for larger views. But the worst consequence of the change was the "killing of initiative from below." Any bold action required the "passion and initiative" of the masses. Kautsky saw little sign of the "intellectual deepening and perfecting" among the party rank and file which was required for progress toward socialism. But he did not despair. Social conflicts, he believed, were becoming so great that the current situation could not long continue. The breakthrough, however, would await "great events" from outside.

Kautsky had come close to confessing that his thirty-year effort to instill Marxist ways of thinking into the party rank and file had failed. A crucial part of that failure had been the inability of the Social Democrats to develop a body of intellectuals, made up of educated recruits from the middle class, who could aid Kautsky in disseminating Marxist theory. Many of those who had come over had ended in the camp of the Revisionists. A younger group, to be discussed shortly, was now following a path to the left of Kautsky. To assist him at the *Neue Zeit* he could still count on Mehring. But the only young academically educated recruits on the staff were two talented Austrians—Gustav Eckstein and Rudolf Hilferding.[27]

The party's failure to attract the "rising generation" of the academically educated was acknowledged in the fall of 1909 by a Social Democrat who had made a special effort to attract them—Adolf Braun.[28] The "immigration of intellectuals" into the party, he observed, had "diminished absolutely and relatively during the previous decade." But Braun rejected the charge of the Revisionists that the policies of the party since Dresden had scared them off. All the German parties, he maintained, suffered from a similar deficiency. The problem, he insisted, could be traced to capitalistic development. Most intellectuals believed that participation in politics was futile. Still, Braun granted that the orthodox Marxist expectation that economic processes would "push the brain workers into the proletariat" had not been realized.

The clash between Kautsky and the party Executive exposed once more the tension between the party's pursuit of working-class interests and the Marxist promise of a fundamental transformation of life. Kautsky had backed away from the problem, confident perhaps that it would be resolved by objective developments. But the issue reappeared in the early weeks of 1910. The resumption of popular agitation for electoral reforms in Prussia and elsewhere presented party leaders with tactical questions which again tested the relevance of orthodox Marxist doctrines. In this new situation Kautsky was forced to reconsider the relationship between theory and practice and his role as an intellectual. The campaign for electoral rights also provided an opportunity for the radical Marxists to challenge the party's practices.

The Radical Marxists: Renewing the Revolutionary Drive

For Luxemburg, who was the dominant figure among the radical Marxists, the period following the election of 1907 was a time of "retrenchment and disillusionment."[29] Defeated in 1906 in her efforts to alter the party's tactics, she concentrated on her teaching duties at the party school. But early in 1910 the popular protests against the electoral laws in Prussia opened new possibilities for action. The "dog days were over." She was soon caught up in a busy round of meetings and demonstrations. "I am happiest," she wrote a friend, "in a storm."[30]

In her attempts to reassert the party's revolutionary goal, Luxemburg was joined by a number of the younger intellectuals who had come over from the middle class. Several held editorial positions on local Social Democratic papers. Paul Lensch, who had received a doctorate in economics in 1900 after study at the universities of Berlin and Strasbourg, became chief editor of the *Leipziger Volkszeitung.*[31] Influenced by Mehring and Luxemburg, he maintained that paper's reputation as a voice for the militant left wing within the party. In Dortmund, another convert from the Bildungsbürgertum, Konrad Haenisch, attempted to give a more radical tone to the local paper, the *Arbeiter-Zeitung.*[32] In Stuttgart, Zetkin and the Dunckers, who had moved there in 1908, provided radical leadership for Social Democrats in the area.[33] They were supported by Fritz Westmeyer, an academically educated recruit who became editor of the local *Schwäbische Tagewacht.*[34] In nearby Göppingen a comparable role was played by August Thalheimer, a doctor of philosophy, who had studied in Munich, Berlin, and Strasbourg.[35] This scattered group of radical intellectuals included Karl Liebknecht, who continued his single-minded campaign to arouse the young against militarism in German society.

Bremen had emerged as an important center of radical Marxism. The local party paper, the *Bremer Bürgerzeitung,* was now edited by a former worker and disciple of Schulz, Alfred Henke, who was dedicated to the propagation of a "socialist world view" and "pure theory."[36] While he initially followed Kautsky and expressed great enthusiasm for his *Road to Power,* Henke became convinced by 1909 that the party required a self-criticism which went well beyond that in the *Neue Zeit.* In his increasingly radical orientation he was influenced by two intellectuals who entered the movement from outside of Germany—Karl Radek and Anton Pannekoek. Radek, who had studied law in Poland, became in these years one of the party's leading commentators on foreign affairs and imperialism.[37] But it was Pannekoek who struggled most energetically with the problem which divided the orthodox and the radical Marxists most deeply—the source and nature of a proletarian socialist consciousness.

Pannekoek was well equipped for this task. Before entering the German movement in 1906 in response to an invitation to teach at the party school, he had been a leader of the radical wing of the Dutch Social Democrats. Born in a middle-class family in 1873, he had been trained as an astronomer and published important papers in his field before adopting Marxism in 1898. He brought to the socialist cause an understanding of modern science and a philosophical sophistication rare among the Marxist intellectuals.[38]

Pannekoek had been quick to defend orthodox Marxist doctrines against the criticism of the Revisionists. At the same time he conceded the validity of the Neo-Kantian claim that orthodox Marxism was excessively mechanistic and deterministic. And he found in the writings of Joseph Dietzgen, a friend and disciple of Marx, a way of reconciling the materialism of orthodox Marxism with a greater emphasis on the role of consciousness.[39] By means of Dietzgen's "monism," in which objective and subjective perceptions were viewed as dual aspects of empirical phenomena, Pannekoek could combine the central Marxist doctrines—economic determinism, the class struggle, the inevitability of revolution—with a strong affirmation of human agency. Dietzgen's unwillingness to grant more than provisional status to any doctrine also appealed to Pannekoek the scientist. He accepted the new relativistic point of view resulting from the collapse of nineteenth-century positivism. By using the "categories of analysis" drawn from both Marx and Dietzgen, Pannekoek attempted to develop "a critical and dynamic account of proletarian philosophy."[40]

That there was a distinctive proletarian philosophy and consciousness Pannekoek did not doubt. In his first contribution to the *Neue Zeit,* in 1904, he attacked Göhre's attempt to limit the scope of Marxism to practical economic and political issues.[41] Socialism, Pannekoek argued, held a new world view. True Marxists were freeing themselves from the "old mysteries" and gaining a radically new understanding of reality.

"Our strength," he declared, "lies in our isolation from bourgeois thought."

In subsequent essays Pannekoek compared the "spiritual breakthrough" taking place within the working class to that which had separated Christianity from the classical world.[42] Only the workers, by virtue of their place in the economic system, stood "unprejudiced with respect to social phenomena" and were capable, therefore, of perceiving and advocating "new truths" about society. "Historical materialism," he maintained, was simply the theoretical expression of what was taking place in modern society; it represented "the world view of socialism." "Proletarian philosophy" was, like previous systems of thought, provisional, but it was a "whole conception of life and a metaphysic." As such it provided a "powerful weapon in the struggle against the rulers of a declining social order," who were incapable of understanding its true nature.

Pannekoek assigned to "spiritual factors" an importance at least equal to economic factors in the revolutionary struggle. The "ultimate political question," one student of his thought noted, was "the problem of working-class consciousness."[43] "What was its precise nature?" How did it arise? In accepting an appointment to teach at the party school Pannekoek wished to include the study of the "human and cultural sciences."[44] When his proposal met resistance from Kautsky, he maintained that "a clear understanding of the role and nature of spirit and the spiritual was imperative."

Pannekoek's position at the party school was terminated by the Prussian authorities in the summer of 1906, but he remained in the German movement. Although he lectured widely for the party, his main center of activity was Bremen. There he became secretary of the education committee, which had been established by Schulz to cultivate a "proletarian world view" within the party rank and file. Pannekoek believed, as he wrote Kautsky, that he could, as an outsider, play an educational role more effectively than those who were occupied with the practical work of the party.[45]

Pannekoek described that role in a long essay published in 1909, "Tactical Differences within the Workers' Movement."[46] More or less contemporary with Kautsky's *Road to Power,* the essay contained significant similarities and differences. In his concern with the process through which the workers acquired a socialist understanding, however, Pannekoek sought to remedy the failures of the orthodox Marxists.

The emphasis that Pannekoek placed on the understanding of the workers was evident in his opening sentence. "The tactics of the proletarian class struggle represent an application of science, of theory, which clarifies the causes and tendencies of social development."[47] He then presented the classical Marxist account of the breakdown of capitalism, modified, however, by an insistence on the importance of human thought and will. While "other classes . . . grope around in darkness," the working class possessed a "science of society" which enabled it to "elucidate both the causes of its misery and the goal of social development."[48]

> Thus able to rely on forces that shape political events and to foresee what is about to happen, it gains a quiet energy, a serenity, which helps it through difficulties . . . to foresee the consequences of its action and to avoid being beguiled by immediate passing appearances.

Pannekoek then discussed the way in which the workers gained understanding. It was the natural outcome of living conditions which destroyed ancient traditions, threw down "old customs and made a 'tabula rasa' of minds which then become capable of accepting absolutely new ideas."[49] The proletariat was the vehicle for the changing "self-consciousness of society." Marxist theory was "increasingly well understood" because it "corresponded more and more closely to the experiences of the workers." The "science of society, the knowledge of the objectives and the methods of the struggle," could not, therefore, be "acquired in a quasi-academic way outside the conflict of which, in reality, they are the fruits."[50] "Action, not words," was the main source of enlightenment. "Theoretical writings of scientific inspiration" helped toward "a better and quicker understanding," but they were "no substitute for the struggle."

The process through which experience was translated into theory remained, however, unclear. Pannekoek did not assign a definite role to intellectuals. Insofar as he referred to them, he emphasized their separation from the proletariat and their captivity to the bourgeois illusion that "mind governs the world."[51] He blamed individuals of petty-bourgeois origins for the two major distortions of Marxist theory—anarchism and revisionism. Both forms of misunderstanding resulted from an inability to enter into that "dialectical mode of thinking" which came naturally to the proletariat.

For Pannekoek the main educational agencies were the party and the trade unions. While he did not oppose their efforts to improve the immediate well-being of the workers, he held that this activity served mainly to shatter illusions about the possibility of fundamental change within the existing system. What mattered most in the practical struggle was the creation of "new men with new habits . . . integral parts of a body animated by one and the same will."[52]

Toward the end of his essay Pannekoek distinguished between "ideology," defined as the direct "spiritual expression of the conditions of material life and class interests," on the one hand, and the "science of society" being acquired by the workers, on the other.[53] The former was "above all a matter of sentiment"; the latter was "an intellectual matter." It provided the proletariat with a "deep and lasting knowledge" which enabled it "to escape from the influence of immediate and limited interests" and follow a "tranquil and sure course."[54] But here again the cognitive or psychological process remained unclear. What was the nature of the transition from the old to the new mentality? As one sympathetic critic of Pannekoek's thought has observed, he "failed to work out" the precise details of how the old consciousness was transcended or to specify the "unique features of a proletarian mentality."[55]

Pannekoek, like Kautsky, believed that a new period in the "proletarian class war" was beginning. He, too, held that the traditional forms of the class struggle—politics and trade unionism—needed to be augmented by a new tactic. "The old methods," he wrote, "have had their day."[56] Required was a mixing of political and economic modes of action in the form of the mass strike. He was convinced that "organized masses . . . endowed with class-consciousness" were "now entering the fray." Indeed, in the early weeks of 1910 the masses entered the fray in a series of demonstrations in Berlin and elsewhere, directed against undemocratic electoral laws.

The demonstrations began in February, when Chancellor Bethmann-Holweg announced his long-awaited proposals for changes in the Prussian electoral system. His "reforms" left the power of the ruling groups virtually untouched. The frustration and anger of the workers, who were joined by many from the middle class, erupted in a series of protests in the major cities of Prussia and other states. The demonstrations, which coincided with an upsurge of strike activity, accelerated in the weeks ahead and subsided only after the middle of April. They represented an unprecedented display of mass discontent within the German nation.[57]

For Luxemburg the moment had come for the masses in Germany to carry out the role she had described in the *Mass Strike*. In an article, "What Next?," prepared for the *Neue Zeit,* she attempted to draw the lessons for the party. She could claim, with some justification, that she was simply developing the implications of Kautsky's analysis in the *Road to Power.*[58] At the same time she addressed a fundamental problem identified by Kautsky. The objective economic and social conditions making for revolution were present, he had argued, but the requisite subjective conditions were not. The workers, according to Kautsky, still lacked the necessary socialist understanding. Luxemburg believed that she had solved the problem. She counted on the rapid emergence of a proletarian consciousness, more or less spontaneously, through the immediate struggle itself.

Luxemburg's reading of the contemporary situation confronted Kautsky with a difficult decision. Should he join her in pressing for the more militant tactic he had recommended in the *Road to Power?* Or should he identify himself with the increasingly cautious course of the party leaders? His rejection of Luxemburg's article for publication in *Neue Zeit* indicated his choice.[59] His decision could be explained in terms of his close relationship to Bebel and the other leaders. But his identification with the party leaders was, in fact, demanded by his orthodox Marxism. The party had always played a crucial mediating role in the process through which Marxist theory reached the workers. Although intellectuals were indispensable to that process, their ideas must first engage those who were organized in the party.[60] The party was the most advanced element of the proletariat. Outside the party there was, for Kautsky, no effective means of developing a theoretically correct tactic.

Kautsky's predicament was clear. In siding with the party in the face of Luxemburg's challenge, he had tied himself, and orthodox Marxism as well, to a leadership which only a year earlier had rejected his own interpretation of the historical situation. There was, to be sure, sufficient ambiguity in the analysis presented in the *Road to Power* to permit Kautsky to disguise his retreat.[61] But his position as the party's leading theorist had changed. The months ahead indicated how much.

Luxemburg's article "What Next?" was published by Haenisch in the Dortmund paper.[62] She argued that the demonstrations taking place reflected a new stage in the working-class struggle. The movement of the masses had "its own logic and psychology."[63] She called on the Social Democratic leaders to place the political mass strike on the party's agenda; it was the appropriate "outer form" of the "inner development" of the workers.

Although Luxemburg saw in the "inner development" of the workers the crucial force needed for making a revolution, she now gave to the party leaders and the trade union leaders an important role in that process. If the leaders "let the moment escape," she warned, the surge of enthusiasm would fall away.[64] If they gave the "necessary word," the élan of the masses would grow. Even if the new strike tactic resulted initially in defeat, working-class organizations would soon "flourish again," augmented by the "new layers of the proletariat" awakened by the struggle. What mattered most was the way in which the struggle produced a "deepening and strengthening of the socialist consciousness" of the masses. Pannekoek, Haenisch, Lensch, and other radical Marxists joined her in calling on the party to adopt the tactic of the mass strike.

Luxemburg's views found no favor among the Social Democratic leaders, who were most concerned about the impact of the street demonstrations on the party's political prospects.[65] With the likelihood of a general election within a year or so, Bebel and his colleagues wished to avoid alienating any elements of the population who might support the party's candidates. The demonstrations, with the possibility of violent clashes with the police, threatened to do just that. Both party and trade union leaders attempted to apply brakes to the campaign for electoral rights. The Social Democratic Executive urged party editors to avoid discussion of the mass strike. Between the views of the radical Marxists, led by Luxemburg, and those of the party leaders there were now fundamental disagreements.

Kautsky defended the policies of the leaders against the position of the radical Marxists.[66] "Is our only choice," he asked, between the mass strike and the demoralization of the masses? Not at all, he replied. Luxemburg failed to appreciate the objective situation facing the workers. They were not in a position to deliver a strong blow to the existing order. Any attempt to employ the mass strike would only lead to brutal countermeasures by the government. But the alternative, according to Kautsky, was not demoralization. In her emphasis on "psychological considerations," Luxemburg had failed to recognize a third course—"attrition"—a further strengthening of the organization and discipline of the workers while the internal contradictions of capitalism continued to unfold. Only during the final crisis could the weapon of the mass strike be effective. In the meantime Social Democrats should concentrate on the coming election, for the "attainment of an absolute majority" of the voters was "only a question of a few years." The greatest danger facing the party was the temptation "to pick the fruit before it was ripe." It would be foolish to use up ammunition in "preliminary skirmishes."

Kautsky had drawn back from the assessment of objective historical conditions he had presented in the *Road to Power.* The mass strike had for him ceased to be an offensive weapon, a way of drawing the political and the economic struggle together. But Kautsky also repeated the claim, made in his earlier analysis, that the masses still lacked the understanding, the subjective state, necessary to play their appointed role in the revolution. This was Luxemburg's focal point when she resumed the debate in June 1910.

The protests against the electoral laws had subsided. The exchanges between Kautsky and Luxemburg, which continued through the summer, had lost their immediate relevance to Social Democratic policy. For both thinkers, however, the disagreement raised issues which were fundamental to the future of the party. To settle those issues was unavoidable. But the effort to do so led to a bitter and irreparable break between the two. "Personal polemics and socialist tactics," as Nettl observed, "became hopelessly mixed up."[67]

Luxemburg maintained that Kautsky had failed to understand "the nature of the great mass movement under way."[68] She noted the "stormy applause" with which the workers had responded in the sixteen meetings she held during April and May. The "broad mass" had developed "a battle mood . . . never before seen in Germany." The responsibility of the leaders was to bring the mood to full consciousness. Kautsky, she charged, had identified with a party leadership which remained "behind the feeling and thought of the masses." In fixing on the electoral tactic, the leaders had "stuck a needle in the balloon" of popular enthusiasm. By retreating to "pure parliamentarianism" Kautsky had failed to recognize that the mass strike represented a completion of the political tactic and "a method for the schooling the masses." Luxemburg now claimed that the party's leading theorist was providing "a theoretical screen for elements in the party and the trade unions who feel uncomfortable with the further ruthless unfolding of the mass movement."[69]

In his reply, Kautsky pointed to a contradiction in Luxemburg's "new strategy."[70] If, as she contended, the mass strike expressed elemental forces at work in the masses, how could she blame the leaders for stifling that development? That the electoral-rights campaign had faded so quickly indicated that Luxemburg had "exaggerated the favorable nature of the historical situation." Her policy was "one of bluff." There could be no substitute, Kautsky maintained, for the slow, painstaking growth of the "self-discipline and political understanding" of the workers. The immediate task was still to win more seats in the Reichstag; "mandates," he declared, "don't lie."[71]

Kautsky was deeply troubled by the quarrel with Luxemburg. Late in the summer he suggested that they "bury their differences" and concentrate on the renewed challenge to the party's policies coming from the right-wing Social Democrats in Baden.[72] Luxemburg was not willing to call it quits. A "theoretical clarification" was necessary to save their "great spiritual movement" from ossification.[73] She again called attention to the "crass contradictions" between Kautsky's present position and his claim in the *Road to Power* that "we are already in a revolutionary period." But now, when his theory "descended to the earth, like an eagle, as in the Prussian electoral rights campaign," it had become "headless and helpless." Kautsky and the party leaders had missed a "brilliant opportunity" for "raising up and enlightening . . . the indifferent masses."

The rift between Kautsky and Luxemburg had become unbridgeable. Kautsky could find some satisfaction in the ending of the belief, held by some party members, that he and Luxemburg were ideological twins.

His friend Adler, viewing the dispute from Vienna, acknowledged his own "Schadenfreude," his malicious pleasure, over the falling out of the old friends.[74] Adler had never had any liking for Luxemburg. Now that "poisonous hussy" had demonstrated once more her "perverse dogmatism" and her "lack of any feeling of responsibility."

Luxemburg, however, emerged from the debate with a sense of triumph; she was confident that she had damaged Kautsky's credibility as a theorist. She noted with satisfaction reports from Berlin that Kautsky had been shaken by her articles.[75] He "gets red in the face with each word, slams his fist on the table, and has lost all remnants of journalistic propriety and humane understanding." "Obviously," she added, "he realizes what has happened to him." But her sense of victory was checked by the feeling that it would be "unpractical to deliver a crushing blow," that it would serve neither the cause of the Radicals nor that of the party.

It is unlikely that Kautsky found much merit in Luxemburg's argument. But he had become vulnerable, by his retreat from the views expressed in the *Road to Power,* to her criticism. She had, to be sure, exaggerated that retreat. The essential features of Kautsky's orthodox Marxism had not changed. A revolutionary upheaval would await the unfolding of objective forces; only a profound crisis in the capitalistic economy would create the conditions in which the workers could take political power. And a revolution could only succeed if the workers had developed the necessary organization and understanding. Until these conditions, objective and subjective, were fulfilled, the proletariat was no match for the power which the Wilhelmine rulers could mobilize against it. In the meantime, the party, the indispensable vehicle for the proletariat, must hold fast to its old "victory-crowned tactic."

There had always been a large measure of illusion in Kautsky's belief that his Marxist theory and the policies of the Social Democratic leaders were in harmony. Even before the antisocialist legislation ended in 1890, immediate political possibilities rather than ideology had begun to shape the policies of Bebel and the other party leaders. As long as the party was shut off from political power, however, Kautsky could ignore the divergence between theory and practice. His form of Marxism was well suited, as Dick Geary has observed, to the "non-revolutionary but repressive situation" in which the Social Democrats found themselves.[76] Orthodox Marxism mirrored the ambiguities of German politics in these years.

Now new political possibilities seemed to be opening up. The clash between Kautsky and the party Executive had shattered the illusion that the party's ideology and its tactics were in harmony. In that clash and in the "ill-advised struggle of the souls" with Luxemburg, as Bebel described it, Kautsky had surrendered to the claims of the party.[77] He had largely given up the critical role which he, as the chief defender of orthodoxy, had exercised.

The nervous breakdown which Kautsky suffered late in the summer of 1910 can be attributed to the crisis in his relationship to the party. Some Social Democrats blamed Luxemburg for his breakdown, and she accepted a measure of responsibility.[78] But Bebel recognized, as he wrote Kautsky's wife, that the "spiritual battle" with his former ally was simply the culmination of a development which reached back a year or more. Kautsky's work for the party, Bebel observed, had become more and more frantic, as if "he stands before his end and must say all that he has to say."[79] The party leader sensed the intellectual and emotional turmoil through which Kautsky had passed during the previous eighteen months.

After some weeks in a sanitorium Kautsky returned to his editorial duties. He resumed his new role—in Luxemburg's words—of providing "theoretical music" for the policies of the party and trade union leaders.[80]

Orthodox Marxism as an Apologetic

During 1911 Kautsky altered his Marxism in ways which brought it into harmony with the policies of the party leaders. To suggest that this move was a calculated or opportunistic one on his part would be a mistake. Despite his retreat from positions taken in the *Road to Power,* the central doctrines in Kautsky's Marxism did not change. What changed was the function of his theory within the party.

Kautsky's move away from the analysis presented in the *Road to Power* was most apparent in his treatment of the second Moroccan crisis. The failure of the Social Democratic leaders to attack the German government for its aggressive action in North Africa had drawn sharp protests from Luxemburg and other radical Marxists. When, in August, the party Executive decided that it was safe to criticize the government, it called on Kautsky to explain its position. His pamphlet *World Politics, World War, and Social Democracy* indicated that his view of capitalistic development was being adapted to the political goals of the party.

Kautsky now gave up the notion of proletarian exclusiveness.[81] The belief that the workers confronted "one reactionary mass," a central claim in the *Road to Power,* was replaced by the argument that the capitalistic class was divided. While imperialistic policies were driving one section down the path of militarism and colonialism, other middle-class groups—the smaller manufacturers, professional elements, including the lower levels of the civil service, and "free intellectuals"—desired peaceful policies, at least insofar as they recognized their own interests. Social Democrats might, therefore, cooperate with those elements in the effort to prevent war.

The abandonment of the notion of proletarian exclusiveness was, in part, a reflection of Kautsky's growing sense of the party's failure to create the theoretically informed working class on which a successful revolution depended. He now conceded that theory had had little impact on the party rank and file, that "the number of actual revisionists, like the number of actual Marxists," was "very small."[82] "Most of our comrades," he added, simply judged matters "according to mood and feeling," not "by our arguments but by circumstances." He acknowledged that the masses were more likely to be taught by "praxis," but he had also become pessimistic about their readiness for revolutionary action.

His pessimism was apparent in the fall of 1911 when he took up once more the claims of the radical Marxists that the masses, unorganized as well as organized, should be readied for revolutionary action.[83] Although he agreed with the Radicals that the masses were likely to play an important role in the political struggles just ahead, he did not share their confidence that the role would be constructive. The overwhelming majority of the masses still lacked the discipline and understanding necessary for the transition to a socialist society. Kautsky drew on the writings of Gustave Le Bon and Scipio Schipele, which had also been employed a decade earlier by Bernstein to criticize the orthodox Marxist view of the proletariat, to suggest that mass action might be dominated by unconscious, irrational, and destructive impulses. "Only a mystical teleology," he argued, could assume that mass action was "always progressive." It was just as likely to be reactionary. Unless an uprising was prepared by a "revolutionizing of the minds," it would be premature and dangerous.

During 1911 Kautsky also turned back to a purely parliamentary tactic, setting aside the view, expressed in the *Road to Power,* that the mass strike should be used as an offensive weapon. At the Jena conference in the fall he gave strong support to the efforts of the Social Democratic leaders to focus all energies on the coming general election.[84] His altered analysis of capitalism was providing "a socioeconomic foundation for the policy of electoral pacts with the liberals."[85]

The party's striking gains in the general election confirmed, according to Kautsky, the wisdom of the new course. He endorsed the agreement with the Progressives; it followed from his argument that Social Democrats could exploit the deepening divisions within the middle class. The election had demonstrated, moreover, that the liberals faced political suicide unless they turned to the left.[86] It was only a question of time before the "majority of the German people" would be won over by the Social Democrats; "our further advance is irresistible."[87]

In the weeks following the election Kautsky continued to chart a path between the "rebellious impatience" of the radical Marxists and the "statesman's impatience" of the Revisionists. What has been called his "centrist" position, however, was becoming indistinguishable in practical terms from that of the Revisionists.[88] Kautsky's "prestige as a Marxist theorist" was being used to justify the efforts of the party leaders to escape from their political isolation.[89] Zetkin concluded that "cowardice" was now the key to Kautsky's character.[90] What was "doubly contemptible," she wrote, was the "semi-official status of his opinions within the party." No wonder the radical Marxists set out to destroy Kautsky's credibility as a theorist.

When, in the spring of 1912, Kautsky joined the Fraktion in supporting proposals for disarmament, he was again the target of sharp criticism from the party's left.[91] At the center of their disagreement lay different interpretations of imperialism. But the radical Marxists now charged that Kautsky was abandoning crucial elements in Marxism. He had given up, according to Pannekoek, the belief in the distinctness of the thought and feelings of the proletariat, which he, "more than any other student of Marx," had helped to clarify.[92] Kautsky's new emphasis on the unpredictability and unreliability of the masses ignored the "essential economic elements" which shaped the mind of the masses. Having "left his Marxist tools at home," the party's leading theorist had, according to Pannekoek, adopted a "passive radicalism" which limited the action of the Social Democrats to parliamentarianism and the trade union struggle.

In the face of renewed criticism from the radical Marxists, Kautsky continued to argue that the conditions—objective and subjective—necessary for revolutionary action were still absent. Again he stressed the need for the "workers themselves" to "acquire scientific insight."[93] Only those who could "think individually and consider arguments" would be capable of effective action at a time of crisis. If a revolutionary situation did arise, reliance on the "blind instincts" of the masses would be hazardous.

In his new role as apologist for the policies of the party leaders, Kautsky was occupied mainly with the challenge from the left. He was providing the Social Democrats with the rhetorical means to reconcile the orthodox Marxist doctrines with the party's increasingly pragmatic political course. His success was evident at the Chemnitz conference, where the major debate dealt with the party's approach to imperialism. Although Kautsky was not present because of illness, a resolution prepared by Hilferding and Haase embodied his conviction that it was possible to moderate the dangerous tendencies in imperialism.[94] The resolution restated the claim of orthodox Marxists, and radical Marxists as well, that a brutal drive toward expansion and international conflict was characteristic of capitalism. At the same time it called on Social Democrats to work against that drive and preserve humankind from the "frightful catastrophe" of war. But the resolution provided, as Wachenheim observed, no clear guidance for the "concrete politics" of the party's Fraktion. The resolution, which passed overwhelmingly, "could not conceal" the "chaos of views" underlying the Social Democratic opposition to imperialism.

The proceedings at Chemnitz demonstrated the confused state of the party's approach to foreign policy issues. But the conference also indicated the way in which Kautsky's Marxism now functioned as an "integrationist ideology." It could hold the varied motives and interests of an increasingly diversified party together without "prejudicing its tactics" or "fragmenting it through dissent."[95] Only the radical Marxists, with their demand for resolute mass action, disagreed.

The triumph of "centrism" at Chemnitz and the altered function of orthodox Marxism in the party were reflected, too, in the ratification of the decision to expel Hildebrand. For Kautsky, this decision meant the repudiation of an "attempt to smuggle bourgeois imperialistic ideas into Social Democracy" and the party's determination to maintain the boundaries which separated it from the liberals.[96] Kautsky rejected the demands of the Revisionists for greater toleration; the party, they claimed, was becoming more pluralistic. Kautsky argued the opposite. Pluralism, or "chaos," he wrote, had been characteristic of the party during the eighties. Since that time it had been moving steadily "toward greater unity." There was now "far less room for fantasy and feeling," because science, "the knowledge of necessity," had gained the upper hand. The party was marked by "growing solidarity and unity," not only "in action but also in thought." Kautsky's self-deception was obvious; he displayed little awareness of the ways in which his own role in the party and that of his theory was changing.

Shortly after the Chemnitz conference, when Heine and Arons presented a petition calling on Social Democrats to remedy an action—the expulsion of Hildebrand—which threatened free inquiry, Kautsky again defended his conception of the party.[97] Noting the prominence of educated recruits among the signers of the petition, he dismissed it as one more stage in the "old struggle of the intellectuals for special rights in the party." Fortunately, he added, the proletariat had always rejected the intellectuals' demands for a "privileged place." How much easier it was, he observed, to "organize and discipline" those who were engaged in material production than the "intellectual producers," inclined as they were to "indiscipline and anarchism."

The theoretical discipline on which Kautsky insisted, however, had led not only to the rhetorical obscurity evident at Chemnitz but to his growing isolation as an intellectual. The earlier defections of the revisionist intellectuals had been followed by the breaking away of the younger Marxists as they took the path scouted by Luxemburg. Then came the disputes with Luxemburg and Zetkin. During 1912 there was also a bitter quarrel with Mehring, the intellectual on whom Kautsky had relied most to develop the orthodox Marxist position in the *Neue Zeit*. The reasons for their falling out were complicated. Mehring's readiness to turn intellectual differences into personal antagonism was again evident.[98] Even before the election, however, he had pulled away from Kautsky's centrist course.[99] By the spring of 1912 the differences between the two men had made it impossible for Mehring to continue writing the lead articles for the *Neue Zeit*. In the months ahead Kautsky was much occupied with the problem of getting rid of Mehring who, he concluded, was "morally dead."[100] Bebel, too, had come to regret their efforts to save Mehring at Dresden and admitted that Braun had been correct in attacking him for the arrogance with which he judged "persons and things."[101]

The death of Bebel in August 1913 deprived Kautsky of his strongest, albeit inconstant, supporter within the party leadership, the figure to whom he had often looked for guidance in practical matters. But Kautsky's Marxism was now bankrupt. It provided no way out, as Groh has observed, of the "blind alley into which the party had entered."[102] In the face of the new situation confronting Social Democrats, Kautsky was "for the first time disoriented and helpless."[103] He was no longer capable of "theoretical-critical reflection."[104]

Kautsky was also surprised. During 1913 economic and social conflicts in Germany seemed to be reaching the revolutionary condition he had forecast in the *Road to Power*. But instead of the rapid rise in "revolutionary élan" that he had expected, there was, as he wrote Adler, only "apathy, despondency, and uneasiness in wide circles."[105] No one among the party leaders, he confessed, knew what to do. In this situation they could only hold fast to the central party institutions against the "experimentation and adventurism" advocated by the demagogues of the "right and the left."[106] Kautsky could take some comfort in the fact that "aggressive mass action" was being preached "almost exclusively by intellectuals." But for protection against such irresponsibility he now counted only on the "healthy instinct" of the average party member.

Kautsky had become little more than a follower. Like the other party leaders, he was trapped in the immobility to which historical developments in Germany and the policies of the Social Democrats had led. When, in August 1914, the party's Fraktion made its peace with the German government and joined in the war effort, Kautsky went along. Only after three years of war did he reassert his intellectual independence and find a new critical force within his orthodox Marxism. The result, however, was his dismissal from the party-owned *Neue Zeit,* his instrument for fulfilling his role as a socialist intellectual. He remained committed to that role, but it was, henceforth, little more than a personal enterprise. The task of developing a cadre of Marxist intellectuals capable of mediating between theory and the proletariat was taken up in the postwar years by others for whom his orthodoxy had little appeal.

In assuming the role of apologist for the policies of the party leaders, Kautsky had implicitly acknowledged the failure of the project to which he had devoted his life. That project was now in the hands of the radical Marxists.

The Radical Marxists: The Myth of the Proletariat

While engaged in a new debate with Kautsky in the summer of 1912 Pannekoek claimed that the workers had undergone a "deep transformation of character."[107] Through their "willingness to sacrifice" and their new qualities of discipline, solidarity, and brotherhood, they had "become different men than the individualistic petty bourgeoisie and the peasants." The words were similar to those used by Kautsky a few years earlier. But the party's leading theorist had ceased to find these socially redeeming features in the Social Democratic rank and file. It was left to the radical Marxists to recover the fundamental faith in the proletariat on which the movement rested.

The conviction that the Social Democratic leaders had lost faith in the proletariat had drawn the radical Marxists together. And they saw in contemporary economic and political developments signs that Germany had entered a time of crisis. Working-class living standards had been stagnant or worse for a decade or more. At the political level, the conservative and reactionary forces were tightening their hold on power. Radical Marxists could see, moreover, in the struggle for electoral rights, evidence of a new "proletarian will" and a readiness on the part of the workers to assume the role forecast by Marx. The moment had arrived for Social Democrats to transform working-class energies into a revolutionary force.

Luxemburg remained the dominant figure among the radical Marxists. By 1910 she was seeking, by means of correspondence and talks before party branches, to strengthen the growing sense among the Radicals that they constituted a distinct force within the movement. The radical Marxists never developed a systematic program, and they often lined up on different sides on the issues facing the party. But during 1911 and 1912 they were energized by events which seemed to them to demonstrate the opportunism of the party leaders.

The second Moroccan crisis, in July 1911, was such an event. Luxemburg immediately attacked the party leaders for their failure to seize the opportunity to mobilize opposition to German militarism. Against the fears of the Executive that criticism of the government might make Social Democrats vulnerable in the coming election, she insisted that the party's task was "to enlighten the masses as soon and as completely as possible as to . . . the sordid capitalistic interests involved in the affair."[108] The effort by the Executive to "restrict our agitation exclusively to domestic policy" reflected its failure to recognize the way in which "financial policy, the rule of the Junkers, and the stagnation of social reform are organically bound up with militarism, naval policy, colonial policy, and personal rule."

The party conference at Jena in the fall of 1911 indicated how difficult it was for the radical Marxists to make their case against the leaders. Luxemburg found herself on the defensive—accused of disloyalty to the party for her disclosure of confidential correspondence relating to the Morocco problem.[109] Efforts by Radicals at Jena to strengthen Social Democratic opposition to imperialism resulted in their almost complete isolation. Preoccupation with the approaching general election also worked against those who favored a more militant policy.

Luxemburg's outspoken criticism of the Social Democratic leaders again made her a popular speaker on local party platforms. During the second half of 1911 she traveled widely, speaking to enthusiastic audiences. The experience, particularly the strong applause which greeted her references to the mass strike, seemed to her to demonstrate that the spirit of the rank and file was "far better than the parliamentary cretinism of the leaders."[110] "How clear and critical the masses are," she exclaimed after a meeting in December.[111] On the eve of the general election she took heart in the "enthusiasm and desire for battle" she saw within the workers.[112]

Luxemburg did not share in the euphoria which followed the party's electoral victory. It simply meant that the radical Marxists would "have to work harder than ever against . . . parliamentary cretinism."[113] "We remain what we are," she wrote in February. As the terms and the results of the party's treaty with the Progressives became known, the Radicals renewed their attacks on the Social Democratic leaders. The failure of the Fraktion to secure support from the liberals in an attempt to gain a vice-presidency in the Reichstag reinforced the conviction of the Radicals that class lines were hardening. The Social Democratic hope for an alliance with bourgeois liberals "in an age of growing imperialism," Luxemburg wrote, was "nothing more than a foolish dream."[114]

In the spring of 1912 Mehring joined the radical Marxists. It was to him that Luxemburg declared, in April, that the party had reached a turning point.[115] While urging Mehring to retain what influence he could at the *Neue Zeit,* she assured him that all "honest men within the party, who are not intellectual slaves of the Executive," would stand on his side in the face of attacks by Bebel and Kautsky. The pettiness and cowardice of the main party agencies meant that it was time to give the masses a "more energetic, ruthless and farsighted leadership." She was confident that "the masses stand behind us."

A new leadership could only come, according to Luxemburg, from a clear understanding of the close relationship between the internal and external aspects of imperialism. A "totalistic" approach to capitalistic development had characterized her thought since the late nineties. And now, in her attempt to shake the party out of its lethargy and self-absorption, she undertook a new analysis of imperialism.[116] The outcome was the *Accumulation of Capital,* published in 1913.

During the spring and summer of 1912, however, the radical challenge to the party leaders was led by Lensch, Radek, and Pannekoek. They took aim at the efforts of the Fraktion to find a common political ground with the liberals. They attacked Kautsky for his support of the government's disarmament proposals and the suggestion, increasingly evident in his writings, that the harsher aspects of imperialism could be mitigated. Through his "improvisations," Lensch charged, Kautsky had abandoned the Marxist claim that there was an inescapable connection between capitalism and imperialistic drives leading toward war.[117] Party efforts to combat those drives were futile. The radical Marxists called on Social Democrats to concentrate on the work of preparing the masses for revolutionary action.

But were the workers ready for new forms of mass action? This question divided Kautsky and Pannekoek when they debated in the summer of 1912. The two men were resuming the argument which Kautsky had initiated with an article on "mass action" during the previous fall. At that time Pannekoek had urged the *Neue Zeit* editor to bring their differences fully out into the open in order to see if they could come closer together.[118] When, in July 1912, Kautsky opened the columns of the *Neue Zeit* to him, Pannekoek presented the radical position in a series of five articles.[119] His hope for a rapprochement with Kautsky, however, ended in the realization that they now represented "two Marxisms."

At the outset Pannekoek attempted to account for the growing differences between "those who had formerly stood together in the common struggle."[120] Their disagreements over the nature of imperialism, electoral tactics, and the use of the mass strike, he argued, could be traced to quite different views of the masses in this "first stage" of a revolutionary era. He addressed what was, in his view, the heart of the problem. How could one explain the continuing domination of German society by a minority that was inferior both in numbers and in economic strength to the working class? He denied that the ruling classes owed their power primarily to their control of the state and the repressive instruments of police and army. What was decisive, Pannekoek declared, was their control over culture—the press, the schools, the churches. The "chief cause of the weakness of the proletariat" lay in its "intellectual or spiritual dependence on the bourgeoisie." "Spiritual power," he added, was now the "mightiest power in the human world." It followed that the proletariat could only break "the intellectual superiority of the dominant class" by gaining "clear insight into the nature of the political and class struggle . . . and the nature of capitalistic development."

Pannekoek thus fixed on the old problem—the formation of a genuine socialist consciousness among the workers. Unlike Kautsky, who denied that the masses had made much progress in gaining a Marxist understanding, Pannekoek believed that a new working-class mentality was emerging. The electoral struggle had displayed a new "proletarian will." The "life-situations of the workers," their material circumstances in particular, were producing a new understanding of social realities, not only among the organized workers but among the unorganized as well.[121] The spontaneous schooling in socialism would, according to Pannekoek, continue to grow through the struggle itself.

Pannekoek's emphasis on spontaneity did not preclude a role for the party. It was the trustee for a part of the proletarian will; it had, therefore, important responsibilities. What was "independently breaking out" among the workers through the "influence of material conditions" must be made "fully conscious."[122] Pannekoek did not reject parliamentary action, but he denied that it could bring about a fundamental change in the political system. Like other radical Marxists, he saw in the mass strike the most effective means of overthrowing the social order.

By placing such emphasis on the subjective state of the proletariat, Pannekoek could view the working-class organizations—the party and the trade unions—differently than Kautsky. Kautsky worried lest the working-class organizations be crushed by launching premature offensives. Pannekoek, however, counted on the spirit—the "essential element" in these organizations—to survive defeat and even be strengthened in the process.[123] Kautsky still saw the revolution as a distant, climactic event; Pannekoek fixed on the process through which the workers were gaining the qualities of mind and will necessary for a revolution. He dismissed Kautsky's fear that the workers might, in the event of war, be caught up in a patriotic fervor; such a worry reflected an underestimation of the force of "socialist instincts" and the growing strength of a class "with special interests and views."[124] Unlike Kautsky, who insisted that the workers would need existing political institutions to make the transition to socialism, Pannekoek was confident that the proletariat could take over the modes of production and build a new order from scratch.

Pannekoek reasserted the radical Marxist belief that a revolutionary outcome was still inherent in the proletarian struggle. In doing so he also demonstrated the growing gulf between the "two Marxisms." There had been no genuine dialogue with Kautsky. Pannekoek's frustration was evident in a letter to the editor. "You have simply" employed labels—"half syndicalist, anarchist or antiparliamentary"; Kautsky had made no effort to understand another way of thinking.[125] After all, Pannekoek added, "my views rest completely on Marxist-socialist ground." But the two men were now working at cross-purposes.

The cross-purposes became even clearer at the Chemnitz conference in the fall when the radical Marxists, led by Pannekoek and Lensch, suffered crushing defeats in their challenges to the party's policy on imperialism and its electoral treaty with the Progressives. Afterward Pannekoek conceded that the revisionist point of view, now supported by the orthodox Marxists, had triumphed on all the critical issues.[126] Chemnitz had shown that fundamental disagreements, evident in the exchanges with Kautsky, separated the radical Marxists from the overwhelming majority of the party's delegates. Pannekoek could take some comfort in the willingness of the Bremen Social Democrats to support the radical position. He continued his efforts, with limited success, to instruct the local workers in Marxist theory.[127]

Chemnitz demonstrated the weakness of the radical Marxists. They now confronted a large and powerful bureaucracy, resistant to any moves which threatened established policies and the vested interests of party officials. The radical Marxists were also losing their key editorial positions. Haenisch had resigned from the Dortmund paper early in 1911, after concluding that his efforts to radicalize its policies had made his situation intolerable.[128] During the early months of 1912 the two radical editors in Württemburg—Westmeyer and Thalheimer—were discharged.[129] Electoral setbacks in the region—exceptions to the general fortunes of the party in 1912—were blamed on the dissensions which the Radicals had generated among the local Social Democrats. A year later Lensch resigned as editor of the *Leipziger Volkszeitung*. And the radical Marxists Luxemburg, Pannekoek, Lensch, and Radek had already been shut out of the *Neue Zeit*.[130] With Lensch's resignation they lost their main alternative outlet. Several attempts by the Radicals to influence Social Democratic papers by means of articles offered through "press services" proved short-lived.

Growing dissatisfaction in the Social Democratic rank and file during 1912 and 1913—expressions both of widespread economic discontent and of disillusionment with the results of the electoral triumph—ensured that the radical Marxists would continue to be heard within the party. But they were unable to mobilize opposition to the policies of the Social Democratic leaders. The party was characterized by increasing apathy; most branches reported falling memberships, declining subscriptions to local papers, and reduced attendance at meetings.[131] Where there were significant pockets of radicalism, the quarrels within the local party weakened its capacity to recruit or act decisively.[132]

The inability of the radical Marxists to give direction to the disaffection within the party also reflected their own limitations. In placing such a strong emphasis on "spontaneity," they neglected the problem of organization. Despite their claim that the revolutionary process was driven by the instincts and attitudes of the masses, the Radicals did not question the basic structure of the party.[133]

Personal tensions also limited the capacity of the radical Marxists to influence the party. Luxemburg was judged by her allies to be irresponsible at times, even "pathological."[134] She in turn often found Lensch, Haenisch, and Liebknecht to be unreliable, and she was frequently scornful of the views of Pannekoek. Nor could the Radicals present a common front on a number of the issues confronting the party. They disagreed during 1912 and 1913 over the Radek affair.[135] When Radek, after angering the Social Democratic leaders through his intemperate criticisms, was expelled from the party, several of the Radicals, including Luxemburg, helped to discredit him. Indeed, the Radicals frequently expressed dismay over the meanness of their fellow socialists. When Luxemburg's lover, Kostja Zetkin, turned down a journalistic post in the party, she observed that at least he would "be spared the hatefulness and difficulties of party life . . . the constant defamation of all that is fine and noble in mankind."[136] And Haenisch lamented that there was "so much moral cowardice in the ranks."[137]

The radical Marxists remained faithful to the revolutionary promise in Marxism and to the conception of the proletariat on which it rested. That faith, however, separated them from the mainstream of the working-class movement. At the same time they showed, as one historian of the party has concluded, their "helplessness before the problematic of the function of the intellectuals in a socialist party."[138] They had also illustrated that problematic, in making explicit the basic ambivalence which the Marxist ideology had presented to intellectuals from the beginning. While the Revisionists and, in time, the orthodox Marxists had followed the apologetic bent of the ideology, the radical Marxists, like the Jungen and the anarcho-socialists earlier, had carried forward the vision of a fundamental transformation of life.

By 1912 that vision could only be sustained by a faith in the proletariat which had little basis in reality. The faith of the radical Marxists has been described variously—as a "mystique," as "dreamlike," and as "teleological."[139] Having detached the myth of the proletariat from the political development of the workers, however, the Radicals completed the process of ideological exhaustion.

Epilogue

THIS book has focused on two interrelated developments—the efforts of Social Democratic intellectuals to cultivate a new socialist mentality in the working class and the controversies which the presence of these intellectuals generated within the party. By 1912 the failure of the Marxist intellectuals to achieve their main goal was apparent and they had ceased, moreover, to be a significant source of controversy. As one disenchanted intellectual observed, the workers still formed "a circle in themselves," impervious to the "abstractions," the "higher science" with which educated members of the middle class had attempted to enlighten them.[1] A later Marxist thinker, Wolfgang Abendroth, put it somewhat differently when he described the prewar development of the Social Democrats as a "victory of an under-consciousness," of "prerational" attitudes instilled into the lower class by educational and other institutions controlled by the ruling classes.[2]

To conclude that the intellectuals failed is not to deny the impact of Marxist ideology on the minds of the workers who joined the Social Democratic party.[3] From the Marxist notions of exploitation, the class struggle, and a coming socialist order, workers drew inspiration and guidance in their attempts to achieve a freer, more equal, and more just society. The workers did not advance very far, however, beyond "class consciousness," a state of mind which Marxist intellectuals had seen as only the first stage on the way to a higher socialist consciousness. By 1912 the Marxist ideology had become little more than an apologetic for class interests, an instrument for the party's political leaders in their efforts to represent those interests. Through their deepening involvement in conventional political activity the Social Democrats became, in fact, captive to an unreformed "mass mentality."[4]

Social Democratic intellectuals in Germany responded in three ways to the difficulties they encountered in the attempt to inculcate Marxist modes of understanding into the minds of the workers. A few—Ernst and Michels were clear examples—gave up on the workers, rejected the Marxist ideology, and sought other paths toward the social regeneration to which they remained committed. Since the Social Democratic workers had, Ernst wrote later, abandoned the "struggle against the life conditions of capitalism," the only hope for Germany was a new "lawgiver," a leader who recognized the need for a "new morality and a new religion."[5]

A second group of intellectuals—the Radicals—kept their faith in the Marxist concept of the proletariat, only to separate themselves from the party's leaders and the great majority of the working class. For Luxemburg and Liebknecht the commitment to revolution would mean martyrdom at the end of the war. Other Radicals—Zetkin, the Dunckers, Thalheimer, and, for a time, Pannekoek and Rühle—looked to the Communist party for a renewal of the Marxist promise of a revolutionary transformation of society.

Revisionists and, in time, the orthodox Marxists who followed Kautsky pursued a third course, adapting the party's ideology to the actual development of the workers. That effort would continue through the war years and beyond. The patriotic feelings aroused by the war presented a new opportunity for Social Democratic intellectuals who were eager to reconcile socialism and nationalism. It was time, Heine declared in the fall of 1914, for Social Democrats to discard class terminology and speak out of their deeper convictions as Germans.[6] The patriotism proclaimed by Heine was embodied most fully in another revisionist intellectual, Frank. Having volunteered for military service, he was killed in one of the early battles on the Western front.[7] But even two of the prominent erstwhile Radicals, Lensch and Haenisch, embraced the cause of the nation with a passion which suggested, to Mehring at least, that their Marxist faith had only been "skin deep."[8] For Lensch the experience of war demonstrated that the Social Democrats were "no longer exclusively the party of the industrial proletariat."[9]

There was still a fourth way in which the intellectuals might deal with the continuing gap between the outlook of the workers and socialist theory. The intellectuals might take it upon themselves to function as guardians of the new truth, pending such time as the workers were ready to develop a socialist mentality. This possibility was recognized by young Polish Marxist Jan Machajski when, during the mid-nineties, Kautsky attempted to clarify the relationship between the workers and the bourgeois intellectuals.[10] In Kautsky's analysis Machajski saw a danger that the educated recruits might use their knowledge to gain a privileged position in the movement and dominate the workers. As a new "aristocracy of the spirit," with its own interests, the intellectuals would become, in fact, a new class of exploiters, a "new enemy of the people."

A few years later, Lenin, facing the difficulties which Russia presented to a revolutionary movement, drew on Kautsky's analysis of the intellectuals to formulate his conception of a party in which a small group, separated from the mass of the workers, assumed the role of guardians of Marxist theory.[11] The tendency to entrust intellectuals and party functionaries with the higher socialist consciousness would be a marked feature of later Marxist development. It can be seen in the thought of the two figures, who, in the years after World War I, struggled most directly with the problem of a proletarian mentality—Georg Lukács and Antonio Gramsci. They carried forward "to its logical conclusions," one historian has claimed, "Lenin's view . . . that Marxist 'intellectual workers' should rule the new society."[12] In time the Marxist ideology would become an apologetic for the "new class" which dominated the Communist societies formed after World War II.[13] The visionary and critical drives, which had been integral parts of the Marxist synthesis, would fall away or be renewed by intellectuals who stood outside or on the margins of these societies.

Whatever the strategy, the gap between the Marxism of the intellectuals and the outlook of the workers remained. The persistence of the gap suggested that the socialist vision was still, in large part, "a product of the spiritual needs" of intellectuals caught up in the social and personal dilemmas of the bourgeois world.[14] The socialism of the intellectuals represented, according to a recent commentator, a "cultural revulsion" against capitalism.[15]

Here lay the central paradox in late nineteenth-century Marxism. By claiming that human consciousness was determined by economic conditions, the orthodox Marxists denied the essentially ethical and idealistic nature of their own project. They were defeated, ironically, by the economic and social conditions which they had counted on to help transform the mentality of the workers. Those conditions were far more complex than the intellectuals recognized; economic motivations were inextricably interwoven with "common sense" or customary ways of living.[16] The limited reach of ideology was most apparent at the political level, where Marxist principles offered little guidance in dealing with the immediate tasks facing legislators. The unexpected appeal of nationalism to the working class was further evidence of attitudes and loyalties hidden from the orthodox Marxists.

Today the project to which the Marxist intellectuals were dedicated has ceased to be credible, and the role of "free intellectuals" has become increasingly problematic. Although the critical force of Marxist theory, given the persistence of many of the failings of the capitalistic or "bourgeois way of life," has retained much of its vitality, the visionary and apologetic elements in the synthesis have not. Political developments in the twentieth century have greatly reduced the appeal of totalistic ideologies as well as faith in a class or its agents as a redemptive force in history.[17] The simpler philosophical options of a century ago have given way to a more pluralistic culture in which ultimate or foundational claims are met with suspicion. In the contemporary world intellectuals have tended to settle for more modest roles—as "interpreters," or mediators between opposing systems of thought, rather than as "legislators," or possessors of exclusive visions.[18]

These developments led some to predict the "end of ideology."[19] But if the deepest source of the socialist movement was an ethical protest against capitalism, such an ending is unlikely. The problems which moved so many of the individuals dealt with in this study—great disparities of wealth and well-being, ill-used lives, cultural and spiritual impoverishment—persist in capitalist society. As long as these cruel inequities exist in societies claiming to be democratic, new critics will arise. And when those critics, the future ideologists, attempt to give systematic and popular expression to their desire for social justice, they will find that they can learn much from the experience of the Marxist intellectuals in Germany.

Abbreviations
Notes . Index

Abbreviations

BAK	Bundesarchiv Koblenz
BVT	*Berliner Volks-Tribüne*
IISH	International Institute of Social History, Amsterdam
NZ	*Die Neue Zeit*
Protokoll	Protokoll über die Verhandlungen des Parteitages der Sozialdemokratischen Partei Deutschland (with place and year)
SA	*Die Sozialistische Akademiker*
SM	*Die Sozialistische Monatshefte*
SM Papers	Sozialistische Monatshefte Papers
UC	University of California, Berkeley, Library—location of the microfilm copies of the Braun-Vogelstein Papers (originals in the archive of the Leo Baeck Institute, New York City)

Notes

Introduction

1. Henri De Man, *Die Intellektuellen und der Sozialismus* (Jena: E. Diederichs, 1926), p. 12.
2. Quotations drawn from Alvin Gouldner, "Marxism and Social Theory," *Theory and Society,* 1, no. 4 (1974): 17–35; "Prologue to a Theory of Revolutionary Intellectuals," *Telos,* no. 26 (Winter 1975–76): 3–36; *The Future of the Intellectuals and the Rise of the New Class* (New York: Oxford University Press, 1979), p. 9; and "Marxism and the Intellectuals," in *Against Fragmentation* (New York: Oxford University Press, 1985), pp. 3–51. An attempt to deal with the problem in Marxist terms can be found in Schlomo Avineri, "Marx and the Intellectuals," *Journal of the History of Ideas,* 17, no. 2 (1967): 269–278. Antonio Gramsci's effort to resolve the "theoretical and practical impasse" is discussed by Jerome Karabel, "Revolutionary Contradictions: Antonio Gramsci and the Problem of the Intellectual," *Politics and Society,* 6, no. 2 (1976): 123–172. Also see William Gleberzon, "Marxist Conceptions of the Intellectual," *Historical Reflections,* 5, no. 1 (1978): 81–98. A bibliography for the subject is provided in Johann Götschl and Christoph Klavier, eds., *Der sozialdemokratische Intellektuelle* (Vienna: Literas Verlag, 1985), pp. 193–203. An agenda for further investigation of the problem is presented in Carl Levy, ed., *Socialism and the Intelligentsia* (London: Routledge and Kegan Paul, 1987), pp. 1–34, 271–290. Also see Gustav Auernheimer, *"Genosse Herr Doktor": Zur Rolle von Akademikern in der deutschen Sozialdemokratie, 1890 bis 1933* (Giessen: Focus Verlag, 1985). Broader historical perspectives can be found in Michael Boedecker and André Leisewitz, "Intelligenz und Arbeiterbewegung," in Christoph Kievenheim and André Leisewitz, eds., *Soziale Stellung und Bewusstsein der Intelligenz* (Cologne: Pahl-Rugenstein, 1973), pp. 9–110; Gerhard Armanski, Norbert Kostede, and Boris Penth, "Vom Bourgeoisideologen zum Massenintellektuellen: Zur Klassenanalyse der Intelligenz," in H. D. Backhaus, ed., *Gesellschaft: Beiträge zur Marxistischen Theorie,* vol. 7 (Frankfurt: Suhrkamp, 1976), pp. 68–118.

3. See Werner Sombart, *Socialism and the Social Movements in the Nineteenth Century,* trans. Anson Atterbury (London: C. P. Putnam's Sons, 1898), p. 146. Later discussions include Robert Michels, *Political Parties,* trans. Eden and Cedar Paul (New York: Collier Books, 1962), pt. 4; Henri De Man, *The Psychology of Socialism,* trans. Eden and Cedar Paul (London: Unwin Brothers, 1928), pp. 219–237.
4. Gouldner, *Against Fragmentation,* pp. 93–100.
5. Walter Adamson, *Marx and the Disillusionment of Marxism* (Berkeley: University of California Press, 1985), p. 47. Also see Jerrold Seigel, "Consciousness and Practice in Marxism," *Comparative Studies in Society and History,* 24, no. 1 (Jan. 1982): 164–177; Harold Mah, *The End of Philosophy and the Origins of "Ideology,"* (Berkeley: University of California Press, 1987), chap. 8.
6. For accounts of the shift see Adamson, *Marx,* p. 57; Seigel, "Consciousness and Practice," pp. 174–177; Avineri, "Marx and the Intellectuals," pp. 271–274.
7. Mah, *The End of Philosophy,* p. 213.
8. Quoted in Avineri, "Marx and the Intellectuals," p. 271.
9. Gouldner, *Against Fragmentation,* p. 142; Avineri, "Marx and the Intellectuals," p. 274.
10. For an overview see Hennoch Brin, *Der Akademiker und die Intellektuellenfrage in der Arbeiterbewegung* (Strasbourg: Imp. du Nouveau Journal de Strasbourg, 1928), pp. 60–78. Also see Robert Michels, "Eine exklusive proletarisch Bewegung in Italien im Jahre 1883," in Eduard Bernstein, ed., *Dokumente des Sozialismus,* 4 (1904): 64–69.
11. Avineri, "Marx and the Intellectuals," p. 275.
12. Engels to Marx, Feb. 11, 1870, in Karl Marx and Friedrich Engels, *Collected Works,* vol. 43 (New York: International Publishers, 1988), p. 427.
13. Marx and Engels to August Bebel, Wilhelm Liebknecht, and Wilhelm Bracke, Sept. 17–18, 1897, in Karl Marx and Friedrich Engels, *Werke,* vol. 34 (Berlin: Dietz, 1977), pp. 394–408. For the context see Gareth Stedman Jones, "Engels and the Genesis of Marxism," *New Left Review,* no. 106 (Nov.-Dec. 1977): 79–104. For a different view see Horst Bartel and Walter Schmidt, "Zur Entwicklung der Auffassung von Marx und Engels über die proletarische Partei," in Bartel, *Marxismus und deutsche Arbeiterbewegung* (Berlin: Dietz, 1970), pp. 78–79.
14. Karl Mannheim, "The Problem of the Intelligentsia: An Inquiry into Its Past and Present Role," *Essays in the Sociology of Culture* (London: Routledge and Kegan Paul, 1956), pp. 91–170.
15. Ibid., p. 150.
16. Ibid., pp. 101–104.
17. For a discussion of Marx's view of ideology as "apologia" see Bhikhu Parekh, *Marx's Theory of Ideology* (London: Johns Hopkins University Press, 1982), chap. 2.
18. Theodor Geiger, *Aufgaben und Stellung der Intelligenz in der Gesellschaft* (Stuttgart: F. Enke, 1949).
19. Ibid., p. 121.

20. Edward Shils, *The Intellectuals and the Powers* (Chicago: University of Chicago Press, 1972), pp. 3–22. Also see his essay "Intellectuals," in *The International Encyclopedia of the Social Sciences,* vol. 7 (New York: Macmillan, 1968), pp. 399–415.
21. Shils, *Intellectuals and the Powers,* p. 3.
22. For a discussion of the intellectuals as a secular clergy see Ben Knights, *The Idea of the Clerisy in the Nineteenth Century* (Cambridge: Cambridge University Press, 1978), especially pp. 2–36. Also see Wolf Lepennies, *Between Literature and Science: The Rise of Sociology,* trans. R. J. Holindale (New York: Cambridge University Press, 1988).
23. Robert Michels, "Intellectuals," in *Encyclopedia of the Social Sciences,* vol. 8 (New York: Macmillan, 1937), pp. 118–126.
24. For perspectives on the Bildungsbürgertum see Klaus Vondung, ed., *Das Wilhelminische Bildungsbürgertum* (Göttingen: Vandenhoeck & Ruprecht, 1976).
25. See W. H. Bruford, *The German Tradition of Self Cultivation* (London: Cambridge University Press, 1975).
26. See C. E. Williams, "Writers and Politics: Some Reflections on a German Tradition," *Journal of European Studies,* 6 (1976): 75–99.
27. See Bruford, *German Tradition,* p. 264, and Klaus Vondung, "Zur Lage der Gebildeten in der Wilhelminischen Zeit," in Vondung, *Wilhelminische Bildungsbürgertum,* pp. 20–33. The great divide between the new groups of producers and the old academic groups and the increasingly defensive and conservative position of the latter is examined in Fritz Ringer, *The Decline of the German Mandarins* (Cambridge, Mass.: Harvard University Press, 1969). Also see Konrad H. Jarausch, *Students, Society, and Politics in Imperial Germany* (Princeton: Princeton University Press, 1982), pp. 81, 158–199. The political outlook encouraged by this tradition is discussed in James Sheehan, *German Liberalism in the Nineteenth Century* (Chicago: University of Chicago Press, 1978), pp. 14–18.
28. The Hegelian project, at once religious and political, and its sociocultural setting are explored in depth in John Edward Toews, *Hegelianism* (New York: Cambridge University Press, 1980).
29. See especially Mah, *End of Philosophy,* pp. 218–229.
30. Thus one twentieth-century Marxist argued that Marx ignored his own insight into the historically conditioned nature of human understanding and removed his own modes of thought from critical scrutiny. See Alfred Sohn-Rethel, *Intellectual and Manual Labor* (Atlantic Highlands, N.J.: Humanities Press, 1978), especially pp. 2–34. Lobkowicz claimed that Marx's turn to the proletariat was "a desperate effort" to preserve his communist ideal from the more logical conclusion of Hegel's most radical critic, Max Stirner. See Nicholas Lobkowicz, *Theory and Practice* (Notre Dame, Ind.: University of Notre Dame Press, 1967), pp. 393–426, and his essay "Karl Marx and Max Stirner," in F. Adelmann, ed., *Demythologizing Marxism* (Boston: Boston College Press, 1969), pp. 88–94.
31. Adamson, *Marx,* p. 71.
32. A number of commentators have claimed that Engels discarded Marx's

dialectic, in which human subjectivity and objective circumstances each received their due, in favor of a one-sided positivistic and deterministic account of human development. For a discussion of the issue see ibid., p. 23.

33. The context within which Engels undertook this task is discussed by Iring Fetscher, "Von der Philosophie des Proletariats zur proletarische Weltanschauung," in Fetscher, ed., *Marxismusstudien,* 2d ed. (Tübingen: Mohr, 1957), pp. 26–60. Also see Renate Merkel, "Neues zur Entstehungsgeschichte des 'Anti Dühring,'" *Beiträge zur Geschichte der Arbeiterbewegung,* 7, no. 6 (1965): 779–788; Richard Adamiak, "Marx, Engels, and Dühring," *Journal of the History of Ideas,* 35, no. 1 (Jan.-March 1974): 98–112.
34. George Lichtheim, "The Concept of Ideology," *History and Theory,* 4, no. 2 (1965), p. 173.
35. Jones, "Engels and the Genesis of Marxism," p. 81.
36. The reception of Marxism in Germany during the eighties is discussed in H. J. Steinberg, *Sozialismus und deutsche Sozialdemokratie* (Hanover: Verlag für Literatur und Zeitgeschehen, 1967), pp. 27–43, and Susanne Miller, *Das Problem der Freiheit im Sozialismus* (Frankfurt: Europaische Verlagsanstalt, 1964), pp. 179–198.
37. For the development of Bebel's Marxism see Ver Vrona, "Die theoretisch-weltanschauliche Entwicklung August Bebels," *Zeitschrift für Geschichtwissenschaft,* 16, no. 3 (1968): 347–362; Horst Strüning, "Die weltanschaulich-theoretische Entwicklung Bebels Ende der sechzinger Jahre," in Wolfgang Abendroth et al., eds., *Sozialdemokratie und Sozialismus: August Bebel und die Sozialdemokratie heute* (Cologne: Pahl-Rugenstein, 1974), pp. 107–115.
38. See Ernst Adam, "Die Stellung der deutschen Sozialdemokratie zur Religion und Kirche" (diss., University of Frankfurt, 1930), pp. 50–74; Vernon Lidtke, "August Bebel and German Social Democracy's Relation to the Christian Churches," *Journal of History of Ideas,* 26, no. 2 (April-June 1966): 246–264.
39. See Shulamit Volkov, *The Rise of Popular Antimodernism in Germany* (Princeton: Princeton University Press, 1976); Robert Gellately, *The Politics of Economic Despair* (London: Sage Publications, 1974).
40. Hartmut Titze, "Enrollment Expansion and Academic Overcrowding in Germany," in Konrad Jarausch, ed., *The Transformation of Higher Learning, 1860–1930* (Chicago: University of Chicago Press, 1983), pp. 157–188.
41. John Craig, "Higher Education and Social Mobility in Germany," ibid., pp. 219–244.
42. The experience of Jewish intellectuals is examined in Michels, *Political Parties,* pp. 245–250. For a discussion of the "specific qualities" that contributed to the prominence of Jewish intellectuals in the party see Werner E. Mosse, "Die Jüden in Wirtschaft und Gesellschaft," in Mosse, *Jüden im Wilhelminischen Deutschland, 1890–1914* (Tübingen: Mohr, 1976), pp. 100–103. The role of Jewish intellectuals in the party is examined by Peter Pulzer in the same volume, pp. 197–215.

43. The influences at work on a number of the educated recruits are discussed in Dirk Hoffmann, "Sozialismus und Literaten" (diss., University of Münster, 1975). See especially vol. 1, pp. 54–95.
44. Adolf Braun, "Die Intellektuellen und die Politik," *NZ*, 27, no. 50 (1908–1909): 847–853.
45. The political careers of Social Democratic journalists are discussed in Waltraud Sperlich, *Journalist mit Mandat* (Düsseldorf: Droste, 1983).
46. Robert Michels, "Die deutsche Sozialdemokratie: Parteimitgliedschaft und soziale Zusammensetzung," *Archiv für Sozialwissenschaft und Sozialpolitik*, 23 (1906): 471–556. The overwhelmingly proletarian character of the local branches is emphasized in Mary Nolan, *Social Democracy and Society* (New York: Cambridge University Press, 1981), chap. 5. Also see Dieter Rossmeissl, *Arbeiterschaft und Sozialdemokratie im Nürnberg* (Nuremberg: Stadtarchiv, 1977), pp. 212–214.
47. The number of academically educated among the Social Democratic candidates for the Reichstag actually declined from 28.6 percent in 1898 to 23.6 percent in 1912. See Wilhelm Heinz Schröder, "Die Sozialstruktur der sozialdemokratische Reischstags-kandidaten, 1898–1912," in *Herkunft und Mandat: Beiträge zum Führungsproblem in der Arbeiterbewegung* (Frankfurt: Europaische Verlagsanstalt, 1976), pp. 83–84.
48. Michels, "Die deutsche Sozialdemokratie," p. 536.
49. Theodor Geiger, "Ideologie und Mentalität," in Geiger, *Die soziale Schichtung des deutschen Volkes* (Stuttgart: F. Enke, 1932), pp. 77–82. For an attempt to apply these concepts see Werner Blessing, "Zur Analyse politischer Mentalität und Ideologie der Unterschichten im 19. Jahrhundert," *Zeitschrift für bayerische Landesgeschichte*, 34, no. 3 (1971): 768–816.

1. The Protest of the Young Intellectuals

1. Georg Simmel, "The Stranger," in *The Sociology of George Simmel*, ed. Kurt H. Wolff (New York: Free Press, 1950), pp. 402–408.
2. For the political development of the Social Democrats in these years see Vernon Lidtke, *The Outlawed Party* (Princeton: Princeton University Press, 1966); Susanne Miller, *Das Problem der Freiheit im Sozialismus* (Frankfurt: Europaische Verlagsanstalt, 1964); William Harvey Maehl, *August Bebel* (Philadelphia: American Philosophical Society, 1980), chaps. 6–11.
3. Lidtke, *Outlawed Party*, pp. 153–154.
4. Biographical information can be found in Paul Kampffmeyer, "Max Schippel," and Robert Schmidt, "Max Schippel in Dienst der Arbeiterbewegung," *SM*, 67 (July 1928): 587–598.
5. *BVT* (July 30, 1887).
6. Ibid. (March 16, 1889).
7. Ibid. (Jan. 5, 1889).
8. Ibid. (Oct. 15, 1887).
9. Ibid. (Oct. 22, 1887).
10. Ibid. (April 21, 1888).
11. Ibid. (Oct. 5, 1889).

12. Ibid. (Sept. 28, 1889).
13. Ibid. (April 13, 1889).
14. Ibid. (April 21, 1888).
15. Ibid. (Oct. 29, 1887).
16. Max Schippel, *Die wirtschaftlichen Umwälzungen und die Entwicklung der Sozialdemokratie* (Berlin: Verlag der Berliner Arbeiter Bibliothek, 1889), p. 32.
17. The crisis of the educated middle class in Germany was, of course, one expression of the wider and deeper European cultural crisis, in which traditional concepts in science as well as in religion, literature, the visual arts, and social thought were all being called into question. Much of the scholarship dealing with the crisis and what can now be seen as the beginnings of a modernist sensibility has focused on Nietzsche and the new generation of German sociologists, particularly Weber and Simmel. One of the most searching analyses of the crisis in Germany is still Helmuth Plessner, *Das Schicksal deutschen Geistes im Ausgang seiner bürgerlichen Epoche* (Zurich: M. Nichans, 1935), especially chaps. 9–12.
18. There is an extensive literature on German Naturalism, much of it dealing with the relationship of the creative writers with the socialist movement. Especially useful for the focus here are Herbert Scherer, *Bürgerlich-oppositionelle Literaten und sozialdemokratische Arbeiterbewegung nach 1890* (Stuttgart: Metzler, 1974), and the essays in Helmut Scheuer, ed., *Naturalismus* (Stuttgart: W. Kohlhammer, 1974). Documentary material can be found in Norbert Rothe, ed., *Naturalismus Debatte, 1891–1896* (Berlin: Akademie Verlag, 1986). Also see Ursula Munchow, *Arbeiterbewegung und Literatur, 1860–1914* (Berlin: Aufbau, 1981); Roy Pascal, *From Naturalism to Expressionism* (London: Wiedenfeld and Nicolson, 1973); Vernon Lidtke, "Socialism and Naturalism in Germany," *American Historical Review,* 79 (Feb. 1974): 14–37.
19. *NZ*, 13, no. 19 (1894–95): 588.
20. Hermann Conradi, *Adam Mensch* (Leipzig: W. Friedrich, 1888), pp. 18, 41.
21. Ibid., p. 460.
22. Hermann Conradi, "Ein Kandidat der Zukunfts-Übergangsmenschen," in Conradi, *Novellen und Skizzen* (Munich: G. M. Müller, 1911), pp. 449–481. The essay was first published in 1889. Also see M. Bowlby, "New Romanticism in German Naturalist Literature; The Theory of the 'Übergangsmensch' in Hermann Conradi's Novel 'Adam Mensch,'" *German Life and Letters,* 16, no. 4 (July 1963): 306–310.
23. The Friedrichshagener circle and its relationship to the Social Democrats is the subject of Scherer, *Bürgerliche-oppositionelle Literaten.*
24. For these difficulties see ibid., pp. 29–32, 51–52, and Dietger Pforte, "Die deutsche Sozialdemokratie und die Naturalisten," in Scheuer, *Naturalismus,* pp. 175–205.
25. For biographical information see Paul Ernst, *Jünglingsjahre* (Munich: G. Müller, 1931), and *Entwicklungen* (Munich: Claudius Verlag, 1966).
26. Paul Ernst, *Der Schmale Weg zum Glück* (Munich: A. Langen, 1937), p. 132. The novel was first published in 1902.

27. Ibid., pp. 142, 146, 168.
28. The leading characters in several of the novels are discussed in Josef Polacek, "Zum 'hyperbolischen' Roman bei Conradi, Conrad, und Hollaender," in Scheuer, *Naturalismus,* pp. 68–92.
29. Wilhelm Hegeler, "Einiges aus meinem Leben," *Die Gesellschaft,* no. 2 (1900): 226–232.
30. The inner movement is described in Ernst, *Entwicklungen,* pp. 222–223. Also see Dirk Müller, *Idealismus und Revolution: Zur Opposition des Jungen gegen der Sozialdemokratischen Parteivorstand, 1890 bis 1894* (Berlin: Colloquium Verlag, 1975), pp. 17–19.
31. Schippel presented these views in a series of articles in the Austrian paper *Die Gleichheit* during 1887. Extensive quotations from the articles appeared in *Der Sozialist* (Dec. 10, 1892) and in Paul Kampffmeyer, *Changes in the Theory and Tactics of Social Democracy,* trans. Winfield Gaylord (Chicago: C. H. Kerr, 1906), pp. 64–68, 130–133.
32. *BVT* (March 17, 1888).
33. Max Schippel, *Die Gewerkschaften, ihr Nutzen und ihre Bedeutung für die Arbeiterbewegung* (Berlin: Berliner Arbeiter Bibliothek, 1889), pp. 25–26.
34. The events in the spring are described most fully in Eduard Bernstein, *Die Geschichte der Berliner Arbeiterbewegung,* 3 vols. (Berlin: Buchhandlung Vorwärts, 1907), and Müller, *Idealismus und Revolution,* pp. 20–45.
35. Max Schippel, "Die beiden Richtungen des Sozialismus," *BVT* (May 17, 1890).
36. Müller, *Idealismus und Revolution,* pp. 68–76.
37. See ibid., pp. 51–55, where the article is quoted at length.
38. Peter Wienand, "Revoluzzer und Revisionister: Die 'Jungen' in der Sozialdemokratie vor der Jahrhundertwende," *Politische Vierteljahrschrift,* 13 (June 1972): 222.
39. See Kurt Sollmann, "Bruno Wille und die Sozialdemokratie: Zur politischeideologischen Dimension," in Sollmann, *Literarische Intelligenz vor 1900* (Cologne: Pahl-Rugenstein, 1982), pp. 85–127, and Kurt Sollmann, "Zur Ideologie intellektueller Opposition im beginnenden Imperialismus am Beispiel Bruno Willes," in Gert Mattenklott und Klaus R. Scherpe, eds., *Positionen der literarischen Intelligenz zwischen bürgerlicher Reaktion und Imperialismus* (Kronberg/Ts.: Scriptor, 1973), pp. 179–209.
40. Sollmann, "Bruno Wille und die Sozialdemokratie," p. 91.
41. Kurt Sollmann, "Bruno Wille und die Volksbühnen," in *Literarische Intelligenz,* pp. 180–195.
42. Quoted in Müller, *Idealismus und Revolution,* p. 55.
43. Rudolf Rocker, *Aus den Memoiren eines deutschen Anarchisten,* ed. Madgalena and Peter Duerr (Frankfurt: Suhrkamp, 1974), p. 37.
44. Paul Kampffmeyer, "Radikalismus und Anarchismus," in *Die Befreiung der Menschheit,* ed. Ignaz Jezower (Berlin: Verlag Klaus Guhl, 1977), p. 74. Reprint of 1921 edition.
45. Ibid., p. 78.
46. Bruno Schönlank, "Zur Psychologie des Kleinbürgertums," *NZ,* 8, nos. 3, 4 (1889–90): 117–124, 163–169.

47. See Paul Mayer, *Bruno Schönlank, 1859–1901* (Hanover: Verlag für Literatur und Zeitgeschehen, 1971), p. 16.
48. Schönlank, "Zur Psychologie," p. 119.
49. Ibid., p. 163.
50. Ibid., p. 123.
51. Ibid., pp. 163–164, 169.
52. Quoted in Müller, *Idealismus und Revolution,* p. 61.
53. Ibid., p. 56.
54. Bebel to Victor Adler, Sept. 5, 1890, in Victor Adler, *Briefwechsel mit August Bebel und Karl Kautsky* (Vienna: Wiener Volksbuchhandlung, 1954), p. 54.
55. Kautsky to Adler, Nov. 29, 1890, ibid., p. 65.
56. Bernstein to Adler, Sept. 10, 1890, ibid., p. 57.
57. Wienand, "Revoluzzer und Revisionister," p. 223.
58. For a description of the meeting, together with extensive quotations from the speeches, see Sollmann, "Bruno Wille und die Sozialdemokratie," pp. 119–121. Also see Hans Müller, *Der Klassenkampf und die Sozialdemokratie: Zur Geschichte der 'Jungen,' der linken Opposition in der frühen SPD* (Berlin: Druck und Verlagskooperative, 1969), pp. 86–96. Reprint of 1892 edition.
59. Protokoll, Halle (1890): 42–55.
60. See Gerhard Ritter, *Die Arbeiterbewegung im Wilhelmischen Reich* (Berlin: Colloquium Verlag, 1959), pp. 86–87.
61. Vollmar's role in the party and the Eldorado speeches, named after the Munich hall in which they were delivered, are discussed in Reinhard Jansen, *Georg von Vollmar* (Bonn: Droste, 1956), pp. 43–52, and Paul Kampffmeyer, *Georg von Vollmar* (Munich: G. Birk, 1930), pp. 90–93.
62. The flyer is reprinted in the Protokoll of the Erfurt conference of 1891. There is an extensive commentary on its contents in Gerhard Hans Rohr, "The Revolt of the Jungen" (diss., University of Rochester, 1975). Also see Lidtke, *Outlawed Party,* pp. 305–319.
63. Protokoll, Erfurt (1891): 61–62.
64. Ibid., p. 196.
65. The Jungen debate took up more than two days of the six-day meeting. For an account see Müller, *Idealismus und Revolution,* pp. 95–101.
66. Reprinted in Müller, *Der Klassenkampf,* p. 118.
67. *Der Sozialist* (Nov. 15, 1891).
68. For the development of the Independents see Müller, *Idealismus und Revolution,* pp. 151–168, and Eugene Lunn, *Prophet of Community: The Romantic Socialism of Gustav Landauer* (Berkeley: University of California Press, 1973), pp. 50–74.
69. Wienand, "Revoluzzer und Revisionister," p. 227.
70. The terms are used in Müller, *Idealismus und Revolution,* p. 171.
71. See Sollmann, "Zur Ideologie intellektueller Opposition," pp. 194–195.
72. Bruno Wille, *Einsiedler und Genosse* (Berlin: Freie Verlags-Anstalt, 1894), p. 103.
73. Sollmann, "Bruno Wille und die Volksbühne," pp. 184–195.

74. Müller, *Idealismus und Revolution,* denies that the Jungen were genuine Marxists and describes their outlook as an "idealistic alternative." See pp. 171–173. I find the analysis by Wienand more convincing.
75. Wienand, "Revoluzzer und Revisionister," p. 222.
76. Quoted in Müller, *Idealismus und Revolution,* p. 122.
77. Engels to Conrad Schmidt, April 12, 1890, in Karl Marx and Friedrich Engels, *Werke,* vol. 37 (Berlin: Dietz, 1978), p. 383.
78. Friedrich Engels, "Ludwig Feuerbach and the End of Classical German Philosophy," in Karl Marx and Friedrich Engels, *Selected Works* (London: International Publishers, 1968), pp. 603–605.
79. Ibid., pp. 622–625.
80. Ibid., p. 620.
81. Ibid., p. 631.
82. Gareth Stedman Jones, "Engels and the End of Classical German Philosophy," *New Left Review,* no. 79 (May-June 1973): 28–29.
83. Engels, "Ludwig Feuerbach," p. 619.
84. Ibid., p. 632.
85. Engels to J. Becker, Oct. 15, 1884, in Marx and Engels, *Werke,* vol. 36, pp. 218–219.
86. Engels to Paul Lafargue, Dec. 5, 1892, ibid., vol. 38, p. 543.
87. Engels to Kautsky, Nov. 8, 1885, in Benedikt Kautsky, ed., *Friedrich Engels Briefwechsel mit Karl Kautsky* (Vienna: Danubia-Verlag, 1955), pp. 154–155.
88. Engels to Bebel, June 21, 1882, June 22–24, 1885, in Werner Blumenberg, ed., *August Bebels Briefwechsel mit Friedrich Engels* (The Hague: Mouton, 1965), pp. 124–125, 227.
89. Ibid., p. xxxii.
90. Engels to Schmidt, Oct. 17, 1889, in Marx and Engels, *Werke,* vol. 37, pp. 290–291.
91. Engels' confidence that the Social Democrats would attain power by 1900, barring a European war or premature action by the party, is stressed in Hans Josef Steinberg, "Friedrich Engels' revolutionäre Strategie nach dem Fall des Sozialistengestzes," in *Friedrich Engels, 1820–1970: Referate-Diskussionen Dokumente* (Hanover: Verlag für Literatur und Zeitgeschehen, 1971), 115–126.
92. Jones, "Engels and the End of Classical German Philosophy," p. 35.
93. Engels to Bebel, May 9, 1890, in Blumenberg, *Bebels Briefwechsel,* p. 389.
94. Engels to Otto v. Boenigk, Aug. 21, 1890, in Marx and Engels, *Werke,* vol. 37, pp. 447–448.
95. Schmidt to Engels, June 25, 1890, IISH, Engels Correspondence, L 5575.
96. Paul Ernst, "Gefahren des Marxismus," *BVT* (Aug. 8, 1890).
97. Joseph Bloch to Engels, Sept. 3, 1890, IISH, Engels Correspondence, L 577.
98. Quoted in Müller, *Idealismus und Revolution,* p. 122.
99. Engels, "Antwort an die Redaktion der 'Sächsischen Arbeiter Zeitung,'" in Marx and Engels, *Werke,* vol. 22, p. 68.
100. Quoted in Engels, "Antwort an Paul Ernst," ibid., p. 80.

101. Engels, "Antwort an die Redaktion," ibid., p. 69.
102. Engels to Otto v. Boenigk, Aug. 21, 1890, ibid., vol. 37, p. 444.
103. Engels, "Antwort an Paul Ernst," p. 85.
104. See Müller, *Idealismus und Revolution,* pp. 122–123, for a summary and discussion of Engels' diatribes against the Jungen.
105. Engels to Friedrich Sorge, Aug. 9, 1890, in Marx and Engels, *Werke,* vol. 37, pp. 439–440.
106. Engels to Gernson Trier, Dec. 18, 1889, ibid., pp. 326–327.
107. See Müller, *Idealismus und Revolution,* pp. 125–127.
108. Engels to Schmidt, Oct. 27, 1890, in Marx and Engels, *Werke,* vol. 37, p. 492. Also see Alfred Schmidt, "Historischer Materialismus in den späten Arbeiter von Engels," in *Friedrich Engels, 1820–1970,* pp. 221–224.
109. Engels to Schmidt, Oct. 17, 1889, Aug. 5, 1890, in Marx and Engels, *Werke,* vol. 37, pp. 290–291, 435–438.
110. Engels to Otto v. Boenigk, Aug. 21, 1890, ibid., pp. 444–448.
111. Engels to Bebel, Oct. 24, 1891, in Blumenberg, *Bebels Briefwechsel,* p. 465.
112. Engels to Bebel, Aug. 25, 1881, ibid., pp. 115–116.
113. Engels to Kautsky, Nov. 8, 1884, in Kautsky, *Engels Briefwechsel,* pp. 153–155.
114. Engels to Bebel, Dec. 11–12, 1884, in Blumenberg, *Bebels Briefwechsel,* pp. 201–205.
115. Engels to Schmidt, Aug. 5, 1891, in Marx and Engels, *Werke,* vol. 38, pp. 435–438.
116. Engels to Max Oppenheimer, March 24, 1891, ibid., pp. 64–65.
117. Engels to Schmidt, Feb. 4, 1892, ibid., pp. 167–169.
118. Engels to Laura Lafargue, Sept. 1894, ibid., vol. 39, p. 298.
119. Engels to Bebel, March 18, 1886, in Blumenberg, *Bebels Briefwechsel,* p. 267.
120. August Bebel, *Aus Meinem Leben,* vol. 1 (Stuttgart: Dietz, 1910), p. 216. Toward the end of his life Bebel observed that although Marx and Engels were "marvelous theorists," they were "worthless practitioners." Quoted in Maehl, *Bebel,* p. 517.
121. Engels to Bebel, July 23, 1892, in Blumenberg, *Bebels Briefwechsel,* pp. 564–565, and Engels to Kautsky, Sept. 4, 1892, in Marx and Engels, *Werke,* vol. 38, p. 448.
122. Maehl, *Bebel,* pp. 233, 244.
123. Julie Bebel to Engels, Nov. 1892, Blumenberg, *Bebels Briefwechsel,* pp. 625–626. Engels did visit the Bebels in Berlin.
124. Blumenberg in his introduction to Ibid., p. xliv.
125. E.S., "Die Intelligenz in der Sozialdemokratie," *BVT* (Aug. 15, 1891).

2. The Academics as Critics

1. See Robert Schmidt's obituary in *SM* (July 1928): 595–598.
2. Max Schippel, "Schäffles Lebensbild," *SM,* 9 (Dec. 1905): 1009–1015.
3. Engels to Kautsky, July 11, 19, 1884, in Benedikt Kautsky, ed., *Friedrich*

Engels Briefwechsel mit Karl Kautsky (Vienna: Danubia-Verlag, 1955), pp. 132, 137–138.
4. The letter is quoted at length in Kampffmeyer, "Max Schippel," *SM* (July 1928): 588.
5. The correspondence deals with Schippel's contributions to the *Neue Zeit.* IISH, Kautsky Correspondence, KD XX 185–194.
6. *BVT* (March 31, 1888).
7. Max Schippel, *Die Gewerkschaften, ihr Nutzen und ihre Bedeutung für die Arbeiterbewegung* (Berlin: Berliner Arbeiter Bibliothek, 1889), pp. 26–28.
8. See the editorials in the *BVT* during April 1890.
9. Bebel to Engels, March 31, 1890, in Werner Blumenberg, ed., *August Bebels Briefwechsel mit Friedrich Engels* (The Hague: Mouton, 1965), p. 385.
10. Schippel's candidacy is discussed in Ernst Heilmann, *Geschichte der Arbeiterbewegung in Chemnitz und dem Erzgebirge* (Chemnitz: Sozialdemokratischer Verein, 1912), p. 216.
11. *BVT* (May 17, 1890).
12. Schippel's relation to the Jungen protest is discussed in Hans Müller, *Der Klassenkampf und die Sozialdemokratie* (Berlin: Druck und Verlagskooperative, 1969), pp. 88–90. First published in 1892.
13. See "Max Schippel und der Parlamentarismus," in *Der Sozialist* (Dec. 10, 1892).
14. Kautsky to Engels, Sept. 8–9, 1890, in Kautsky, *Engels Briefwechsel,* pp. 260–261, and Kautsky to Victor Adler, July 29, 1890, in Victor Adler, *Briefwechsel mit August Bebel und Karl Kautsky* (Vienna: Wiener Volksbuchhandlung, 1954), pp. 51–52.
15. Kautsky to Engels, Sept. 8–9, 1890, in Kautsky, *Engels Briefwechsel,* p. 260.
16. Kautsky to Engels, Dec. 21, 1890, ibid., p. 267.
17. Engels to Kautsky, April 30, 1891, ibid., p. 297.
18. Max Schippel, "Ein Problem der Sozialreform," *NZ,* 9, no. 1 (1890–91): 23.
19. Max Schippel, "Drei Monat Fabrikarbeiten," *NZ,* 9 nos. 40, 41 (1890–91): 468–475, 499–504.
20. Ibid., pp. 469–470.
21. Ibid., pp. 468, 472–475.
22. Ibid., pp. 500–503.
23. For the development of the trade unions in these years see John Moses, *Trade Unions in Germany from Bismarck to Hitler,* vol. 1, *1869–1918* (Totowa, N.J.: Barnes and Noble, 1982), chaps. 4, 5. Also see Heinz Langerham, "Richtungsgewerkschaft und gewerkschaftliche Autonomie, 1890–1914," *International Review of Social History,* 2 (1957): 22–31, 187–208.
24. Max Schippel, "Die Gewerkschaftsbewegung in Deutschland und der Kongress zu Halberstadt," *NZ,* 10, no. 1 (1891–92): 4–10.
25. Ibid., p. 10.
26. See Protokoll, Cologne (1893): 180.

27. Bebel to Engels, April 24, 1894, in Blumenberg, *Bebels Briefwechsel,* p. 759.
28. Ibid., p. 760.
29. Bebel to Engels, Nov. 13, 1893, in Blumenberg, *Bebels Briefwechsel,* p. 730.
30. Kautsky to Engels, Nov. 25, 1893, in Kautsky, *Engels Briefwechsel,* pp. 394–395; Kautsky to Adler, Oct. 13, 1893, in Adler, *Briefwechsel,* p. 122.
31. *Sozialdemokrat* (Feb. 3, 1894).
32. Paul Kampffmeyer, "Die Gründung der 'Neue Zeit' und die Intellektuellen," *Die Gesellschaft: Ein Sonderheft* (Berlin, 1924), pp. 86–91.
33. Kampffmeyer to Georg von Vollmar, Oct. 16, 1905, IISH, Vollmar Correspondence, V 1061.
34. Willy Hellpach, *Wirken in Wirren: Lebenserinnerungen,* vol. 1, *1877–1914* (Hamburg: C. Wagner, 1948), p. 377.
35. Kampffmeyer, "Die Gründung," pp. 89–90.
36. Ibid., p. 91.
37. Paul Kampffmeyer, "Die ökonomischen Grundlagen des deutschen Sozialismus der vierziger Jahre und siene wissenschafliche Ausbildung durch Marx und Engels vor Abfassung des kommunistischen Manifest," *NZ,* 5, nos. 12, 13 (1887): 502–509, 535–545.
38. The exchanges took place mainly during 1886. IISH, Kautsky Correspondence, D XLV 55–63.
39. Kampffmeyer, "Die ökonomischen Grundlagen," p. 543.
40. Ibid.
41. *BVT* (Jan. 4, 1890).
42. Paul Kampffmeyer, "Radikalismus und Anarchismus," in *Die Befreiung der Menscheit,* ed. Ignaz Jezower (Berlin: Verlag Klaus Guhl, 1977), pp. 171–187. First published in 1921.
43. The situation in Magdeburg is described in Müller, *Der Klassenkampf,* pp. 77–87.
44. Paul Kampffmeyer, *Ist der Sozialismus mit der menschlichen Natur vereinbar?* (Berlin: Verlag der Berliner Arbeiter Bibliothek, 1891), p. 28.
45. Ibid., pp. 24–25.
46. The draft is reprinted in the Erfurt Protokoll (1891), pp. 23–24.
47. Quoted in Müller, *Der Klassenkampf,* p. 116.
48. Ibid., p. 118.
49. Paul Kampffmeyer, *Die Bedeutung der Gewerkschaften für die Taktik der Proletariats* (Berlin: Verlag des "Socialist," 1892).
50. Ibid., p. 14.
51. Ibid., p. 17.
52. Ibid., pp. 17–19.
53. Ibid., p. 26.
54. Ibid., p. 27.
55. Ibid., pp. 28–29.
56. See Paul Kampffmeyer, "Wandlungen in der sozialistischen Theorie," *SA* (Jan. 1896): 11–18.

57. For the correspondence with Fischer see IISH, Kleine Korrespondenz, Socialdemokratische Partei.
58. Engels to Kautsky, April 20, 1889, in Karl Marx and Friedrich Engels, *Werke,* vol. 37 (Berlin: Dietz, 1978), pp. 154–158.
59. Engels to Laura Lafargue, July 15, 1887, ibid., vol. 36, p. 682.
60. Engels to Kautsky, Sept. 28, 1891, ibid., vol. 38, p. 157.
61. Engels to Schmidt, Oct. 17, 1889, ibid., vol. 37, pp. 290–291.
62. Käthe Kollwitz, *Aus meinem Leben* (Munich: Paul List, 1958), pp. 34–37, 41–42, and *Briefe der Freundschaft* (Munich: Paul List, 1966), pp. 149–150.
63. See the obituary of Karl Schmidt in *SM* (April 1898), pp. 244–246.
64. Conrad Schmidt, *Der natürliche Arbeitslohn* (Jena: G. Fischer, 1886).
65. Ibid., p. 48.
66. See Karl Marx, *Capital,* vol. 2, trans. Ernst Untermann (Chicago: C. H. Kerr, 1910), pp. 24–28.
67. Schmidt to Engels, Feb. 19, 1888, IISH, Engels Correspondence, L 5562.
68. There is an extensive literature on the problem of the profit rate in Marx's theory. For an overview see Joseph Gillman, *The Falling Profit Rate* (London: D. Dobson, 1957), pp. 1–36.
69. Conrad Schmidt, *Die Durchschnittsprofitrate auf Grundlage des Marx'schen Wertgesetzes* (Stuttgart: Dietz, 1889), and "Das Wertgesetz und die Profitrate," *NZ,* 8, no. 10 (1889–90): 433–442. Schmidt's argument is summarized in Eugen von Bohm-Bawerk, *Karl Marx and the Close of His System,* ed. Paul Sweezy, trans. Rudolf Hilferding (New York: A. M. Kelley, 1949), pp. 32–36.
70. Schmidt, "Die Wertgesetz," p. 440.
71. Ibid., p. 441.
72. Engels to Schmidt, Oct. 17, 1889, in Marx and Engels, *Werke,* vol. 37, pp. 290–291.
73. For Engels' tribute to Schmidt see his preface to Karl Marx, *Capital,* vol. 3, trans. Ernst Untermann (Chicago: C. H. Kerr, 1909), pp. 21–24.
74. Schmidt to Engels, Nov. 10, 1889, IISH, Engels Correspondence, L 5572.
75. Schmidt to Kautsky, April 12, 1889, IISH, Kautsky Correspondence, D XX 319.
76. Engels to Schmidt, Dec. 9, 1889, in Marx and Engels, *Werke,* vol. 37, pp. 324–325.
77. Schmidt to Engels, April 1, 1890, IISH, Engels Correspondence, L 5574.
78. Conrad Schmidt, *Spinoza* (Berlin: Robenow, 1890).
79. Quoted in Siegfried Nestriepke, *Geschichte der Volksbühne in Berlin* (Berlin: Volksbühnen Verlags und Vertriebs, 1930), p. 35.
80. Arne Garborg, *Müde Seelen,* trans. Marie Herzfeld (Berlin: Fischer, 1893).
81. The novel was reviewed by Ernst in *NZ,* 11, no. 12 (1892–93): 383–384.
82. Schmidt to Engels, Oct. 17, 1892, IISH, Engels Correspondence, L 5583.
83. Kautsky to Engels, Aug. 22, 1890, in Kautsky, *Engels Briefwechsel,* p. 259.
84. Engels to Kautsky, Sept. 18, 1890, ibid., p. 261.
85. Schmidt to Engels, Oct. 20, 1890, IISH, Engels Correspondence, L 5576.
86. Schmidt to Engels, Sept. 5, 1892, ibid., L 5582.

87. Schmidt to Engels, Feb. 26, 1890, ibid., L 5573.
88. Schmidt to Engels, June 25, 1890, ibid., L 5575.
89. Engels to Schmidt, Oct. 27, 1890, in Marx and Engels, *Werke,* vol. 37, pp. 488–495.
90. Engels to Kautsky, April 7, 1891, ibid., vol. 38, p. 77.
91. Schmidt to Engels, Oct. 25, 1891, IISH, Engels Correspondence, L 5579.
92. Schmidt to Engels, Sept. 5, 1892, ibid., L 5582.
93. Schmidt to Engels, March 5, 1891, ibid., L 5577.
94. Schmidt to Engels, Sept. 5, 1892, ibid., L 5582.
95. Schmidt to Engels, July 13, 1892, ibid., L 5581.
96. Schmidt, "Die psychologische Richtung in der neuen National-Ökonomie," *NZ,* 10, nos. 40, 41 (1891–92): 421–429, 459–464.
97. Engels to Bebel, July 7, 1892, in Marx and Engels, *Werke,* vol. 38, p. 374.
98. Schmidt, "Die Durchschnittsprofitrate und das Marx'sche Wertgesetz," *NZ,* 11, nos. 3, 4 (1892–93): 68–75, 112–124.
99. Engels to Kautsky, Sept. 29, 1892, in Marx and Engels, *Werke,* vol. 38, p. 484.
100. Schmidt to Engels, July 13, 1892, IISH, Engels Correspondence, L 5581.
101. Schmidt to Engels, Oct. 17, 1892, ibid., L 5583.
102. Schmidt to Engels, no date, ibid., L 5584.
103. Schmidt to Engels, March 28, 1894, ibid., L 5586.
104. Schmidt's review appears in *Le Devenir Social* (May 1895): 181–193. He also expresses his doubts in a letter to Kautsky, March 25, 1895, IISH, Kautsky Correspondence, D XX 321.
105. Engels to Schmidt, March 12, 1895, in Marx and Engels, *Werke,* vol. 38, pp. 430–434.
106. Engels to Schmidt, April 6, 1895, ibid., p. 461.
107. Schmidt to Kautsky, March 25, 1895, IISH, Kautsky Correspondence, D XX 321.
108. Schmidt raises these issues in a letter to Engels, undated, IISH, Engels Correspondence, L 5584.
109. Schmidt's article, "Sozialistische Moral," appears in *Ethische Kultur* (1894), nos. 20, 21. The article is quoted at length in Thomas G. Masaryk, *Die philosophischen und soziologischen Grundlagen des Marxismus* (Vienna: C. Konegen, 1899), pp. 496–497.
110. Quoted by Karl Kutzbach in his introduction to Paul Ernst, *Politische Studien und Kritiken: Aufsätze von Paul Ernst aus den Jahren, 1894–1902* (Langensalza: Julius Beltz, 1938), pp. 9–10.
111. Paul Ernst, *Entwicklungen* (Munich: Claudius Verlag, 1966), p. 211.
112. See Ernst's autobiographical sketch, "Bemerkungen über mich selbst," in Paul Ernst, *Der Weg zur Form* (Munich: G. Müller, 1928), pp. 11–29.
113. The Durch circle is discussed in Katharina Gunther, *Literarische Gruppenbildung im Berliner Naturalismus* (Bonn: Bouvier, 1972), pp. 50–72.
114. The influence of the Russian writers on Ernst is discussed in F. K. Richter, "Dostojewski im literarischen Denken Paul Ernsts," *German Quarterly,* 17, no. 2 (March 1944): 79–87.
115. Paul Ernst, *Jünglingsjahre* (Munich: G. Müller, 1931), p. 167.

116. *BVT* (Feb. 1, 8, 1890).
117. Ibid. (May 31, 1890).
118. Ernst, *Jünglingsjahre,* pp. 203–204.
119. Ernst discusses the Norwegian dramatists in *NZ,* 7, no. 3 (1889): 128–138. Bahr's criticism appeared in *Freie Bühne,* no. 1 (1890).
120. Ernst to Engels, May 31, 1890, IISH, Engels Correspondence, L 1799.
121. Engels to Ernst, June 5, 1890, in Marx and Engels, *Werke,* vol. 37, pp. 411–413.
122. Ernst, *Jünglingsjahre,* p. 202.
123. Ernst, "Gefahren des Marxismus," *BVT* (Aug. 9, 1890).
124. Ibid. (Sept. 6, 1890).
125. Engels, "Antwort an Herrn Paul Ernst," in Marx and Engels, *Werke,* vol. 22, p. 80. The reply was published in the *Berliner Volksblatt* (Oct. 15, 1890).
126. Engels to Schmidt, Oct. 27, 1890, in Marx and Engels, *Werke,* vol. 37, p. 49.
127. Ernst's review of Bahr's *Kritik der Moderne* appeared in the *BVT* (Sept. 27, Oct. 4, 1890).
128. See, for example, Paul Ernst, "Die neueste literarische Richtung in Deutschland," *NZ,* 10, no. 16 (1891–92): 509–510. Ernst's contribution to the development of Marxist literary criticism is discussed in Georg Fülberth, *Proletarische Partei und bürgerliche Literatur* (Neuwied: Luchterhand, 1972), pp. 58–61.
129. Gustav Landauer, "Die Zukunft und die Kunst," *NZ,* 11, no. 19 (1892–93): 532–535, and Paul Ernst, "Die Zukunft und die Kunst: Eine Erwiderung," *NZ,* no. 31 (1892–93): 658–60.
130. Paul Ernst, "Mehrings Lessing-Legende und die materialistische Geschichtsauffassung," *NZ,* 12, nos. 27, 28 (1893–94): 7–13, 45–51.
131. See Paul Ernst, "Die Sozialdemokratie und die Gebildeten unserer Tage," *BVT* (Dec. 13, 20, 1890).
132. Ibid. (Dec. 20, 1890). Ernst responds to the author's defense of his position in the issue of Jan. 3, 1891.
133. Ibid. (Jan. 10, 1891).
134. Ibid. (Aug. 29, 1891).
135. Ibid. (Nov. 14, 1891).
136. Ibid. (Dec. 26, 1891).
137. Ibid. (Dec. 14, 1891).
138. Ernst, *Jünglingsjahre,* p. 265.
139. Ibid., pp. 272–276.
140. Ernst, "Bemerkungen über mich selbst," p. 16.
141. Ernst, *Jünglingsjahre,* p. 294.
142. The series of articles, "Der soziale Zustände im romanischen Reich vor dem Einfall der Barbaren," appeared in the *Neue Zeit* during 1892 and 1893.
143. Rudolph Meyer is discussed in William Shanahan, *German Protestants Face the Social Question* (South Bend, Ind.: University of Notre Dame Press, 1954), p. 375.

144. Ernst, *Jünglingsjahre,* pp. 288, 295–297.
145. Ibid., p. 303.
146. Ernst, "Bemerkungen über mich selbst," p. 19.
147. Ibid., p. 20.

3. Two Paths for Marxist Intellectuals

1. Quoted in Benedikt Kautsky, ed., *Friedrich Engels Briefwechsel mit Karl Kautsky* (Vienna: Danubia-Verlag, 1955), p. 4.
2. For Kautsky's early intellectual development see Walter Holzheuer, *Karl Kautskys Werk als Weltanschauung* (Munich: Beck, 1972), and H. J. Steinberg, *Sozialismus und deutschen Sozialdemokratie* (Hanover: Verlag für Literatur und Zeitgeschehen, 1967), pp. 48–53.
3. Karl Kautsky, *Erinnerungen und Eröterungen* (The Hague: Mouton, 1960), p. 216.
4. Kautsky, *Engels Briefwechsel,* p. 166.
5. Engels to Kautsky, Feb. 1, 1881, ibid., p. 13.
6. Engels to Bebel, Aug. 25, 1881, in Karl Marx and Friedrich Engels, *Werke,* vol. 35 (Berlin: Dietz, 1979), p. 221.
7. Engels to Bebel, June 22, 1885, Jan. 20, 1886, ibid., vol. 36, pp. 336, 424.
8. Quoted in Kautsky, *Engels Briefwechsel,* p. 90.
9. Ingrid Gilcher-Holtey, *Das Mandat des Intellektuellen: Karl Kautsky und die Sozialdemokratie* (Berlin: Siedler, 1986), p. 21.
10. Hermann Müller, "Vor Dreissig Jahren," *Die Gesellschaft: Sonderheft* (Berlin, 1927), pp. 77–82. The development of the journal during the eighties is described in Brigitte Rieck, "Die Gründung der 'Neue Zeit' und ihre Entwicklung von 1883 bis 1890: Ein Überblick," *Jahrbuch für Geschichte,* 10 (1974): 253–294.
11. Kautsky to Bebel, Feb. 14, 1885, in John Kautsky, Jr., ed., *August Bebels Briefwechsel mit Karl Kautsky* (Assen: Van Gorcum & Co., 1971), p. 27.
12. Kautsky to Engels, Dec. 29, 1883, in Kautsky, *Engels Briefwechsel,* p. 92.
13. Kautsky to Bebel, Feb. 14, 1885, in Kautsky, *Bebels Briefwechsel mit Kautsky,* p. 28.
14. Ibid., p. 26.
15. Ibid., p. 28.
16. Holzheuer, *Kautsky,* p. 50.
17. Kautsky's view of the political process is discussed in Peter Gilg, *Die Erneuerungen des demokratische Denkens im Wilhelminischen Deutschland* (Wiesbaden: Steiner, 1965), pp. 52–87.
18. Kautsky to Engels, Aug. 22, 1890, in Kautsky, *Engels Briefwechsel,* p. 259.
19. The episode is described in Gary Steenson, *Karl Kautsky, 1854–1938* (Pittsburgh: University of Pittsburgh Press, 1978), pp. 93–98.
20. Bebel to Kautsky, March 26, 1891, in Kautsky, *Bebels Briefwechsel mit Kautsky,* p. 75.
21. For a criticism of the Erfurt Program see Wolfgang Abendroth, *Aufstieg*

und Krise der deutschen Sozialdemokratie (Frankfurt: Stimme Verlag, 1964), pp. 32–37.

22. Karl Kautsky, *The Class Struggle,* trans. E. Bohn (New York: W. W. Norton, 1971). For an analysis of Kautsky's position see Adam Przeworski, "Proletariat into a Class: The Process of Class Formation from Karl Kautsky's 'The Class Struggle' to Recent Controversies." *Politics and Society,* 7, no. 4 (1977): 343–401. Also see the important essay by Erich Matthias, "Kautsky und der Kautskyanismus," in I. Fetscher, ed., *Marxismusstudien,* 2nd ser. (Tübingen: Mohr, 1957).
23. Kautsky, *Class Struggle,* p. 117.
24. Ibid., pp. 34–42.
25. Ibid., p. 152.
26. Ibid., p. 155.
27. Ibid., p. 156–157.
28. Ibid., p. 195.
29. Ibid., p. 164.
30. Ibid., p. 199.
31. The study by Gilcher-Holtey, *Mandat des Intellektuellen,* places great emphasis on Kautsky's continuing insistence that the proletariat needed to be prepared for revolutionary action by "gaining insight into the laws of historical development." See especially pp. 80–83.
32. Holzheuer, *Kautsky,* pp. 51–52, 82.
33. For the argument that this dilemma underlies much of modern thought, including Marxism, see Charles Taylor, *Sources of the Self* (Cambridge, Mass.: Harvard University Press, 1989), pp. 332–339.
34. Kautsky, *Class Struggle,* pp. 183–189.
35. Ibid., p. 195.
36. Ibid., p. 188.
37. Bebel to Kautsky, Nov. 28, 1892, in Kautsky, *Bebels Briefwechsel mit Kautsksy,* pp. 75–76.
38. Kautsky to Bebel, Nov. 1892, ibid., pp. 78–81.
39. Mehring's earlier development is discussed in Glen R. McDougall, "Franz Mehring and the Problems of Liberal Social Reform in Bismarckian Germany, 1884–90: The Origins of Radical Marxism," *Central European History,* 16 (Sept. 1983): 225–255.
40. Kautsky to Adler, Aug. 5, 1891, in Victor Adler, *Briefwechsel mit August Bebel und Karl Kautsky* (Vienna: Wiener Volksbuchhandlung, 1954), p. 76.
41. Mehring's contribution to Marxist literary critisism is discussed in Georg Fülberth, *Proletarische Partei und bürgerliche Literatur* (Neuwied: Luchterhand, 1972), pp. 40–49. Also see Georg Fülberth and Michael Schuller, "Mehring l'ancien," *Le Mouvement Social,* no. 59 (April-June 1967): 11–24.
42. Engels to Mehring, July 14, 1892, in Marx and Engels, *Werke,* vol. 37, pp. 96–100.
43. Kautsky to Adler, Aug. 5, 1891, in Adler, *Briefwechsel,* p. 76.

44. Kautsky to Adler, June 20, 1895, ibid., p. 181.
45. Bebel to Engels, March 20–21, 1892, in Werner Blumenberg, ed., *August Bebels Briefwechsel mit Friedrich Engels* (The Hague: Mouton, 1965), p. 527.
46. Adler to Kautsky, Nov. 28, 1894, and Adler to Bebel, Nov. 1, 1898, in Adler, *Briefwechsel,* pp. 164, 265.
47. Kautsky to Bebel, Dec. 9, 1885, in Kautsky, *Bebels Briefwechsel mit Kautsky,* p. 46.
48. Kautsky to Engels, April 6, 1892, in Kautsky, *Engels Briefwechsel,* p. 336.
49. Liebknecht's editorial policy is discussed in Raymond Dominick, "Democracy of Socialism: A Case Study of *Vorwärts* in the 1890s," *Central European History,* 12 (Dec. 1977): 286–311. Also see Barbel Bauerle, "Das sozialdemokratische Zentralorgan in Berlin: Materialien zum ersten Dezennium der 'Vorwärts,'" *Jahrbuch für Geschichte,* 35 (1987): 269–296.
50. Kautsky to Adler, Oct. 15, 1892, in Adler, *Briefwechsel,* pp. 106–107.
51. Kautsky to Bebel, Aug. 9, 1894, and Kautsky to Hugo Heller, Dec. 22, 1894, in Kautsky, *Bebels Briefwechsel mit Kautsky,* pp. 84, 372.
52. Kautsky to Adler, June 20, 1895, in Adler, *Briefwechsel,* p. 180.
53. Kautsky to Engels, Nov. 25, 1893, in Kautsky, *Engels Briefwechsel,* p. 395.
54. Kautsky to Braun, Jan. 17, 1894, IISH, Kautsky Correspondence, C 316.
55. Kautsky to Adler, Oct. 15, 1892, in Adler, *Briefwechsel,* p. 108.
56. Ibid., p. 109.
57. Braun is described as a "co-founder" of the *Neue Zeit* by his fourth wife and biographer. See Julie Braun-Vogelstein, *Heinrich Braun* (Stuttgart: Deutsche Verlags-Anstalt, 1967), p. 55. The book was first published in 1932. Kautsky disputes that claim in his memoir, "Heinrich Braun: Ein Beitrag zur Geschichte der deutschen Sozialdemokratie," *Die Gesellschaft,* 10, no. 2 (1923): 160–162. Kautsky's correspondence with Engels indicates that he and Braun were closely associated in the venture. See Kautsky to Engels, Oct. 3, 1883, in Kautsky, *Engels Briefwechsel,* p. 86. Also see Kautsky, *Erinnerungen,* pp. 523, 532.
58. Braun to Kautsky, Jan. 28, 1885, IISH, Kautsky Correspondence, D VII 437.
59. Biographical facts are drawn from Braun-Vogelstein, *Braun.*
60. Freud to Julie Braun-Vogelstein, Oct. 30, 1927, in Ernst L. Freud, ed., *Letters of Sigmund Freud* (New York: Basic Books, 1960), pp. 378–380.
61. The Pernerstorfer circle is discussed in William McGrath, *Dionysian Art and Populist Politics in Austria* (New Haven: Yale University Press, 1974), pp. 18–52.
62. Braun-Vogelstein, *Braun,* pp. 48–55.
63. Ibid., p. 30.
64. Kautsky to Engels, May 31, 1882, in Kautsky, *Engels Briefwechsel,* p. 58.
65. Kautsky to Engels, Sept. 6, 1882, ibid., pp. 59–60.
66. Heinrich Braun, "Das Problem der Arbeiterversicherung und die Auffassung Lujo Brentanos," *NZ,* 1, no. 1 (1883).
67. Braun to Kautsky, Oct. 21, 1887, IISH, Kautsky Correspondence, D VI 539.

68. Kautsky to Engels, Oct. 3, 1883, in Kautsky, *Engels Briefwechsel,* p. 86.
69. Braun to Kautsky, Dec. 9, 1885, IISH, Kautsky Correspondence, D VI 490.
70. Braun to Kautsky, Jan. 14, 1887, ibid., 520.
71. Braun to Paul Natorp, as cited in Braun-Vogelstein, *Braun,* p. 65.
72. Braun to Kautsky, April 7, 1887, IISH, Kautsky Correspondence, D VI 526.
73. Braun to Kautsky, April 24, 1887, ibid., 527.
74. The letter to Paul Natorp, is cited in Braun-Vogelstein, *Braun,* p. 65.
75. Braun-Vogelstein, *Braun,* p. 63.
76. Braun to Kautsky, Oct. 13, 1887, IISH, Kautsky Correspondence, D VI 537.
77. Ibid.
78. Braun to Kautsky, Oct. 24, 1887, ibid., 539.
79. Bebel to Kautsky, Dec. 3, 1887, in Kautsky, *Bebels Briefwechsel mit Kautsky,* p. 67.
80. Braun to Kautsky, Oct. 21, 1887, IISH, Kautsky Correspondence, D VI 539.
81. Testimonies to Braun's editorial skills are contained in letters from Ferdinand Tönnies and others cited in Braun-Vogelstein, *Braun,* pp. 70–72.
82. For Sombart's development see Arthur Mitzman, *Sociology and Estrangement* (New York: Knopf, 1973), pp. 135–175.
83. Sombart's criticism of the Marxist theory of value, as presented in the third volume of *Capital,* appeared in his article, "Zur Kritik des ökonomischen System von Karl Marx," *Archiv für soziale Gesetzgebung und Statistik,* 7 (1894): 555, 565.
84. Braun-Vogelstein, *Braun,* p. 69.
85. Braun to Kautsky, Oct. 21, 1887, IISH, Kautsky Correspondence, D VI 539.
86. Kautsky to Bebel, Oct. 1888, in Kautsky, *Bebels Briefwechsel mit Kautsky,* p. 73.
87. Braun recalled his role in remarks at the Dresden party conference in 1903. Protokoll, Dresden (1903): 167.
88. Schmidt to Engels, June 25, 1890, IISH, Engels Correspondence, L 5575.
89. Schmidt to Engels, Oct. 20, 1890, Oct. 25, 1891, ibid., L 5576, 5579.
90. Braun-Vogelstein, *Braun,* p. 78.
91. Ibid., pp. 78–79.
92. Quoted in ibid., pp. 81–83.
93. *NZ,* 10 (1891–92): 533.
94. Ibid., p. 374.
95. Kautsky to Adler, June 13, 1892, Adler, *Briefwechsel,* p. 92.
96. Kautsky to Adler, Sept. 19, 1892, ibid., p. 100.
97. Kautsky to Adler, Oct. 15, 1892, ibid., pp. 107–108.
98. Ibid., p. 110.
99. Braun to Adler, Oct. 9, 1892. Quoted in Braun-Vogelstein, *Braun,* p. 326.
100. Heinrich Braun, "Zur Lage der deutschen Sozialdemokratie," *Archiv für soziale Gesetzgebung und Statistik,* 6 (1893): 506–520.
101. Ibid., p. 513.

102. Ibid., p. 519.
103. Ibid., p. 517.
104. Braun to Sombart, July 25, 1892. Quoted in Braun-Vogelstein, *Braun,* pp. 121–122.
105. Ibid., p. 66.
106. Braun, "Zur Lage der deutschen Sozialdemokratie," p. 520.
107. Kautsky to Braun, Jan. 17, 1894, IISH, Kautsky Correspondence, C 316.
108. Ibid.

4. Discovering the Akademikerproblem

1. The party's "discovery of the problem of its academics" is discussed in Brigitte Emig, *Die Veredelung des Arbeiters* (Frankfurt: Campus Verlag, 1980), pp. 104–127.
2. Protokoll, Cologne (1893): 132.
3. See Karl-Dietrich Mrossko, "Richard Calwer," in *Lebensbilder aus Schwaben und Franken,* vol. 12 (Stuttgart, 1972), pp. 362–384.
4. Richard Calwer, *Das Kommunistische Manifest und die heutige Sozialdemokratie* (Braunschweig: Gunther, 1894).
5. Ibid., p. 5.
6. Ibid., pp. 6–7.
7. Ibid., pp. 21–23.
8. Ibid., p. 24.
9. Ibid., p. 28.
10. Ibid., pp. 42–44.
11. Ibid., pp. 46–47.
12. Ibid., pp. 39–40. On this question also see Robert Wistrich, "Anti-Capitalism or Anti-Semitism: The Case of Franz Mehring," in *Leo Baeck Institute Yearbook,* vol. 22 (London, 1977), pp. 35–51.
13. Calwer, *Das Kommunistische Manifest,* p. 47.
14. Ibid., p. 50.
15. Ibid., pp. 29–30.
16. Ibid., p. 52.
17. Franz Mehring, "Die selbstkritik des Sozialismus," *NZ,* 12, no. 30 (1893–94): 129–132.
18. Richard Calwer, *Einführung in den Sozialismus* (Leipzig: H. Wigand, 1896), p. 230.
19. Protokoll, Frankfurt (1894): 82.
20. Ibid., pp. 76–77, 82.
21. Ibid., p. 76.
22. Ibid., p. 77.
23. Ibid., p. 73.
24. Ibid.
25. Ibid., p. 71.
26. Ibid., p. 84.
27. Ibid., p. 79.

28. Ibid., pp. 80–81.
29. Ludwig Quessel, “Nach 10 Jahren,” *SM*, 17 (Sept. 11, 1913): 1069–1073.
30. *Vorwärts* (Dec. 1, 1894).
31. *NZ*, 13, no. 18 (1894–95): 551.
32. “Die proletarische Intelligenz,” *NZ*, no. 19 (1894–95): 582.
33. Ibid., pp. 584–585.
34. H. Max, “Zur Frage der Organisation des Proletarians der Intelligenz,” *NZ*, no. 22 (1894–95): 692.
35. The three-part article “Die Intelligenz und die Sozialdemokratie” appeared in the *Neue Zeit*'s 1894–95 volume, nos. 27–29: 10–16, 43–49, 74–80.
36. Ibid., no. 27 (1894–95): 10–11.
37. Ibid., pp. 12–13.
38. Ibid., p. 13.
39. Ibid., pp. 14–16.
40. Ibid., no. 28, pp. 44–46.
41. Ibid., no. 29, pp. 74–75.
42. Ibid., pp. 76–77.
43. Ibid., pp. 77–78.
44. Charles Taylor, *Sources of the Self* (Cambridge, Mass.: Harvard University Press, 1989), pp. 322–329.
45. Kautsky, “Die Intelligenz und die Sozialdemokratie,” no. 29, pp. 78–79.
46. Ibid., pp. 79–80.
47. Rosa Luxemburg, “Der Sozialpatriotismus im Polem,” *NZ*, 14, no. 41 (1895–96): 459–470.
48. Karl Kautsky, “Finis Poloniae,” *NZ*, 14, no. 43 (1895–96): 513–525.
49. Gerhard Ritter, *Die Arbeiterbewegung im Wilhelminischen Reich* (Berlin: Colloquium Verlag, 1959), p. 130.
50. There are two excellent studies of the agrarian problem: Helmut Hesselbarth, *Revolutionäre Sozialdemokraten: Opportunisten und die Bauern am Vorabend des Imperialismus* (Berlin: Dietz, 1968), and Hans Georg Lehmann, *Die Agrarfrage in der Theorie und Praxis der deutschen und internationalen Sozialdemokratie* (Tübingen: Mohr, 1970).
51. Hesselbarth, *Revolutionäre Sozialdemokratie*, pp. 7–15.
52. Karl Kautsky, “Die Bauern und Sozialdemocratie,” *BVT* (Dec. 1, 1888).
53. Karl Kautsky, “Ein sozialdemokratische Katechismus,” *NZ*, 12, no. 12 (1893–94): 365.
54. All three published pamphlets in the Verlag des Berliner Arbeiter Bibliothek series: Max Schippel, *Die deutsche Zuckerindustrie und ihre Subventionirten* (Berlin, 1891); Paul Kampffmeyer, *Junker und Bauern* (Berlin, 1890); and Conrad Schmidt, *Die soziale Frage auf dem Land* (Berlin, 1890). The pamphlets are discussed in Lehmann, *Agrarfrage*, pp. 21–23.
55. See *NZ*, 11, no. 49 (1892–93): 696–697.
56. Calwer, *Kommunistiches Manifest*, p. 24.
57. *Sozialdemokrat* (Feb. 3, 1894).
58. Paul Ernst, “Zur Psychologie der Bauern,” *Sozialdemokrat* (March 22, 1894).

59. Paul Ernst, "Die Rentengesetzgebung in Preussen, letzter Abschnitt," *Sozialdemokrat* (April 12, 1894).
60. Katzenstein discusses his activity in these years in "Sozialistische Akademiker: Erinnerungen und Betractungen eines alteren Parteigenossen," *Vorwärts* (June 18, 1932).
61. Simon Katzenstein, "Zur Landagitation, Ein Beitrag zur Diskussion," *Sozialdemokrat* (March 10, 17, 1894).
62. For a biographical sketch see Susanne Miller, ed., *Das Kriegstagebuch des Reichstagsabgeordneten Eduard David. 1914–1918* (Düsseldorf: Droste, 1960), pp. xi–xxxvi.
63. Eduard David, "Zur Landagitation in Mitteldeutschland," *Sozialdemokrat* (Aug. 9, 16, 23, 30, Sept. 5, 13, 20, 27, 1894).
64. Hesselbarth, *Revolutionäre Sozialdemokraten,* p. 177.
65. The situation in Württemberg is discussed in Maja Christ-Gmelin, "Die Württembergerische Sozialdemokratie, 1890–1914" (diss., University of Stuttgart, 1976), pp. 23–34.
66. Vollmar's role is discussed in Reinhard Jansen, *Georg von Vollmar* (Bonn: Droste, 1956), chaps. 4, 5.
67. See William Harvey Maehl, *August Bebel* (Philadelphia: American Philosophical Society, 1980), p. 271.
68. For biographical information see Paul Mayer, *Bruno Schönlank, 1859–1901* (Hanover: Verlag für Literatur und Zeitgeschehen, 1971).
69. Quarck's early development is discussed in Paul Kampffmeyer, "Der sozialistische Theoretiker und Praktiker Max Quarck," *SM,* 71 (Feb. 17, 1930): 140–144.
70. See Protokoll, Gotha (1896): 88–90.
71. The setting for the discussion is described in Hesselbarth, *Revolutionäre Sozialdemokraten,* chap. 5.
72. Simon Katzenstein, "Eine sozialdemokratische Agrarkommission," *Sozialdemokrat* (Sept. 20, 1894).
73. Engels to Paul Lafargue, Nov. 22, 1894, in Karl Marx and Friedrich Engels, *Werke,* vol. 39 (Berlin: Dietz, 1978), pp. 324–326.
74. Bebel to Engels, Nov. 10, 1894, in Werner Blumenberg, ed., *August Bebels Briefwechsel mit Friedrich Engels* (The Hague: Mouton, 1965), pp. 781–782.
75. *Vorwärts* (Nov. 16, 1894).
76. Friedrich Engels, "Die Bauernfrage in Frankreich und Deutschland," *NZ,* 13, no. 10 (1894–95): 292–306.
77. Karl Kautsky, "Das Erfurter Programm und die Landagitation," *NZ,* 13, no. 9 (1894–95): 278–281.
78. The speech is reported in *Vorwärts* (Nov. 16, 1894).
79. Hesselbarth, *Revolutionäre Sozialdemokraten,* p. 198; Lehmann, *Agrarfrage,* p. 114.
80. The government's threat is discussed in Robert Lougee, "The Anti-Revolution Bill of 1894 in Wilhelmine Germany," *Central European History,* 15 (Sept. 1982): 224–240.

81. Engels to F. A. Sorge, Dec. 4, 1894, in Marx and Engels, *Werke,* vol. 39, pp. 334–336.
82. Lehmann, *Agrarfrage,* p. 138.
83. Bebel to Engels, July 17, 1895, in Blumenberg, *Bebels Briefwechsel,* pp. 803–804.
84. The Report is summarized in Hesselbarth, *Revolutionäre Sozialdemokraten,* pp. 213–217.
85. Karl Kautsky, "Unser neuestes Programm," *NZ,* 13, nos. 44, 45, 46 (1894–95): 557–565, 586–594, 610–624.
86. Eduard David, "Zur Beweisführung unserer Agrarier," *NZ,* 13, no. 36 (1894–95): 293–303.
87. David to Vollmar, July 3, 1895, IISH, Vollmar Correspondence, V 435.
88. Paul Ernst, "Zur Frage der Konkurrenzfähigkeit des Kleinbetriebes in der Landwirtschaft," *NZ,* 13, no. 50 (1894–95): 750–755.
89. This point is emphasized in Lehmann, *Agrarfrage,* pp. 159–163.
90. *Sozialdemokrat* (July 18, 1895).
91. Lehmann, *Agrarfrage,* p. 182.
92. Nearly 80 percent of the 178 meetings of local branches held to discuss the report expressed opposition to its recommendations. See Hesselbarth, *Revolutionäre Sozialdemokraten,* p. 227.
93. *Sozialdemokrat* (Aug. 8, 1895).
94. See the discussion in Lehmann, *Agrarfrage,* p. 179.
95. Paul Singer to Victor Adler, Sept. 27, 1895, in Victor Adler, ed., *Briefwechsel mit August Bebel und Karl Kautsky* (Vienna: Wiener Volksbuchhandlung, 1954), pp. 192–193.
96. Protokoll, Breslau (1895): 100–103.
97. Ibid., p. 138.
98. Ibid., p. 113.
99. Ibid., p. 153.
100. Ibid., p. 101.
101. Ibid., pp. 137–138.
102. Ibid., p. 119.
103. Ibid., pp. 126–127.
104. Ibid., pp. 105–110.
105. Ibid., p. 123.
106. Ibid., pp. 138–143.
107. Ibid., p. 129.
108. Karl Kautsky, "Der Breslauer Parteitag und die Agrarfrage," *NZ,* 14, no. 4 (1895–96): 108–113.
109. Franz Mehring, "Dogmen-Fanatismus," *NZ,* 14, no. 9 (1895–96): 256–262.
110. Lehmann, *Agrarfrage,* pp. 200–202.
111. Bebel to Adler, Oct. 20, 1895, in Adler, *Briefwechsel,* pp. 194–195.
112. Ibid.
113. David to Vollmar, Oct. 13, 1895, IISH, Vollmar Correspondence, V 435.
114. Ritter, *Die Arbeiterbewegung,* pp. 148–149.

115. See his "Wochenschau," *Sozialdemokrat* (Oct. 17, 1895), and his "Theorie der Taktik" (Nov. 20, 1895).
116. "Ein Blick auf unsere Partei" *Sozialdemokrat* (Nov. 21, 1895).

5. The Cultural Meaning of Marxism

1. "Was wir wollen," *SA,* 1 (Jan. 1, 1895): 1–7.
2. Ibid., pp. 5–7.
3. Ibid., p. 11.
4. See, for example, "Das gebildete Proletariat und die Sozialdemokratie," *SA,* 1 (March 15, 1895): 128–130.
5. S.K., "Das Kleinbürgertum und seine Beziehungen zur Intelligenz," *SA,* 1 (March 1, 1895): 85–90.
6. "Das gebildete Proletariat," *SA,* 1 (March 15, April 15, May 1, 1895).
7. Georg Zepler, "Zweites Armeecorps vor," *SA,* 1 (June 1, July 1, 1895): 189–192, 229–232.
8. Heinz Starkenburg, "Agrarprogramm und Landagitation," *SA,* 1 (Sept. 1, 1895): 309–312.
9. Georg Zepler, "Zur Agrarfrage," *SA,* 1 (Sept. 1, 1895): 312–316.
10. B.H., "Der Breslauer Parteitag," *SA,* 1 (Oct. 15, 1895): 371–372.
11. For biographical information see Anna Siemsen, ed., *Ein Leben für Europa* (Frankfurt: Europaische Verlagsanstalt, 1956).
12. Catilina, "Die kommunistischen Richtungen und der 'freiheitliche' Sozialismus," *SA,* 1 (Jan. 1, 1895): 14–22.
13. Catilina, "Zum 1 Mai," *SA,* 1 (May 1, 1895): 157.
14. Catilina, "Die anarchistischen Lehren und ihre Verhältnisse zum Kommunismus," *SA,* 1 (Aug. 1, 15, Oct. 1, 15, Dec. 15, 1895): 273–276, 299–303, 360–362, 382–384, 474–477.
15. Ibid., pp. 273–274.
16. Ibid., p. 274.
17. Ibid., p. 362.
18. Ibid., pp. 302, 299.
19. Ibid., pp. 475–476.
20. Catilina, "Ein Brief von Friedrich Engels," *SA,* 1 (Oct. 1, 1895): 351–353.
21. Catilina, "Ein zweiter Brief von Friedrich Engels," *SA,* 1 (Oct. 15, 1895): 380.
22. Heinz Starkenburg, "Die Soziologie des ökonomischen Materialismus," *SA,* 1 (May 15, June 1, 1895): 175–177, 193–196.
23. "Einiges über die deutsche Sozialdemokratie zum Breslauer Parteitag," *SA,* 1 (Aug. 15, 1895): 290–299.
24. Miguel de Unamuno, "Die Treibkräfte in der sozialistischen Bewegung," *SA,* 1 (Dec. 15, 1895): 478–481.
25. "Zu unserm ersten Kampfesjahr," *SA,* 1 (Dec. 15, 1895): 465–467.
26. Conrad Schmidt, "Egoismus und Sozialismus," *SA,* 2 (Jan. 1896): 3–9.
27. Conrad Schmidt, "Ein neues Buch über die materialistische Geschichtsauffassung," *SA,* 2 (July, Aug. 1896): 399–407, 475–482.

28. Paul Kampffmeyer, "Wandlungen in der sozialistischen Theorie," *SA,* 2 (Jan. 1896): 11–18.
29. Paul Kampffmeyer, "Die Irrtümer Ferdinand Lassalles," *SA,* 2 (April, May 1896): 201–206, 282–291.
30. Ibid., p. 283.
31. Paul Ernst, "Wirtschaftliche Neubildungen," *SA,* 2 (Feb. 1896): 69–76.
32. Paul Ernst, "Die soziale Bedeutung der landwirtschaftlichen Krisis," *SA,* 2 (June 1896): 333–339.
33. Paul Ernst, "Ostasiatische Lyrik," *SA,* 2 (Aug. 1896): 485–488.
34. Paul Ernst, "Der Gebildete in Deutschland," *SA,* 2 (April 1896): 232–238.
35. Georg Zepler, "Atheismus, Christentum, Sozialdemokratie," *SA,* 2 (Feb. 1896): 84–89.
36. Simon Katzenstein, "Kritische Bemerkungen zu Bebels Buch 'Die Frau und der Sozialismus," *NZ,* 15, no. 10 (1896–97): 293–303. Bebel responded in the next issue.
37. Herbert Scherer, *Bürgerliche-oppositionelle Literaten und sozialdemokratische Arbeiterbewegung nach 1890* (Stuttgart: Metzler, 1974), p. 202.
38. See James McFarlane, "Berlin and the Rise of Modernism," in Malcolm Bradbury and James McFarlane, eds., *Modernism* (New York: Penguin Books, 1976), pp. 105–119.
39. Ria Claasen, "Neue Kunst," *SA,* 2 (Oct. 1896): 632–638. Here, as at a number of points in this study, I have drawn on writers who develop significant aspects of the unfolding thought of the intellectuals even though I have not been able to discover the background or status of the contributor.
40. Simon Katzenstein, "Die Akademiker in der Sozialdemokratie," *SA,* 2 (Dec. 1896): 729–736.
41. "Rundschau," *SA,* 2 (Dec. 1896): 784–785.
42. Quoted in Siegfried Nestriepke, *Geschichte der Volksbühne in Berlin* (Berlin: Volksbühnen-Verlags und Vertriebs, 1930), p. 11.
43. For discussions of the split see Scherer, *Bürgerliche-oppositionelle Literaten,* pp. 79–96; Nestriepke, *Geschichte der Volksbühne,* pp. 58–65; Heinz Selo, "Die 'Freie Volksbühne' in Berlin" (diss., University of Erlangen, 1930).
44. Franz Mehring, "Der heutige Naturalismus," in Fritz Raddatz, ed., *Franz Mehring Werkauswahl III* (Darmstadt: Luchterhand, 1975), pp. 12–15.
45. Ibid., p. 14.
46. Franz Mehring, "Freie Volksbühne," *NZ,* 11, no. 43 (1892–93): 481–485. Mehring's aesthetic views are discussed in Vernon L. Lidtke, *The Alternative Culture: Socialist Labor in Imperial Germany* (New York: Oxford University Press, 1985), pp. 145–147.
47. Selo, "Die 'Freie Volksbühne,'" pp. 76–78.
48. Franz Mehring, "Paul Bader: Andere Zeiten," in Raddatz, *Franz Mehring,* pp. 227–232.
49. See the discussion in Scherer, *Bürgerliche-oppositionelle Literaten,* pp. 110–112.

50. Ibid., p. 114.
51. See ibid. for a discussion of the reorientation. Also see Georg Fülberth, *Proletarische Partei und bürgerliche Literatur* (Neuwied: Luchterhand, 1972), pp. 52–54, and Hans Koch, *Franz Mehrings Beiträge zur Marxistischen Literaturtheorie* (Berlin: Dietz, 1959), pp. 100–102.
52. Quoted in Scherer, *Bürgerliche-oppositionelle Literaten,* pp. 114–116.
53. Ibid., p. 119.
54. See the accounts in Nestriepke, *Geschichte der Volksbühne,* pp. 133–143, and Selo, "Die 'Freie Volksbühne,'" p. 83.
55. Franz Mehring, "Die Freie Volksbühne," *NZ,* 18, no. 44 (1899–1900).
56. Quoted in Selo, "Die 'Freie Volksbühne,'" p. 37.
57. See the obituary of Steiger in *NZ,* 37 (Nov. 7, 1919): 121–123.
58. Edgar Steiger, *Der Kampf um die neue Dichtung* (Berlin: R. Weidler Werther, 1889).
59. On the *Neue Welt* see Dirk Hoffmann, "Sozialismus und Literaten," (diss., University of Münster, 1975), pp. 293–295.
60. The two novels are discussed in Scherer, *Bürgerliche-oppositionelle Literaten,* pp. 153–182.
61. The articles were republished in Edgar Steiger, *Das Arbeitervolk und die Kunst* (Leipzig, 1896); reprinted in Norbert Rothe, ed., *Naturalismus Debatte, 1891–1896* (Berlin: Akademie Verlag, 1986), pp. 185–191.
62. Berard's article is reprinted in Rothe, *Naturalismus,* pp. 192–195.
63. See Edgar Steiger, "Kunst oder Traktätchen?" ibid., pp. 195–197.
64. Edgar Steiger, "Kunst und Sittlichkeit," ibid., pp. 206–209.
65. See the unsigned article, "Das arbeitende Volk und die Kunst," ibid., pp. 198–201.
66. Steiger, "Kunst oder Traktätchen," p. 209. Virtually the entire debate is reprinted in Rothe, *Naturalismus.*
67. Ibid., p. 212.
68. Ibid., pp. 213–215.
69. Ibid., p. 219.
70. See the discussion in Scherer, *Bürgerliche-oppositionelle Literaten,* pp. 142–153, in which Steiger is seen as exemplifying the outlook of the Friedrichshagen circle, which placed art above class. Scherer argues that only a party organized along Leninist lines could have extricated the Social Democrats from their cultural impasse. Also see the discussion in Fülberth, *Proletarische Partei,* pp. 91–98.
71. For Bebel's comments see Rothe, *Naturalismus,* pp. 230–232.
72. *Vorwärts* (Oct. 17, 1896).
73. Scherer, *Bürgerliche-oppositionelle Literaten,* pp. 184–190.
74. Franz Mehring, "Kunst und das Proletariat," *NZ,* 15, no. 5 (1896–97): 129–133.
75. Ibid., p. 132.
76. The series of ten articles ran in the *Neue Zeit* during 1897 and 1898. They are reprinted in Raddatz, *Franz Mehring,* pp. 30–140. For the quotation see p. 137.
77. Ibid., p. 138.

78. Edgar Steiger, *Das Werden des neuen Dramas* (Berlin: W. F. Fontane, 1898), pp. 96–120.
79. Ibid., pp. 116, 119–120.
80. Raddatz, *Franz Mehring,* p. 139.
81. Franz Mehring, "Die Freie Volksbühne," *NZ,* 18, no. 44 (1899–1900): 530–536.
82. Conrad Schmidt, "Genosse Mehring und die Freie Volksbühne," *NZ,* no. 48 (1899–1900): 659–663.
83. See Hoffmann, *Sozialdemokratie und Literatur,* especially pp. 109–116.
84. Susanne Miller, "Critique litteraire de la social-democratie allemande à la fin du siècle dernier," *Le Mouvement Social,* no. 59 (April-June 1967), pp. 50–69.
85. Scherer, *Bürgerliche-oppositionelle Literaten,* pp. 213–215. This process is examined in Guenther Roth, *The Social Democrats in Imperial Germany* (Totowa, N.J.: Bidminster Press, 1963), chaps. 7, 9. Also see Hermann Bausinger, "Verbürglichung-Folen einer Interpretation," in Gunter Wiegelmann, ed., *Kultureller Wandel im 19, Jahrhundert* (Göttingen: Vandenhoeck & Ruprecht, 1973), pp. 24–49. The whole subject is viewed from a different perpective in Lidtke, *Alternative Culture.* Lidtke recognizes that the movement "drew heavily on . . . bourgeois society and culture" and that the "most advanced Social Democratic thinkers neglected to develop a fully rounded cultural theory on a Marxist foundation." But he argues that the manner in which the socialists adapted the "intellectual and artistic substance" of the wider world constituted an "alternative culture." See especially pp. 3–20, 192–201. For an interesting discussion of Max Weber's recognition and assessment of Social Democracy as a "cultural movement," see Lawrence A. Scaff, *Fleeing the Iron Cage: Culture, Politics, and Modernity in the Thought of Max Weber* (Berkeley: University of California Press, 1989), pp. 175–180. Weber held that the cultural aspirations of the socialists were negated by their acceptance of "technical progress" and the process of "rationalization."
86. See, for example, August Bebel, *Akademiker und Sozialismus* (Berlin: Dietz, 1898), p. 11.
87. See the essays in Paul Ernst, *Politische Studien und Kritiken* (Langensalza: Julius Beltz, 1938).
88. See Paul Ernst, "Bermerkungen über mich selbst," *Der Weg zur Form* (Munich: G. Müller, 1928), p. 19.
89. Paul Ernst, "Modernes Drama," ibid., pp. 61–67.
90. Paul Ernst, *Friedrich Nietzsche: Veränderte zweite Auflage* (Berlin: Gotz und Tetzlaff, 1904), p. 38. For discussions of the complex relationship between Nietzsche and the socialist intellectuals see: R. Hinton Thomas, *Nietzsche in German Politics and Society, 1890–1918* (Manchester: Manchester University Press, 1983); Kurt Sollmann, *Literarische Intelligenz vor 1900* (Cologne: Pahl-Rugenstein, 1982), pp. 220–273; Helmut Scheuer, "Zwischen Sozialismus und Individualismus—Zwischen Marx und Nietzsche," in Helmut Scheuer, ed., *Naturalismus* (Stuttgart: W. Kohlhammer, 1974), pp. 150–174; Steven E. Aschheim, "Nietzschean Socialism—

Left and Right, 1890–1933," *Journal of Contemporary History,* 23 (April 1988): 147–168.

91. Paul Ernst, *Der schmale Weg zum Glück* (Munich: A. Langen, 1937), pp. 270–273.
92. Paul Ernst, "Einst und Jetzt," in *Politische Studien,* pp. 222–243.
93. Ernst's quest bore a curious relationship to later Marxist thought. His conception of the tragic hero, who displaced the proletariat as the bearer of future values, influenced the young Hungarian cultural critic Georg Lukács. In a reversal of Ernst's course, Lukács moved toward Marxism and sought to restore the conscious and willful elements, the depreciation of which had contributed to Ernst's disaffection. See the essay on Ernst in Georg Lukács, *Soul and Form* (Cambridge, Mass.: M.I.T. Press, 1974). For the correspondence between the two men see Karl Kutzbach, ed., *Paul Ernst und Georg Lukács: Dokumente einer Freundschaft* (Emsdetten: Lechte, 1974). The relationship is discussed briefly in Harry Liebersohn, *Fate and Utopianism in German Sociology, 1870–1923* (Cambridge, Mass.: M.I.T. Press, 1988), pp. 170–176. For Ernst's later sympathy for National Socialism see George L. Mosse, *Masses and Man* (New York: H. Fertig, 1980), pp. 80–83.

6. Revising Marxism

1. The literature on Bernstein and revisionism is extensive. It includes Pierre Angel, *Eduard Bernstein et l'évolution du socialisme allemand* (Paris: M. Didier, 1961); Peter Gay, *The Dilemma of Democratic Socialism* (New York: Collier Books, 1962); Bo Gustafson, *Marxismus und Revisionismus* (Frankfurt: Europaische Verlagsanstalt, 1972); Peter Strutynski, *Die Auseinandersetzungen zwischen Marxisten und Revisionismus in der deutschen Arbeiterbewegung um die Jahrhundertwende* (Cologne: Pahl-Rugenstein, 1976); Horst Heimann and Thomas Meyer, eds., *Bernstein und demokratische Sozialismus* (Berlin: Dietz, 1977); Thomas Meyer, *Bernsteins konstruktiver Sozialismus* (Berlin: Dietz, 1977); Helmut Hirsch, *Der "Fabier" Eduard Bernstein* (Berlin: Dietz, 1977); still useful for the broader development of revisionism is Erika Rikli, *Der Revisionismus* (Zurich: H. Girsberger, 1936).
2. Paul Kampffmeyer, "Historisches und Theoretisches zur Sozialdemokratie Revisionismus Bewegung," *SM,* 6 (May 1902): 354.
3. Bernstein to Bebel, Oct. 20, 1898, in Victor Adler, *Briefwechsel mit August Bebel und Karl Kautsky* (Vienna: Wiener Volksbuchhandlung, 1954), p. 260.
4. Published later as *Zur Geschichte und Theorie des Sozialismus* (Berlin: Akademischer Verlag für Sociale Wissenschaft, 1901). A number of the articles are translated and reprinted in H. Tudor and J. M. Tudor, eds., *Marxism and Social Democracy: The Revisionist Debate, 1896–1898* (Cambridge: Cambridge University Press, 1988). Where possible I have cited this volume.

5. Eduard Bernstein, "Crime and the Masses," in Tudor, *Marxism and Social Democracy,* pp. 109–118.
6. Bernstein, "The Realistic and Ideological Moments in Socialism," ibid., p. 241.
7. Bernstein, "Critical Interlude," ibid., p. 221.
8. Kautsky's flexibility is emphasized in Ingrid Gilcher-Holtey, *Das Mandat des Intellektuellen* (Berlin: Siedler, 1986), pp. 167–177.
9. Kautsky to Adler, April 9, 1898, in Adler, *Briefwechsel,* pp. 245–246.
10. Kautsky to Adler, Aug. 4, 1898, ibid., p. 249.
11. Most of the debate at Stuttgart is reprinted in Tudor, *Marxism and Social Democracy,* pp. 276–304.
12. Quoted in Walter Holzheuer, *Karl Kautskys Werk, als Weltanschauung* (Munich: Beck, 1972), p. 68.
13. Kautsky to Bernstein, Oct. 23, 1898, in Adler, *Briefwechsel,* p. 273.
14. Ibid.
15. Bernstein to Adler, March 28, 1899, ibid., pp. 307–308.
16. Bernstein to Adler, March 3, 1899, ibid., pp. 288–289.
17. Kautsky to Adler, April 10, 1899, ibid., pp. 311–312.
18. Kautsky to Adler, March 21, 1899, ibid., p. 304.
19. William Harvey Maehl, *August Bebel* (Philadelphia: American Philosophical Society, 1980), p. 310.
20. Bebel to Adler, Nov. 4, 1898, in Adler, *Briefwechsel,* pp. 268–270.
21. Bebel to Adler, April 8, 1899, ibid., p. 309.
22. Bernstein to Adler, March 3, 1899, ibid., p. 288. Looking back thirty years later, Bernstein recognized that he had asked the party to give up qualities which had been vital to its existence, qualities which "had the significance of a religious-like belief." See his *Entwicklungsgang eines Sozialisten* (Leipzig: E. Reiss, 1930), p. 37.
23. Protokoll, Hanover (1899): 67–68.
24. Paul Kampffmeyer, "Ein Wort über den Zusammenhang von Theorie und Praxis in der socialen Frage," *SM,* 1 (Jan. 1897): 3–9.
25. Paul Kampffmeyer, "Polemisches zur Theorie und Praxis der sozialen Frage," *SM,* 2 (April 1898): 147–153.
26. See G. Sorel, "Über die Marx'sche Werttheorie," *SM,* 1 (June 1897): 345–353; "Was man von Vico lernt" *SM,* 2 (June 1898): 270–272; and "Betrachtungen über die materialistische Geschichtsauffassung" *SM,* 2 (July, Aug. 1898): 316–322, 345–352.
27. Kampffmeyer, "Polemisches zur Theorie," p. 149.
28. Ladislaus Gumplowicz, "Wandlungen in der anarchistischen Taktik und Doktrin," *SM,* 2 (July 1898): 322–327. For the development of Gumplowicz, son of the Austrian sociologist Ludwig Gumplowicz, see Max Nettlau, "Geschichte des Anarchismus," vol. 7, p. 234. IISH, unpublished manuscript.
29. Paul Kampffmeyer, *Mehr Macht* (Berlin: Verlag der Sozialistischen Monatshefte, 1898).
30. Ibid., p. 3.

31. Ibid., p. 18.
32. Ibid., pp. 26–28.
33. Ibid., pp. 36–37. Kampffmeyer's views are discussed in Peter Gilg, *Die Erneuerung des demokratischen Denkens im Wilhelminischen Deutschland* (Wiesbaden: Steiner, 1965), pp. 167–169.
34. Conrad Schmidt, "Grenznutzpsychologie und Marx'sche Wertlehre," *SM,* 1 (Jan. 1897): 18–22, and "Über das eherne Lohngesetz" *SM,* 2 (May 1898): 206–212.
35. See Schmidt's article, "Final Goal and Movement," published in *Vorwärts* in February 1898 and reprinted in Tudor, *Marxism and Social Democracy,* pp. 205–211.
36. G. Plekhanov, "Konrad Schmidt gegen Karl Marx und Friedrich Engels," *NZ,* 17, no. 3 (1898–99): 133–145. Plekhanov's relationship to the German Social Democrats and his dispute with Schmidt is discussed in Samuel Baron, *Plekhanov* (Stanford: Stanford University Press, 1963), pp. 176–180.
37. Conrad Schmidt, "Einige Bemerkungen über Plekhanovs letzten Artikel in der 'Neue Zeit,'" *NZ,* 17, no. 11 (1898–99): 324–334.
38. Chajm Schitlowsky, "Die Polemik Plekhanov contra Stern und Conrad Schmidt," *SM,* 3 (June, July 1899): 274–283, 322–330.
39. Plekhanov, "Konrad Schmidt," p. 145.
40. Schmidt, "Einige Bemerkungen," pp. 332–333.
41. Conrad Schmidt, "Nachträgliche Bemerkungen zur Bernstein Diskussion," *SM,* 3 (Oct. 1899): 493–499.
42. Ritter, *Die Arbeiterbewegung im Wilhelminischen Reich* (Berlin: Colloquium Verlag, 1959), p. 187.
43. The development of the trade unions in these years is discussed in John Moses, *Trade Unionism in Germany from Bismarck to Hitler,* vol. 1, *1869–1918* (Totowa, N.J.: Barnes and Noble, 1982), chaps. 4, 5.
44. Protokoll, Hamburg (1897): 121.
45. Ibid., p. 141.
46. Ibid., pp. 143–144.
47. Ibid., pp. 137–139.
48. Ibid., p. 122.
49. Protokoll, Stuttgart (1898): 172–184.
50. "Isegrin," "Skizzen aus der sozialpolitischen Literatur und Bewegung," "IV. War Friedrich Engels milizgläubisch?" *SM,* 2 (Nov. 1898): 495–498.
51. Kautsky and Schippel debated the issues in the *Neue Zeit* during January and February 1899. For a discussion see Strutynski, *Die Auseinandersetzung zwischen Marxisten und Revisionisten,* pp. 100–110. Also see Dieter Fricke, "Zur Militarisierung des deutschen Geisteslebens im wilhelminischen Kaisserreich: Der Fall Leo Arons," *Zeitschrift für Geschichtswissenschaft,* 8 (1960): 1069–1107, and Nikolaj Oucarenko, "Zum Militärprogramm der deutschen Sozialdemokratie an der Wende vom 19. zum 20. Jahrhundert," *Jahrbuch für Geschichte,* 10 (1974): 295–341.
52. Ritter, *Die Arbeiterbewegung,* pp. 190–191.

53. See Kurt Dietrich Mrossko, "Richard Calwer," in *Lebensbilder aus Schwaben und Fraken,* vol. 12 (Stuttgart, 1972), pp. 362–384.
54. Richard Calwer, *Einführung in den Sozialismus* (Leipzig: H. Wigand, 1896), pp. 223–225.
55. Mrossko, "Richard Calwer," p. 376. For background and a discussion of the views of Schippel and Calwer on trade policy see Hans Maximillian Calmann, *Die Finanzpolitik der deutschen Sozialdemokratie 1867–1914* (Munich: Rosl, 1922), pp. 127–139.
56. Biographical information is drawn from Wolfgang Heine, "Persönliche, für die Familie bestimmte 'Erinnerungen,'" BAK.
57. Ibid., pp. 332–336.
58. Ibid., pp. 422–423.
59. Wolfgang Heine, *Die Sozialdemokratie und die Schichten der Studierten* (Berlin, 1899).
60. Heine, "Erinnerungen," pp. 435–439.
61. See Hedwig Wachenheim, *Die deutsche Arbeiterbewegung, 1844 bis 1914* (Cologne: Köln und Opladen Westdeutschen Verlag, 1967), pp. 349–350.
62. Protokoll, Stuttgart (1898): 107–110.
63. Wolfgang Heine, "Die Bernstein Frage und die politische Praxis der Sozialdemokratie," *SM,* 3 (Dec. 1899): 478–493.
64. Ibid., p. 491.
65. Göhre's development is examined in Kurt Dietrich Mrossko, *Paul Göhre* (Reutlingen, 1967), and Joachim Brenning, "Christentum und Sozialdemokratie" (diss., University of Marburg, 1980).
66. Paul Göhre, *Drei Monate Fabrikarbeiter und Handwerksbursche* (Leipzig: Grunow, 1891).
67. See Dieter Düding, *Der Nationalsoziale Verein, 1896–1903* (Munich: Oldenbourg, 1972).
68. Paul Göhre, "Wandlungen der Nationalsozialen," *SM,* 5 (Dec. 1901): 917–936.
69. See Paul Meyer, *Bruno Schönlank, 1859–1901* (Hanover: Verlag für Literatur und Zeitgeschehen, 1971), pp. 125, 138.
70. Paul Göhre, *Wie ein Pfarrer Sozialdemokrat wurde* (Berlin: Vorwärts, 1909).
71. See Eugen Losinsky, "Das religiöse Problem in Sozialismus," *SM,* 5 (Feb. 1902): 123–131, and Göhre's reply, "Das religiöse Problem im Sozialismus," "Materialismus und Religion," and "Christentum und materialistische Geschichtsauffassung," *SM,* 5 (April, July, Aug. 1902): 267–277, 501–508, 598–607.
72. Schmidt's interpretation of Kant is criticized in Karl Vorlander, *Kant und Marx* (Tübingen: Mohr, 1926), pp. 154–166. Also see Tibor Hanak, *Die Entwicklung der Marxistischen Philosophie* (Stuttgart: Schwabe, 1974), pp. 50–52.
73. The relationship between Neo-Kantianism and the Social Democrats is discussed in Thomas Wiley, *Back to Kant: The Revival of Kantianism in German Social and Historical Thought, 1860–1914* (Detroit: Wayne State University Press, 1978). Also see Timothy Keck, "The Marburg School and

Ethical Socialism; Another Look," *Social Science Journal* (Oct. 1977): 105–120; Hermann Lubbe, *Politische Philosophie in Deutschland* (Basel: B. Schwabe, 1963), pp. 113–125; H. J. Steinberg, *Sozialismus und deutsche Sozialdemokratie* (Hanover: Verlag für Literatur und Zeitgeschehen, 1967), pp. 96–110. A number of the essays dealing with the relationship can be found in Rafael de la Vega and Hans Jorg Sandkuller, eds., *Marxismus und Ethik: Texte zum neukantianischen Sozialismus* (Frankfurt: Suhrkamp, 1970).

74. Kautsky's weakness with respect to philosophy is discussed in Hanak, *Entwicklung der Marxistischen Philosophie,* pp. 57–62.
75. Staudinger is discussed in Vorlander, *Kant und Marx,* pp. 138–149.
76. See Sadi Gunter, "Die materialistische Geschichtsauffassung und der praktische Idealismus," *NZ,* 16, no. 41 (1897–98): 452–464, and "Antonio Labriola und Ethik," no. 45: 556–560, no. 46: 586–591.
77. Staudinger to Kautsky, May 19, 1911, IISH, Kautsky Correspondence, KD XXI 323.
78. Karl Vorlander, *Kant und Sozialismus* (Berlin: Reuther & Reichard, 1900).
79. Woltmann is discussed in Vorlander, *Kant und Marx,* pp. 166–176.
80. Ibid., p. 167.
81. Woltmann to Kautsky, Sept. 23, 1899, IISH, Kautsky Correspondence, D XXIII 215.
82. Ludwig Woltmann, "Der historische Materialismus: Darstellung und Kritik der marxistischen Weltanschauung," *NZ,* 17, no. 50 (1898–99): 790–794.
83. Ludwig Woltmann, "Die Wirtschaftlichkeit und politischem Grundlagen der Klassenkämpfe," *SM,* 5 (Feb., May, June 1901): 122–132, 362–368, 415–424.
84. Ludwig Woltmann, *Die Stellung der Sozialdemokratie zur Religion* (Leipzig: Bibliothek für modernes Geistesleben, 1901).
85. For a discussion of Woltmann's racist turn see George Mosse, *The Crisis of German Ideology* (New York: Grosset and Dunlap, 1965), pp. 99–103, and Ernst Nolte, "Marxismus und Nationalsozialismus," *Vierteljahrshefte für Zeitgeschichte,* 31 (July 1983): 401–402.
86. See Jean H. Quataert, *Reluctant Feminists in German Social Democracy, 1885–1917* (Princeton: Princeton University Press, 1979); Werner Thonnessen, *The Emancipation of Women: The Rise and Decline of the Women's Movement in German Social Democracy, 1864–1953* (London: Pluto Press, 1973); and Richard Evans, "Socialist Women and Political Radicalism," in his *Proletarians and Politics* (New York: St. Martin's Press, 1990), pp. 93–123.
87. Quataert, *Reluctant Feminists,* p. 12.
88. Biographical information is drawn from Luise Dornemann, *Clara Zetkin* (Berlin: Dietz, 1973).
89. Zetkin's editorial policy is discussed in Fritz Staude, "Die Rolle der 'Gleichheit' im Kampf Clara Zetkins für die Emanzipation der Frau," *Beiträge zur Geschichte der Arbeiterbewegung,* 16 (1974): 427–445.
90. The debate over the woman's question at the Gotha conference, where Zetkin's views were formally accepted by the party, is reprinted in Heinz

Niggemann, ed., *Frauenemanzipation und Sozialdemokratie* (Frankfurt: Fischer, 1981), pp. 69–93.

91. Quataert, *Reluctant Feminists,* p. 106.
92. For biographical information see Julie Vogelstein, *Lily Braun: Ein Lebensbild* (Berlin: F. Schneider, 1922), and Alfred G. Meyer, *The Feminism and Socialism of Lily Braun* (Bloomington, Ind.: Indiana University Press, 1985).
93. Quoted in Dieter Fricke, "Die Gründung der revisionistisch Zeitschrift 'Die Neue Gesellschaft,' 1900–1905," *Beiträge zur Geschichte der Arbeiterbewegung,* 16, no. 6 (1974): 1054.
94. Lily Braun, *Memoiren einer Sozialistin,* vol. 2, *Kampfjahr* (Berlin: A. Langen, 1911), pp. 57–60.
95. Her speech is reprinted in Niggemann, *Frauenemanzipation,* pp. 115–120. For a report of the conference see Wally Zepler, "Die internationale Frauenbewegung," *SA,* 2 (Oct. 1896): 601–608.
96. The relationship between Lily Braun and Clara Zetkin is discussed in Quataert, *Reluctant Feminists,* pp. 107–133, and Evans, "Socialist Women and Political Radicalism," pp. 106–112.
97. Braun, *Memoiren,* pp. 244–246.
98. Ibid., p. 60.
99. Ibid., pp. 159–160.
100. See the discussion in Meyer, *Feminism and Socialism of Lily Braun,* pp. 68–69.
101. Lily Braun, *Die Frauenfrage; ihre geschichtliche Entwicklung und ihre wirtschaftliche Seite* (Leipzig: S. Hirzel, 1901).
102. See Quataert, *Reluctant Feminists,* pp. 125–127.
103. Braun, *Memoiren,* pp. 314–315.
104. For a description see Willy Hellpach, *Wirken in Wirren: Lebenserinnerungen,* vol. 1, *1877–1914* (Hamburg: C. Wegner, 1948), pp. 375–376.
105. Lily Braun, "Die Entthronung der Liebe," *Die Neue Gesellschaft* (Aug. 16, 1905): 237–239. Several of her articles on this issue are reprinted in Lily Braun, *Selected Writings on Feminism and Socialism,* trans. and ed. Alfred Meyer (Bloomington, Ind.: Indiana University Press, 1987).
106. Julie Braun-Vogelstein, *Heinrich Braun* (Stuttgart: Deutsche Verlags-Anstalt, 1967), p. 499.
107. See J. P. Nettl, *Rosa Luxemburg,* vol. 1 (London: Oxford University Press, 1966).
108. Ibid., pp. 94–97.
109. Luxemburg to Robert Seidel, June 23, 1898, in Rosa Luxemburg, *Gesammelte Briefe,* vol. 1 (Berlin: Dietz, 1982), p. 153.
110. The articles, published as *Social Reform or Revolution,* are reprinted in Dick Howard, ed., *Selected Political Writings: Rosa Luxemburg* (New York: Monthly Review Press, 1971). Citations are drawn from that volume.
111. Ibid., pp. 74–76.
112. Luxemburg's concept of "totality" is discussed in Lelio Basso, "Rosa Luxemburg: The Dialectical Method," *International Socialist Journal* (Nov.

1966): 504–541. Basso draws heavily on Georg Lukacs' essay on Luxemburg in his *History and Class Consciousness,* trans. Rodney Livingston (Cambridge, Mass.: M.I.T. Press, 1971). On the general development of the concept see Martin Jay, *Marxism and Totality* (Berkeley: University of California Press, 1984).

113. Howard, *Political Writings,* pp. 101, 130.
114. Nettl, *Luxemburg,* vol. 1, p. 211.
115. Howard, *Political Writings,* pp. 54–55, 127.
116. See the discussion of the problem by Kathy Ferguson, "Class Consciousness and the Marxist Dialectic: The Elusive Synthesis," *Review of Politics,* 42 (Oct. 1980), pp. 504–532.
117. Howard, *Political Writings,* p. 55.
118. Luxemburg to Leo Jogiches, June 27, 1898, in Luxemburg, *Gesammelte Briefe,* vol. 1, pp. 162–163.
119. Luxemburg to Jogiches, June 24, 1898, ibid., p. 156.
120. Luxemburg to Jogiches, July 2, 1898, ibid., p. 166.
121. Luxemburg dismissed the Jungen and the Independents as examples of the "anarchist streak of childishness" which threatened the movement from time to time. Howard, *Political Writings,* p. 132.
122. Ibid., pp. 148–149.
123. Ibid., p. 129.
124. Ibid., p. 121.
125. Ibid., p. 133.
126. Luxemburg to Bebel, Oct. 31, 1898, in Luxemburg, *Gesammelte Briefe,* vol. 1, p. 210.
127. Luxemburg's criticism of Schippel's discussion of the military budget was developed in articles in the *Leipziger Volkszeitung* during February 1899. They were added to *Social Reform and Revolution* together with a rejoinder by Schippel. See Howard, *Political Writings,* pp. 135–158.
128. Luxemburg to Jogiches, May 1, 1899, in Luxemburg, *Gesammelte Briefe,* vol. 1, p. 323.
129. Adler to Kautsky, May 13, 1896, in Adler, *Briefwechsel,* p. 207.
130. Nettl, *Luxemburg,* pp. 152–160.
131. Luxemburg to Jogiches, May 1, 1899, in Luxemburg, *Gesammelte Briefe,* vol. 1, p. 323.
132. Protokoll, Gotha (1896): 88–90
133. Protokoll, Hamburg (1897): 109, 141.
134. Protokoll, Stuttgart (1898): 95–100; Protokoll, Hanover (1899): 127, 170, 195.

7. The Akademikerproblem, 1901–1903

1. See Hans Ulrich Wehler, *The German Empire, 1871–1918,* trans. Kim Traynor (Dover: N. H. Berg, 1985), pp. 41–45, 142–145.
2. The debate about the extent of politicization is discussed in Stanley Suval, *Electoral Politics in Wilhelmine Germany* (Chapel Hill, N.C.: University of

North Carolina Press, 1985), pp. 12–20. For a cogent description of the political system see Gerhard A. Ritter, *Arbeiterbewegung Parteien und Parlamentarismus* (Göttingen: Vandenhoeck und Ruprecht, 1976), pp. 10–20. For the party's relationship to the monarch see Peter Domann, *Sozialdemokratie und Kaisertum unter Wilhelm II* (Wiesbaden: Steiner, 1974).

3. Richard Calwer, "Die Akademiker in der Sozialdemokratie," *SM*, 5 (May 1901): 319–324.
4. Karl Kautsky, "Akademiker und Proletarier," *NZ*, 19, no. 29 (1900–1901): 89–91.
5. Ibid. Also see the discussion in Reinhard Hünlich, *Karl Kautsky und der Marxismus II Internationale* (Marburg: Verlag Arbeiterbewegung und Gesellschaftwissenschaft, 1981), pp. 150–151.
6. See Dieter Fricke, "Zur Rückkehr Eduard Bernstein in dem Deutschen Reich 1901," *Zeitschrift für Geschichtswissenschaften*, 22 (1974): 1341–1347.
7. Eduard Bernstein, *Wie ist wissenschaftlicher Sozialismus möglich?* (Berlin: Verlag der Sozialistischen Monatschefte, 1901).
8. Kautsky to Adler, May 3, 1901, in Victor Adler, *Briefwechsel mit August Bebel und Karl Kautsky* (Vienna: Wiener Volksbuchhandlung, 1954), p. 351.
9. Paul Kampffmeyer, "Karl Kautsky und der 'freie' kritische Sozialismus," *SM*, 5 (July 1901): 494–505.
10. Wolfgang Heine, "Wie ist wissenschaftlicher Sozialismus möglich?," *SM*, 5 (Sept. 1901): 661–669.
11. Kautsky to Adler, June 5, 1901, in Adler, *Briefwechsel*, pp. 354–357.
12. Karl Kautsky, "Die Seeschange," *NZ*, 19, no. 41 (1900–1901): 468–473.
13. "Parvus" was the pseudonym for Alexander Helphand. His articles appeared in the *Neue Zeit* during August 1901.
14. Nettl points out that the attacks were encouraged by Bebel. See J. P. Nettl, *Rosa Luxemburg*, vol. 1 (London: Oxford University Press, 1966), pp. 185–186.
15. Bebel to Kautsky, Sept. 4, 1901, in John Kautsky, Jr., ed., *August Bebels Briefwechsel mit Karl Kautsky* (Assen: Van Gorcum & Co., 1971), p. 139.
16. Protokoll, Lübeck (1901): 134–150, 155–180.
17. Eduard David, "Rückblick auf Lübeck," *SM*, 5 (Nov. 1901): 837–846.
18. Protokoll, Lübeck (1901): 163.
19. Ibid., p. 145.
20. Ibid., p. 168.
21. William Harvey Maehl, *August Bebel* (Philadelphia: American Philosophical Society, 1980), p. 330.
22. Protokoll, Lübeck (1901): 191–192.
23. Ibid., p. 196.
24. Ibid., pp. 193–194.
25. Karl Kautsky, "Der Parteitag in Lübeck," *NZ*, 20, no. 1 (1901–1902): 13–20.
26. Kautsky to Adler, Nov. 15, 1901, in Adler, *Briefwechsel*, p. 377.

27. Kautsky to Adler, Nov. 21, 1901, ibid., p. 384.
28. See the account in Peter Kulemann, *Am Beispiel des Austro-Marxismus* (Hamburg: Junius, 1979), pp. 108–117.
29. Kautsky to Adler, Oct. 25, 1901, in Adler, *Briefwechsel,* p. 369.
30. Karl Kautsky, "Die Revision der Programme der Sozialdemokratischen Partei in Östereich," *NZ,* 20, no. 3 (1901–1902): 68–82.
31. Karl Kautsky, "Der Wiener Parteitag," *NZ,* 20, no. 7: 197–203.
32. Kulemann, *Am Beispiel des Austro-Marxismus,* pp. 116–117.
33. Karl Kautsky, "Der Parteitag in Lübeck," *NZ,* 20, no. 1 (1901–1902): 17.
34. For reactions to the Bernstein debate at the local level see Mary Nolan, *Social Democracy and Society* (Cambridge: Cambridge University Press, 1981), pp. 85–89; Adelheid von Saldern, *Von Einwohnern zum Bürger* (Berlin: Duncker & Humblot, 1973), p. 141; Maja Christ-Gmelin, "Die Württembergerische Sozialdemokratie 1890–1914," (diss., University of Stuttgart, 1976). The general dislike for theoretical discussion is noted by Georg Fülberth, "Zur Genese des Revisionismus in der deutschen Sozialdemokratie vor 1914," *Argument,* no. 63 (1971): 1–21.
35. Protokoll, Munich (1902): 131.
36. Ernst's essay appeared in *Zukunft* (Feb. 1, 1902).
37. Eduard Bernstein, "Von deutschen Arbeitern einst und jetzt," *SM,* 7 (March 1902): 174–185.
38. Karl Kautsky, *The Social Revolution,* trans. A. M. Simon and Mary Wood Simon (Chicago: C. H. Kerr, 1910).
39. Ibid., pp. 46–48.
40. Ibid., p. 171.
41. Protokoll, Munich (1902): 111–147.
42. Ibid., pp. 121–122.
43. Julie Braun-Vogelstein, *Heinrich Braun* (Stuttgart: Deutsche Verlags-Anstalt, 1967), p. 203.
44. Ibid., p. 132.
45. Ibid., p. 126, quoting Heinrich Braun to Werner Sombart, Dec. 12, 1896.
46. Ibid., p. 134, quoting Braun to Sombart, Dec. 13, 1900. Sombart's relationship to the socialist movement is discussed in Dieter Fricke, "Bürgerliche Sozialreformer und deutsche Sozialdemokratie: Zu Briefen Werner Sombarts von 1899," *Zeitschrift für Geschichtswissenschaft,* 23, no. 8 (1975): 929–945. Also see Arthur Mitzman, *Sociology and Estrangement* (New York: Knopf, 1973), pp. 161–168.
47. Braun to Bernstein, July 19, 1900, UC, Braun-Vogelstein Papers. For the relationship between Braun and Bernstein see Dieter Fricke, "Die Gründung der revisionistischen Zeitschrift 'Die Neue Gesellschaft,' 1900–1905," *Beiträge zur Geschichte der Arbeiterbewegung* 16 (1974): 1052–1065.
48. Braun to Bernstein, Nov. 18, Dec. 6, 16, 26, 29, 1900, UC, Braun-Vogelstein Papers.
49. Braun to Bernstein, Dec. 19, 26, 1900, ibid.
50. Braun to Bernstein, Jan. 20, 1901, ibid.
51. Braun to Bernstein, Jan. 14, 1901, ibid.

52. See the account in Braun-Vogelstein, *Braun,* pp. 141–142, and Fricke, "Zur Rückkehr Eduard Bernsteins."
53. Braun to Lily Braun, Aug. 24, 1901, quoted in Braun-Vogelstein, *Braun,* p. 143.
54. Bebel to Kautsky, Oct. 20, 1901, in Kautsky, *Bebels Briefwechsel mit Kautsky,* p. 142.
55. Braun-Vogelstein, *Braun,* pp. 260–268.
56. Willy Hellpach, *Wirken in Wirren: Lebenserinnerungen,* vol. 1, *1877–1914* (Hamburg: C. Wegner, 1948), pp. 252, 370–378.
57. Ibid., p. 380.
58. Ibid., p. 395.
59. In his unpublished memoirs Heine recalls that Bernhard was the party's best speaker in Berlin during the election campaign of 1898. Wolfgang Heine, "Persönliche für die Familie bestimmte 'Erinnerungen,'" p. 448, BAK.
60. Georg Bernhard, "Marxismus und Klassenkampf," *SM* 2 (Feb. 1898): 103–108.
61. Georg Bernhard, "Parteimoral," *Die Zukunft* (Jan. 10, 1903): 79–80.
62. Ibid.
63. Ibid.
64. Franz Mehring, "Konsessionsschulzes," *NZ,* 21, no. 16 (1902–1903): 481–484.
65. Georg Bernhard to Kautsky, Jan. 28, 31, 1903, IISH, Kautsky Correspondence, KD IV 151–152.
66. Georg Bernhard, "Parteimoral," *NZ,* 21, no. 19 (1902–1903): 602–603.
67. See the "Nachwort," *NZ,* 21, no. 19 (1902–1903): 603–606.
68. A copy of the protest is included with Braun's letter to Vollmar, Feb. 13, 1903, IISH, Vollmar Papers, V 309.
69. Protokoll, Dresden (1903): 167.
70. Ignaz Auer to Braun, May 14, 1903, UC, Braun-Vogelstein Papers.
71. Lily Braun, *Memoiren einer Sozialistin,* vol. 2, *Kampfjahre* (Berlin: A. Langen, 1911), p. 483.
72. Braun to Vollmar, July 13, 1903, IISH, Vollmar Papers, V 309, IISH.
73. Paul Göhre to Braun, July 8, 1903; Braun to Göhre, July 10, 11, 1903; Braun to Joseph Bloch, July 13, 1903. All in IISH, Vollmar Papers, V 309.
74. See the account in Braun-Vogelstein, *Braun,* p. 268.
75. Kautsky to Adler, April 4, 1903, in Adler, *Briefwechsel,* pp. 414–416.
76. Karl Kautsky, "Freiheit und Gerechtigkeit," *NZ,* 21, no. 31 (1902–1903): 261–274.
77. Paul Göhre, "Die Sozialdemokratie und die Monarchie," *SM,* 7 (March 1903): 169–179.
78. Paul Kampffmeyer, "Neuer Wind in den Segeln der Sozialdemokratie," *SM,* 7 (June 1903): 399–345; Wolfgang Heine, "Der 16 Juni," *SM,* 7 (July 1903): 475–478.
79. Eduard Bernstein, "Was folgt aus dem Ergebnis der Reichstagswahlen," *SM,* 7 (July 1903): 478–486.
80. Heine to Vollmar, July 6, 1903, IISH, Vollmar Papers, V 973.

81. See Paul Göhre, "Das Ende der Nationalsozialen?" *SM,* 7 (Aug. 1903): 553–559. Hildebrand was editor of the National Socialist paper, *Hilfe,* and Maurenbrecher was secretary of the organization. See Carl Schneider, *Die Publizistik der national-sozialen Bewegung, 1895–1903* (Wangen i. A.: Argen Bote v. J. Walchner, 1934), p. 43.
82. Naumann discussed Maurenbrecher's "new confession" in *Hilfe* (Sept. 20, 1903).
83. Karl Kautsky, "Zum Parteitag," *NZ,* 21, no. 47 (1902–1903): 729–739.
84. Karl Kautsky, "Noch ein Wort zum Parteitag," *NZ,* 21, no. 50 (1902–1903): 748–753.
85. August Bebel, "Ein Nachwort zur Vizepräsidentenfrage und Verwandtes," *NZ,* 21, no. 49 (1902–1903): 708–729.
86. Ibid., p. 724.
87. Bebel to Kautsky, Sept. 9, 1903, in Kautsky, *Bebels Briefwechsel mit Kautsky,* pp. 160–162.
88. Ignaz Auer, "Zum sozialdemokratischen Parteitag in Dresden," *SM,* 7 (Sept. 1903): 635–651.
89. See the discussion in Freya Eisner, *Kurt Eisner* (Frankfurt: Suhrkamp, 1979), pp. 13–19.
90. Franz Mehring, "Zwanzig Jahre," *NZ,* 21, no. 1 (1902–1903): 1–4.
91. Franz Mehring, "Eine Partei und Pressefrage," *NZ,* no. 46 (1902–1903): pp. 641–645.
92. See his article "Die wahre Frage," *Leipziger Volkszeitung* (Aug. 11, 1903).
93. Franz Mehring, "Bürgerliche Agonien," *NZ,* 21, no. 49 (1902–1903): 705–708.
94. Franz Mehring, "Zum Parteitag," *Leipziger Volkszeitung* (Sept. 12, 1903).
95. In a letter to Kautsky in 1899 Braun had protested against Mehring's harsh criticism of Sombart. Braun to Kautsky, Sept. 20, 1899, IISH, Kautsky Correspondence D VI 563.
96. Braun, *Memoiren,* pp. 413, 488–489, and Braun-Vogelstein, *Braun,* pp. 167–172.

8. The Rout of the Revisionist Intellectuals

1. Klaus Saul, quoted in Sven Papcke, *Der Revisionismusstreit und die politische Theorie der Reform* (Stuttgart: Kohlhammer, 1974), p. 7.
2. Protokoll, Dresden (1903): 161.
3. *Vorwärts* (Oct. 8, 1903).
4. For the report of Braun's speech see the Protokoll, Dresden (1903): 162–169.
5. Ibid., p. 163.
6. Lily Braun, *Memoiren einer Sozialistin,* vol. 2, *Kampfjahre* (Berlin: A. Langen, 1911), p. 511. Also see Dieter Fricke, "Die Gründung der revisionistische Zeitschrift 'Die Neue Gesellschaft,' 1900–1905," *Beiträge zur Geschichte der Arbeiterbewegung,* 16 (1974): 1063–1064.
7. Protokoll, Dresden (1903): 172.
8. Ibid., p. 183.

9. Ibid., p. 197.
10. Ibid., pp. 172–176.
11. Ibid., p. 201.
12. For the report of Bebel's speech see ibid., pp. 210–229.
13. Ibid., p. 211.
14. Ibid., pp. 216–218.
15. Ibid., pp. 224–225.
16. Ibid., p. 229.
17. After the defeat of the party's candidate in the first vote, Heine sent a telegram urging local Social Democrats to support the National Liberal candidate, Hellmuth von Gerlach, in the runoff. *Vorwärts* endorsed the proposal. Angered at what they saw as a violation of the party's policy, Michels and others in Marburg submitted a resolution to the Dresden conference calling for the censure of Heine. For details see Robert Michels, "Eine syndikalistische gerichtete Unterströmung im deutschen Sozialismus, 1903–1907," *Festschrift für Carl Grünberg: Zum 70. Geburtstag* (Leipzig: C. L. Hirschfeld, 1932): 343–364.
18. Protokoll, Dresden (1903): 229.
19. Ibid., p. 233.
20. Ibid., pp. 234–239.
21. Ibid., pp. 241–244.
22. Lily Braun describes her reaction in her *Memoiren,* pp. 503–514.
23. Protokoll, Dresden (1903): 253–257.
24. See ibid., pp. 321–345, for the debate on tactics.
25. Wally Hellpach, *Wirken in Wirren: Lebenserinnerungen,* vol. 1, *1877–1914* (Hamburg: C. Wegner, 1948), p. 239.
26. Protokoll, Dresden (1903): 322.
27. Ibid., pp. 339–340.
28. Braun, *Memoiren,* p. 512.
29. Eduard Bernstein, "1878 und 1903," *SM,* 7 (Oct. 1903): 741–750.
30. William Harvey Maehl, *August Bebel* (Philadelphia: American Philosophical Society, 1980), pp. 376–377.
31. Wolfgang Heine, "Persönliche für die Familie bestimmte 'Erinnerungen,'" pp. 532–533, BAK.
32. Hellpach, *Wirken in Wirren,* p. 395.
33. Friedrich Naumann, "August Bebel," *Hilfe* (Sept. 27, 1903).
34. Friedrich Naumann, "Masse und Akademiker," *Hilfe* (Oct. 4, 1903).
35. Friedrich Naumann, "Was wird aus der Sozialdemokratie," *Hilfe* (Oct. 11, 1903).
36. Quoted in *Vorwärts* (Oct. 8, 1903).
37. Ibid. (Sept. 23, 1903).
38. Ibid. (Sept. 20, 1903).
39. Karl Kautsky, "Nachklänge zum Parteitag," *NZ,* 22, no. 1 (1903–1904): 1–5.
40. Karl Kautsky, "Der Dresden Parteitag," *NZ,* 21, no. 52 (1902–1903): 815.
41. Ibid., p. 813.
42. Karl Kautsky, "Franz Mehring," *NZ,* 22, no. 4 (1903–1904): 97–108.

43. Ibid., pp. 101–102.
44. Ibid., p. 100.
45. Ibid., p. 108.
46. Rosa Luxemburg, "Geknickte Hoffnungen," *NZ,* 22, no. 2 (1903–1904): 33–39.
47. Ibid., p. 35.
48. Kautsky to Friedrich Sorge, Nov. 24, 1903. Cited in Reinhard Hunlich, *Karl Kautsky und der Marxismus II Internationale* (Marburg: Verlag Arbeiterbewegung und Gesellschaftwissenschaft, 1981), pp. 248–249.
49. Albert Südekum to Vollmar, Dec. 21, 1903. Quoted in Reinhard Jansen, *Georg von Vollmar* (Bonn: Droste, 1956), p. 111.
50. Adolph von Elm, "Der Parteitag des Sieges," *SM,* 7 (Oct. 1903): 729–735.
51. Eduard Bernstein, "1878 und 1903," *SM,* 7 (Oct. 1903): 746.
52. Friedrich Hertz, "Revidieren wir!" *SM,* 7 (Nov. 1903): 817–824.
53. See Dieter Fricke, "Zur Rolle von Friedrich Stampfers privater Pressekorrespondenz," *Zeitschrift für Geschichtswissenschaft,* 23, no. 3 (1975): 204–209.
54. Quoted in Friedrich Stampfer, *Erfahrungen und Erkenntnisse* (Cologne: Verlag der Politik und Wirtschaft, 1957), p. 94.
55. Eduard David, "Der Eroberung der politischen Macht," *SM,* 8 (Jan. 1904): 13, and (March 1904): 204–205.
56. Richard Calwer in the "Rundschau," *SM,* 8 (Oct. 1903): 782.
57. See "Bebel und Genossen," *Zukunft* (Sept. 26, 1903): 1–20.
58. Karl Kautsky, *Franz Mehring und die deutsche Sozialdemokratie* (Dessau, 1918), p. 28.
59. Franz Mehring, *Meine Rechtfertigung* (Leipzig: Verlag der Leipziger Buchdrucherei Aktiengesellschaft, 1903).
60. Ibid., p. 36.
61. The details of the hearings are reported in the Protokoll of the Bremen party conference (1904): 35–42.
62. For Mehring's reaction see Luxemburg to Luise Kautsky, Sept. 1904, in Rosa Luxemburg, *Gesammelte Briefe,* vol. 2 (Berlin: Dietz, 1982), p. 68.
63. Protokoll, Bremen (1904): 42.
64. Ibid., p. 36.
65. See the review in *SM,* 8 (April 1904): 317.
66. Adler to Kautsky, Sept. 28, 1903, in Victor Adler, *Briefwechsel mit August Bebel und Karl Kautsky* (Vienna: Wiener Volksbuchhandlung, 1954), pp. 424–428.
67. For details see Julie Braun-Vogelstein, *Heinrich Braun* (Stuttgart: Deutsche Verlags-Anstalt, 1967), pp. 285–287.
68. Karl Kautsky, "Heinrich Braun: Ein Beitrag zur Geschichte der deutschen Sozialdemokratie," *Die Gesellschaft,* 10, no. 2 (1933): 155–172.
69. For details see Ursula Mittmann, *Fraktion und Partie* (Düsseldorf: Droste, 1976), pp. 70–75.
70. Wolfgang Heine, "Demokratische Randbemerkungen zum Fall Göhre," *SM,* 8 (Aug. 1904): 281–291.

71. Heine, "Erinnerungen," p. 529, and Heine to Vollmar, Oct. 3, 17, 1903, IISH, Vollmar Papers, V 973.
72. Heine, "Erinnerungen," pp. 532–533.
73. See the account in Ernst Heilmann, *Geschichte der Arbeiterbewegung in Chemnitz und dem Erzgebirge* (Chemnitz: Sozialdemokratischen Verein, 1912), pp. 295–297.
74. See Gerhard Ritter, *Die Arbeiterbewegung im Wilhelminischen Reich* (Berlin: Colloquium Verlag, 1959), p. 187.
75. Bebel to Kautsky, Feb. 1, 1904, in John Kautsky, Jr., ed., *August Bebels Briefwechsel mit Karl Kautsky* (Assen: Van Gorcum & Co., 1971), p. 162.
76. Bebel to Kautsky, July 7, 1904, ibid., p. 163.
77. Protokoll, Bremen (1904): 199–262.
78. Ibid., p. 248.
79. Ibid., p. 231.
80. Ibid., pp. 238–239.
81. Ibid., p. 244.
82. Ibid., pp. 254–260.
83. Ibid., p. 262.
84. For the local situation see Heilmann, *Arbeiterbewegung in Chemnitz*, pp. 295–300.
85. *Plutus* (Nov. 25, 1905).
86. Heine, "Erinnerungen," p. 531.
87. See Jochen Loreck, *Wie man früher Sozialdemokrat wurde* (Bonn: Verlag Neue Gesellschaft, 1977), pp. 70–74, and Raymond Dominick, "Democracy of Socialism? A Case Study of *Vorwärts* in the 1890s," *Central European History,* 10 (June 1977): 286–311.
88. On Gradnauer see Waltraud Sperlich, *Journalist mit Mandat: Sozialdemokratische Reichstagsabgeordnete und ihre Arbeit in der Parteipresse 1867 bis 1918* (Düsseldorf: Droste, 1983), pp. 177–178.
89. See Freya Eisner, *Kurt Eisner* (Frankfurt: Suhrkamp, 1979), pp. 7–20.
90. Bebel to Adler, Oct. 23, 1899, in Adler, *Briefwechsel,* p. 329.
91. Allan Mitchell, *Revolution in Bavaria, 1918–1919: The Eisner Regime and the Soviet Republic* (Princeton: Princeton University Press, 1965), pp. 177–178.
92. Luxemburg to Jogiches, Nov. 2, 8, 10, 1899, in Luxemburg, *Gesammelte Briefe,* vol. 1, pp. 399–400.
93. Kautsky to Luise Kautsky, Nov. 11, 1899. Cited in Kautsky, *Bebels Briefwechsel mit Kautsky,* p. 122.
94. Protokoll, Lübeck (1901): 164.
95. Franz Mehring, "Bebel und der Vorwärts," *Leipziger Volkszeitung* (Sept. 9, 1903).
96. Quoted in Eisner, *Eisner,* p. 19.
97. Protokoll, Dresden (1903): 264–272.
98. See Eisner's account in *Der Vorwärts Konflikt* (Berlin, 1905), p. 81.
99. Mehring, *Meine Rechtfertigung,* pp. 45–47.
100. Mehring's *Rechtfertigung* was reviewed in *Vorwärts* (Oct. 23, 1903).

101. For the viewpoint of the Berlin Social Democrats see J. L. Adolph, *Otto Wels und des Politik der deutschen Sozialdemokratie* (Berlin: De Gruyter, 1971), pp. 17–26.
102. For biographical details see Franz Osterroth, *Biographisches Lexikon des Sozialismus,* vol. 1 (Hanover: Dietz, 1960), pp. 304–305.
103. For biographical details see ibid., p. 57.
104. See Ströbel's article, "Ein Nachwort zum Dresden Parteitag," *Vorwärts* (Oct. 8, 10, 1903).
105. *Leipziger Volkszeitung* (Dec. 23, 1904).
106. *Vorwärts* (Jan. 11, 1905). The episode is discussed in *Der Vorwärts Konflikt,* pp. 60–61.
107. Bebel to Kautsky, Jan. 7, 1905, Kautsky, in *Bebels Briefwechsel mit Kautsky,* p. 168.
108. Karl Kautsky, "Die Stimmung in der deutschen Sozialdemokratie," *NZ,* 23, no. 42 (1904–1905).
109. Kurt Eisner, "Über politische Streik," *Vorwärts* (June 25, 1905).
110. Karl Kautsky, "Die Stimmung."
111. Eisner, "Über politische Streik."
112. Karl Kautsky, "Die Stimmung."
113. Kurt Eisner, "Unmögliche Diskussion," *Vorwärts* (July 19, 1905).
114. An account of the debate can be found in Ingrid Gilcher-Holtey, *Das Mandat des Intellektuellen* (Berlin: Siedler, 1986), pp. 197–204.
115. Karl Kautsky, "Die Fortsetzung einer unmöglichen Diskussion," *NZ,* 23, nos. 48, 49 (1904–1905): 681–692, 717–727.
116. Kurt Eisner, "Unmögliche Diskussion," *Vorwärts* (July 19, 1905), and "Ein Haufen Unrichtigkeiten," *Vorwärts* (July 20, 1905).
117. Kurt Eisner, "Wenn und Aber, V," *Vorwärts* (Sept. 9, 1905).
118. Karl Kautsky, "Noch einmal die unmögliche Diskussion," *NZ,* 23, no. 50 (1904–1905): 776–785.
119. Kurt Eisner, "Debatte über Wenn und Aber," *Vorwärts* (Sept. 6, 1905).
120. Mehring's articles are reprinted in the issues of *Vorwärts* from August 27 to September 13, 1905.
121. Karl Kautsky, "Noch einmal."
122. Adler to Kautsky, July 17, 1905, in Adler, *Briefwechsel,* p. 459.
123. Kautsky to Adler, July 20, 1905, ibid., pp. 461–466.
124. Bebel to Kautsky, Aug. 1, 1905, in Kautsky, *Bebels Briefwechsel mit Kautsky,* pp. 169–171.
125. Luxemburg to Jogiches, Oct. 6, 1905, in Luxemburg, *Gesammelte Briefe,* vol. 2, pp. 184–185.
126. Protokoll, Jena (1905): 144.
127. Ibid., pp. 187–188.
128. Subsequent events are described by Richard Fischer in a letter reprinted in Kautsky, *Bebels Briefwechsel mit Kautsky,* pp. 379–380.
129. *Vorwärts Konflikt,* pp. 103–107.
130. The formation of the association is described in Eisner, "Literarische Psychologie," *Neue Gesellschaft* (Nov. 22, 1905): 403–408.
131. See the discussion of Bebel's treatment of Eisner in William Harvey Maehl,

August Bebel (Philadelphia: American Philosophical Society, 1980), pp. 375, 378.
132. Eisner's letter is reprinted in the *Vorwärts Konflikt,* pp. 65–68.
133. Bloch to Bebel, Nov. 7, 1905, BAK, SM Papers.
134. Adolf von Elm, "Der *Vorwärts* Konflikt und die Partei," *SM,* 10 (Jan. 1906): 27–35.
135. See Luxemburg's letters to Jogiches, Sept. 30, Oct. 6, 22, 24–25, 1905, in Luxemburg, *Gesammelte Briefe,* vol. 2, pp. 177–178, 183–184, 211–216.
136. Luxemburg to Jogiches, Nov. 3, 1905, ibid., pp. 230–231.
137. Comments from the party press were reprinted in *Vorwärts* during October and November 1905.
138. *Vorwärts Konflikt,* p. 3.
139. Ibid., p. 138.
140. Braun to Vollmar, Nov. 5, 1905, in IISH, Vollmar Correspondence, V 309.
141. See especially "Krisis in der Sozialdemokratie," *Neue Gesellschaft* (Nov. 1, 1905).
142. Wolfgang Heine, "Der 'Vorwärts' und die Berliner Genossen," *Neue Gesellschaft* (Nov. 8, 1905).
143. See Eisner, "Literarische Psychologie," *Neue Gesellschaft* (Nov. 22, 1905).
144. Georg Zepler, *Radikalismus und Taktik: Ein Nachwort zum Vorwärts Konflikt als Mahnwort an die Genossen* (Munich, 1906), p. 14.
145. Richard Calwer, "Disziplin und Meinungsfreiheit," *SM,* 10 (Jan. 1906): 36–40.
146. *Vorwärts Konflikt,* p. 75.
147. Karl Kautsky, "Der Journalismus in der Sozialdemokratie," *NZ,* 24, no. 7 (1905–1906): 216–225.
148. Karl Kautsky, "Eine Nachlese zum Vorwärtskonflikt," *NZ,* 24, no. 10 (1905–1906): 313–326.
149. Franz Mehring, "Ein warnendes Exempel," *NZ,* 24, no. 9 (1905–1906): 273–276.

9. The Making of a Socialist Mentality

1. Karl Kautsky, "Allerhand Revolutionäres," *NZ,* 22, no. 19 (1903–1904): 588–589.
2. Alexander Kosiol, "Organizationen für die theoretische Bildung der Arbeiterklasse," *NZ,* 25, no. 28 (1905–1906): 64–69.
3. Quoted in Dirk Müller, *Idealismus und Revolution* (Berlin: Colloquium Verlag, 1975), p. 158.
4. Karl Kautsky, "Ein Sozialdemokratischer Katechismus," *NZ,* 12, no. 13 (1893–1894): 402–410.
5. Kurt Eisner, "Wenn und Aber," *Vorwärts* (Sept. 9, 1905).
6. Karl Kautsky, "Der mögliche Abschluss einer unmöglichen Diskussion," *NZ,* 23, no. 51 (1904–1905): 795–804.
7. Ibid., p. 797.
8. Karl Kautsky, *Ethics and the Materialistic Conception of History,* trans.

John B. Askew (Chicago: Kerr, 1906). See especially pp. 155–161, 174–206.

9. Protokoll, Dresden (1903): 431–432.
10. Raphael Friedeberg, *Parlamentarismus und Generalstreik* (Berlin: F. Kater, 1904). Reprinted in Peter Friedmann, ed., *Materialien zum politischen Richtungstreit in der deutschen Sozialdemokratie, 1890–1917* (Frankfurt: Ulstein, 1977), pp. 545–560.
11. See the discussion in Hans Manfred Bock, *Syndikalismus und Linkskommunismus von 1918–1923* (Meisenheim am Glan: A. Hein, 1969), p. 19.
12. Paul Kampffmeyer, "Eine Wiedergeburt der unabhangigen sozialistischen Bewegung," *SM*, 9 (Oct. 1905): 849–857.
13. Robert Michels, "Les Dangers du Parti socialiste allemand," *Le Mouvement Socialiste*, no. 144 (Dec. 1904): 193–212.
14. Michels' relationship to the French syndicalists is discussed in Zeev Sternhell, *Neither Right nor Left*, trans. David Maisel (Berkeley: University of California Press, 1986), pp. 81–86. Also see Arthur Mitzman, *Sociology and Estrangement* (New York: Knopf, 1973), pp. 282–315.
15. Robert Michels, "Controverse socialiste," *Le Mouvement Socialiste*, no. 184 (March 1907), 282.
16. Robert Michels, "Die deutsche Sozialdemokratie im internationalen Verband: eine kritische Untersuchung," *Archiv für Sozialwissenschaft und Sozialpolitik*, 27 (1907): 148–231.
17. Ibid., p. 230.
18. Robert Michels, "August Bebel," *Archiv für Sozialwissenschaft und Sozialpolitik*, 37 (1913): 671–700.
19. See Rudolf Goldscheid, "Die Revolution als Problem," *Neue Gesellschaft*, 2 (June 13, 1906): 280–283.
20. Rudolf Goldscheid, *Verelendung oder Meliorationstheorie* (Berlin: Verlag der Sozialistische Monatshefte, 1906), p. 29.
21. Luxemburg to Henriette Roland-Holst, Dec. 17, 1904, in Stephen Bronner, ed., *The Letters of Rosa Luxemburg* (Boulder, Colo.: Westview Press, 1978), pp. 94–95.
22. Luxemburg to Jogiches, Sept. 30, 1905, ibid., pp. 177–178.
23. Luxemburg to Jogiches, Oct. 28, 1905, ibid., pp. 224–225.
24. Luxemburg to Mathilde and Emanuel Wurm, July 18, 1906, ibid., pp. 258–259.
25. J. P. Nettl, *Rosa Luxemburg*, vol. 1 (London: Oxford University Press, 1966), p. 357.
26. Rosa Luxemburg, *The Mass Strike*, trans. Patrick Lavin (New York: Harper and Row, 1971), p. 45.
27. Ibid., p. 36.
28. Ibid., p. 52.
29. Ibid., p. 62.
30. Ibid., p. 72.
31. Ibid., p. 48.
32. Ibid., p. 72.
33. Ibid., p. 68.

34. Ibid., p. 66.
35. Ibid., p. 67.
36. Ibid., p. 32.
37. Ibid., p. 68.
38. See Hedwig Wachenheim, *Die deutsche Arbeiterbewegung, 1844 bis 1914* (Cologne: Köln und Opladen Westdeutschen Verlag, 1967), pp. 413–414.
39. Luxemburg to Zetkin, Dec. 16, 1906, in Rosa Luxemburg, *Gesammelte Briefe,* vol. 2 (Berlin: Dietz, 1982), pp. 277–278.
40. Jochen Loreck, *Wie man früher Sozialdemokrat wurde* (Bonn: Verlag Neue Gesellschaft, 1977), pp. 24–26, 64–65. Also see Dirk Hoffmann, "Sozialismus und Literatur" (diss., University of Münster, 1975), vol. 1, pp. 99–102.
41. Hoffmann, "Sozialismus und Literatur," vol. 1, pp. 283–303.
42. For an overview of the press see Kurt Koszyk, *Die Presse der deutschen Sozialdemokratie* (Hanover: Verlag für Literatur und Zeitgeschehen, 1966), pp. 11–15.
43. Norbert Schwarte, *Schulpolitik und Pädagogik der deutschen Sozialdemokratie an der Wende vom 19. zum 20. Jahrhundert* (Cologne: Bohlau, 1980), p. 237, and Wolfgang Habekost, "Proletarische Bildungskonzeption vor dem Mannheimer Parteitag 1890–1905," in Josef Olbrich, ed., *Arbeiterbildung nach dem Fall der Sozialistengesetze* (Braunschweig: G. Westermann, 1982), pp. 19–25.
44. Richard Levy, "Jugendliteratur und Sozialismus," *NZ,* 21, no. 50 (1902–1903): 772–773.
45. K. Bl., "Jugendliteratur von Erziehung zum Sozialismus," *NZ,* 22, no. 5 (1903–1904): 153–157.
46. Julian Borchardt, "Jugendschriften und Bildungswesen," *NZ,* 19, no. 49 (1900–1901): 715–719.
47. K. Bl., "Jugendliteratur von Erziehung," 156.
48. Protokoll, Bremen (1904): 178.
49. Helmut Trotnow, *Karl Liebknecht* (Cologne: Kiepenheuer und Witsch, 1980), pp. 95–112, and Karl Korn, *Die Arbeiterjugendbewegung* (Berlin: Arebeiterjugend-Verlag, 1922), pp. 31–64.
50. Quoted in Dieter Fricke, *Die Deutsche Arbeiterbewegung, 1869–1914* (Berlin: Dietz, 1976), p. 334.
51. Korn, *Arbeiterjugendbewegung,* pp. 65–90, and Fricke, *Deutsche Arbeiterbewegung,* pp. 337–340.
52. For biographical details see Hedwig Wachenheim, ed., *Ludwig Frank: Aufsätze, Reden, und Briefe* (Berlin: Verlag für Sozialwissenschaft, 1924), pp. 19–21.
53. Ludwig Frank to Kautsky, Oct. 22, 1904. Cited in Schwarte, *Schulpolitik und Pädagogik,* p. 82.
54. Ludwig Frank, "Sozialistische Jugendorganisationen," *NZ,* 22, no. 49 (1903–1904): 725–726.
55. See Vernon Lidtke, *The Alternative Culture* (New York: Oxford University Press, 1985), chap. 6.
56. See Hans-Joachim Schäfers, *Zur sozialistischen Arbeiterbildung in Leipzig,*

1890 bis 1914 (Leipzig: Museum für Geschichte der Leipziger Arbeiterbewegung, 1961).

57. Henri De Man, *Gegen den Strom* (Stuttgart: Deutsche Verlags-Anstalt, 1953), p. 73.
58. Luise Dornemann, *Clara Zetkin* (Berlin: Dietz, 1973), pp. 164–166, and Rosemarie Walter, "Clara Zetkin: Representantin der pädagogischen Anschauungen der deutschen Arbeiterklasse im ersten Viertel des 20 Jahrhunderts," *Pädagogik,* 12, no. 2 (1957): 507–533.
59. Ruth Kirsch, *Ihr zwingt uns Nicht: Ein Lebensbild der Kommunistin und Pädagogin Kate Duncker* (Berlin: DFD-Bindesvorstand, 1970), pp. 10–15.
60. Quoted in Gunter Griep, "Revolutionärer Kampfer und Lehrer der Proletarier Hermann Duncker," *Beiträge zur Geschichte der Arbeiterbewegung,* 13, no. 1 (1971): 97.
61. See Hermann Duncker, "Mein Weg zum Lehrer des Marxismus," *Beiträge zur Geschichte der Arbeiterbewegung,* 9, no. 2 (1967): 274–276.
62. Hermann Duncker, "Volkswirtschaftlehre und Arbeiterbildung." From *Der Freie Bund* (April 1899). Reprinted in Olbrich, *Arbeiterbildung,* pp. 71–73.
63. Schäfers, *Zur socialistischen Arbeiterbildung,* p. 27. Also see Vernon Lidtke, "Die kulturelle Bedeutung des Arbeitervereins," in Gunter Wiegelmann, ed., *Verhandlungen der 18 Deutschen Volkskunde-Kongresse in Trier vom 13 bis 18 Sept. 1971* (Göttingen, 1973), p. 55.
64. There are two important studies of Rühle: Gottfried Mergner, *Arbeiterbewegung und Intelligenz* (Starnberg: Raith, 1973), and Horst Maneck, "Otto Rühles bildungspolitisches und pädagogisches Wirken in der Zeit von der Jahrhundertwende bis zum Jahre 1916" (diss., University of Dresden, 1976).
65. Otto Rühle, "Ein neuer Weg zur Volksbildung," *NZ,* 22, no. 29 (1903–1904): 92–96.
66. Ibid.
67. Heinrich Schulz, "Volksbildung oder Arbeiterbildung," *NZ,* 22, no. 43 (1903–1904): 522–529.
68. Protokoll, Jena (1905): 214.
69. For biographical details see Hinrich Wulff, "Heinrich Schulz, 1872–1932: Ein Leben im Spannungsfelde zwischen Pädagogik und Politik," *Bremisches Jahrbuch,* 48 (Bremen, 1962), pp. 319–374.
70. See Hans-Jurgen Eckl, Karin Iwan, and Wolfgang Weipert, "Die Arbeiterbildungschule in Berlin (1891–1914)," in Olbrich, *Arbeiterbildung,* p. 142. Also see the account by Schulz in his *Politik und Bildung* (Berlin: Dietz, 1931), pp. 79–80.
71. Karl-Ernst Moring, *Die Sozialdemokratische Partei in Bremen, 1890–1914* (Hanover: Verlag für Literatur und Zeitgeschehen, 1968), pp. 74–77.
72. Schulz, "Volksbildung oder Arbeiterbildung," pp. 527–528.
73. Otto Rühle, "Nochmals die Arbeiterschule," *NZ,* 22, no. 47 (1903–1904): 663–667.
74. Moring, *Sozialdemokratische Partei in Bremen,* pp. 74–77.

75. Quoted in Wulff, "Heinrich Schulz," p. 341.
76. Moring, *Sozialdemokratische Partei in Bremen,* p. 80.
77. Maneck, "Otto Rühles bildungspolitisches und pädagogisches Wirken," vol. 1, p. 20.
78. See Schwarte, *Schulpolitik und Pädagogik,* pp. 308–309, for a discussion of Schulz's attempt to develop a Marxist pedagogy.
79. See especially Otto Rühle, *Arbeit und Erziehung* (Munich: G. Birk, 1904).
80. For Schulz's debt to earlier reformers see Heinrich Schulz, "Zu Pestallozzis hundertfünfzigstem Geburtstag," *NZ,* 14, no. 15 (1895–1896): 452–461, and Heinrich Schulz, "Landerziehungsheime," *NZ,* 2, no. 29 (1902–1903): 75–81. Rühle's debt to the older tradition is discussed in Maneck, "Otto Rühles bildungspolitisches und pädagogishes Wirken," vol. 1, p. 230.
81. See Heinrich Schulz, "Sozialdemokratische Jugendliteratur," *NZ,* 19, no. 32 (1900–1901): 172–177, and Maneck, "Otto Rühles bildungspolitisches und pädagogisches Wirken," vol. 1, p. 20.
82. Schwarte, *Schulpolitik und Pädagogik,* p. 310.
83. See Karl Kautsky, "Der Bremer Parteitag," *NZ,* 24, no. 1 (1905–1906): 4–12.
84. Protokoll, Jena (1905): 214.
85. Olbrich, *Arbeiterbildung,* p. 30.
86. Kosiol, "Organisation für die theoretische Bildung."
87. Heinrich Schulz, "Arbeiterbildung," *NZ,* 24, nos. 32, 34 (1905–1906): 180–186, 262–269.
88. Emil Rauch, "Zum Thema Arbeiterschule," *NZ,* no. 46 (1905–1906): 175–177.
89. J. Brendler, "Zur Arbeiterbildungsfrage," *NZ,* no. 47 (1905–1906): 708–709.
90. Hans-Albrecht Schwarz, "Die Parteischule, 1906–14," in Olbrich, *Arbeiterbildung,* pp. 194–195.
91. See Olbrich, *Arbeiterbildung,* pp. 91–99, where these theses are reprinted.
92. Ibid., p. 96. For a general discussion of the Mannheim theses see Gerhard Schneider, "Heinrich Schulz: Sein ideologischer und politischer Standpunkt auf dem Parteitag der Sozialdemokratischen Partei 1906 zu Mannheim," *Pädagogik,* 12, no. 2 (1957): 110–118.
93. Max Maurenbrecher, "Parteischule," *Neue Gesellschaft,* 2 (July 25, 1906): 353–354.
94. See Dieter Fricke, "Die Sozialdemokratische Parteischule (1906 bis 1914)," *Zeitschrift für Geschichtswissenschaft,* 5 (1956): 229–248.
95. David's article, "Volkserziehung und Sozialdemokratie," published in the *Neue Gesellschaft,* is reprinted in Olbrich, *Arbeiterbildung,* pp. 100–107.
96. Jurgen Heinrich, "Proletarische Bildungskonzeption in der Jahren 1905–14," in Olbrich, *Arbeiterbildung,* p. 26.
97. See Nettl, *Luxemburg,* vol. 1, pp. 390–395, and Fricke, "Die Sozialdemokratische Parteischule," pp. 239–240.
98. The minutes of the first meeting are reprinted in Olbrich, *Arbeiterbildung,* pp. 107–113.

99. For a breakdown by year and an analysis of their roles in the party see Schwarz, "Die Parteischule," pp. 226–228. Also see Lidtke, *Alternative Culture,* pp. 169–176.
100. Reports by Schulz appear in the *NZ,* 26, no. 50 (1907–1908): 882–886 and vol. 29, no. 49 (1910–11): 806–813.
101. A number of testimonies are reprinted in Olbrich, *Arbeiterbildung,* pp. 260–268.
102. Ibid., p. 262.
103. Maneck, "Otto Rühles bildungspolitisches und pädagogisches Wirken," p. 67.
104. Ibid., p. 60.
105. Rühle's teaching technique is described by Otto Forkert, "Zur theoretischen Durchbildung der Arbeiterklasse," *NZ,* 24, no. 51 (1905–1906): 812–815, and discussed in Maneck, "Otto Rühles bildungspolitisches und pädagogisches Wirken," pp. 28–30.
106. Otto Rühle, "Was ist zu tun?," *NZ,* 25, no. 22 (1906–1907): 750–753.
107. For assessments of the school's influence see Schwarz, "Die Parteischule," pp. 224–232, and Fricke, "Die Sozialdemokratische Parteischule," p. 246.
108. Fricke, "Die Sozialdemokratische Parteischule," pp. 241–242.
109. According to Wilhelm Dittmann, the trade union leaders "boycotted" the party school. Wilhelm Dittmann, "Erinnerungen," pp. 309–312, IISH, typescript.
110. Bloch to Adolf von Elm, June 11, 1906, BAK, SM Papers, IV, 117.
111. Luxemburg's article, "Gewerkschaftschule und Parteischule," was published in the *Leipziger Volkszeitung* in June 1911, and reprinted in Olbrich, *Arbeiterbildung,* pp. 269–272.
112. The idealistic turn is emphasized in Schwarz, "Die Parteischule," pp. 228–231.
113. Ibid., p. 225.
114. Quoted in ibid., p. 225.
115. Bertram Batterwitz, "Gesellschaft und bildungstheoretische Grundlagen der Arbeiterbildung vor 1914," in Olbrich, *Arbeiterbildung,* pp. 61–68.
116. Wulff, "Heinrich Schulz," pp. 354–359.
117. For this shift see Maneck, "Otto Rühles bildungspolitisches und pädagogisches Wirken," vol. 1, pp. 67–80; Mergner, *Arbeiterbewegung und Intelligenz,* pp. 73–74; and Schäfers, *Zur sozialistischen Arbeiterbildung,* pp. 218–221.
118. See the biographical sketch in Maneck, "Otto Rühles bildungspolitische und pädagogisches Wirken," vol. 2, pp. 4–10.
119. For the later years see ibid., pp. 10–16; Mergner, *Arbeiterbewegung und Intelligenz,* pp. 168–176; and Friedrich Georg Hermann, "Otto Rühle als politischer Theoretiker," *Internationale Wissenschaftliche Korrespondenz zur Geschichte der Deutschen Arbeiterbewegung,* 9 (April 1973): 1–22.
120. The limited extent to which the "thought world" of the working class was altered by the Social Democrats has been suggested by studies of the reading habits of party members and trade unionists. For a good summary of these studies see Lidtke, *Alternative Culture,* pp. 180–191. Also see

Hans-Josef Steinberg, "Lesegewohnheiten deutsche Arbeiter," in Peter von Rüden, ed., *Beiträge zur Kulturgeschichte der deutschen Arbeiterbewegung, 1848–1918* (Frankfurt: Buchergilde Gutenberg, 1979), pp. 260–280.

10. Revisionists, Nationalism, and Accommodation

1. For analyses of the election see George Crothers, *The German Elections of 1907* (New York: Columbia University Press, 1941), and Carl Schorske, *German Social Democracy, 1905–1917* (Cambridge, Mass.: Harvard University Press, 1955), pp. 59–63.
2. Karl Kautsky, "Der 25. Januar," *NZ*, 25, no. 18 (1906–1907): 588–596. Also see the discussion in Reinhard Hünlich, *Karl Kautsky und der Marxismus II Internationale* (Marburg: Verlag Arbeiterbewegung und Gesellschaftwissenschaft, 1981), pp. 140–144.
3. Eduard Bernstein, "Der Wahlkampf und das Mandat," *SM*, 11 (March 1907): 183–192.
4. The development of the *Sozialistische Monatshefte* is discussed most fully, though rather critically, in Roger Fletcher, *Revisionism and Empire: Socialist Imperialism in Germany, 1897–1914* (London: George Allen & Unwin, 1984). For its financing see pp. 75–79.
5. August Müller, "Wir müssen aus dem Turm heraus," *Neue Gesellschaft*, 5 (Sept. 11, 1907): 321–326.
6. See Richard Calwer, "Der 25 Januar," *SM*, 11 (Feb. 1907): 101–107, and Edmund Fischer, "Sozialdemokratische Mittelstandpolitik," *SM*, 11 (June 1907): 451–459.
7. Bernstein, "Der Wahlkampf und das Mandat."
8. Joseph Bloch, "Sozialisten Bewegung," *SM*, 12 (Jan. 9, 1908): 55–57.
9. There were numerous articles on the "new middle class" in the journal during this period. See especially Wolfgang Heine, "Vom neuen Mittelstand," *SM*, 12 (July 23, 1908): 922–926.
10. Richard Wolter, "Unsere Stellung zur Privatbeamtenbewegung," *SM*, 12 (Jan. 25, 1908): 95–101.
11. For biographical details see John Kautsky, Jr., ed., *August Bebels Briefwechsel mit Karl Kautsky* (Assen: Van Gorcum & Co., 1971), p. 182.
12. August Müller, "Sprechende Zahlen," *Neue Gesellschaft*, 2 (Feb. 28, 1906): 101–104.
13. August Müller, "Ein Beitrag zur Sozialpsychologie der Sozialdemokratie," *Neue Gesellschaft*, 4 (April 10, 1907): 29–36.
14. Müller referred to an analysis by Robert Block which appeared in the *Archiv für Sozialwissenschaft und Sozialpolitik* during 1905. Ritter maintains that even Bebel's counterclaim that the party received no more than a sixth of its vote from nonworkers was too high. See G. A. Ritter, "Die Sozialdemokratie im Deutschen Kaiserreich in sozialgeschichtlicher Perspektive," *Historische Zeitschrift*, 249, no. 2 (1989): 295–362.
15. Müller, Wir müssen aus dem Turm heraus."

16. Eduard Bernstein, "Die Massen werden irre," *SM,* 13 (Aug. 12, 1909): 1012–1018.
17. Wally Zepler, "Individualismus," *SM,* 13 (July 15, 1909): 888–901.
18. Biographical sketches of Quessel can be found in *SM,* 73 (March 16, 1930): 216–225.
19. Ludwig Quessel, "Zur Psychologie des modernen Proletariats," *SM,* 13 (July 1, 1909): 811–820.
20. Max Maurenbrecher, "Massenbildung," *SM,* 13 (Oct. 21, 1909): 1364–1371.
21. Paul Kampffmeyer, "Die sozialistische Theorie und die Praktiker der Arbeiterbewegung," *SM,* 13 (Nov. 18, 1909): 1481–1486.
22. Max Maurenbrecher, "Schulung der Funktionäre," *SM,* 13 (Nov. 4, 1909): 1405–1414.
23. Eduard Bernstein, "Die Theorie in der Partei," *SM,* 13 (Dec. 2, 1909): 1531–1537.
24. Gerhard Hildebrand, "Die Abänderung von Parteitagbeschlüssen," *SM,* 14 (Sept. 8, 1910): 1241–1252.
25. The criticism by the Revisionists is discussed in Fricke, "Die Sozialdemokratische Parteischule," pp. 241–245.
26. Michels' initial discussion of "oligarchical" tendencies appeared in the *Archiv für Sozialwissenschaft und Soziopolitik* during 1908. It was answered by Bernstein, "Die Demokratie in der Sozialdemokratie," *SM,* 12 (Sept. 3, 1908): 1106–1014. Michels replied to Bernstein's critique in the issue of December 17.
27. Ludwig Quessel, "Führer und Masse," *SM,* 14 (Oct. 27, 1910): 1407–1412.
28. Wilhelm Schröder, "Das Preussentum in der Partei," *SM,* 13 (June 17, 1909): 747–753.
29. Paul Kampffmeyer, "Die sozialistische Theorie."
30. Max Schippel, "Das Lob der Gegner," *SM,* 12 (July 9, 1908): 839–847.
31. See Schippel's discussion of politics in *SM,* 14 (Sept. 8, 1910): 1272–1275.
32. Paul Kampffmeyer, "Die Intellektuellen und die Sozialdemokratie," *SM,* 12 (Jan. 9, 1908): 39–42.
33. Paul Kampffmeyer, "Neue Entwicklungstendenzen seit Marx," *SM,* 13 (Jan. 14, 1909): 3–7.
34. Paul Kampffmeyer, "Marx und die wissenschaftliche Begründung des Sozialismus," *SM,* 13 (Jan. 28, 1909): 90–94.
35. Conrad Schmidt, "Zur Erinnerung an Karl Marx," *SM,* 12 (March 5, 1908): 265–267.
36. Conrad Schmidt, "Grundriss zu einem System der theoretischen Nationalökonmie," *SM,* 13 (Oct. 7, 1909): 1197–1214.
37. Conrad Schmidt, "Positive Kritik des Marxschen Wertgesetzes," *SM,* 14 (May 19, 1910): 604–618, and "Kantische Ethik und Sozialismus," *SM,* 15 (April 6, 1911): 472–476.
38. Paul Kampffmeyer, "Die sozialistische Theorie und die Praktiker der Arbeiterbewegung," *SM,* 13 (Nov. 18, 1909): 1481–1486.
39. Max Maurenbrecher, "Propheten und Praktiker," *SM,* 12 (Jan. 13, 1908): 18–25.

40. Karl Leuther, "Einst und Jetz," *SM,* 14 (April 7, 1910): 417–423, and "Wandlungen der Journalistik," *SM,* 14 (April 21, 1910): 488–496.
41. Wally Zepler, "Die psychischen Grundlagen der Arbeiterbildung," *SM,* 14 (Nov. 24, 1910): 1551–1559.
42. For other discussions of the religious issue by Revisionists, see the *Neue Gesellschaft* for June 1905, and the *Neue Zeit* during December of 1913 and the early weeks of 1914.
43. Max Maurenbrecher, "Die religiöse Frage in der politischen Agitation," *SM,* 14 (July 28, 1910): 953–960.
44. Hans Müller, "Das religiöse Moment im Sozialismus," *SM,* 14 (Dec. 22, 1910): 1665–1669.
45. Max Maurenbrecher, "Das religiöse Element im heutigen Sozialismus," *SM,* 15 (Jan. 12, 1911): 47–55.
46. Paul Kampffmeyer, "Die religiöse Einigung im Sozialismus," *SM,* 15 (Feb. 23, 1911): 240–245.
47. Franz Staudinger, "Sozialismus und Religion," *SM,* 15 (March 19, 1911): 289–294.
48. For a survey of the party's changing relationship to the nation see William H. Maehl, "The Triumph of Nationalism in the German Socialist Party on the Eve of the First World War," *Journal of Modern History,* 24, no. 1 (March 1952): 15–41.
49. Their emerging critique of party policies is discussed in H. M. Calmann, *Die Finanzpolitik der deutschen Sozialdemokratie* (Munich: Rosl, 1922), pp. 131–139.
50. See Max Schippel, "Konsument und Produzent," *SM,* 4 (Dec. 1900): 783–795.
51. See Max Schippel, *Grundzüge der Handelspolitik* (Berlin: Akademischer Verlag für sociale Wissenschaft, 1900).
52. *Hilfe* (Sept. 16, 1900).
53. *Plutus* (Nov. 25, 1905).
54. Richard Calwer, "Ein mitteleuropäischer Zollbund," *Neuland* (1897), pp. 261–266.
55. Naumann discusses Calwer's views in *Hilfe* (Aug. 11, 1901).
56. Richard Calwer, "Weltpolitik und Sozialdemokratie," *SM,* 9 (Oct. 1905): 741–749.
57. Richard Calwer, "Englands Aussichten und die deutsche Sozialdemokratie," *SM,* 9 (Nov. 1905): 919–922.
58. Richard Calwer, "Das Fazit der Marokkoaffair," *SM,* 10 (May 1906): 335–336.
59. Richard Calwer, "Der 25. Januar," *SM,* 11 (Feb. 1907): 101–107.
60. Max Schippel, "Kolonialpolitik," *SM,* 12 (Jan. 9, 1908): 3–10.
61. A five-part series of articles by David, "Sozialdemokratische Briefe über Vaterlands Liebe," appeared in the *Neue Gesellschaft* during the spring and summer of 1906.
62. Quoted in Fricke, "Opportunismus und Nationalismus: Zur Rolle Wolfgang Heines in der deutschen Sozialdemokratie bis zum Beginn des ersten Weltkrieg," *Zeitschrift für Geschichtswissenschaft,* 22, no. 8 (1974): 844–869.

63. Wolfgang Heine, "Wie bekämpfen wir den Militarismus," *SM,* 11 (Nov. 1907): 911–918.
64. See "Meinungsfreiheit," *SM,* 11 (Aug. 1907): 789–790.
65. See Richard Calwer, *Das Sozialdemokratische Programm* (Jena, 1914).
66. Max Schippel, "Marxismus und koloniale Eingeborenenfrage," *SM,* 12 (March 5, 1908): 273–285. The changes in the party's view of colonies is discussed in Hans-Christoph Schröder, *Sozialismus und Imperialismus* (Hanover: Verlag für Literatur und Zeitgeschehen, 1968), chap. 5.
67. See his review of a book on anarchism in *SM,* 8 (Aug. 1904): 677–679.
68. Bloch expresses his agreement with Calwer in a letter to Kurt Eisner, March 21, 1906, BAK, SM Papers. Also see Fletcher, *Revisionism and Empire,* chap. 2.
69. Bloch discusses the "lessons of the election" in the *SM,* 11 (March 1907): 247–249.
70. Bloch to Karl Leuther, Oct. 5, 1907, BAK, SM Papers.
71. Bloch to Adolph von Elm, Aug. 7, 1908, ibid.
72. Bloch to Leo Arons, n.d., 1908, ibid.
73. See Fletcher, *Revisionism and Empire,* chap. 4.
74. Ibid., p. 81.
75. See the correspondence between Maurenbrecher and Naumann reprinted in Dieter Fricke, "Nationalsoziale Versuche zur Förderung der Krise der deutschen Sozialdemokratie," *Beiträge zur Geschichte der Arbeiterbewegung,* 25, no. 4 (1983): 542–548.
76. Max Maurenbrecher, "Englische oder proletarische Politik," *SM,* 13 (May 21, 1909): 624–629.
77. Ibid., p. 627.
78. Gerhard Hildebrand, "Was ist Kolonisation?" *SM,* 13 (Jan. 14, 1909): 31–36.
79. Gerhard Hildebrand, "Vortrage der Kolonisation," *SM,* 13 (March 25, 1909): 352–356.
80. Gerhard Hildebrand, "Weltpolitische Bilanz," *SM,* 13 14 (June 3, 1909): 683–688.
81. Gerhard Hildebrand, "Kolonisation und Kultur," *SM,* 13 14 (March 10, 1910): 293–302.
82. See Wilhelm Dittmann, "Erinnerungen," pp. 233–234, IISH, typescript.
83. His letter is reprinted in the Protokoll, Chemnitz (1912): 484–485.
84. Gerhard Hildebrand, *Die Erschütterung der Industrieherrschaft und des Industriesozialismus* (Jena: G. Fischer, 1910). Hildebrand's study is discussed within the context of Social Democratic imperialistic thought in Annelies Laschitza, "Sozialdemokratie und imperialistische deutsche Mitteleuropapolitik: Ein Beitrag zur Stellung der verschiedenen Strömungen der deutschen Sozialdemokratie zur imperialistischen Aussenpolitik," *Jahrbuch für Geschichte,* 15 (1977): 107–144.
85. Hildebrand, *Die Erschütterung,* p. 210.
86. Ibid., p. 216.
87. Ibid., pp. 239–240.
88. Ibid., p. 238.
89. Ibid., p. 241.

90. Ibid., pp. 242–243.
91. Max Maurenbrecher, "Agrarischer Sozialismus," *SM,* 15 (April 6, 1911): 431–438.
92. Wally Zepler, "Individualismus in der Partei," *SM,* 13 (Dec. 16, 1909): 1596–1607.
93. Wilhelm Kolb, "Von Dresden bis Essen," *SM,* 11 (Aug. 1907): 702–706.
94. Schorske, *German Social Democracy,* pp. 77–79.
95. Ibid., p. 85.
96. Joseph Bloch, "Parteitag in Essen," *SM,* 11 (Oct. 1907): 880–883.
97. Eduard David, "Wo Steht der Feind?" *SM,* 12 (March 5, 1908): 291–294.
98. Joseph Bloch, "Landtagwahlen in Preussen," *SM,* 12 (June 25, 1908): 820–822.
99. See the account in Hedwig Wachenheim, *Die deutsche Arbeiterbewegung, 1844 bis 1914* (Cologne: Köln und Opladen Westdeutschen Verlag, 1967), pp. 458–463.
100. Quoted in Hedwig Wachenheim, ed., *Ludwig Frank; Aufsätze, Reden, und Briefe* (Berlin: Verlag für Sozialwissenschaft, 1924), p. 187.
101. Joseph Bloch, "Parteitag in Nürnberg," *SM,* 12 (Oct. 8, 1908): 1295–1297.
102. These developments are treated well in Schorske, *German Social Democracy,* chaps. 4 and 5.
103. Between 1907 and 1912 the Social Democrats gained ten or more seats in the Reichstag through by-elections.
104. See Wachenheim, *Deutsche Arbeiterbewegung,* pp. 469–476.
105. See Beverly Heckart, *From Bassermann to Bebel* (New Haven, Conn.: Yale University Press, 1974), p. 315.
106. Robert Schmidt, "Die Ergebnisse des Leipziger Parteitages," *SM,* 13 (Oct. 7, 1909): 1226–1228.
107. Wolfgang Heine to Joseph Bloch, Sept. 20, 1909, quoted in Fricke, "Eine Mutterzeitschrift des Opportunismus," pp. 1220–1222.
108. Ludwig Quessel, "Die Möglichkeit einer Anderung der deutschen Politik," *SM,* 14 (July 4, 1910): 865–871.
109. Max Maurenbrecher, "Auf dem Weg zur Macht," *SM,* 14 (June 16, 1910): 171–179.
110. Joseph Bloch, "Zurück zur Negation," *SM,* 14 (July 28, 1910): 941–945.
111. Wolfgang Heine, "Wahlfragen," *SM,* 15 (April 20, 1911): 481–486.
112. Max Schippel, "Kein Mann und kein Groschen oder Reformismus," *SM,* 15 (April 20, 1911): 486–492.
113. Ludwig Quessel, "Der alte und neue Liberalismus," *SM,* 15 (July 13, 1911): 903–906.
114. For accounts of this episode see Dieter Groh, *Negative Integration und revolutionärer Attentismus: Die deutsche Sozialdemokratie am Vorabend des Ersten Weltkrieges* (Frankfurt: Propyläen, 1973), pp. 229–243; Schorske, *German Social Democracy,* pp. 197–201; and Wachenheim, *Deutsche Arbeiterbewegung,* pp. 502–506.
115. Schorske, *German Social Democracy,* p. 227. Also see Groh, *Negative Integration,* pp. 267–273.
116. For analyses of the election see Schorske, *German Social Democracy,*

pp. 226–238; Groh, *Negative Integration,* pp. 276–289; and Wachenheim, *Deutsche Arbeiterbewegung,* pp. 506–510.

117. Max Schippel, "Die Reichstagswahlen," *SM,* 16 (Jan. 31, 1912): 75–81.
118. Eduard Bernstein, "Bedeutung des Sieges," *SM,* 16 (Feb. 15, 1912): 141–147.
119. Wilhelm Schröder, "Lehrjahr der Partei," *SM,* 16 (Jan. 31, 1912): 81–84.
120. Paul Kampffmeyer, "Ziele und Methoden der sozialdemokratischen Agitation," *SM,* 16 (Feb. 29, 1912): 234–239.
121. For a full account see Erich Matthias und Eberhard Pikart, eds., *Die Reichstagsfraktion der deutschen Sozialdemodratie, 1898 bis 1918,* vol. 1 (Düsseldorf: Droste, 1966), cxxxv–cil.
122. Wolfgang Heine, "Präsidentenwahl, Hofgang, Kaiserhoch," *SM,* 16 (March 28, 1912): 335–340.
123. Ludwig Quessel, "Sozialdemokratie und Monarchie," *SM,* 16 (March 14, 1912): 271–275.
124. Max Schippel, "Die neuesten Vorstöss unserer Impossibilisten," *SM,* 16 (March 14, 1912): 280–284.
125. See the review by Wissel, *SM,* 15 (Jan. 26, 1911): 139–140.
126. Gerhard Hildebrand, *Sozialistische Aussenpolitik* (Jena: E. Diederichs, 1911).
127. Ibid., p. 5.
128. Ibid., p. 63.
129. Maurenbrecher to Naumann, Aug. 17, 1911, reprinted in Fricke, "Nationalsoziale Versuche," p. 543.
130. Dittmann, "Erinnerungen," p. 339.
131. Details are drawn from ibid., p. 364.
132. Gerhard Hildebrand, "Wegen groben Verstosses gegen die Grundsätze des Parteiprogramms," *SM,* 16 (May 9, 1912): 524–531.
133. Wolfgang Heine, "Autodafé," *SM,* 16 (May 9, 1912): 531–538.
134. Paul Kampffmeyer, "Meinungsfreiheit innerhalb der Partei," *SM,* 16 (May 23, 1912): 597–605.
135. August Erdmann, "Die moralische und politische Bedeutung des Falles Hildebrand," *SM,* 16 (June 20, 1912): 726–733.
136. Wilhelm Kolb, "Heraus aus dem toten Geleise," *SM,* 16 (Aug. 29, 1912): 1096–1101.
137. Eduard Bernstein, "Darf Hildebrand ausgeschlossen werden?" *SM,* 16 (Aug. 29, 1912): 1147–1150.
138. Max Maurenbrecher, "Warum sind wir Sozialdemokraten?" *SM,* 16 (Aug. 29, 1912): 1154–1161.
139. Ibid., p. 1159.
140. For discussion of the case see Protokoll, Chemnitz (1912): 450–507.
141. Ibid., p. 476.
142. Ibid., p. 492.
143. Ibid., pp. 494–495.
144. Ibid., pp. 493–494.
145. Ibid., pp. 498–499. Laufenberg's "enormous influence" on the Social Democrats in Düsseldorf is discussed in Mary Nolan, "The Socialist Move-

ment in Düsseldorf, 1890–1914" (diss., Columbia University, 1975), pp. 161–163.

146. Eduard Bernstein, "Wissenschaft, Werturteile, und Partei," *SM,* 16 (Nov. 14, 1912): 1407–1415.
147. Protokoll, Chemnitz (1912): 497.
148. See Groh, *Negative Integration,* p. 278.
149. Gerhard Hildebrand, "Sozialismus und Sozialdemokratie," *Die Tat,* 5, no. 2 (1913–14): 149–158.
150. Ibid., p. 153.
151. Gerhard Hildebrand, "Die Religion der Sozialdemodrakischen Arbeiterschaft," *Die Tat,* no. 4 (1913–14): 373–384.

11. The Exhaustion of Orthodox Marxism

1. Karl Kautsky, "Der 25. Januar," *NZ,* 25, no. 18 (1906–1907): 588–596. Also see the discussion in Reinhard Hünlich, *Karl Kautsky und der Marxismus II Internationale* (Marburg: Verlag Arbeiterbewegung und Gesellschaft, 1981), pp. 140–145.
2. Kautsky's articles, which appeared in the *Leipziger Volkszeitung,* are summarized in Massimo Salvadori, *Karl Kautsky and the Socialist Revolution,* trans. Jon Rothschild (London: NLB, 1979), pp. 120–121.
3. Hedwig Wachenheim, *Die deutsche Arbeiterbewegung, 1844 bis 1914* (Cologne: Köln und Opladen Westdeutschen Verlag, 1967), p. 440.
4. Protokoll, Essen (1907): 261–262.
5. Quoted in Gary P. Steenson, *Karl Kautsky, 1854–1938* (Pittsburgh: University of Pittsburgh Press, 1978), p. 164.
6. Karl Kautsky, "Wie geht man an das Studium des Sozialismus," *NZ,* 26, no. 20 (1907–1908): 708–712.
7. Karl Kautsky, "Die budgetbewilligung," *NZ,* 26, no. 49 (1907–1908): 809–827.
8. Max Maurenbrecher, "Wo Stehen Wir," *NZ,* 27, no. 11 (1908–1909): 394–400.
9. For discussions of the pamphlet see the following: Salvadori, *Kautsky,* pp. 125–132; Wachenheim, *Deutsche Arbeiterbewegung,* pp. 476–482; Ingrid Gilcher-Holtey, *Das Mandat des Intellektuellen* (Berlin: Siedler, 1986), pp. 244–246; and Georg Fülberth's introduction to an edition of *Der Weg zur Macht* (Frankfurt: Europaische Verlagsanstalt, 1972), pp. vii–xxiii.
10. Karl Kautsky, *Der Weg zur Macht* (Berlin: Buchhandlung Vorwärts, 1910), p. 110.
11. See Hünlich, *Kautsky,* pp. 149–150, 160.
12. Kautsky, *Weg zur Macht,* p. 61.
13. Ibid., p. 79.
14. Ibid., pp. 101–103.
15. Fülberth, Introduction, p. xvii.
16. Correspondence relevant to the dispute can be found in Ursula Ratz, "Briefe zum Erscheinen von Karl Kautskys *Weg zur Macht,*" *International Review of Social History,* 12 (1967): 432–477.

17. Kautsky to Hugo Haase, Feb. 25, 1909, in Ratz, "Briefe," pp. 445–449.
18. Bebel to Adler, March 6, 1909, in Victor Adler, *Briefwechsel mit August Bebel und Karl Kautsky* (Vienna: Wiener Volksbuchhandlung, 1954), p. 495.
19. Haase to Kautsky, Feb. 22, 1909, in Ratz, "Briefe," p. 443. Haase's career is described in Kenneth Roy Calkins, *Hugo Haase, Democrat and Revolutionary* (Durham, N.C.: Carolina Academic Press, 1979).
20. There is an excellent discussion of this point in Gilcher-Holtey, *Das Mandat des Intellektuellen,* pp. 232–234.
21. Kautsky to Hugo Haase, March 9, 1909, in Ratz, "Briefe," pp. 465–466.
22. The alterations are indicated in Hünlich, *Kautsky,* pp. 285–286.
23. Clara Zetkin to Kautsky, March 16, 1909, in Ratz, "Briefe," pp. 475–476.
24. Gilcher-Holtey, *Mandat des Intellektuellen,* p. 232.
25. Wachenheim, *Deutsche Arbeiterbewegung,* p. 484. Also see Hünlich, *Kautsky,* pp. 153–169.
26. Kautsky to Adler, Sept. 26, 1909, in Adler, *Briefwechsel,* pp. 500–502.
27. Hilferding's relationship to Kautsky and the *Neue Zeit* is discussed in William Smaldone, "Rudolf Hilferding and the Theoretical Foundations of German Social Democracy, 1902–33," *Central European History,* 21, no. 3 (Sept. 1988): 270–280. For Eckstein see Karl Kautsky, Jr., "Gustav Eckstein, Der Erzieher," *Der Kampf,* 19 (Aug. 1926): 319–323.
28. Adolf Braun, "Die Intellektuellen und die Politik," *NZ,* 27, no. 50 (1908–1909): 847–853.
29. J. P. Nettl, *Rosa Luxemburg,* vol. 1 (New York: Oxford University Press, 1966), p. 405.
30. Luxemburg to Mathilde and Robert Siedel, May 28, 1910, in Rosa Luxemburg, *Gesammelte Briefe,* vol. 3 (Berlin: Dietz, 1982), p. 160.
31. Lensch's development is discussed in Hans Herzfeld, "Paul Lensch: Eine Entwicklung vom Marxisten zum nationalen Sozialisten," *Archiv für Politik und Geschichte,* 9 (1927): 263–306. Also see Robert Sigel, *Die Lensch, Cunow, Haenisch-Gruppe* (Berlin: Duncker und Humblot, 1976), pp. 21–25.
32. Haenisch did not receive an academic education. For his break with the bourgeois world see *SA* (Jan. 1, 1895): 23–24. Also see Rudolf Franz, "Aus Briefen Konrad Haenischs," *Archiv für der Geschichte des Sozialismus und der Arbeiterbewegung,* 14 (1929): 445–447, and Sigel, *Die Lensch, Cunow, Haenisch-Gruppe,* pp. 28–31.
33. The radical group in Stuttgart is discussed in Maja Christ-Gmelin, "Die Württembergerische Sozialdemokratie" (diss., University of Stuttgart, 1976), pp. 18, 180–198.
34. For Westmeyer's role see ibid., p. 153.
35. Thalheimer's background is discussed in Dieter Wuerth, *Radikalismus und Reformismus in der sozialdemokratischen Arbeiterbewegung Göppingens, 1910–1919* (Göppingen: Stadtarchiv Göppingen, 1978), p. 67.
36. Karl-Ernst Moring, *Die Sozialdemokratische Partei in Bremen, 1890–1914* (Hanover: Verlag für Literatur und Zeitgeschehen, 1968), pp. 103–105.

37. See Warren Lerner, *Karl Radek* (Stanford: Stanford University Press, 1970).
38. For biographical information see John Gerber, "The Formation of Pannekoek's Marxism," in Serge Bricianer, *Pannekoek and the Workers' Council* (St. Louis: Telos Press, 1978), pp. 1–30. Also see Hans Manfred Bock, "Zur Geschichte und Theorie der Hollandischen Marxistischen Schule," in Bock, ed., *Organisation und Taktik der proletarischen Revolution* (Frankfurt: Verlag Neue Kritik, 1969), pp. 7–48.
39. Dietzgen's thought is discussed in Lloyd Easton, "Empiricism and Ethics in Dietzgen," *Journal of the History of Ideas,* 19 (Jan. 1958): 77–90.
40. Gerber, "Formation of Pannekoek's Marxism," p. 7.
41. Anton Pannekoek, "Historischer Materialismus und Religion," *NZ,* 22, no. 31 (1903–1904): 133–143. Also see Ernst Adam, "Die Stellung der deutschen Sozialdemokratie zur Religion und Kirche" (diss., University of Frankfurt, 1929), pp. 119–121.
42. Anton Pannekoek, "Klassenwissenschaft und Philosophie," *NZ,* 23, no. 19 (1904–1905): 604–610.
43. Gerber, "Formation of Pannekoek's Marxism," p. 16.
44. Quoted in Russell Jacoby, *Dialectic of Defeat: Contours of Western Marxism* (Cambridge: Cambridge University Press, 1981), p. 73.
45. Quoted in Moring, *Sozialdemokratische Partei in Bremen,* p. 114.
46. Reprinted in Bricianer, *Pannekoek and the Workers' Council,* pp. 73–117.
47. Ibid., p. 73.
48. Ibid., p. 78.
49. Ibid., p. 83.
50. Ibid., p. 81.
51. Ibid., p. 109.
52. Ibid., p. 102.
53. Ibid., p. 111.
54. Ibid., p. 117.
55. Gerber, "Formation of Pannekoek's Marxism," p. 21.
56. Bricianer, *Pannekoek and the Workers' Council,* pp. 106–107.
57. For discussions of the protests see Dieter Groh, *Negative Integration und revolutionärer Attentismus* (Frankfurt: Propyläen, 1973), pp. 128–156, and Wachenheim, *Deutsche Arbeiterbewegung,* pp. 484–487.
58. For the argument that Luxemburg and the radical Marxists were carrying out the implications of the *Road to Power* see Hünlich, *Kautsky,* p. 175.
59. Details of the rejection can be found in Nettl, *Luxemburg,* vol. 1, pp. 421–422.
60. Kautsky's view of the party as a necessary mediator is discussed in Hünlich, *Kautsky,* pp. 150–151.
61. See ibid., pp. 170–181, which emphasizes Kautsky's reversal of his earlier positions.
62. The article, "Was Weiter?," is reprinted in Rosa Luxemburg, *Gesammelte Werke,* vol. 2 (Berlin: Dietz, 1972), pp. 289–299.
63. Ibid., pp. 291–292.
64. Ibid., pp. 295–297.

65. Groh, *Negative Integration,* pp. 150–156.
66. Kautsky, "Was Nun?," in Antonio Grunenberg, ed., *Die Massenstreikdebatte* (Frankfurt: Europaische Verlagsanstalt, 1970), pp. 96–121.
67. Nettl, *Luxemburg,* vol. 1, p. 428.
68. Luxemburg, "Ermattung oder Kampf?," in Grunenberg, *Massenstreikdebatte,* pp. 122–152.
69. Ibid., p. 149.
70. Kautsky, "Eine neue Strategie," in Grunenberg, *Massenstreikdebatte,* pp. 153–190.
71. Ibid., p. 187.
72. See Kautsky's editorial note to Luxemburg's article, "Die Theorie und die Praxis," in Grunenberg, *Massenstreikdebatte,* p. 191.
73. Ibid., p. 210.
74. Adler to Bebel, Aug. 5, 1910, in Adler, *Briefwechsel,* p. 510.
75. Luxemburg to Jogiches, Aug. 8, 1910, in Luxemburg, *Briefe,* vol. 3, p. 213.
76. Dick Geary, *Karl Kautsky* (Manchester: Manchester University Press, 1987), p. 90.
77. Bebel to Kautsky, Aug. 5, 1910, in John Kautsky, Jr., ed., *August Bebels Briefwechsel mit Karl Kautsky* (Assen: Van Gorcum & Co, 1971), p. 226.
78. Luxemburg to Jogiches, Aug. 31, 1910, in Luxemburg, *Briefe,* vol. 3, p. 226.
79. Bebel to Luise Kautsky, Sept. 4, 1910, in Kautsky, *Bebel Briefwechsel,* p. 229.
80. Luxemburg, "Die Theorie und die Praxis," in Grunenberg, *Massenstreikdebatte,* p. 232.
81. Kautsky's changing views of imperialism are presented succinctly in Geary, *Kautsky,* pp. 46–59. Also see Hünlich, *Kautsky,* pp. 178–181.
82. Kautsky to Charles Rappaport, June 8, 1911, IISH, Kautsky Correspondence, C 571.
83. Kautsky, "Die Aktion der Masse," in Grunenberg, *Massenstreikdebatte,* pp. 233–264.
84. See Kautsky, "Der zweite Parteitag von Jena," *NZ,* 29, no. 50 (1910–11): 873–877.
85. Salvadori, *Kautsky,* p. 150.
86. Karl Kautsky, "Die Revanche der Niedergerittenen," *NZ,* 30, no. 16 (1911–12): 545–549.
87. Karl Kautsky, "Die Wurzeln des Sieges," *NZ,* 30, no. 17 (1911–12): 581.
88. The revisionist character of Kautsky's thinking at this time is stressed in Hünlich, *Kautsky,* p. 180. Groh disagrees. See Groh, *Negative Integration,* pp. 208, 222.
89. Groh, *Negative Integration,* p. 197.
90. Zetkin to Mehring, June 13, 1912, quoted in Annelies Laschitza, "Karl Kautsky und der Zentralismus," *Beiträge zur Geschichte der deutschen Arbeiterbewegung,* 10, no. 5 (1968): 798–832.

91. See Ursula Ratz, "Karl Kautsky und die Abrüstungskontroverse in der deutschen Sozialdemokratie, 1911–1912," *International Review of Social History,* 11 (1966): 197–227.
92. Anton Pannekoek, "Massenaktion und Revolution," in Grunenberg, *Massenstreikdebatte,* pp. 264–294.
93. Kautsky, "Die neue Taktik," in Grunenberg, *Massenstreikdebatte,* pp. 295–334.
94. The resolution, together with a discussion of the debate, is reprinted in Wachenheim, *Deutsche Arbeiterbewegung,* pp. 539–541. The convergence of the Social Democratic approach to peace and that of the German peace movement is described in Roger Chickering, *Imperial Germany and a World without War* (Princeton: Princeton University Press, 1975), pp. 259–285.
95. Gilcher-Holtey, *Mandat des Intellektuellen,* pp. 266–267. The problem of holding the party together in these years is examined in Dieter K. Buse, "Party Leadership and the Mechanisms of Unity: The Crisis of German Social Democracy Reconsidered, 1910–1914," *Journal of Modern History,* 62 (Sept. 1990): 477–502.
96. Karl Kautsky, "Ein Ketzergericht," *NZ,* 31, no. 1 (1912–13): 1–6.
97. Karl Kautsky, "Ein Pronunziamento," *NZ,* 31, no. 2 (1912–13): 55–61.
98. Karl Kautsky, *Franz Mehring und die deutsche Sozialdemokratie* (Dessau, 1918), pp. 28–32.
99. Josef Schleifstein, *Franz Mehring: Sein marxistisches Schaffen, 1891–1919* (Berlin: Rütten & Loening, 1959), pp. 291–299.
100. Kautsky to Adler, Oct. 8, 1913, in Adler, *Briefwechsel,* pp. 582–586.
101. Bebel to Kautsky, July 16, 1913, in Kautsky, *Bebels Briefwechsel mit Kautsky,* pp. 351–352.
102. Groh, *Negative Integration,* p. 288.
103. Ibid., p. 467.
104. Ibid., p. 501.
105. Kautsky to Adler, Oct. 8, 1913, in Adler, *Briefwechsel,* pp. 582–586.
106. Kautsky to Adler, June 26, 1913, ibid., p. 573.
107. Pannekoek, "Marxistische Theorie und revolutionäre Taktik," in Bock, *Organisation und Taktik,* pp. 49–69.
108. Luxemburg's article, "Um Marokko," appeared in the *Leipziger Volkszeitung* (July 24, 1911). It is reprinted in Robert Looker, *Rosa Luxemburg: Selected Political Writings,* trans. William Graf (New York: Grove Press, 1974), pp. 160–167.
109. See Wachenheim, *Deutsche Arbeiterbewegung,* pp. 503–504.
110. Luxemburg to Mehring, Dec. 9, 1911, in Luxemburg, *Briefe,* vol. 4, p. 138.
111. Luxemburg to Luise Kautsky, Dec. 7, 1911, ibid., p. 137.
112. Luxemburg to Kostja Zetkin, Dec. 17, 1911, ibid., p. 146.
113. Luxemburg to Kostja Zetkin, Jan. 26, 1912, ibid., p. 159.
114. Luxemburg, "Was Nun?," *Gleichheit* (Feb. 5, 1912). Reprinted in Looker, *Luxemburg,* pp. 168–178.

115. Luxemburg to Mehring, April 19, 1912, in Luxemburg, *Briefe,* vol. 4, pp. 201–202.
116. Nettl, *Luxemburg,* vol. 1, pp. 530–539.
117. Paul Lensch, "Eine Improvisation," *NZ,* 30, no. 35 (1911–12): 308–313.
118. Pannekoek to Kautsky, Nov. 19, 1911, cited in Moring, *Sozialdemokratische Partei in Bremen,* p. 162.
119. Three of the articles, collectively entitled "Massenaktion und Revolution," are reprinted in Grunenberg, *Massenstreikdebatte,* pp. 264–294. The other two, "Marxistische Theorie und revolutionäre Taktik," are reprinted in Bock, *Organisation und Taktik,* pp. 49–69.
120. Pannekoek, "Massenaktion und Revolution," p. 265.
121. Pannekoek, "Marxistische Theorie und revolutionäre Taktik," p. 56.
122. Pannekoek, "Massenaktion und Revolution," pp. 291–292.
123. Ibid., p. 274.
124. Ibid., p. 287.
125. Pannekoek to Kautsky, Oct. 17, 1912, quoted in Moring, *Sozialdemokratische Partei in Bremen,* p. 164.
126. Ibid., pp. 165–167.
127. Ibid., pp. 116–117.
128. Haenisch to Rudolf Franz, Sept. 15, 1910, in Franz, "Aus Briefen Konrad Haenischs," p. 458.
129. See Otto-Ernst Schüddekopf, "Der Revolution entgegen: Materialien und Dokumente zur Geschichte der linken Flügel der deutschen Sozialdemokratie vor dem Ersten Weltkrieg," *Archiv für Sozialgeschichte,* 9 (1969): 455–457, and Wuerth, *Radikalismus und Reformismus,* pp. 63–79.
130. The elimination of the Radicals from the party press is noted in Annelies Laschitza and Horst Schumacher, "Thesen über die Herausbildung und Entwicklung der deutschen Linken von der Jahrhundertwende bis zur Gründung der KPD," *Beiträge zur Geschichte der deutschen Arbeiterbewegung,* 7, no. 1 (1965): 32.
131. For a summary of the state of the party see Groh, *Negative Integration,* pp. 469–476.
132. For examples of these conflicts see Moring, *Sozialdemokratische Partei in Bremen,* pp. 168–192; Hans J. L. Adolph, *Otto Wels und die Politik der deutschen Sozialdemokratie* (Berlin: De Gruyter, 1971), pp. 33–52; Christ-Gmelin, "Die Württembergische Sozialdemokratie," pp. 198–204; and Mary Nolan, *Social Democracy and Society* (Cambridge: Cambridge University Press, 1981), pp. 232–245.
133. Georg Fülberth, "Zur Genese des Revisionismus in der deutschen Sozialdemokratie vor 1914," *Argument,* no. 63 (1971): 17–18.
134. Haenisch to Rudolf Franz, Sept. 18, 1911, in Franz, "Aus Briefen Konrad Haenischs," 467.
135. For details see Moring, *Sozialdemokratische Partei in Bremen,* pp. 176–200, and Wuerth, *Radikalismus und Reformismus,* pp. 63–83.
136. Luxemburg to Kostja Zetkin, May 8, 1910, in Luxemburg, *Briefe,* vol. 3, p. 148.

137. Haenisch to Rudolf Franz, Sept. 3, 1912, in Franz, "Aus Briefen Konrad Haenischs," p. 474.
138. Fülberth, "Zur Genese des Revisionismus," p. 18.
139. The terms are drawn from Schorske, *German Social Democracy, 1905–1917* (Cambridge, Mass.: Harvard University Press, 1955), p. 248; Gerhard Beier, "Rosa Luxemburg," *Internationale wissenschaftliche Korrespondenz zur Geschichte der deutschen Arbeiterbewegung,* 10, no. 2 (1974): 196; and Curt Geyer, *Der Radikalismus in der deutschen Arbeiterbewegung* (Jena: Thuringer Verlagsanstalt, 1923), pp. 16–18.

Epilogue

1. Hans Staudinger, "Das Kulturproblem und die Arbeiterpsyche," *Die Tat,* 5, no. 10 (1913–14): 990–1002.
2. See "Dialektik im Gespräch mit Wolfgang Abendroth," *Dialektik,* 3 (1981): 148–149. Steinberg provided another perspective on the problem when he concluded that the development of the Social Democrats could be described as an "emancipation from theory." See H. J. Steinberg, *Sozialismus und deutsche Sozialdemokratie* (Hanover: Verlag für Literatur und Zeitgeschehen, 1967), pp. 146–150.
3. The ways in which the Marxist ideology influenced individual workers were recorded in Adolf Levenstein, *Die Arbeiterfrage: Mit besonderer Berücksichtigung der sozialpsychologischen Seite der modernen Grossbetriebes und der psycho-physischen Einwirkungen auf die Arbeiter* (Munich: E. Reinhardt, 1912). The book contains the replies to over five thousand questionnaires given to miners, textile workers, and metal workers. See especially pp. 172–226 for accounts of the hopes inspired by Marxism. For a discussion of the mentality of the German workers and the "taming of the proletariat" see Barrington Moore, Jr., *Injustice: The Social Basis of Obedience and Revolt* (White Plains, N.Y.: W. E. Sharpe, 1978). Also see Jörg Schadt, ed., *Wie wir den Weg zum Sozialismus fanden* (Cologne: Kohlhammer, 1981), p. 65.
4. Georg Fülberth, "Zur Genese des Revisionismus in der deutschen Sozialdemokratie vor 1914," *Argument,* no. 63 (1971): 8.
5. Paul Ernst, *Der Zusammenbruch des Marxismus* (Munich: G. Müller, 1919), pp. 129–132.
6. See Wolfgang Heine, *Kultur und Nation* (Chemnitz, 1914), and Heine's correspondence with Stampfer and others, reprinted in Dieter Fricke, "Opportunismus und Nationalismus: Zur Rolle Wolfgang Heines in der deutschen Sozialdemokratie bis zum Beginn des ersten Weltkriegs," *Zeitschrift für Geschichtswissenschaft,* 22, no. 8 (1974): 855–869.
7. Frank's letters from August 1914 are reprinted in Hedwig Wachenheim, ed., *Ludwig Frank; Aufsätze, Reden, und Briefe* (Berlin: Verlag für Sozialwissenschaft, 1924), pp. 348–360.
8. Franz Mehring, "Wieder einer," in Mehring, *Politische Publizistik,* vol. 2 (Berlin: Dietz, 1964), p. 681.

9. Paul Lensch, *Am Ausgang der deutschen Sozialdemokratie* (Berlin: G. Fischer, 1919), pp. 21–22.
10. Machajski's reaction to Kautsky's treatment of the bourgeois intellectuals is discussed in Marshall S. Shatz, *Jan Waclaw Machajski: A Radical Critic of the Russian Intelligentsia and Socialism* (Pittsburgh: University of Pittsburgh Press, 1989), pp. 32–36.
11. Lenin acknowledges his debt to Kautsky most fully in the two essays, "What Is to Be Done?" and "One Step Forward, Two Steps Back." See V. I. Lenin, *Selected Works* (New York: International Publishers, 1967), pp. 129, 362–363, 426–428.
12. William Gleberzon, "Marxist Conceptions of the Intellectual," *Historical Reflections,* 5, no. 1 (1978): 96. For criticisms, from a Marxist point of view, of the ways in which Lukács and Gramsci dealt with the problem of the working-class mentality, see István Mészáros, *The Power of Ideology* (New York: New York University Press, 1989), pp. 355–359, 401–409.
13. See Georg Konrad and Ivan Szelenyi, *The Intellectuals on the Road to Class Power,* trans. Andrew Arato and Richard Allen (New York: Harcourt, Brace, Jovanovich, 1979), and Alvin Gouldner, *The Future of the Intellectuals and the Rise of the New Class* (New York: Oxford University Press, 1979).
14. Henri De Man, *Die Intellektuellen und der Sozialismus* (Jena: E. Diederichs, 1926), p. 24.
15. Thus John Dunn, *The Politics of Socialism* (New York: Cambridge University Press, 1984), claims that the hope that cultural values might rule over economic and political structures was fundamental to the "true socialism" of the intellectuals. See especially pp. 71–87.
16. The resistance presented by "common sense" to ideology is discussed in Mészáros, *Power of Ideology,* pp. 401–408.
17. For a case study of this process see Sudhir Hazareesingh, *Intellectuals and the French Communist Party* (New York: Oxford University Press, 1991).
18. This is the argument of Zygmunt Bauman, *Legislators and Interpreters: On modernity, postmodernity, and intellectuals* (Ithaca, N.Y.: Cornell University Press, 1987).
19. The debate over this thesis is discussed by one who advanced it in Seymour Martin Lipset, "The End of Ideology and the Ideology of the Intellectuals," in Joseph Ben-David and Terry Nichols Clark, *Culture and Its Creators: Essays in Honor of Edward Shils* (Chicago: University of Chicago Press, 1977), pp. 15–42. For a survey of the tendencies toward "de-ideologization" and "re-ideologization" since World War II see Karl Dietrich Bracher, *The Age of Ideologies: A History of Political Thought in the Twentieth Century,* trans. Ewald Osers (London: Weidenfeld and Nicholson, 1982), pp. 189–277.

Index